Dante: The Poetics of Conversion

Dante
The Poetics of Conversion

JOHN FRECCERO
Edited, and with an Introduction by Rachel Jacoff

HARVARD UNIVERSITY PRESS
Cambridge, Massachusetts, and London, England

Printed in the United States of America
10 9 8 7 6 5 4 3 2

Text design by Joyce C. Weston

LIBRARY OF CONGRESS CATALOGING-IN-PUBLICATION DATA

Freccero, John.
Dante : the poetics of conversion.

Bibliography: p.
Includes index.
1. Dante Alighieri, 1265–1321—Criticism and interpretation—Addresses, essays, lectures.
I. Jacoff, Rachel. II. Title.
PQ4390.F82 1986 851'.1 85-17679

ISBN 0-674-19225-7 (alk. paper) (cloth)
ISBN 0-674-19226-5 (paper)

For Diane

Quale ne' plenilunii sereni
Trivïa ride tra le ninfe etterne
che dipingon lo ciel per tutti i seni . . .

CONTENTS

INTRODUCTION

John Freccero's essays on Dante have been and remain a mine for scholars, but they transcend the scholarly in their ability to speak to pressing literary and human concerns. This collection includes all of his major essays published between 1959 and 1984. In order to respect the integrity of these essays, they are reprinted here in virtually their original form; occasional repetitions seemed less worrisome than altering the shape of the original arguments. Freccero has reviewed all the essays, changed slightly a few of their titles, and done some minimal rewriting. As editor of the volume, I have standardized the footnote form and, with a few exceptions, uniformly used the text and translation from Charles S. Singleton's edition of the *Commedia.* All quotations have been translated into English in the text, although not in the notes; the citations remain to the original sources. The essays are arranged here in order of the *Commedia*'s own trajectory rather than in order of their dates of publication; their original dates and places of publication are listed at the back of the book. Since they were written over a period of twenty-five years and published in a variety of journals, the essays quite naturally manifest differences in tone and in density of erudition. But placing them together "in un volume" also reveals the remarkable unity and evolving consistency of their concerns.

This unity derives from the empowering conviction of the reciprocity of Dante's theology and his poetics. Freccero's reading of the *Commedia* articulates Dante's intellectual and theological coordinates in specific relation to their narrative and poetic consequences. This double focus marks him as the heir of the two great Dantisti of the previous generation, Erich Auerbach and Charles Singleton, who, in different terms, had addressed the question of the unity of Dante's poem. Auerbach and Singleton both offered ways out of the conceptual limits then dominating Dante studies in the aftermath of Benedetto Croce's influential division of the *Commedia* into "poesia" and "non-poesia." Where Croce had celebrated the poem's lyric and dramatic intensities and ignored, or depreciated, its structure, Singleton in particular argued for and in terms of the poem's master-structures. With some exceptions, it is fair to say that modern Italian Dante criticism still bears the stamp of its Crocean origins, while contemporary American Dante criticism for the most part has proceeded from Singleton and Auerbach. Or, to put it another way, Italian scholars still venerate philology while American scholars have become adept at exegesis; since both disciplines are necessary to a full discussion of Dante's poetry, there is much to be learned on either side of the question and on both sides of the Atlantic. Freccero's essays do suggest a synthesis of both approaches, but they begin and end in the profound belief in the poem's coherence and its potential for intelligibility.

Coherence and unity are somewhat suspect notions in current critical discourse, which is frequently engaged in undermining such assumptions. As the awareness of rhetorical strategies that subvert meaning becomes more acute, "aporia" has replaced "epiphany" as the critic's focus. Although Freccero's more recent work takes account of developments in literary theory, he remains resolutely concerned with the possibilities for the recovery of meaning opened up by the presumption of coherence: "we must assume the existence of a coherent pattern and abandon our hypothesis only when our resources, or those of the poem, are exhausted. Only then may we conclude either that the significance of these details escapes us, or that the poem is unintelligible in this respect." One of the consequences of such an assumption is precisely the sense of the poem's inexhaustibility, an exhilarating experience conveyed by these essays and an important dimension of their seminality. Even when undecidability becomes an issue in interpretation, as it does in the analysis of *Inferno* XXXIII, it functions within the Pauline hermeneutic categories of letter and spirit, which determine the moral valence of the interpretive question.

While Singleton emphasized the larger allegorical structures of the poem, Freccero usually begins with a small unit of meaning. The characteristic procedure of his early essays is to address a crux, a phrase or line that had long been debated by the commentary tradition without having reached an interpretive consensus. Thus his first published article, "The Firm Foot on a Journey without a Guide," took as its subject a phrase that made no sense if understood literally (nor was it even clear what its exact literal meaning was); no known gloss for it had yet convinced the majority of readers. Marshaling a wide variety of classical, patristic, and scholastic sources, Freccero arrived at an interpretation of the phrase as a figure for the pilgrim's wounded will, the crucial impediment to his desired journey toward truth. Understanding the precise meaning of this phrase required a reconstruction of its intellectual history, beginning with Aristotle and tracing its subsequent neoplatonic and Christian elaborations. In the attention to the nuances of such a reconstruction, one sees the influence of both Leo Spitzer's "historical semantics" and Pierre Courcelle's work on the Christianization of classical ideas.

Several of the essays contain analyses which work the same way, notably the ones that trace the development of ideas about the relation between the cosmos and the soul. These ideas originated in Plato's *Timaeus* (a text known to the Middle Ages in its Latin translation by Chalcidius) and were assimilated and transformed by neoplatonic and Christian thinkers. The analogies between corporeal and spiritual movement set forth in the *Timaeus,* and developed by subsequent commentators, provided a repository of potential images for Dante's translation of classical notions of *paideia* into a Christian journey of the mind to God. These connections are evident in the first two essays collected here, and form the basis of several later studies, most notably "Pilgrim in a Gyre," "The Dance of the Stars: *Paradiso* X," and "The Final Image."

The analysis of the "firm foot" proved to be typical of Freccero's subsequent work in another sense. Although it ostensibly aims to explicate one vexed phrase, it ends by implying a reading of the whole canto and of the meaning of Dante's journey. Freccero's way of deducing and implying the whole from a detail recalls Spitzer's conviction that every crux is potentially the totality to which it belongs ("Das Ganze im Fragment"). In "The Prologue Scene," the essay with which this collection begins, larger themes are opened out more fully; the spiritual crisis of the opening canto is given resonance by connecting the protagonist's unsuccessful attempt to climb the "dilettoso monte" of the opening scene, a "failed exodus," with another exemplary "failed journey," that of Ulysses in Canto XXVI. Both Dante's initial regression and Ulysses' final shipwreck are seen as narrative embodiments of the journey of the unaided human intellect—failures of philosophical presumption that underline the need for guidance and for a descent into humility, both of which are offered to Dante by the gratuitous appearance of Virgil in the first canto. Virgil tells Dante that he must "go another way," leading him into the complex infernal itinerary that figures the death of the self necessary for a true conversion.

Conversion is the central organizing principle and preoccupation of these essays—conversion understood both as religious experience and as poetic structure. Where Singleton focused on Exodus typology as the poem's master-structure, Freccero's work concentrates on the tropological dimension of that typology, the ways in which Dante's particular conversion narrative determines discrete aspects of the poem's language and structure. Augustine's *Confessions* provides the model and supreme analogue for such a "novel of the self," as these essays intermittently define Christian autobiography. For Freccero the genre is characterized by the coincidence of its formal pattern and its theological counterpart: "The Christian theme of conversion satisfies the contrary exigencies of autobiography by introducing a radical discontinuity into the sequence of a life thanks to which one can tell one's story as though it were true, definitive, and concluded. Death in life is closure in the story, but it is thanks to a spiritual resurrection that the story can be told. It was Augustine who set the pattern for this Christian thematization of narrative structure in his *Confessions*." Conversion as theme and narrative mode provides the necessary "Archimedean point" from which the author of such a story can speak as if the story were both complete and accurate. For both Augustine and Dante such a point is constituted by a death of the old self which makes possible a new consciousness, the story of whose coming into being—"the story of how the self that was becomes the self that is"—is at once its subject and its structure. While most scholars continued to gloss Dante's ideas primarily in relation to Aristotelian philosophy and Thomistic theology, Freccero's profound grasp of neoplatonic thought and of Augustine's understanding of the relationship between language and desire allowed him to uncover the dynamism of such a paradigm; several essays explicitly return to these considerations, and each time the new context gives added density and intensity to our understanding of the centrality of the notion of conversion. The necessarily diachronic nature of such a narrative places temporality in the foreground. The importance of temporality in the work of two of Freccero's favorite critics, Georges Poulet and Paul De Man, suggests one reason for his affinity with their work.

Freccero's interpretation of Dante's allegory as a temporal rather than a spatial phenomenon takes on a specifically metaliterary dimension in his analysis of the poem's retrospective or revisionary readings of its own materials. Furthermore, since the *Commedia* subsumes and reevaluates Dante's earlier work from its own privileged culminating point, Dante's poetic career as well as his poem become invested with a dynamic aspect. Freccero illuminates this process in his study of the palinodic dimension of Dante's self-citation in "Casella's Song" where the gap between the original text and context and the new staging becomes itself the occasion of poetic redefinition: "an allusion to a former work is inevitably palinodic, for it invests the poetry itself with the dramatic double-focus that is part of the story: the conversion of the Dante who *was* into the poet whose work we read." This understanding of Dante's relation to his own work as an aspect of the larger narrative structure of conversion informs much of the current interest in the dialectical quality of intertextuality in the *Commedia*.

Freccero's ongoing elaboration of the centrality of conversion employs Dante's own terminology of experience and exemplum. The existential reality underlying the *Commedia* is, of course, forever unknowable to us; but the exemplum which Dante constructs to convey it links whatever private historical experience there may be to a universal structure. The interplay of the personal and the public, of the unique and the universal, is part of the poem's continuing fascination. This doubleness is related to other polarities which the poem attempts to integrate: the novelistic and epic, the linear and circular, the syntagmatic and paradigmatic, the pilgrim and the poet. In Freccero's words, "The process of the poem, which is to say the progress of the pilgrim, is the transformation of the problematic and humanistic into the certain and transcendent, from novelistic involvement to epic detachment, from a synchronic view of the self in a dark wood to a diachronic total view of the entire world as if it were, to use Dante's powerful image, a humble threshing floor upon which a providential history will one day separate the wheat from the chaff." In several essays, most notably "Dante's Ulysses: From Epic to Novel" and "The Significance of *Terza Rima,*" Freccero traces the interpenetration of such a double perspective.

Freccero's understanding of the *Commedia* as a conversion narrative includes the inevitable question of its status as truth. This question haunts modern approaches to the poem, and has received a number of responses—from Eliot's attempt to separate assent from belief to Singleton's frequently cited assertion that "the fiction of the *Divine Comedy* is that it is not a fiction." Freccero speaks to this polemic in other terms by concentrating on the homology of literary and linguistic structures. His approach is close to Kenneth Burke's formulation of "logology" in its focus on the interchangeability of linguistic and theological categories. If, as Augustine had long ago made clear, words about words and words about God have a homologous structure, then it is possible (for us, if not for Augustine or Dante) to delineate this reciprocity without a priori deciding on the ontological status of either term. Freccero deals most fully with this issue in the final essay of this collection, "The Significance of *Terza Rima,*" where he articulates the following position: "thematics (that is, theology) and poetics might conceivably be joined in such a way as to offend neither historical understanding nor contemporary skepticism, for in either case, we are discussing a coherence that is primarily linguistic. The traditional problem of poetry and belief would then be shifted onto a philosophical plane. Does the order of language refect the order of reality or is 'transcendent reality' simply a projection of language? What we had always taken to be a problem of Dante criticism turns out to be the central epistemological problem of all interpretation." Freccero's ongoing address to such central interpretive issues places his erudition and command of intellectual history at the service of a larger discourse. The perspective from which he takes up these questions also saves his work from the excessively moralistic or pietistic stance often found in those scholars who address the poem's theology. Freccero keeps finding ways to translate theological concerns into phenomenological or literary issues so that they become interesting to us on contemporary terms even while we are learning about them with the utmost respect for their historicity, and our own.

Since they are not arranged in order of their publication, it might not be obvious that a certain evolution takes place within the essays, a development which has its own plot. Where the earliest essays deal primarily with a particular interpretive crux and treat a specific occurrence as an occasion for problem solving, the later essays address the problematic of interpretation itself. In the essays on Medusa and on Ugolino, Freccero points out the ways in which the criticism of the poem has troped the text by reenacting the interpretive obtuseness figured within the poem. In his analysis of the inherently ambiguous line with which Ugolino concludes his extraordinary "aria," Freccero shows us that the critical debate about its meaning inscribes the critic within the poem's own drama: "The central interpretive problem of the canto of Ugolino turns out to be its theme: Ugolino's critics dramatize the difficulty they seek to resolve." His reading of the Medusa as an exploration of the letter–spirit dichotomy establishes the centrality of these Pauline metaphors for the problematic of reading as it functions throughout the *Inferno.* Taken together, these two essays are mutually reinforcing, allowing the reader to see that the poetics of the *Inferno* are precisely a poetics of the letter just as its characteristic representatives are all literalists. The crisis of interpretation dramatized for the pilgrim in the threat of the Medusa (the threat of petrification which Freccero reads as equivalent to the Pauline hardness of heart and to reading the letter without the spirit) is lived out by the sinners themselves, in particular the terrifying Ugolino, who turns to stone while his children ask him for bread. The interchangeability of interpretive and ethical categories here offers a way into the *Inferno* seen as the realm of the dead letter. Freccero himself develops these themes into an exploration of the subversive aspects of mimesis in his most recent article, "Infernal Irony: The Gates of Hell."

His reading of the *Purgatorio* (in "Manfred's Wounds and the Poetics of *Purgatorio*") outlines the different poetic and moral coordinates of that *cantica,* its emphasis on process, on *fantasia,* and its redefinition of the poem's relation to the "real world." In the essay that was an introduction to John Ciardi's translation of the *Paradiso,* Freccero takes the measure of that *cantica's* fragile boldness, unfolding its radical metaphoricity. In "The Dance of the Stars," he analyzes Dante's syncretic deployment of astronomical, neoplatonic, and theological traditions, unpacking the complex specificity of metaphorical structure in one canto and thereby suggesting a mode of reading the whole *cantica.* Although the essays remain discrete in their focus, their continuing address to the large issues of poetic representation suggests the outlines of a reading of the whole work as well as the diverse poetics of each of the *cantiche.*

John Freccero's essays have had a profound effect on Dante studies in America; they continue to inspire new work and references to them show up in an unusual number of other people's footnotes. This is not only because of their insightfulness, but also because of a certain modesty or courtesy with which they leave many of their conclusions or analogues to be worked out by the reader. They are suggestive rather than exhaustive. In their power to engage the reader, as well as in their meticulous conceptual elegance and their sense of the inherent fascination of the issues they raise, they are continuous with Freccero's teaching. These essays teach us how to find the questions, or how to make limited questions into much larger ones: they have the rare ability both to lead the way and to open it.

Editor's Acknowledgments

I would like to thank the staff of Special Collections at the John M. Olin Library of Cornell University, and in particular James Tyler, for assistance. I am grateful to Princeton University Press for allowing us to use Charles S. Singleton's edition and translation of the *Divine Comedy* throughout the book. I deeply appreciate the generous participation of several friends at various stages of this project; Jeffrey Schnapp and David Quint were especially helpful. Andrea Wilson supplied translations for all the Latin quotations that had not been previously translated; she did so with extraordinary alacrity and good will. Eileen Reeves compiled the indexes. Lindsay Waters of Harvard University Press warmly facilitated and encouraged this project at every stage; his support turned it into a reality.

1. The Prologue Scene

The Region of Unlikeness

IN THE SHADOWY WORLD OF THE prologue scene, things both are and are not what they seem. For all its familiarity, the scenery seems to have no real poetic existence independent of the allegorical statement it was meant to convey. Moreover, the statement itself, judging from the vast bibliography dedicated to it, is by no means obvious to the contemporary reader. The ambiguous nature of the moral landscape lends itself too readily to arbitrary allegorization, but scarcely to formal analysis. In this respect, the prologue is radically unlike any other part of the *Commedia* and matches the abortive journey of the pilgrim with an apparent failure that is the poet's own.

Any fresh interpretation of the prologue, if it is to contribute measurably to our understanding, must not only attempt an exploration of this well-travelled critical terrain, but also account for the presence, in this most substantial of poetic visions, of a region whose outlines are decidedly blurred. It is such an accounting that I hope to offer. My thesis is that the landscape in which the pilgrim finds himself bears a striking, indeed at times a textual, resemblance to the "region of unlikeness" in which the young Augustine finds himself in the seventh book of the *Confessions.* Moreover, the resemblance is not simply an isolated fact of purely historical interest but is also of some significance for an interpretation of the poem. If the point of departure, as well as the goal, of Dante's spiritual itinerary deliberately recalls the experience of Augustine in the *Confessions,* then it may be that we are to regard Dante's entire spiritual autobiography as essentially Augustinian in structure.

There is good evidence, apart from the prologue scene, for considering Dante's poem as a spiritual testament in the manner of Augustine. Toward the end of the *Purgatorio,* at a moment that is of great dramatic importance, Beatrice calls to the pilgrim by name:

> in su la sponda del carro sinistra,
> quando mi volsi al suon del nome mio,
> che di necessità qui si registra,
> vidi la donna . . . (XXX, 61–64)

> so on the left side of the chariot—when I turned
> at the sound of my name, which of necessity
> is registered here—I saw the lady . . .

Thus, in defiance of medieval convention, the author identifies himself with his protagonist, insisting that he does so "di necessità." The apology is so pointed and the word "necessità" so strong that the passage seems to call for some interpretation. It happens that in the *Convivio* Dante had discussed the circumstances under which it might be considered necessary to speak of oneself. One of his examples, precisely the *Confessions,* is described in terms that seem almost to herald Dante's own "testament":

> Per necessarie cagioni lo parlare di sè è conceduto: e intra l'altre necessarie cagioni due sono più manifeste. L'Una è quando sanza ragionare di sè grande infamia o pericolo non si può cessare . . . L' Altra è quando, per ragionare di sè, grandissima utilitade ne segue altrui per via di dottrina; e questra ragione mosse Agostino ne le sue confessioni a parlare di sè, *chè per lo processo de la sua vita, lo quale fu di* [*non*] *buono in buono, e di buono in migliore, e di migliore in ottimo, ne diede essemplo e dottrina, la quale per sì vero testimonio ricevere non si potea.*[1]

> Speaking of oneself is allowed, when it is necessary, and among other necessary occasions two are most obvious: One is when it is impossible to silence great infamy and danger without doing so . . . The other is when, by speaking of himself, the greatest advantage follows for others by way of instruction; and this reason moved Augustine to speak of himself in his confessions, so that in the progress of his life, which was from bad to good,

> and from good to better, and from better to best, he furnished example and teaching which could not have been obtained from any other equally truthful testimony.

Critics have usually been content with rather generic explanations for Dante's mention of his own name in the *Purgatorio,* none of which seem as relevant as does this passage in the *Convivio.*[2] It is clear from the beginning of the poem that Dante, like Augustine, intends his work to have exemplary force for "*nostra* vita." Elsewhere Dante makes this explicit, when he says that he writes "in pro del mondo che mal vive" (*Purg.* XXXII, 103). By naming himself at the moment of his confession, however, he gives to the abstract *exemplum* the full weight of *vero testimonio,* exactly as had St. Augustine before him. Furthermore, the three stages of Augustine's progress are described in the *Convivio* in terms that are partially echoed in the *Paradiso:*

> È Bëatrice quella che sì scorge
> *di bene in meglio,* sì subitamente
> che l'atto suo per tempo non si sporge. (X, 37–39)

> It is Beatrice who thus conducts from good to better, so swiftly that her act does not extend through time.

The phrase "di bene in meglio," for all of its apparent banality, has technical force,[3] describing the second stage of the pilgrim's progress. Beatrice is virtually defined here as the guide for the second stage of spiritual progress[4] in terms that the *Convivio* had used for the second stage of Augustine's conversion from sinner to saint: "di buono in migliore." It seems likely that in the *Convivio* Dante perceived in Augustine's life the same pattern of conversion that he was later to read retrospectively in his own experience.

Dante speaks of Augustine's life as giving an "essemplo," implying the transformation of personal experience into intelligible, perhaps even symbolic, form. We may observe in passing that it is the exemplary quality of the *Confessions* that distinguishes it from its modern descendants. Augustine's purpose is not to establish his own uniqueness (nor, therefore, innocence, in terms of the standards by which ordinary men are judged), but rather to demonstrate how the apparently unique experience was, from the perspective of eternity, a manifestation of Providence's design for all men. The scholarly debates about the historicity of Augustine's conversion scene, where a real garden in Milan seems to enclose the fig tree of Nathanael (John 1:48),[5] are paralleled by the scholarly debates about Beatrice who, on one hand, was a woman of flesh and blood and yet, on the other hand, seems to be surrounded at Dante's confession scene with unmistakably Christological language and mystery. The point is that in the "then" of experience, grace came in intensely personal form, whereas in the "now" of witness, the particular event is read retrospectively as a repetition in one's own history of the entire history of the Redemption. For both Dante and Augustine the exegetical language seems to structure experience, identifying it as part of the redemptive process, while the irreducibly personal elements lend to the *exemplum* the force of personal witness. Together, *exemplum* and experience, allegory and biography, form a confession of faith for other men.

Conversion, a death and resurrection of the self, is the experience that marks the difference between such confessions and facile counterfeits. In the poem, the difference between the attempt to scale the mountain, the journey that fails, and the successful journey that it prefigures is a descent in humility, a death of the self represented by the journey through hell. Augustine alludes briefly to a similar *askesis* in order to describe his suffering during his stay in Rome:

> And lo, there was I received by the scourge of bodily sickness, and I was going down to Hell, carrying all the sins which I had committed, both against Thee, and myself, and others, many and grievous, over and above that bond of original sin, whereby we all die in Adam. . . . So true, then, was the death of my soul, as that of His flesh seemed to me false; and how true the death of His body, so false was the life of my soul.[6]

The descent into hell, whether metaphorical as in the *Confessions,* or dramatically real as in Dante's poem, is the first step on the journey to the truth. It has the effect of shattering the inverted values of this life (which is death, according to Christian rhetoric) and transforming death into authentic life. The inversion of values is represented in Dante's poem by the curious prefiguration in the first canto of the ascent of the mountain of purgatory: the light at the summit, the mountain itself, the attempted climb. Although the landscape is analogous to the scenery that comes into sharper focus in the second *cantica,* all directions are reversed. What seems up is in fact down; what seems transcendence is in fact descent. Just as the reversed world of Plato's myth in the *Statesman* represented a world of negative values, so the reversed directions of the prologue stand for spiritual distortion. Augustine alludes in the seventh book to Plato's myth when he describes his spiritual world before his conversion as a "regio dissimilitudinis."[7] Although Dante nowhere uses the phrase, he borrowed several of Augustine's topographical details to describe his own spiritual condition.

Augustine's journey to God, like Dante's, is immediately preceded by a journey that fails, an attempt at philosophical transcendence in the seventh book of the *Confessions* that amounts to a conversion *manquée.* Lost in what he refers to as a "region of unlikeness," Augustine turns to the light of Platonic vision, only to discover that he is too weak to endure it. He is beaten back by the light and falls, weeping, to the things of this world. At that point in the narrative, the author asks himself why God should have given him certain books of neoplatonic philosophy to read before leading him to Scripture. He answers: "[So that] I might know the difference between presumption and confession; between those who saw where they were to go, yet saw not the way, and the way itself, that led not to behold only, but to dwell in the beatific country."[8] The answer applies exactly to the dramatic purpose of Dante's prologue scene.

There are some excellent reasons for believing Dante meant that first ascent to be read as a purely *intellectual* attempt at conversion, where the mind sees its objective but is unable to reach it. After the pilgrim's fear is somewhat quieted, the poet uses a famous simile:

E come quei che con lena affannata,
uscito fuor del pelago a la riva,
si volge a l'acqua perigliosa e guata,
così *l'animo mio, ch'ancor fuggiva,*
si volse a retro a rimirar lo passo
che non lasciò già mai persona viva.
Poi ch'èi posato un poco *il corpo lasso,*
ripresi via per la piaggia diserta,
sì che 'l piè fermo sempre era 'l più basso. (I, 22–30)

And as he who with laboring breath has es-

> caped from the deep to the shore turns to look back on the dangerous waters, so my mind which was still fleeing turned back to gaze upon the pass that never left anyone alive.

Charles Singleton has called our attention to the shift, in these lines, from the flight of an *animo,* the mind of the pilgrim, to the lagging of a *corpo lasso,* a tired body.[9] He was primarily concerned with the radical shift in poetic tone, the beginning of what he referred to as Dante's vision "made flesh." It should be observed that such a shift, besides being a radical poetical departure, has a precise conceptual significance in this context. The whole reason for the failure of all such journeys of the mind resides precisely in that laggard body. The *animo* is perfectly willing, but it is joined to flesh that is bound to fail.

The phrase "l'animo mio ch'ancor fuggiva" has an unmistakable philosophical ring. For one thing, the word *animo* is decidedly intellectual, rather than theological in meaning, quite distinct from the more common *anima.* For another, the phrase recalls, or at least would have recalled to the Church fathers, the flight of the soul from the terrestrial to the spiritual realm according to the Platonists and especially to Plotinus. In the *Enneads,* the latter urges such a flight: "Let us therefore flee to our dear homeland . . . But what manner of flight is this? . . . it is not with our feet that it can be accomplished, for our feet, no matter where they take us, take us only from one land to another; nor must we prepare for ourselves a team of horses or a ship . . . it is rather necessary to change our sight and look with the inner eye."[10]

This flight of the soul by means of the "interior eye" was destined to have an interesting history. It is perhaps the ancestor of Dante's abortive journey. The point of it is that the Plotinian sage can safely ignore his body in his attempts at ecstasy. By chance this passage was well known in the Middle Ages, having been paraphrased, indeed almost translated, as Pierre Courcelle has shown, by St. Ambrose. In one of his sermons, he adds an interesting detail to Plotinus' exhortation: "Let us therefore flee to our true homeland . . . But what manner of flight is this? It is not with our bodily feet that it is accomplished, for our steps, no matter where they run, take us only from one land to another. Nor let us flee in ships, in chariots, or with horses that stumble and fall, but let us flee with our minds (*fugiamus animo*), with our eyes or with our interior feet."[11] It is not essential, for my purposes, to suggest that Dante knew this passage, although there is no reason why he could not have. The phrase *fugiamus animo* is not so bizarre that its resemblance to Dante's phrase could establish it as the poet's source. But even if Dante did not know it, the point can still be made that since Ambrose's phrase was meant to sound Platonic, it is likely that the similar phrase, "l'animo mio ch'ancor fuggiva," especially in a context of failure, was likewise meant by Dante to have philosophical rather than theological force.

The division between body and soul was of course a commonplace in ancient "flights" of the soul. For Christians, however, it was not the body *per se* that constituted the impediment, but rather the fallen flesh. It is not physical reality that the soul must flee, but sin itself. Before looking at Augustine's view of the dichotomy, it might be well to show how a less original thinker saw the effect of the division of body and soul in the psychology of conversion. Gregory the Great provides us with the kind of theological context in which I believe we are to read the "animo" and "corpo" of Dante's verses. His remarks are suggestive, too, for a reading of the impediments that beset the pilgrim:

> Indeed, one suffers initially after conversion, considering one's past sins, wishing to break immediately the bonds of secular concerns, to walk in tranquillity the ways of the Lord, to throw off the heavy burden of earthly desires and in free servitude to put on the light yoke of God. Yet while one thinks of these things, there arises a familiar delight in the flesh which quickly takes root. The longer it holds on, the tighter it becomes, the later does one manage to leave it behind. What suffering in such a situation, what anxiety of the heart! *When the spirit calls and the flesh calls us back.* On one hand the intimacy of a new love invites us, on the other the old habits of vice hold us back.[12]

This is the "flesh" that was ignored by Plotinus in his rather optimistic invitation to the soul to fly to the Truth.

To return to Ambrose's influential statement for a moment, we notice that he added the detail of the "interior feet" to Plotinus' remarks. No reader of Dante's first canto can fail to remember that after resting his tired body, the pilgrim sets off to his objective "sì che 'l piè fermo sempre era 'l più basso." In another essay (chapter

2 in this book), I attempt to explain the meaning of that verse in terms of the allegory of the "interior feet" of the soul. The "piè fermo" signifies the pilgrim's will, unable to respond to the promptings of the reason because of the Pauline malady, characteristic of fallen man whose mind far outstrips the ability of a wounded will to attain the truth. The fallen will limps in its efforts to reach God. Augustine, who uses the theme in a submerged way, was himself very probably Dante's direct source for the image of an *homo claudus,* unable to advance to the summit. In a passage from the *Confessions* paraphrasing precisely the Plotinian, then Ambrosian passage, Augustine insists upon the inability of a crippled will to complete the journey. He does so with an extended comparison of the movement of the limbs with the movement of the will:

> I was troubled in spirit, most vehemently indignant that I entered not into Thy Will and Covenant, O my God, which all my bones cried out unto me to enter, and praised it to the skies. And therein we enter not by ships, or chariots, or feet, nor move not so far as I had come from the house to that place where we were sitting. For, not to go only, but to go *in* thither was nothing else but to will to go, but to will resolutely and thoroughly; not to turn and toss, this way and that, *a maimed and half-divided will, struggling, with one part sinking as another rose.*[13]

In this magnificent passage, Augustine uses Platonic words and turns them against the Platonists. The goal is not some world of Ideas, but the covenant of Jehovah. Moreover, the problem is not of the body as a purely physical impediment, but rather of the fallen and crippled will, shortcomings the Platonists had not considered. As Augustine was unable to achieve the ecstasy of the Platonists, so Dante's pilgrim is unable to reach the truth of the mind with a will that "sempre era 'l più basso." The parallel is close enough to suggest on Dante's part a conscious evocation.

Apart from the parallels between Dante's journey and Augustine's with respect both to the need for the journey and to the fatal flaws in the wayfarers, there are also parallels to be drawn with regard to the objective. The light of God, even as perceived with the neoplatonic eyes of the soul, proves too much for Augustine in the seventh book of his *Confessions:* "And Thou didst beat back the weakness of my sight, streaming forth Thy beams of light upon me most strongly, and I trembled with love and awe: and I perceived myself to be far off from Thee, in the region of unlikeness, as if I heard this Thy voice from on high: 'I am the food of grown men, grow, and thou shalt feed upon Me.' "[14] In spite of his repeated attempts to reach the light, the weight of "fleshly habit" causes him to fall back, "sinking with sorrow into these inferior things—*ruebam in ista cum gemitu*."[15] Dante might well have been remembering that phrase when he described himself as beaten back by the wolf: "i' rovinava in basso loco." Augustine seems to hear the voice of God in the light that he sees. The synaesthetic effect is rhetorically appropriate in this interior journey, for all of the senses here stand for movements of the mind, moved by a single God in all of His various manifestations. It may not be purely coincidental that Dante also insists on a mystical synaesthesia in his experience. After he is beaten back to the dark wood, he describes it as the place "dove 'l sol tace." The implication is that the light which he saw before spoke to him with a voice that was divine.

Pierre Courcelle has traced Augustine's "vain attempts at Plotinian ecstasy" back to their neoplatonic sources.[16] What emerges clearly from his study is that the ancients saw no need for a guide on such a journey. Plotinus explicitly says that one requires self-confidence to reach the goal, rather than a guide.[17] This self-confidence was precisely what Augustine interpreted as philosophical pride, the element that in his view vitiated all such attempts. His own interior journey begins with an insistence upon his need for help: "And being thence admonished to return to myself, I entered even into my inward self, *Thou being my Guide:* and able I was, for *Thou wert become my Helper.* And I entered and beheld with the eye of my soul (such as it was), above the same eye of my soul, above my mind, the Light Unchangeable."[18] Christian virtue, unlike Socratic virtue, is more than knowledge and vice is more than ignorance. The Platonic conversion toward the light is doomed to failure because it neglects to take account of man's fallen condition. To put the matter in Platonic terms, the pilgrim must struggle even to reach the cave from which Plato assumed the journey began. That struggle, the descent in humility, helps remove the barrier that philosophy leaves intact. God's guidance, represented dramatically in the poem by the pilgrim's three guides, transforms philosophical presumption into Christian confession. St. Bernard, an outspoken critic of philosophical presumption, speaks of the opposition between humility and pride in the itinerary to God. His remarks serve as an excellent illustration of how familiar Augustine's struggle was in the Middle Ages and of how readily the struggle lent itself to dramatization in terms that are strikingly like Dante's:

> "Who dares climb the mountain of the Lord or who will stand in His holy place?" . . . Only the humble man can safely climb the mountain, because only the humble man has nothing to trip him up. The proud man may climb it indeed, yet he cannot stand for long . . . The proud man has only one foot to stand on: love of his own excellence . . . Therefore to stand firmly, we must stand humbly. So that our feet may never stumble we must stand not on the single foot of pride, but on the two feet of humility.[19]

There can be scarcely any doubt that Dante's pilgrim climbs the mountain in the same tradition.

The final passage from Augustine's seventh book provides a series of images which offer the closest analogue to the landscape with which Dante begins his poem. The theme is humility, which provides a transition to the eighth book, from attempts at Plotinian ecstasy to the conversion under the fig tree. Speaking of Christ against the philosophers he says:

> They disdain to learn of Him, because He is gentle and humble of heart; for these things hast Thou hid from the wise and prudent, and hast revealed them unto babes. For it is one thing from a wooded mountain-top (*de silvestre cacumine*) to see the land of peace and to find no way thither; and in vain to essay through ways unpassable, opposed and beset by fugitives and deserters, under their captain the lion and the dragon: and another to keep on the way that leads thither, guarded by the host of the heavenly General (*cura caelestis imperatoris*); where they spoil not who have deserted the heavenly army (*qui caelestem militiam deseruerunt*)[20]

The Augustinian phrase, "de silvestre cacumine," may at first seem a trifle remote as an analogue for the "selva oscura," but if we read on in the *Confessions* we find that Augustine elaborates on the description of his former life with an alternate image: "In this so vast wilderness [*immensa silva*], full of snares and dangers, behold many of them I have cut off and thrust out of my heart."[21] Of greater significance is the fact that elements of the former passage echo not only in the first canto of the *Inferno,* but perhaps also in the eighth canto of the *Purgatorio.* In other words, there seem to exist between the two authors not only analogies of detail but also of structure, for in these few lines Augustine distinguishes between success and failure in the journey to God by a series of oppositions that match the opposition between the journey of the prologue and the successful journey that it foreshadows. One need only paraphrase Augustine in Dantesque terms in order to make this apparent: it is one thing to be beset by wild beasts and quite another to be guarded by the "essercito gentile" (*Purg.* VIII, 22) of the "imperador che là sù regna" (*Inf.* I, 124), safe from the chief deserter, "'l nostro avversaro" (*Purg.* VIII, 95).

A further word must be said here about the most famous image of the prologue scene, that of the "selva oscura." If we are in fact dealing in the prologue with an attempt at transcendence that is neoplatonic in origin, then the temptation is strong to identify Dante's "selva" with the prime matter of Plato's *Timaeus,* the traditional enemy of philosophical flights of the soul. The Greek word for matter, *hylē,* was rendered into Latin as "silva" by Chalcidius and the phrase "silva Platonis" became proverbial in the Middle Ages. Bernardus Silvestris uses the word with a force that sometimes suggests a totally unchristian equation of matter with evil: *silva rigens, praeponderante malitia, silvestris malignitas.*[22] Some critics recently have attempted to associate Dante's "selva" with the Platonic "silva," thereby reviving a gloss that goes back to the Renaissance commentary of Cristoforo Landino.[23] The gloss runs the risk, however, of leading to a serious misunderstanding. In the dark wood, we are not dealing with man's hylomorphic composition, but rather with *sin.* Landino's facile equation, "corpo, cioè vizio" will not do for the "selva," for it obscures the fundamental point of Christianity's quarrel with metaphysical dualism. Ultimately, to obscure the difference between "corpo" and "vizio" is to forget the doctrine of the Incarnation and this Dante was no more likely to forget than was Augustine, who spent much of his life refuting the Manicheans.

Nevertheless, it is possible to show that Dante used the opposition "selva–luce" in exactly the same way that he used the opposition "corpo–animo"; that is, as a Platonic commonplace used to signify a struggle of which the Platonists were unaware. The distinctive characteristic of the dark wood in Dante's poem is not that it is a *selva,* but rather that it is *oscura,* as the following textual parallel reveals:

Già m'avean trasportato
i lenti *passi*
dentro a *la selva antica*
tanto, ch'io

non potea rivedere *ond' io mi 'ntrassi;*

ed ecco più andar mi tolse
un rio
(*Purg.* XXVIII, 22–25)

Nel mezzo del *cammin*
di nostra vita
mi ritrovai per *una*
selva oscura

. . . . .

Io non so ben ridir com'
i' v'intrai

. . . . .

Ed ecco, quasi al cominciar
de l'erta
(*Inf.* I, 1–2, 10, 31)

Now my slow steps had carried me on into the ancient wood so far that I could not see back to where I had entered it, when lo, a stream took from me further progress

Midway in the journey of our life I found myself in a dark wood . . . . . I cannot rightly say how I entered it . . . . . And behold, near the beginning of the steep

The resemblance can hardly be fortuitous. Dante's descent into hell and his ascent of the mountain of purgatory bring him to a point from which he can begin his climb to the light, his entrance into sanctifying grace, without fear of the impediments that blocked his way before. That new point of departure, the garden of Eden, was the home of man before the fall. Through Adam's transgression, the prelapsarian state of man was transformed into the state of sin. In poetic terms, Adam transformed the *selva antica* into a *selva oscura.* Although the "rio" forever separates the pilgrim from original justice and Matelda, he can, with the help of Beatrice, go far beyond:

"Qui sarai tu poco tempo *silvano;*
e sarai meco sanza fine cive
di quella Roma onde Cristo è romano.
(*Purg.* XXXII, 100–102)

Here shall you be short time a forester, and

> you shall be with me forever a citizen of that
> Rome whereof Christ is Roman.

To say that the pilgrim is a *silvano* is to say that he still inhabits the *selva* of human existence; only in the *selva* darkened by sin, what Dante called "la selva erronea di questa vita,"[24] does it become impossible to follow the path to the heavenly city.

Augustine chose to describe the impediments on his journey to the mountain top in terms of the wild beasts of the Psalms, the lion and the dragon. Dante, on the other hand, described them in terms of the three beasts of Jeremiah 5:6. I take these to be the basic wounds to the rational, irascible, and concupiscent appetites suffered by all men as a result of the fall (see chap. 2 in this book). What is of particular poetic interest here is that in the text of Jeremiah, those three beasts are said to be enemies of all the sinners of Jerusalem. The question is, why should the three beasts associated with Jerusalem, the promised land, be the obstacles to the pilgrim on his climb?

The answer, I believe, resides in the fact that the pilgrim's goal is in a sense Jerusalem, or at least the heavenly Jerusalem, although he cannot know that until he reaches it, which is to say, until he assumes the perspective of the poet. Earlier I suggested that both Augustine and Dante used scriptural exegesis in order to structure their experience, superimposing (or discovering, they would insist) a biblical pattern of meaning upon their own history. Thus far I have tried to compare the shadowy world of the pilgrim with Augustine's region of unlikeness. There is nothing shadowy about the interpretative view of the poet, however, for, as Charles Singleton has shown, part of the poet's strategy is to introduce into both the prologue and the *Purgatorio,* superimposed upon the narrative, the *figura* which was considered to be the pattern of conversion.[25] We have already cited the verses that relate the emergence from the dark wood to the crossing of a "passo" through the open sea. Again, as the pilgrim struggles up the slope of the mountain, the poet refers to him as being in a "gran diserto," as far from woods or water as can be imagined. Finally, when the wolf blocks the pilgrim's passage, Lucy, looking down from heaven, sees him as though he were standing before a flooded river of death, weeping and unable to cross. In the sea, desert, and river, any medieval exegete would discern the three stages of the exodus of the Jews, en route from Egypt to Jerusalem, the promised land.

In this respect too, Dante probably owed much to the Augustinian tradition. For the representation of his attempts at purely intellectual conversion, Augustine drew upon the traditional neoplatonic motifs of the conversion to the light. At the same time, he reinterpreted those motifs in the light of Revelation. On at least one occasion, the death of Monica, his allusion to the figure of exodus is explicit: "May they [God's servants] with devout affection remember my parents in this transitory light, my brethren under Thee our Father in our Catholic Mother, and my fellow-citizens in that eternal Jerusalem which Thy pilgrim people sigheth after from their Exodus, even unto their return thither."[26] There may be as well an allusion to the exodus in the passage in the seventh book, which seems so important for Dante's representation: "For it is one thing, from the wooded mountain top to see the land of peace and to find no way thither." In the sixteenth century, the passage was annotated with a reference to Deut. 32:48–52, where Moses is permitted by God to see the land of Canaan from the mountain, but not to reach it: "Yet thou shalt see the land before thee; but thou shalt not go thither unto the land which I give the children of Israel."[27]

These references are admittedly too few to enable us to demonstrate that the presence of the figure of exodus is of importance in Augustine's narrative, but if Augustine was merely allusive with respect to the figure, commentators on his work throughout the Middle Ages were explicit. Courcelle's repertory of commentaries on the "region of unlikeness" provides many citations that are suggestive for the interpretation of Dante's prologue scene. Among them are several which specifically relate Augustine's conversion to the traditional biblical figure of conversion. Richard of St. Victor will serve as an example:

> The first miracle was accomplished in the exodus of Israel from Egypt (*In exitu Israel de Aegypto*), the second was in the exodus of Israel from the desert. Who will give me the power to leave behind the region of unlikeness? Who will enable me to enter the promised land, so that I may see both the flight of the sea and the turning back of the Jordan.[28]

Richard makes clear, first of all, that Egypt is a state of mind, and secondly, that even after leaving it, the soul must traverse a desert egion which is precisely like the "gran diserto" in which the pilgrim blocked: "Coming forth from the darkness of Egypt, from worldly rror to the more secret places of the heart, you discover nothing lse but a place of terror and vast solitude. This is that desert land, rid and unpassable . . . filled with all terrible things."[29] In this desert lace, where "all is confused, all is disturbed; where nothing is in its roper place, nothing proceeds in proper order,"[30] the impediments ne encounters are the vices and passions (usually three-fold, according to Augustine's commentators)[31] to which man is subject, nce "vulnerati sumus ingredientes mundum"[32] (we are already ounded when we enter the world).

The Wings of Ulysses (*Inf.* XXVI, 125)

The canto of Ulysses contains a striking instance of Dante's use f neoplatonic imagery to describe, not simply the flight of the soul the absolute, but also the inevitable failure attendant upon any ich journey when it is undertaken without the help of God. This stance of neoplatonic imagery is therefore analogous, perhaps even ordinate, to the imagery the poet uses to describe his own unsuccessful journey in the first canto.

Since Giorgio Padoan's essay of some years ago,[33] there can no nger be any doubt that Dante's Ulysses is the Ulysses of medieval adition, whose journey was considered to have a moral significance. he knowledge which is the object of his quest is of a metaphysical, ther than navigational, order. In Dante's reading, as in the reading the neoplatonists, the voyage was an allegory for the flight of the ul to transcendent truth; one could extend Padoan's argument to ggest that Dante's Ulysses ends up a shipwreck rather than in the ms of some paradisiac Penelope in order to indicate what Dante ought of such purely philosophical excursions. It is this dimension meaning that gives the episode its structural importance throughit the poem, beyond the limits of the canto in which it is contained. ne ancient voyager is recalled at the beginning of the *Purgatorio* d again toward the end of the *Paradiso* precisely to mark the conist between his abortive journey and that of the pilgrim. Dante's scent into hell enables him to reach the shore which Ulysses was le only to make out in the distance, a contrast that evokes once ain, as we shall see, Augustine's distinction between philosophical esumption and Christian conversion.

At one point in his famous speech, Ulysses describes his journe in terms that directly allude to the traditional flight of the soul:

> e volta nostra poppa nel mattino,
>   de' remi facemmo ali al folle volo . . .   (vv. 124–125)

> And turning our stern to the morning, we made
> of our oars wings for the mad flight . . .

Critics have seized on the phrase "folle volo" and have used it t characterize the daring of Ulysses' voyage. The adjective is partic ularly apt, as Rocco Montano has observed,[34] for it can reflect bot Ulysses' regret for the disastrous consequences of his voyage, as we as the author's moral judgment on the entire undertaking. Howeve the first part of the verse is of potentially much greater significanc By itself, the word "volo" might be taken as a simple rhetorical twis a faint suggestion at best of Platonic flights. A careful look at th preceding metaphor, however, transforms the suggestion into a ce tainty. When Dante has Ulysses say "dei remi facemmo ali," he echoing a classical metaphor, the "remigium alarum" used by Virg to describe the flight of Daedalus. The metaphor was eventuall endowed with meaning in a philosophical context, a meaning whic is relevant to our understanding of the entire episode.

In the sixth book of the *Aeneid,* Virgil summarizes in a fe words the story of Daedalus and Icarus. He then describes the temp built by Daedalus and the votive offering made to Phoebus:

> Redditus his primum terris, tibi, Phoebe, sacravit
> remigium alarum posuitque immania templa.
> (*Aeneid* VI, 18–19)

> Here first restored to earth, he consecrated to
> you, O Phoebus, the oarage of his wings, and
> built a vast temple.

It is to Pierre Courcelle that we are indebted for the history of t neoplatonic interpretation of Daedalus' "wingèd oarage."[35] In t article to which Padoan alludes in his essay, Courcelle shows th both the story of Ulysses and the flight of Daedalus were interpret by neoplatonists to signify the flight of the soul: "il faut que l'ân prenne son vol pour regagner sa patrie."[36] St. Ambrose refers to t myth of Daedalus to describe the liberation of the soul from matter and uses the phrase "remigium alarum," as does St. Augustine on several occasions.[37] I should like merely to add to Courcelle's vast documentation a passage that lies outside the scope of his study but is exactly within mine, since it occurs in the only medieval neoplatonic commentary of the *Aeneid* which Dante was likely to have known. Bernardus Silvestris simply echoed a long tradition when he identified the temple with contemplation and the "remigium alarum" with reason, but in doing so, he probably made that gloss directly accessible to Dante:

> Daedalus came to the temple of Apollo, that is, to the contemplation of sublime things with the reason. And journeying with the intellect he turned his attention completely to the study of philosophy, and there he dedicated the oarage of his wings, that is, the exercise of his reason and intellect (*alarum remigium i.e. rationis et intellectus exercitium sacravit*).[38]

Just as Virgil's *remigium alarum* metaphorically transformed Daedalus' flight into a sea voyage, so the phrase, "de' remi facemmo ali" transformed Ulysses' voyage into a Platonic "volo." Ulysses' journey is an extended dramatization of an interior journey through what Padoan has called "le vie della sapienza"; the very oars that he used were traditional metaphors for the power of intellect.

I should like to underscore what I take to be an important implication of the phrase that Dante puts into the mouth of Ulysses. The "wingèd oarage" of tradition was usually associated with Daedalus, rather than Icarus.[39] In Virgil's story it was mentioned in connection with a flight that was not "folle" at all, for Daedalus, unlike his son, reached his objective. This element is what the allegory of Ulysses has in common with the allegory of Daedalus: the return of Daedalus to safety ("*Redditus* his primum terris") and the return of Homer's Ulysses to his home made those stories excellent analogues for the Platonic *regressus* of the soul to its heavenly *patria*.[40] The fact that Dante associated the "remigium alarum" of tradition with Ulysses' voyage seems to suggest that he was aware of an allegorical significance common to the two stories; yet, by describing the flight as a "folle volo," he seems deliberately to have turned the allegory against its authors. In spite of the opinion of most modern commentators, he may even have known of Ulysses' return to Ithaca through several indirect sources;[41] he certainly knew that the "wingèd oarage" of the soul was usually associated with the return of Daedalus. Nevertheless, it is *because* he accepts the common allegorical significance and interprets it as a Christian must that his version of the story ends in shipwreck. If Ulysses is shipwrecked and if the wings of Daedalus seem rather to recall Icarus, it is because the *regressus* that both stories came to represent is, in Dante's view, philosophical presumption that is bound to end in failure. I should like to suggest that the voyage of Dante's Ulysses exists on the same plane of reality as its counterpart, the journey of the pilgrim; that is, as a dramatic representation of the journey of the mind. It is for this reason that Dante takes it as an admonition:

> Allor mi dolsi, e ora mi ridoglio
> quando drizzo la mente a ciò ch'io vidi,
> e più *lo 'ngegno* affreno ch'i' non soglio,
> perché non corra che *virtù* nol guidi. (*Inf.* XXVI, 19–22)

> I sorrowed then, and sorrow now again, when I turn my mind to what I saw; and I curb my genius more than I am wont, lest it run where virtue does not guide it.

His insistence on the distinction between *ingegno* and *virtù,* between the motive power of his journey and his guide, contrasts sharply with the speech of Ulysses, in which "virtute e canoscenza" (v. 120) seem almost synonymous, the single, somewhat exterior objective of the "folle volo." Just as the ancients equated knowledge and virtue, so too Ulysses seems to equate them, making no provision in his calculations for the journey within, the personal *askesis* upon which all such attempts at transcendence must be based. The distinction between Ulysses' journey and the journey of the pilgrim is not in the objective, for both are directed toward that mountain in the southern hemisphere, but rather in how the journey is accomplished. The difference is quite literally the journey through hell, the descent *intra nos* which transforms philosophical presumption into a journey of the mind and heart to God.

For Plotinus the power of intellect was a sufficient vehicle for the flight to the truth; the great neoplatonist specifically denied the need for any guide on such a journey. For Augustine, on the contrary, and for all Christian thinkers thereafter, the journey had to be accomplished "et per intellectum *et per affectum*."[42] Such insistence on the volitive power of the soul is the constant theme of Augustine's polemic against neoplatonism in the *Confessions*. This polemic, I believe, lies at the heart of Dante's representation in the canto of Ulysses. Toward the beginning of the *Confessions*, Augustine uses the example of the prodigal son in order to illustrate his thesis that one moves toward or away from God with the will:

> For darkened affections is removal from Thee. For it is not by our feet, or change of place, that men leave Thee or return unto Thee, nor did Thy younger son look out for *horses* or *chariots*, or *ships*, or *fly with visible wings*, or journey by the *motion of his limbs* that he might in a far country waste in riotous living all Thou gavest at his departure.[43]

Again, in the passage offered earlier as a background text for understanding Dante's "piè fermo" verse, some of these images of flight reappear:

> And therein [Thy Covenant] we enter not by *ships*, or *chariots* or *feet*, nor move not so far as I had come from the house to that place where we were sitting. For, not to go only, but to go *in* thither was nothing else but to will to go, but to will resolutely and thoroughly; not to turn and toss, this way and that, a maimed and half-divided will, struggling, with one part sinking as another rose.[44]

Each of Augustine's neoplatonic images of flight has its counterpart in the canto of Ulysses. Ulysses describes his navigation as a wingèd flight, but to the pilgrim the sight of the Greek hero recalls a celestial chariot:

> E qual colui che si vengiò con li orsi
> vide 'l *carro* d'Elia al dipartire,
> quando *i cavalli* al cielo erti levorsi . . . (vv. 34–36)

> And as he who was avenged by the bears saw
> Elijah's chariot at its departure, when the horses
> rose erect to heaven . . .

Whatever else Dante may have intended to suggest by the somewhat gratuitous comparison, the fact remains that, like the ship of Ulysses and the wings of Daedalus, the chariot of Elijah is on a flight to the absolute. The presence of these comparisons, although stripped of all trace of Platonic banality by Dante's poetic power, nevertheless reinforces the figurative significance of Ulysses' voyage and generalizes that significance beyond the limits of one man's experience. At first glance the passages from the *Confessions* just quoted and the episode of Ulysses seem to have nothing more in common than these images of flight, schematic and allusive in Augustine, dramatic and powerful in Dante's verses. But the allusions in Augustine's words can lead us back to a complex of literary and philosophical motifs to which, I believe, the figure of Dante's Ulysses owes its origin.

As Pierre Courcelle has shown, the neoplatonic images in the Augustinian passage derive from a text of Plotinus, incorporated virtually unchanged by St. Ambrose and quoted partially above. A fuller citation of the passage reveals that Plotinus is in fact thinking of Ulysses when he urges his reader on to the journey without a guide to the heavenly *patria:*

> Let us therefore flee to our dear homeland . . . But what manner of flight is this? How shall we reascend? Like Ulysses, who, they say, escaped from Circe the magician and from Calypso, that is, who refused to stay with them in spite of the pleasures of the eyes and the beauty of the senses that he found there . . . it is not with our feet that it can be accomplished . . . nor must we prepare for ourselves a team of horses or a ship . . . we must rather look with the inner eye.[45]

Both St. Ambrose and St. Augustine suppressed the reference to Ulysses when they paraphrased Plotinus' exhortation. Several other passages in Augustine's work, however, suggest that Ulysses came to represent for him the archetype of the presumptuous philospher who would reach the truth unaided.[46] One text in particular, the prologue to the *De beata vita,* seems, according to Courcelle, to refer to Ulysses in a lengthy allegory of voyage.[47] Padoan in his essay quoted from it, yet failed to refer to some of the passages which seem most relevant for understanding Dante's Ulysses. Of considerable importance for the purpose of this study is that Augustine helps us to understand the significance of shipwreck on a journey such as that undertaken by Ulysses. More important still is the fact that he seems to read in the voyage his own philosophical experience.

Augustine begins his allegory by explaining that an unknown power has launched us on the sea of life and that each of us seeks, with more or less success, the port of philosophy: "how would we know how to get there, except by the power of some tempest, (which fools believe to be adverse) hurling us, unknowing wanderers, toward that most desired land?"[48] He then distinguishes three types of philosophers. The first never wander very far, yet find the place of tranquillity and become beacons to their fellow men. The second,

> deceived by the deceptive appearance of the sea, choose to set out on the open sea and dare to wander far from their country, often forgetting it. If . . . the wind, which they deem favorable, keeps blowing from the poop, they enter proudly and rejoicing into an abyss of misery . . . What else can we wish them but . . . a violent tempest and contrary winds, to lead them in spite of their sighs and tears, to certain and solid joys?[49]

Padoan observed that the element of forgetfulness in this passage seems to recall Ulysses' neglect of family and home, while the following paragraph seems more reminiscent of Aeneas.[50] Nevertheless, the hazards described in the latter, are instructive for glossing Ulysses' journey as well:

> Those of the third category . . . perceive certain signs which remind them of their dear homeland . . . and, either they find their home again without wandering or delay, or more often, they lose their way in the fog or fix upon stars that sink in the sea. Again, they are sometimes held back by various seductions and miss the best time for setting sail. They wander for a long time and even risk shipwreck. It often happens to such men that some calamity, arising in the midst of their good fortune, like a tempest opposing their efforts, drives them back to the homeland of their desires and of their peace.[51]

There is an undeniable, although somewhat generic, resemblance between these sea-going adventures of philosophical quest and Ulysses' own story. The reference to the navigational "fix" on stars that sink beneath the waters is perhaps less generic. It is paralleled by the apparently descriptive but probably significant detail mentioned by Ulysses:

Tutte le stelle già de l'altro polo
   vedea la notte, e 'l nostro tanto basso,
   che non surgëa fuor del marin suolo. (vv. 127–129)

The night now saw the other pole and all its stars, and ours so low that it did not rise from the ocean floor.

The point is that the ship is "off course," since the pole star, upon which all mariners must fix for guidance, has disappeared beneath the ocean floor. But the most startling detail of Augustine's allegory follows the paragraph just cited, and one that Padoan omitted; it may be the clue to why Ulysses should be sailing toward a *mountain,* rather than back to Ithaca:

> Now all of these men who, in some manner, are borne toward the land of happiness, have to fear and desperately to avoid a huge mountain set up before the port, creating a great danger to those entering. It shines so and is clothed with such a deceptive light that it seems to offer to those who enter a haven, promising to satisfy their longing for the land of happiness . . . For what other mountain does the reason designate as fearful to those who are entering upon or have entered philosophical study than the mountain of proud vainglory?[52]

At this point Augustine concludes his allegorical exposition and proceeds to apply the allegory of his own life. In his youth, he had fixed his eyes on stars that sank into the ocean and therefore led him astray. The study of various philosophies kept him afloat, but the attractions of a woman and the love of honor prevented him from flying "totis velis omnibusque remis" (with full sail and all the oars) into the embrace of philosophy. Finally, a tempest that he took to be adverse (his illness), forced him to abandon the career that was leading him toward the sirens and drove his shaky and leaking boat toward the haven of tranquillity.[53]

The prologue of the *De beata vita* is a dramatic representation of the events recounted with apologetic intent in the *Confessions*. The attempts at Plotinian ecstasy are represented in the seventh book of the *Confessions* in largely traditional philosophical terms while in the prologue to the dialogue, under the influence of a long tradition of Homeric allegoresis, autobiography takes a more literary form. There is a similar relationship between the experience of Dante's pilgrim and that of Ulysses. For both men, the object of the journey seems to be the mountain in the southern hemisphere. Again, the pilgrim takes Ulysses' fate to be a specific admonition for himself. Ulysses dies shipwrecked before the looming mountain, but in the first canto of the poem the pilgrim seems to have survived, by pure accident, a metaphorical shipwreck of his own:

> E come quei che con lena affannata,
>   uscito fuor del pelago a la riva,
>   si volge a l'acqua perigliosa e guata,
> così l'animo mio, ch'ancor fuggiva,
>   si volse a retro a rimirar *lo passo*
>   che non lasciò già mai persona viva. (*Inf.* I, 22–27)

> And as he who with laboring breath has escaped from the deep to the shore turns to look back on the dangerous waters, so my mind which was still fleeing turned back to gaze upon the pass that never left anyone alive.

Ulysses' experience with the "alto passo" (*Inf.* XXVI, 132) seems to be what one would expect of such a "varco folle." (*Par.* XXVII, 82–83). It is the pilgrim's survival that is gratuitous, both on the mountain of the prologue and the mountain of purgatory. In the latter instance, just before he is girded with the rush of humility, he remembers Ulysses' pride:

> Venimmo poi in sul lito diserto,
>   che mai non vide navicar sue acque
>   omo, che di *tornar* sia poscia esperto. (*Purg.* I, 130–132)

> Then we came on to the desert shore, that never saw any man navigate its waters who afterwards had experience of return.

The return is the element of the story that is given new meaning, in the Christian perspective. The mountain of philosophic pride, says Augustine, "swallows up into its depths the proud men who walk upon it and covers them over in its darkness, snatching from them that shining abode of which they had caught but a glimpse."[54] For some that shipwreck was definitive; for others it was the prelude to a new life, "com'Altrui piacque."

At the beginning of this essay I suggested that Dante's borrowing from Augustine in the *Confessions* was not simply an isolated fact of purely historical interest but was also of some significance for the interpretation of the poem. If Dante chose to echo Augustine's attempt to reach the truth through philosophy alone, then the implication is that Dante undertook a similar attempt and also met with failure. For all of his efforts in the *Convivio* to define philosophic truth in theological terms, Dante's philosophical experience may have been as ultimately disillusioning for him as was Augustine's with the neoplatonists. Whatever that experience, we know that it was shared by Guido Cavalcanti, who seems to have remained obdurate in his philosophical presumption. In the fourth book of the *Confessions,* a deathbed conversion of a dear friend separates Augustine from one who was "of one soul with me." Although the roles are reversed, it is the same drama of conversion that seems to come between Dante and his "first friend" in the tenth canto of the *Inferno.*

The myth of Ulysses serves as an exemplar of philosophical pride and, as we have seen, an antitype of Dante's own philosophical experience. In concretely historical terms, however, Guido fulfilled the role of alter ego and antitype. Some of the words used by Augustine in his generic condemnation of the Platonists are repeated in intensely personal terms when Dante refers to his friend. In the seventh book of the *Confessions,* Augustine says that he was able to find in the teaching of the Platonists all of the prologue to the Gospel of John except for the doctrine of the Word made flesh. The philosophers "disdain to learn of Him because He is gentle and humble of heart." Similarly, in the *Inferno,* we learn that Guido "disdained" guidance for a descent into hell: "ebbe a disdegno" (*Inf.* X, 63). The past absolute tense with reference to a subject who is still alive requires us to understand "disdained" as a perfected action—disdained *to come*—rather than as some habitual attitude toward Virgil or Beatrice. In sense and in syntax, it is exactly equivalent to the refusal of the philosophers to learn from Christ's humility—*dedignantur ab eo discere*—as exemplified by His descent into hell. Like Ulysses or the pilgrim of the prologue, Guido was lost, perhaps definitively ("forse . . ."), by his philosophical presumption.

Beyond this biographical analogy, there is the more important analogy, or perhaps *homology,* of literary structure. As in all spiritual autobiographies, so in the *Confessions* and in the *Divine Comedy* there is a radical division between the protagonist and the author who tells his story. The question of the relative "sincerity" of such autobiographies is the question of how real we take that division to be. Augustine and Dante took it to be almost ontologically real, for it was their conviction that the experience of conversion, the subject matter of their respective stories, was tantamount to a death of their former selves and the beginning of a new life.

For Dante, the distance between protagonist and author is at its maximum at the beginning of the story and is gradually closed by the dialectic of poetic process until pilgrim and poet coincide at the ending of the poem, which gives a unity and a coherence to all that went before. From the outset, the poet's voice expresses the detached point of view toward which his pilgrim strives, while the journey of the pilgrim is history in the making, a tentative, problematic view constantly subject to revision, approaching certitude as a limit. It is at the last moment that the metamorphosis of the pilgrim's view of the world is completed, when he himself has become metamorphosed into the poet, capable at last of writing the story that we have read.

This metamorphosis accounts for much of the ambiguity in the characterizations of the *Inferno.* The critical uncertainties about whether Francesca is a heroine of spontaneous human love or merely a deluded medieval Emma Bovary, whether Ulysses embodies the spirit of the Renaissance or simply *mala curiositas,* whether Ugolino is a father suffering with Dostoevskian dignity or a Pisan cannibal, arise from the dialectical relationship of the pilgrim's view to that of the poet. Further, it is no accident that we generally side with the pilgrim in his human response to these great figures, against the crushing exigencies of the poet's structure. The pilgrim's view is much like our own view of history and of ourselves: partial, perhaps confused, still in the making. But the poet's view is far different, for it is global and comprehensive, the total view of a man who looks at the world, his neighborhood, and indeed himself with all the detachment of a cultural anthropologist. The process of the poem, which is to say the progress of the pilgrim, is the transformation of the problematic and humanistic into the certain and transcendent, from novelistic involvement to epic detachment, from a synchronic view of the self in a dark wood to a diachronic total view of the entire world as if it were, to use Dante's powerful image, a humble threshing floor upon which a providential history will one day separate the wheat from the chaff.

The view from paradise is a spatial translation of what might be called a memory of universal history. The coherence of the whole poem may be grasped only with a view to its totality, a view from the ending, just as the coherence of the poet's life could be grasped only in retrospect, from the perspective of totality in death. Clearly the same may be said of universal history, whose coherence may be perceived only from the perspective of eschatology, when the evolution is finally concluded. In the linear time that is ours, such a perspective is impossible, for it implies a survival of our own death and the death of the world. For Dante, however, as for Augustine, there was a death which enabled the mind to grasp such totalities, not by virtue of linear evolution, but rather by transcendence: a death of detachment. To perceive the pattern of one's life in its totality was to see the structure or *figura* of God's redemptive act, the master-plan of all history. In the *Paradiso,* Dante describes the cognition of the blessed as he addresses Cacciaguida:

> . . . come veggion le terrene menti
> non capere in trïangol due ottusi,
> così vedi le cose contingenti
> anzi che sieno in sé, mirando il punto
> a cui tutti li tempi son presenti; (*Par.* XVII, 14–18)

> even as earthly minds see that two obtuse angles can not be contained in a triangle, so you, gazing upon the Point to which all times are present, do see contingent things before they exist in themselves.

This "now" of the blessed, like a geometric *figura,* enables Cacciaguida to prophesy Dante's future without ambiguity. It provides the place to stand from which the pilgrim comes ultimately to see himself and the world around him under the aspect of eternity.

Augustine first saw the need to define that "present moment," the position from which one could see one's former self, in the totality that is present in God. He was also the first to see the metaphysical significance of what used to be referred to as "organic unity." For Augustine, as well as for Dante, a poem had to be understood as a unity, not because it was a "literary object," but rather because its significance could be grasped only when its process was completed. This was not simply a literary fact, but rather the outward sign of a spiritual reality. A passage from the *Confessions* makes clear how the progression to greater and greater totalities can lead from a poem to universal history:

> I am about to repeat a Psalm that I know. Before I begin, my expectation is extended over the totality; but when I have begun, however much of it I shall separate off into the past is extended along my memory . . . until the whole expectation be at length exhausted, when that whole action being ended, shall have passed into memory . . . the same takes place in the whole life of man, whereof all the actions of man are parts; the same holds through the whole age of the sons of men, whereof all the lives of men are parts.[55]

Formal criticism helps us to see how the poem must be read in retrospect, but to see all of reality in that way requires a perspective more privileged than that of the critic. From such a perspective, the "present moment" of conversion, levels of meaning are not arbitrarily superimposed by the human mind, but are rather discovered to be exponential recurrences of the structure of God's Providence in history, life, and the whole universe. The passage from Augustine contains within it at once the essence of biblical allegory and the essence of Dante's spiritual autobiography, even to the stylistic level.

I should like to close with a verse to which I have already alluded. As he moves with the stars, Dante looks down upon "l'aiuola che *ci* fa tanto feroci" (*Par.* XXII, 151). For all the distance implied by the poetic fiction, the pronoun "ci" strains to have it both ways: to claim the perspective of eternity without a surrender of the poet's place in time. The synthesis of eternity and time is the goal of the entire journey: the vision of the Incarnation. At the end of the poem, the dramatic convergence of pilgrim and poet is matched by the conceptual convergence of humanity and the divine.

Augustine's autobiography, like Sartre's, is primarily concerned with words, but the ending of Christian autobiography is silence:

> For that voice passed by and passed away, began and ended; the syllables sounded and passed away, the second after the first, the third after the second, and so forth in order, until the last

> after the rest, and silence after the last. . . . And these Thy words, created for a time, the outward ear reported to the intelligent soul, whose inward ear lay listening to Thy Eternal Word.[56]

So the literary unity of Dante's poem is no formal artifact, but is rather the testament of a spiritual journey from a region of unlikeness to likeness, from the "selva oscura" to "la nostra effige."

2. The Firm Foot on a Journey Without a Guide

THE JOURNEY OF THE *Divine Comedy* begins with a conversion. The pilgrim "comes to" after somehow having lost his way in a dark wood. He looks up from that tangle and sees the rays of the sun striking upon a mountain-top, and knows that he must attain the summit. From that moment, the problem is no longer where to go, but rather how to get there, and the problem proves to be insoluble. Try as he may, he cannot achieve the goal which is the beginning and the cause of all joy, for three formidable beasts drive him back into the wood from which he has come, and he retreats, no longer able to help himself, exhausted, and very nearly defeated.

This attempted journey, the "corto andare" which the pilgrim never completes, contrasts with that longer journey, the circuitous route through hell and purgatory to the same objective. In recent years, we have come to understand more and more of the meaning of Dante's itinerary to God.[1] It is in the light of that meaning that I will seek to understand the pilgrim's initial frustration and suggest a new reading for a traditionally obscure line. The allegory of this all-important scene seems clear when we see the prologue in the poem and the poem in the tradition.

The type of frustration felt by the pilgrim arises not from a defect of the mind, but rather from an incapacity of the will. It is not enough to know what must be done; one must also know how to do it. Ever since the Socratic equating of knowledge with virtue, moralists have objected that these are not the same. To say that moral weakness arises from ignorance plainly contradicted the observed facts, as far as Aristotle was concerned,[2] and St. Paul formulated the classic reply to Socrates' thesis (Rom. 7:18–19): "to will is present with me, but how to perform that which is good I find not. For the good that I would, I do not; but the evil which I would not, that I do." Canto I of Dante's poem dramatizes this situation, and the successful journey is the resolution of the problem.

For this reason a glance up to the light, symbolic of intellectual conversion in Plato's *Republic* and *Timaeus,* and thereafter a commonplace in vision and neoplatonic literature,[3] can only represent, in the beginning of Dante's poem, an incomplete turning. Conversion is not a matter of "either/or," for the pilgrim who has recovered himself where he catches sight of the mountain-top is one step closer to truth than he was throughout the dark night, but he is still far removed—three beasts removed—from his final goal. His fear is only somewhat allayed, "un poco queta," and the qualification is important. He has not yet climbed the mountain, the distant summit of which is his ultimate destination (as far as he can tell) and the desert slope, between the dark wood and the mountain proper, is an intermediate area, between the "selva oscura" and the objective. In the moral allegory, the existence of that middle ground contradicts the Socratic contention that virtue and knowledge are synonymous, for the pilgrim's awakening suggests both a kind of conversion to truth, and an awareness of the great gap that remains to be traversed.

Dante ends the first stage of the pilgrim's temporary progress with the striking simile we already discussed in another context:

> E come quei che con lena affannata,
> uscito fuor del pelago a la riva,
> si volge a l'acqua perigliosa e guata,
> così l'animo mio, ch'ancor fuggiva,
> si volse a retro a rimirar lo passo
> che non lasciò già mai persona viva. (I, 22–27)

> And as he who with laboring breath has escaped from the deep to the shore turns to look back on the dangerous waters, so my mind which was still fleeing turned back to gaze upon the pass that never left anyone alive.

Part of the reason these lines are striking, aside from their poetic power, is that they seem gratuitous in terms of the poem's imagery thus far. They mark the end of the poem's first action, which has been presented as an extended simile of darkness and light; to be presented with a simile within another startles the reader somewhat, when the literal terms are so disparate. To be sure, there is nothing unusual about representing a moral struggle with the figure of a drowning man. In Dante's day, references to St. Augustine's *fluctus concupiscentiae*[4] were frequent, and the comparison of life to a tempestuous sea was a commonplace. The interesting thing about Dante's metaphoric mariner, however, is that he neither drowns nor reaches his port, but rather emerges from the sea onto the shore of a middle ground, from which he looks back, terrified, at the danger he has so narrowly escaped. Further on beyond this simile, the poet refers to the area between the dark wood and the mountain proper as a "piaggia diserta," and since the word "piaggia" may be translated either "slope" or "shore," the two images, the first a glance up to the light, and the second, an emergence from the water, exist side by side, and serve as two analogues for the same conversion, an abrupt movement from sin and ignorance into wisdom and virtue—or so it seems at any rate, until we learn what the pilgrim will soon discover: that this slope or shore is no exit, but rather a dead end for any man left on his own. The pilgrim's escape will be temporary and his struggle to remain on the desert slope will fail, for a sudden movement from one extreme to another is characteristic of angels, and not of the fallen flesh.

Some of the ancients, presented with this image of a man rising up out of the water, might have mistaken the bank of that harsh sea for the shore of the plain of truth, and seen in the simile the pilgrim's victory. Cicero reported that the Stoics believed in conversions as sudden and extreme as this, wherein neither folly nor wisdom were susceptible of degree. He described their views in the third book of the *De finibus*,[5] and the description of the transition from folly to wisdom is represented there by a comparison similar to Dante's:

> For just as men submerged in water, even if they are just below the surface and might emerge at any moment, are no more capable of breathing than those who are already at the bottom; and just as a puppy on the verge of opening its eyes sees no

better than one just born; so too a man who has made some progress toward the condition of virtue is no less miserable than one who has not progressed at all.[6]

Cicero will not allow the Stoic contention to stand, however, and he dismisses this as one of those "extremely false analogies which the Stoics are so fond of employing." He supplies other analogies which seem to him more in keeping with the facts:

> One man's vision is dim, another's health poor. When the remedy is applied, they are relieved of their ailments and improve daily; every day the one is stronger and the other sees more clearly. So it is with all those who pursue virtue: they are released and relieved of their vices and errors.[7]

So it was for Dante, who could not believe in the conversion of "sink or swim," and who wrote the poem which is in a sense the dramatization of a gradual illumination. One has a feeling that the poet would have discussed these analogies in precisely the same way as did St. Augustine. In a letter to St. Jerome, Augustine wonders what the Apostle James means when he says (II, 10): "whosoever shall keep the whole law, and yet offend in one point, he is guilty of all." It reminds the Bishop of Hippo of the Stoic analogy:

> This comparison, in which folly is represented as water and wisdom as air, so that the mind emerges, as it were, from the suffocating depths of folly to breathe suddenly the air of wisdom, does not seem to me sufficiently compatible with the authority of our Scriptures. It is better to compare folly (or vice) to darkness, and wisdom (or virtue) to light—to the extent, of course, that resemblances taken from corporeal things may be applied to intellectual concepts. One does not reach wisdom in the same way as a man, rising up out of water into the air, suddenly breathes as much as he needs as soon as he breaks through the surface of the water; rather, one arrives at wisdom as a man gradually advances from darkness into light. Until he is fully illuminated, we say that he is like one who, coming forth from the most dark and hidden cavern, is influenced by the proximity of the light more and more as he draws nearer to the entrance of the cave; thus, whatever light he has derives from the light toward which he is advancing, and whatever remains obscure derives from the darkness from which he has emerged.[8]

Augustine could not be content with a simple widsom-folly dichotomy, but neither did the Ciceronian analogy offered as an alternative satisfy his poetic imagination. From the barest suggestion of a visual analogue in Cicero's discussion, he evoked the Platonic myth of the cave—an ancestor of many allegorical journeys, and the ultimate source of Dante's journey through the infernal regions. Nowhere in Christian writing is the idea of the *itinerarium mentis* more clearly expressed, or its Platonic origin more clearly suggested.

We suspect, then, that no man leaves the dark wood as suddenly as Dante's water simile first suggests, and, as if to confirm the suspicion, Dante refers to the dark wood as "the pass which no man ever left alive,"[9] exactly as Augustine reminds us at the end of his discussion that in the sight of God shall no man living be justified. It is for this reason that the mind of the poet stops in its flight, like Lot's wife, to look back at the danger which it has only temporarily left behind. The pilgrim will soon learn of the tremendous gap that exists between knowledge in the abstract and wisdom in a concrete sense. He will learn that the body must be coaxed along to follow the movement of the mind, and that man must take the longer journey. Above all, he needs God's guidance, so that he may climb slowly and gradually from the cave, *a riveder le stelle.*[10]

The pilgrim's metaphoric shore or slope is far from the Platonic plain of truth. It is the locus, in the moral landscape, of the Pauline situation, knowledge without virtue, where the spirit is willing but the flesh is fatally weak. We are reminded very effectively of the weakened flesh by the line immediately following our simile, the signal introducing this middle area:

> Poi ch'èi posato un poco il corpo lasso,
> ripresi via per la piaggia diserta,
> sì che 'l piè fermo sempre era 'l più basso. (*Inf.* I, 28–30)

> After I had rested my tired body a little, I again took up my way across the desert strand, so that the firm foot was always the lower.

This sudden incarnation, the presence of a body on this journey of the mind, marks Dante's poetic originality, and is the first intimation of an allegorical language different from that found in the innumerable dream-visions of the Middle Ages.[11] Further, it is a significant reminder of the fact that we are moving with the poet in this life, and that any contemplative venture will be hampered by a body which does not respond unhesitatingly to the prodding of a mind bent on the absolute. The pilgrim crosses (or attempts to cross) this middle area in a specific way: "so that the firm foot was always the lower," and the enormous bibliography on that puzzling verse testifies that this is no ordinary ambulation.[12] Rather, it tells us something important about the condition of man left to himself, and therefore cannot be dismissed as simply one more insoluble riddle.

In the first place, it is clear that the pilgrim is making some forward and upward progress on this desert slope. This eliminates the suggestion that the "piè fermo," the "firm foot," might mean the foot upon which most of the body's weight is resting, for if this foot were always the lower, the pilgrim could make no progress at all, as a little experimentation will show. Yet, this is the interpretation which most Dantists have favored, from Boccaccio to the present.[13] A small number have suggested that the "piaggia" is not a slope, but rather a plain, and that when one walks normally on level ground, one's firm foot is always the lower, if only by a fraction of an inch, since it is firm only when it is completely flat. This interpretation makes the line appear totally superfluous, as if Dante were saying, I took up my way again in such manner that I was walking—a tautology if not an absurdity. Finally, aware of all these difficulties, a few Dantists have suggested that "fermo" means the strong, and therefore by extension the right, foot, as one might call the right hand the "strong hand." The pilgrim could then be imagined as climbing a steep slope in a circular path, turning to the right (as he will later climb the Mount of Purgatory) with his right foot always the lower because of the incline. Francesco D'Ovidio objected to this view for he found no poof that "fermo" was used in this way in Dante's time, and the text said nothing of a circular path. Both these arguments are cogent, and this reading too must be rejected.

The identification of the "piè fermo" as a specific foot, rather than as the foot upon which the climber always leans, would do far less violence to the literal image. Unfortunately, however, one cannot use twentieth century logic on a fourteenth century poem, and assume that "fermo" means right without having some texts to support such an assumption. Hundreds of years of Dante scholarship have failed to come up with any such texts, and D'Ovidio was therefore correct in his rejection of this reading, although he too surrendered before the enigmatic verse.

The word "fermo" had a meaning, however, in the scientific tradition, when applied to the feet. If we look into the theory of motion current in Dante's day, so important for the understanding of his poetical cosmos, we are in for some surprises, for we find there that the quality of firmness or fixity is a characteristic of the left, and not of the right part of the body. According to Aristotle, all motion originates from the right. Indeed, right is defined as the place whence motion begins, as far as the cosmos is concerned.[14] This principle was so widely held in the early centuries of Christianity that it was evoked even in mystical contexts, to gloss passages from the Bible. Marius Victorinus, for instance, explained that this was the reason that Christ sat at the right hand of God, for the Son of God is movement in action, and action pertains to the right.[15]

Aristotle also maintained that all movement consists of pushing and pulling, and that in movement, some point must remain stationary, to provide thrust.[16] In the local movement of animals, this alternate pushing and pulling is accomplished by the feet,[17] but the philosopher was subtle enough to see that the stationary foot was not invariably the left; some animals put the right foot out first, whereas others are capable of using either,[18] but most of Aristotle's followers were not so careful. Pliny, for instance, states unequivocally that "all animals begin motion from the right side, resting on the left."[19] In antiquity, then, right came to mean agile, *dextrous,* and not firm or strong.

It was not until the reawakening of interest in Aristotle in the twelfth and thirteenth centuries that these ideas became fixed in scientific speculation, at least as far as the Latin West was concerned. Albertus Magnus, one of the most authoritative of Scholastic Aristotelians, dedicates two of his *Quaestiones super de animalibus* to the problem of deciding which is the "firm" and which the "agile" foot. The first inquires "whether the right foot is more perfect (*absolutior*) and more fit for motion than the left," and he answers that this is indeed the case, except for some men who happen to be ambidextrous. In all other cases, "the left foot is less suited for motion than the right." This is because the heart, which is situated on the left side, nevertheless pours out its influence (*spiritus*) to the right.[20] The second question asks whether all animals naturally put their right feet forward first, and this time no exception is made to the affirmative answer: "Because every animal rightly disposed naturally puts forward its right foot first . . . the left foot is more stable and firm (*pes autem sinister stabilior et firmior est*) . . . and so the body supports itself upon that foot." One of the objections which Albert raises against his own thesis is that in fighting, a man puts out his left foot and leans upon the right. He proves himself a shifty tactician as well as a philosopher by his response: "It must be said that a man when defending himself needs to stand on his feet to avoid blows, and thus sometimes he puts his left foot forward first so that his right foot might be more ready for motion; therefore he does not plant his right foot as firmly on the ground."[21]

Finally, and perhaps most influentially for Dante, Thomas Aquinas was just as explicit in his commentary on the *De caelo*. He specified the word "fortior" when applied to the feet: "For, although it has the same shape, the right hand is stronger (*fortior*) than the left; likewise, the right shoulder is stronger than the left in motion, although the left is stronger for carrying weight; and likewise the right foot is stronger in motion, but the left stronger in standing fixed."[22] Elsewhere in the commentary, he set forth the principle in its broadest terms: "Motion begins from the right. By nature animals move the right part of their bodies before the left just as, for example, they move their right foot first."[23]

As far as the scholastics were concerned then, the first step of archetypal movement was taken by the right foot, and the left was considered the "pes firmior." It may well be that Dante was using this technical term when he wrote of the pilgrim's "piè fermo." A scholastic with a command of Aristotle inferior to Dante's would not have failed to read this expression as a reference to the left, or "fixed" foot.

It seems strange that Dante would use the medieval equivalent of clinical terminology to refer to one of the pilgrim's feet, when it would have been clearer to say simply, "the left foot." Knowing Dante as we do, however, we can be sure that the poet had his reason and that this is no vain display of irrelevant scientific erudition. We must know more about the passage and the tradition before we discuss the reason at any length, but for the moment we should notice that this is not the first instance of such language in the prologue scene. After the pilgrim has beheld the rays of the sun on the mountain top, he says that the fear which had lasted in the "lake of the heart" was somewhat allayed (v. 19).[24] It has been generally agreed since Boccaccio's time that this *lago del cor* to which Dante refers and which we shall later discuss, was the cavity of the heart in which dwelt the vital spirits. In the *Vita Nuova,* Dante refers to this cavity as a secret room of the heart in which the vital spirits were set trembling by his meeting with Beatrice. These vital spirits are the Aristotelian *pneuma* and the *lago del cor* is therefore as physiological an expression as the phrase we have been discussing, the *piè fermo,* for which it so clearly sets the stage. We must now investigate the meaning of these curious verses.

If the pilgrim advances up the slope with his left foot always lower than his right, it is clear that he is not advancing normally. We cannot account for this solely by imagining an exceedingly steep incline, for one can move the feet consecutively, even when scaling a cliff. Rather must we look to the state of the pilgrim to explain this queer situation. He has barely escaped with his life from the dangerous "passo" and has rested his body only "un poco." He is at the point of total exhaustion, and although he manages to make some advance, his motion is unlike the pace of a strong person. He is dragging himself up, with his right foot leading, and his left lagging behind. In a sense he limps toward the summit, as a man wounded in the left leg. There is no literal justification for this incapacity of the pilgrim, just as there is no literal reason for his body being so tired, or later, for his being able to bypass the leopardess and the lion, but not the wolf. But it may be suggested that just as exhaustion is the result of the mortal combat in the waters of the heart, so this weakness arises from a wound suffered by a limb of the soul.[25]

The poem is an itinerary, a "cammino" of this life, made by a soul. Just as the body moves with its feet, so the "body" of the soul, so to speak, moves with twin powers, and to say that the two are not working in harmony as in normal movement is to say something very important about this first attempted journey, in an allegorical language which has a long tradition.[26]

Plato in the *Phaedrus* constructed the famous myth of the soul—the chariot drawn by two winged horses, which perpetually pull against each other, the black steed on the left veering off the course pursued by the white.[27] In the *Timaeus,* in a different context, we are told that the soul becomes incarnate as man, and if this rational being is given education, "he will pass his life free from all confusion and grief." If education is neglected, however, the man limps along the road of his life: "if he neglects it, slowly limping down the path of life with his habitual folly, he is finally called back to hell."[28] The commentary of Chalcidius on this passage associated the image of the feet with the allegory obvious in the Phaedrus myth, and thus bequeathed to the Middle Ages a dyadic division of the human composite represented by the figure of the walking man:

> For he made man out of soul and body. The few who take care for both will be whole and strong; he who cares for neither will be maimed and crippled; he who cares for one of the two will limp. Therefore the uneducated man who devotes his attention to the body will surely limp through life; and the soul of the man whose opinions are true, but who has not been initiated into the rites of the secrets of the intellect, will likewise be lame.[29]

For Christians who had undergone the influence of the neoplatonists, the association of the feet of the body with wings of the soul was a commonplace.[30] Clement of Alexandria contrasted the feet of the body with the winged soul in prayer.[31] St. Ambrose, as we have seen, added the image of the interior feet to the traditional analogues of human movement found in ancient psychology.[32] He rejected the images representative of physical or bodily movement—Platonic commonplaces catalogued in compilations concerning the soul, such as that of Iamblichus.[33] Ambrose meant a flight of the soul, exactly as is undertaken by Dante's "animo . . . ch'ancor fuggiva," and for such a flight, the inward feet are required.

As so often, here too it was St. Augustine who established the theme for biblical exegetes throughout the Middle Ages. Speaking of the journey to God, a favorite theme, he says:

> Let us hold true to what we have attained. This walking is not performed by corporeal feet, but by affections of mind and habits of life (*mentis affectibus et vitae moribus*) in order that they might be perfect possessors of righteousness who, advancing on the upright path of faith, renewing themselves from day to day, finally become wayfarers (*viatores*) in such justice.[34]

This journey to Justice, an ancestor of Dante's moral allegory, was a metaphor which Augustine worked out in detail. Elsewhere he tells us that "our feet on this journey are our affections."[35] Insofar as we have love, in that measure do we approach God or move away from Him. Augustine applied to the feet of the soul his famous dichotomy: "The foot of the soul (*pes animae*) is rightly understood as love (*amor*);

which, when it is base or crooked is called cupidity or lust, and when it is upright is delectation or charity."[36]

The Bible contains many instances of such anatomical imagery, and even in passages where the mention of feet would appear to be a primarily literal reference, we can of course be quite sure that the exegetes found meanings much like those suggested by Ambrose and Augustine before them, and these were echoed with, alas, little variation throughout the Middle Ages. Two passages in particular called for special treatment, however, and it is enlightening to look at the interpretations given to them by the pseudo-Ambrose, Augustine, and Gregory the Great, who were to establish the exegetical tradition.

For St. Ambrose, original sin was the bite of the serpent, and he tells us that if we wish to avoid a repetition of the fall in our own lives, we must get our spiritual feet off the ground, "so that the serpent can not find our heel here on earth and wound it."[37] Elements from Genesis and from Plato's flight of the soul are here fused together, under the influence of Philo Judaeus.[38] In the *De sacramentis,* attributed for many years to Ambrose, the wounding of the foot is associated with the residual effect of original sin after baptism. Why is it, the author wonders, that Christ, while about to wash the feet of Peter (John 13:8–10), says, "He who has bathed does not need to wash, except for his feet"? The answer, he replies, is that Adam trod upon he serpent, and that because of this all of us must "wash away the venom." This, according to the author, is the symbolic origin of the washing-of-the-feet ceremony in the northern Italian Church.[39]

St. Augustine explained the ceremony in the same way, with a different, and certainly more striking image, thoroughly consistent with the journey motif. Man is indeed cleaned by baptism. Why then is the washing of the feet required? Because even the man walking to God gets the dust of this life upon his feet.[40]

Elsewhere in the writings of the Bishop of Hippo, this partial uncleanness is expressed with the image of the limping man, who must be cured by the physician of the soul.[41] Sometimes Christ suggests remedies for lameness which are rather extreme, to our way of thinking. So it seems, at any rate, when we are presented with Augustine's gloss on Jacob's limp, for there he recalls Matt. 8:8, and its drastic cure: "If thy leg offend thee, cut it off . . . for it is more expedient to you to enter the kingdom of God with one foot, than to enter into eternal fire with two."[42]

Finally, Gregory the Great added even more permutations to the bizarre catalogue of feet-of-the-soul images. Commenting on Jacob's wrestling with the angel, he identifies the feet as love of God and love of the world. After contact with the absolute, Jacob limps, for his love for the world decays, just as the soul which holds on to the angel "supports itself, with all virtue, on the foot of the love of God alone. And it stands on that foot alone because it now holds suspended above the earth the foot of the love of the world which it had been accustomed to placing on the ground."[43]

These passages in the Bible, Christ's washing of the disciples' feet and Jacob's limping after his encounter with the angel, as well as many more passages involving the same elements, were glossed with echoes of the commentaries of these three fathers for hundreds of years.[44] Until the scholastics, commentators seemed content to apply to various biblical verses these rather general identifications and interpretations. Elements from each of them are obviously suggestive for the reading of Dante's line, and it comes as no surprise that many commentators, including Pietro di Dante, the poet's son, Benvenuto da Imola, and Francesco da Buti, glossed Dante's "piè fermo" with elements from these commentaries.[45] None of the interpretations, however, provides more than generic explications of a verse which we suspect, because of its context, is more philosophically precise. The "piè fermo" verse calls attention to a particular foot (as do none of the Church fathers when they speak of the feet of the soul), and it does so in scientific language. It is to the philosophy, rather than to the exegesis of the Middle Ages, that we must turn to arrive at the fullness of Dante's meaning.

In the early thirteenth century, a new identification of the feet of the soul gradually displaced the traditional ones. According to Albertus Magnus,[46] Godfrey Admontensis,[47] and Hugo de Sancto Caro, just as the body proceeded by means of its limbs, so the soul proceeded by twin powers: *intellectus* and *affectus,* or the apprehensive and the appetitive faculties. The interior acts of the soul had long been known as the "steps" of the soul.[48] Now for the first time, the traditional image became subjected to the same close scrutiny as was the psychology of human action. This was the age during which the study of Aristotle was at its peak, and it is to him that we must return, where we began this part of our discussion.

According to Aristotle in the third book of the *De anima,* all movement involves three factors: the originator; the means; and the thing which is moved. The first of these three factors, that which originates movement, can be understood either as the object or external good which moves without itself being moved, or as the faculty of appetite, which is at once moved (since it is acted upon by the mind's apprehension of the object) and moving (since it moves the body). The second factor, the instrument of movement, is to be found where the beginning and end of motion coincide: the heart, which is the center of articulation, like the joint of an extremity, the end of one organ, the beginning of another.[49] It is the mid-point between the alternate movements of pushing and pulling in the motion of an animal, one side remaining fixed while the other moves, itself in turn becoming fixed while the former moves.[50] The third factor, the thing moved, is of course the body. Recapitulating the whole process of movement, we find that the object or thing-to-be-done is apprehended by the mind. The mind's last movement is the first movement of the appetite, or the moment of choice, the "actus intellectus appetitivi, vel appetitus intellectivi." After choice, the faculty of appetite, working on the "spirit" (*pneuma*) located in the heart, the mysterious substance which is the locus of contact between body and soul, causes the spirit to flow through the arteries thereby moving the muscles and tendons with alternate pushing and pulling movements, and the human mechanism moves out step by step. It has by this time become apparent that Aristotle's *pneuma,* the *spiritus* of the scholastics, is precisely the vapor to which Dante refers in the beginning of the *Vita Nuova* as the "spirito di vita," which resides in what the poet has here called the "lago del cor."

From this rather primitive summary, it is clear that the movement of the soul is exactly analogous to the movement of the body, for just as the heart is at once the end of one movement and the beginning of another, so the act of choice, residing in the soul, is the end of one movement (that of the mind), and the beginning of another (the appetite).[51] The archetypal circle of movement thus applies to both body and soul, as indeed it does to the entire Aristotelian cosmos.[52] In order to make the two analogous planes of action, of body and soul, completely congruent, one had only to associate the beginning principle of cosmic or corporeal movement, the right, with the beginning of choice, the apprehension, or the reason.[53] Nothing suggests itself as more natural to St. Bonaventure, for instance, in his analogy between the acts of the soul and the steps of the body. He analyzes the "syllogism of sin" as consisting of four short steps:

> Our internal movements are short paths leading quickly to death because they contain only four steps by which the feet of the soul run to death. One foot is the movement of reason, the other the movement of appetite; the first is on the right, the second on the left, since the right foot is moved first, and the left afterward, for "apprehension precedes appetite," according to the Philosopher. The first step of the right foot is awareness of the sin, the second, that of the left foot, is desire, the third, of the right foot, deliberation, and the fourth, of the left foot, choice.[54]

Thus, to represent the intimate correspondence existing between the soul's twin powers, the scholastics chose the analogy of walking, and in doing so were elaborating a tradition as old as Plato, particularly apt in an age which considered every man a pilgrim.

For Dante, imbued with the study of Aristotle, the analogy was meant in a very strict sense. The figure of a man in the act of walking was quite literally the incarnation of the act of choice, for walking was simply choosing brought down to the material plain. The vital spirit residing in the heart has for its entire function the transmission of the soul's commands, and the concatenation of thoughts and desires produced by the intellect and the will is reproduced, in the act of walking, by the succession of right and left. What better way to represent a struggle which goes on in the soul, than to observe the effects of that very struggle upon a body.

It is a tired body, at that, and it is time that we turned our attention to it. In line 15 Dante tells us that the pilgrim's heart was pierced with fear by the dark wood. Fear is a passion, and as such, for medieval science, it had both its interior and exterior manifestations, being at once a psychic and a physical phenomenon. A man who is afraid suffers contractions of the vital spirit, which is to say that he is likely to tremble all over, making chattering noises with his teeth, and lose control of himself generally.[55] The reason for this is that the vital spirit rushes to the center of the body, and no longer exercises control over the members—as frightened citizens rush from the fields to the citadel, St. Thomas explained.[56] This is the phenomenon the pilgrim later experiences when he meets the wolf, for it makes his veins and arteries tremble.[57]

The sight of the sun, however, allays the fear which had collected in the lake of the pilgrim's heart, the point to which all vital spirits flow, but the poet draws our attention to the qualification "un poco," by repeating it in line 28, with its reference this time to the body. If the vital spirits are somewhat calmed, but not entirely, how does this affect the entire human composite? A quotation from Thomas will help us to answer the question:

> With respect to the bodily instruments, fear by its very nature is apt to interfere with external behavior because of the loss of body heat in the external members brought on by fear. With respect to the soul, if the fear is moderate and does not excessively disturb the processes of reasoning it is a help in acting well . . . But if fear should develop to the point where it upsets reason, then even mental functioning will be disturbed.[58]

The pilgrim's problem, then, is that his body will not respond perfectly to his mind, for his fear has been only somewhat allayed. If it were only a question of an interior action, one of the mind alone on the purely literal level, he would have no problem. This pilgrim, unfortunately, has a mountain to climb, difficult for anyone, let alone for a man half struck with fear, and therefore only half able to walk—limping in one leg.

After this long excursion, we are in a position to understand Dante's language in these verses more clearly. Literally speaking, a man is lost in a dark wood, and is therefore afraid. Having finally caught sight of the sun, he is somewhat comforted, but because he is not completely free of fear, and the vital spirits which had collected in the "lake of the heart" are only partially calmed, he is not in complete control of his body. His left leg, which even in a normal man does not receive as much of the vital spirit as does the right (it is for this reason the "firm," rather than the "agile," foot), now so lacks the *spiritus* of the heart that it is unable to respond to the command of the mind, and the pilgrim consequently limps toward his objective.

But this is the journey of an "animo . . . ch'ancor fuggiva" (v. 25), and hence, when we read of the sudden intrusion of a body where there was no body before—the "corpo lasso" (v. 28)—we are surely to understand this, to use the words of Charles Singleton, as the "vision made flesh."[59] Here begins the journey of the "body" of the soul, accomplished, as St. Ambrose suggested, *pedibus interioribus,* and the feet are precisely the soul's two powers: *intellectus* and *affectus.* We have only to understand St. Bonaventure's four syllogistic steps as heading in an opposite direction—not the four short steps on the road toward perdition, but rather the innumerable, difficult steps leading to beatitude; difficult, if not impossible, until the defective left foot is made "libero, dritto e sano" (*Purg.* XXVII, 140) after another, far longer journey.

In the fifth canto of the *Paradiso,* the poet gives us an intimation of what the step is like after the longer journey. Beatrice tells the pilgrim that she burns with the supernatural love of charity. She explains: "Ciò procede / da perfetto veder, che, come apprende, / così nel bene appreso move il piede" (for it comes from perfect vision which, according as it apprehends, so does it move its foot to the apprehended good).[60] We know here which foot it is that moves out toward the good, for the good is the object of the will, as the truth is the object of the reason. Perfect desire follows perfect intellection, and such perfection can only be the product of sanctifying grace. If one or the other of the feet is lacking or defective, the journey cannot end in success, for we have it on the authority of St. Thomas that the mind must move to God *et per intellectum et per affectum.* Unfortunately for man in his fallen state, Thomas goes on to say, "the intellect is stonger in understanding (*cognoscendo*) than the affections in loving (*diligendo*), wherefore Augustine says that the intellect precedes and the affections follow upon it, either slowly or not at all (*sequitur tardus aut nullus affectus*)."[61] Ever since Adam's sin, man's ability to see the good has outdistanced his ability to do it on his own, for in the life without sanctifying grace, the middle ground of which St. Paul was so painfully aware, only one foot takes the forward step.

We have already seen that both Augustine and the author of the *De sacramentis* associated the washing of the feet with the removal of the residual effect of original sin, rather than with the removal of sin itself. In metaphor, the washing removed the "venom" or "dust" from postlapsarian feet already made right by baptism. Although the image was different in the twelfth and thirteenth centuries, the doctrine remained the same. The wounds of the feet were the residual effect of the fall. The right foot, *intellectus,* suffered the wound of ignorance; the left, *affectus,* that of concupiscence.

To describe Adam's condition between his creation *in naturalibus* and the infusion of grace, the scholastics used the formula *Stare poterat, pedes movere non poterat,* which meant that the first man could prevent himself from falling away by the natural power of his will, but that he was powerless to advance any closer to God.[62] The author of the *Summa Theologica* long attributed to Alexander of Hales had this formula in mind when he spoke of Adam's need of two supernatural perfections, with respect to both *intellectus* and *affectus,* so that he might please God and "walk uprightly on the path of virtue." As his knowledge had to be perfect, so his faculty of desire had to be "upright and ready for action . . . so that he might not limp (*ut non claudicaret*)." By his sin, he lost this double perfection, and fell into ignorance and concupiscence: *ignorantia boni et concupiscentia mali.*[63] In the twelfth century, these two were almost universally regarded as hereditary results of the fall in Adam's children. Of the two, however, it was concupiscence, the wound of the left foot, which was so firmly linked to the doctrine of original sin as to be considered by many of the scholastics both the sin and its consequence.[64]

Concupiscence was variously defined, but one of the ways of describing it was to quote St. Paul's confession on the inefficacy of his will. An anonymous summist of the school of Hugh of St. Victor states:

> It must be noted that ignorance of good and concupiscence of evil, which are the effects of the sin of the first man, are the original sin for all those not reborn (baptized). But we must realize that the concupiscence of evil is called a burden because it is difficult to avoid the concupiscence of the carnal bond. Whence the Apostle said, "For the good that I would, I do not: but the evil which I would not, that I do."[65]

Sometimes, on the other hand, St. Paul's words were called to mind by the figure of the limping man without reference to the specific wound. Hugo de Sancto Caro, the second and least famous of the Dominican triumvirate, perhaps alludes to Paul when glossing Proverbs 2:20: "on the path of truth, with the foot of the intellect, and on the path of goodness, with the foot of the will, having the same object in both the will and the intellect, not knowing one thing and willing another (*non aliud scientes et aliud volentes*), as many do."[66] At any rate, it seems clear that Dante's *homo claudus* would have suggested, to a contemporary reader as learned as the poet, one of

Adam's children, afflicted by the disease contracted by his father unable to order his appetites to his mind.[67]

In the prologue scene we have to do with three separate areas and if we wished to extend the image of the feet of the soul to these areas, we might say that in the first, the dark wood, neither of the feet is *rectus,* and there is only the aimless wandering of a man enmeshed in fear and sin: *homo collapsus.* Once the pilgrim beholds the rays of the sun, however, he has undergone an intellectual conversion, and is healed, so to speak, in one foot. This is the condition of *homo claudus,* divided by an inward struggle. If he were somehow to bypass the three beasts, he would then become healed in both limbs and his will (*affectus*), free, straight and sound, could follow its own discernment (*intellectus*), which is accomplished in fact only at the summit, at the coronation of the pilgrim, when he is dismissed by his first guide to await the second.[68] If our reading is correct, then it follows that the three beasts and the area over which they preside primarily pertain to the *affectus,* which is to say, to the heart rather than to the mind.

Here then is a picture of man in his present state, without the guidance he needs, left to himself. By an overwhelming effort he can avoid sin itself, but each victory will be costly, and he cannot progress beyond negative goodness, for three beasts block his path and threaten to make each victory a temporary one. These three beasts are not sins, for it is not sin that checks man's escape route from the forest of sin. Rather are they dispositions toward sin, and they afflict every man, to a greater or lesser degree, without exception. We must turn now, if only for a moment, to these three impediments along the direct route.

The scholastics who had undergone the influence of Aristotle tried to harmonize the classic definition of the fall as *ignorantia* and *concupiscentia* with his divisions of the powers of the soul. At the same time another theory of the fall, that of St. Anselm, was becoming more prominent, and in the writings of Albert, Bonaventure and Thomas this conception of the result of Adam's sin as the loss of original justice was to replace the older doctrine.[69] The result of these two tendencies is clearly visible in Dante's poem, and the poet was more complete and more subtle in this scene than our analysis has thus far suggested.

The summit of the mountain is the goal of both the itinerary led by Virgil and the attempted journey which the pilgrim undertakes on his own. It represents, in the moral allegory, an interior harmony in the soul, whereby the appetites, the movement of the left foot, are perfectly coordinated with the reason, which, as the right, must always choose the objective and point the way. In the *Republic* Plato compares this inner rectitude with right order in the state, and calls it, by analogy, justice.[70] Reason and desire are the two faculties which must be related to each other as ruler to subject. This, in germ, is the theory which was to become in the writings of St. Anselm the concept of original justice in the soul, and it is this justice that Adam lost by his sin.[71]

The importance of this metaphor for the journey to the summit in Dante's poem need not detain us here, for it has been fully explored. Of particular interest for us is Plato's subdivision of the irrational "subjects" of the reason into two classes: desire (*epithumia*) and passion (*thumos*). Thus, just as the state is composed of three classes (traders, auxiliaries, counsellors), so the soul is made up of three powers, the concupiscent, irascible, and rational.

Aristotle felt that Plato's division was inadequate because appetite pertains to all three parts of the soul, the rational power having a kind of desire of its own, apart from its cognitive function. This he called "wish" (*boulēsis*). To Aristotle, a division more fundamental than Plato's was "mind" on one hand, and "appetite" on the other. In the second book of the *De anima,* he listed the three species of appetite: desire (*epithumia*), passion (*thumos*), and wish (*boulēsis*).[72] These were to become most influential in the development of scholastic psychology, for they came to be known as the concupiscent, irascible, and rational appetites.

W. H. V. Reade has shown that St. Thomas moved away from Aristotle by equating the rational appetite with the Christian *voluntas,* or will.[73] St. Thomas seemed to misunderstand the pagan philosopher in another respect as well, for he admitted a formal division between *ira,* or passion, and *concupiscentia,* or desire, suggesting the separate powers of Plato, whereas Aristotle merely distinguished them as different kinds of appetites. Reade attributed these errors of interpretation to the Latin translation of Aristotle used by Thomas, but as a matter of fact, such interpretations were already present in St. John Damascene's *De fide orthodoxa,* whose influence on thirteenth-century psychology with respect to the faculties of the soul has been traced by Dom Odon Lottin.[74]

Regardless of the historical reasons for the garbling of Aristotle's text by the scholastics, it was interpreted as making these divisions: *intellectus* and *appetitus* at the broadest level, and *appetitus* further subdivided into *appetitus rationalis* (that is, *voluntas*) and *appetitus sensitivus,* which is in turn subdivided into the irascible and concupiscent powers. Thus, man's appetite is composed of rational (i.e. volitive), irascible, and concupiscent forces, the first of which is peculiarly human, while the other two are rational in man only because they are ruled by the first, and moved by it.[75] The composite threefold appetite in man is what we call the will in the broadest sense. The *Convivio* demonstrates that Dante accepted these commonplace divisions of the human soul, when he spoke of the obedience the lower owes to the higher: "Nullo dubita che l'appetito razionale non sia più nobile che 'l sensuale" and again, "questo appetito [i.e., the sensitive, "che in noi dal nostro principio nasce"] che irascibile e concupisibile si chiama . . . a la ragione obedire conviene."[76] (No one doubts that the rational appetite is more noble than the sensitive . . . this appetite [i.e., the sensitive, "which is born in us at our beginning"], which is called irascible and concupiscent . . . ought to obey the reason.) The *Commedia,* that most rational of all poems, retains this common ordering of the soul's powers.

We cannot enter here into the debate concerning the moral system of Dante's *Inferno* except to suggest that the tripartite division of the appetitive faculty, agreed upon by Christians and pagans alike best enables us to see with the pilgrim a Christian hell from a Virgilian, and therefore pagan, perspective. As hell is the realm of those who have lost the good, who in their lives inverted the order of reason and desire, subjecting the former to the latter, so is hell's structure patterned on that of the human appetite, albeit in horrible inversion. Malice, bestiality, and incontinence, the dispositions incarnate in fraud, violence, and lust, correspond to disorders in the rational, irascible, and concupiscent appetites.

There is surely no difficulty in identifying lower hell with sins of malice, whose distinctive feature is that reason participates directly in their commission, and in identifying upper hell with sins of incontinence, which only secondarily imply the use of reason. The major quarrel about hell's structure has arisen about the suitability of the expression "matta bestialità" to that middle area of "forza" in Dante's divisions. The trouble seems to be that in Thomas' commentary on the relevant passages of the *Nicomachean Ethics,* from which Dante got his divisions, one finds both "bestialis malitia" and "bestialis incontinentia," and there appears to be no single distinctive "bestialità."[77] Without entering into the debate it will suffice for us to notice that just as the irascible power stands between the concupiscent and the rational, so bestiality manifests itself as either will to injury or animal violence. It is perhaps for this reason that the middle region of hell is presided over by the Minotaur and by the centaurs. Bestiality, like every mediate point in an ontological chain,[78] partakes of both the higher and the lower, and man and beast meet in the seventh circle, as they do in the soul's irascible appetite.

Giacinto Casella was perhaps the first to suggest that Dante's three beasts were related to the three categories of sin in the *Inferno,* and others, in the vast literature pertaining to these animals, have identified them with the three Aristotelian "dispositions that heaven does not want: incontinence, malice and mad bestiality."[79] Both interpretations are in a sense correct, for as hell represents the totality of sins which men have committed, so must these three beasts somehow comprise the totality of impediments on the direct road to beatitude. The will, and the will alone, is the locus of sin, and hell therefore is patterned on its threefold division: the rational (*voluntas* properly speaking), the irascible, and the concupiscent appetites.[80] Similarly, since the middle ground represents the area between sin and virtue, where man is left to struggle on his own to overcome the weaknesses of his fallen nature, the totality of dispositions toward sin, which likewise reside in the appetitive faculty, can be discerned there in the prologue scene.

One of the proofs offered by medieval thinkers for the existence of original sin and its deleterious effects was the fact that man, the highest of all forms of animal life, nevertheless suffers from a fear of animals.[81] There is something unnatural about such a situation, or rather, something which has become natural to man only since Adam's fall. That fear recommends itself as an excellent symbol for the shortcomings of human nature, and it may be that Dante intended to allude to those shortcomings with the symbol of the beasts. The source of Dante's images is undoubtedly Jeremiah 5:4–6:

> But I said: Perhaps these are poor and foolish, that know not the way of the Lord, the judgment of their God.
>
> I will go therefore to the great men, and will speak to them: for they have known the way of the Lord, the judgment of their God; and behold these have altogether broken the yoke more, and have burst the bonds.
>
> Wherefore a lion out of the wood hath slain them, a wolf

> in the evening hath spoiled them, a leopard watcheth for their cities: every one that shall go out thence shall be taken, because their transgressions are multiplied, their rebellions are strengthened.

Here are all the elements of the first part of Dante's prologue scene: the forest, the three animals, and the *ignorantia viae Domini.* According to our reading up to this point, the glance at the light and the subsequent escape from the forest represent a conversion from ignorance and sin. One of the classic wounds of nature was thereby overcome, and there remained the other traditional affliction to which man in this life is subject: concupiscence, the wound of the *affectus.* Just as the *affectus* or appetite is tripartite, however, so the general wound to which we have heretofore referred as concupiscence was in reality threefold.

The mention of the "lonza" in the pilgrim's descent signals the entrance into the area of fraud, for it was with the rope-girdle used to summon Geryon that the pilgrim once had hoped to "prender la lonza a la pelle dipinta."[82] Since fraud is "dell'uom proprio male," there is no difficulty associating the leopardess with the rational appetite, the will, peculiar to man alone.[83] The description of the wolf "di tutte brame . . . carca" quite clearly suggests the concupiscent appetite,[84] and the lion would seem an apt symbol for the irascible appetite, even if Thomas had not specifically called it to mind as a symbol of bestiality in the commentary on the seventh book of the *Nicomachean Ethics,* the source of Dante's "tre disposizioni."[85]

St. Cyprian, in the early years of Christianity, was the first to use the expression "vulnera naturae" to refer to the effect of Adam's sin on the rest of mankind.[86] It was St. Augustine who established the traditional ignorance and concupiscence pair, for according to the Bishop of Hippo, every sin consisted of an aversion from truth, ignorance, and a conversion to evil, concupiscence.[87] The Venerable Bede added two more defects to these: malice and weakness,[88] and these four then became traditional. The pseudo-Alexander of Hales insisted on the need for grace to heal the wounds of the *status naturae lapsae:*

> On account of our ignorance (*ignorantiam*) of what ought to be done that grace is necessary which is the spiritual light illuminating the soul itself. On account of our weakness (*infirmitatem*), because of which man is unable to rise to the work of vir-

> tue . . . that grace is necessary which administers virtue to the soul. On account of malice (*malitiam*), through which man has a propensity toward evil and an aversion from God, that grace is necessary which, raising up the soul, directs it towards God and away from evil. On account of concupiscence (*concupiscentiam*) . . . that grace is necessary which induces a desire for things eternal, thus dimishing the force of concupiscence.[89]

According to Thomas Aquinas, when Adam was created he had original justice, which is to say that his reason held perfect sway over the lower powers of his soul, and was in turn perfectly subjected to God. This perfect subjection was exemplified by four virtues, which resided in reason (prudence), the will (justice), the irascible appetite (fortitude), and the concupiscent (temperance). When he was stripped of these virtues, he suffered the four corresponding "wounds": ignorance, malice, weakness, and concupiscence.[90]

That the dark wood suggests not only actual sin but ignorance as well, will be readily admitted by anyone familiar with the tradition called to mind by the pilgrim's glance up to the light. Further, others have argued convincingly about how well the wolf and the leopardess represent concupiscence and malice respectively.[91] The only difficulty seems to be with the identification of the lion as the *vulnus* of weakness. This difficulty vanishes, however, when we pause to consider what *infirmitas* means in this context. Thomas has this to say about it: "Just as in the body a violent departure from the normal is a greater illness, so, too, the more violent and uncontrolled the emotion, the greater the sickness of the soul."[92] Thus it is precisely because of its great irrational violence that the lion is the perfect symbol of human weakness.

One last point must be made. Some Dantists believed that the greatest objection to the identification of the three beasts as analogous to the three major categories of sin, and more specifically, to the identification of the wolf as concupiscence, was the fact that in the allegory it was this beast, representative of the least serious of sins, which proved to be the only really insurmountable barrier on the road to the summit.[93] Far from being a problem, however, this is rather a buttress for such an identification.

Purely from the standpoint of human experience, and quite independently of any theological tradition, it is clear that the more prone one is toward sin, through no personal fault, the less is one's culpability for its commission. On the other hand, the further one progresses toward virtue, the less serious are the faults remaining to be purged, but the more difficult are they to overcome. The last step toward perfection, for those who believe in such moral progress, is always the most difficult to take. In Dante's poem, it is perhaps for this reason that the last barrier between the pilgrim and the summit, the flames of *Purgatory* XXVII, is so fearsome that he refuses, momentarily, to take the last step.[94] The same is true of the last barrier in the middle ground. The universality of the wolf's reign diminishes the culpability involved in becoming subject to her, and that universality makes it most difficult, if not impossible, to elude her.

We are not dependent upon this argument, however, to prove that the insurmountable barrier represents a disposition toward the least serious of mortal sins, or that the least fearsome of the animals represents the gravest disposition. Thomas' elaboration of a principle laid down by Aristotle in the seventh book of the *Ethics* makes this clear:

> Therefore, just as a beast is less blameworthy than an evil man, but is more terrifying, so also bestial malice and incontinence are more terrifying but less blameworthy and more innocent (*terribilior quidem est, sed minoris culpae et innocentior*) than human incontinence or malice. Thus if someone is out of his mind or bestial by nature, he is punished less.[95]

Similarly bestial concupiscence is at once less grave and more fearsome than human malice.

Concupiscence, in the broad sense, was the wound suffered by the *affectus,* according to the doctrine established by St. Augustine and supported by his authority throughout the Middle Ages. After the general acceptance of St. Anselm's theory of original justice and its loss, however, Thomas used the word "concupiscentia" to denote the loss of the reason's control over each of the three powers of the faculty of appetite. Thus concupiscence in the broad sense included the wounds of the rational, irascible, and concupiscent appetites. According to Dom Lottin, this was Aquinas' way of adopting Anselm's theory without at the same time appearing to abandon Augustine's.[96] Concupiscence as more strictly defined by Aquinas, on the other hand, was closer to the Augustinian concept: the disorder of the lowest appetite. In the allegory of Eden, concupiscence plays the role of the serpent, and in many moments of the soul's existence, the drama of Eden is reenacted.[97] The serpent, the *primus motus* of the sensitive appetite, suggests a course of illicit action, and if it is not immediately suppressed, the consequence is sin. Only grace can help suppress his first movement of concupiscence, but the movement itself can never be totally eradicated in this life: *nunquam in hac vita totaliter tollitur.*[98]

The wolf represents just this kind of concupiscence. When the pilgrim reaches her, he has gone as far as any man in this life, without sanctifying grace, can go. Just as she succeeds in pushing him back "a poco, a poco," so the wound of concupiscence, precisely because of its less serious nature, can become the source of all sins, until it succeeds in pushing man back to the point "là dove 'l sol tace." The glance at the sun begins a movement toward the soul's perfection which, without grace, will be halted by the last impediment between the soul and its object. At any moment, that impediment can become the occasion of a reverse movement, a backsliding, to use Jeremiah's expression, back into the condition of actual sin.[99] Without God's help, man can only stagger repeatedly out of the forest by his own power, only to return again to the misery out of which he has come.

This last barrier, the wolf, is the one of which St. Paul was acutely aware. According to Augustine, Paul's agony was caused precisely by the "malum concupiscentiae"[100] and this *incontinentia* is what the pagan Socrates, in Thomas' reading, did not understand.[101] For the Christian, it is the middle ground between virtue and vice which poses the insoluble problem. The final wound can only be completely cured in the hereafter, in purgatorial fire, as Dante would have it:

> con tal cura conviene e con tai pasti
> che la piaga da sezzo si ricuscia. (XXV, 136–139)

> with such treatment and with such diet must
> the last wound of all be healed.

Until that time, man must lean upon a guide sent from heaven.

To make the shorter journey is to do what no man has ever done. The best for which man on his own can hope is to ward off those three beasts for the time being, and avoid being pushed back into actual sin. Without guidance, all men must despair of reaching the summit, but some can hold their ground at least a little while. That ground, the middle ground between sin and true Christian virtue, is a deserted slope because few men have made it their land.

Only Virgil and the other virtuous pagans were familiar with the moral landscape, so to speak, and if we wished to go beyond the text in a way that would not have offended the poet, we might say that this middle area is analogous to Limbo, where the noble souls are neither happy with the joy of the summit nor afflicted with the despair of the damned. They are relegated to Limbo, because it was in a kind of limbo that they struggled to live where one does not wander blindly as in a forest, but rather hobbles painfully in the light.

3. The River of Death: *Inferno* II, 108

IN THE TWENTY-FIFTH CANTO OF the *Paradiso* Beatrice introduces Dante to St. James as the man to whom it was "granted to come from Egypt to Jerusalem, that he may see, before his term of warfare is completed" (XXV, 55–57). With these words Beatrice glosses Dante's journey in retrospect, according to the figure of exodus, the Old Testament story that was taken by medieval exegetes to be a forshadowing of the coming of Christ. By describing this particular journey in terms of the master-plan of Christian history, Beatrice reveals the structural principle whereby the personal experience of the pilgrim is to be understood in more general terms as another embodiment of the continually unfolding pattern of God's Providence.

This structural principle, which Erich Auerbach[1] called by its medieval name, *figura,* gave to the otherwise linear course of Christian history (of the self or of the world) a recurrent pattern of meaning. The Redemption was thought to have been adumbrated by the flight of the Jews from Egypt long before the Crucifixion, the event by which it was finally made manifest. Furthermore, both the exodus of the Jews and the Redemption were thought to have their final fulfillment, at least in history, with the Second Coming. At the same time, the drama of exodus might be embodied in the experience of every individual soul, thereby recapitulating the essential outlines of universal history in the justification of each sinner. So Dante's journey, while reserving its uniqueness as the experience of a single man, nevertheless embodies the figure of exodus, the timeless pattern that is fulfilled in God. In the *Epistola* to Can Grande, Dante suggests that the poem is to be read according to this figure, by which is signified, among other things, "the conversion of the soul from the grief and misery of sin to the state of grace."[2] We may take it as established by Dante's own words and as demonstrated by Charles Singleton[3] that the outlines of the poetic journey are essentially those of exodus, the figure of conversion.

If this is so, then the journey without a guide, the frustrated attempt to climb the mountain in the first canto of the *Inferno,* must be considered an exodus that failed, a temporary escape that was not a definitive departure from "Egypt," but merely a disastrous sortie. From the pilgrim's perspective, the final barrier on the difficult road to the summit seems to be the wolf; the view from heaven, however, refers to another, equally formidable, barrier. So we must assume from the words of Lucy when she calls upon Beatrice to help the pilgrim who finds himself blocked, *impedito,* on the desert slope:

> Non odi tu la pieta del suo pianto,
> non vedi tu la morte che 'l combatte
> su la fiumana ove 'l mar non ha vanto? (*Inf.* II, 106–108)

> Do you not see the death that assails him on
> that river over which the sea has no boast?

We know a great deal about the nature of this "river over which the sea has no boast" in terms of the moral theology of Dante's time.[4] A good deal remains to be said, however, about its figural meaning, that is, its place here in the description of an exodus that fails. It is perhaps because we have been exclusively concerned with the pilgrim's point of view in our attempt to explain these puzzling verses that we have not taken sufficient notice of the fact that they are Lucy's words and that they are spoken in heaven. My purpose here is to show that when Lucy speaks of the wolf as though it were a *fiumana,* she is glossing the frustrated journey precisely as Beatrice will later gloss its successful counterpart in the *Paradiso;* that is, according to a *figura* which cannot be perceived by the pilgrim on this side of the river.

Because the exegetical language is no longer familiar to us, it is tempting to dismiss any biblical dimension of meaning as being no longer relevant to a modern reading of the text. To do so in this case, however, would be to dismiss the entire structure of the poem.

This becomes apparent as soon as we realize that the "view" from paradise, being that of the ending of the poem, is the view of the poet himself. In a sense, the purpose of the entire journey is to write the poem, to attain the vantage-point of Lucy, and of all the blessed, from which to perceive the *figura* and the coherence in life, and to bear witness to that coherence for other men. As in all spiritual autobiography, the protagonist struggles to stand outside time and from there to find the meaning of his history and to judge it as though it were concluded. The duality of the imagery in the prologue scene, with the pilgrim using the wolf and Lucy the river as descriptions of the same dramatic action, indicates a dialectic fundamental to this poem and to any novel of the self: the perspective of the self that was corrected and reinterpreted by the perspective of the author, the self that is. Dante's journey, the story of how he came to write the poem, ends where it began, when the pilgrim who was becomes the poet who has been with us from the beginning. The journey and the poem itself are therefore inseparable; the figure of exodus is not only the subject matter of the story, but also, in Dante's view, a precondition for the existence of it. Since both the journey of the pilgrim and the struggle of the self to capture its own essence in retrospect depend on a conversion, they may therefore be described according to the traditional biblical figure for such an experience—an exodus from Egypt to Jerusalem—and they take place within the prescribed limits of Dante's life.

Once we think of the barrier facing the pilgrim in the first canto as an impediment not only to the completion of the journey but also to the telling of the story, we begin to see the aptness of describing the encounter as a mortal combat. If the journey had ended there, the poem could never have been written. The fact that we have it before us proves that the pilgrim ultimately survived this struggle. On the other hand, there is a sense in which all self-analysis presupposes a death of the self. To grasp the totality of a historical evolution, it is necessary that the evolution be completed and that the observer stand outside it. Only from Jerusalem could the Jews have written their national epic, for then the myriad extraneous details of the journey could be separated from those events which seemed to reveal the providential structure of their exodus.[5] Similarly, the Book of Exodus could be interpreted as prophetic only when read from the perspective of the New Testament as a fulfillment of the Old. However, when the evolution is that of the self, the goal of the journey is death, the necessary conclusion, which terminates the perpetual change of the self so that inventory may be taken. Death being what it is, the inventory must usually be left to someone else. A spiritual autobiography then, in order to be authentic, requires nothing less than death and subsequent rebirth.

Because such a death and resurrection are in ordinary terms unthinkable, we find few novels of the self that strike us as successful. Those which concern themselves solely with history seem to be devoid of any structure or coherence because there is no definitive separation between the past and present self. No number of historic details amassed by an author can add up to the continuity of a single life. On the other hand, when such novels err on the side of plot, they strike us as too neat and contrived. The rationale superimposed upon the "facts" seems to stifle whatever authenticity those facts may have had. Somewhere between these two forms of literary failure there lies the authentic novel of the self, a story told with all of the intimacy and historicity that comes from the organic continuity of the author with his subject, yet at the same time with the detachment and sense of finality that come only with death. The *Divina Commedia* is the first and perhaps the foremost of such novels of the self. The retrospective structure of a historic evolution is, in terms of literary creation, the retrospective structure of this greatest of spiritual autobiographies.

The river of death alluded to by Lucy's words is therefore the boundary separating facile autobiography from the true novel of the self. Short of that barrier, preaching about virtue sounds hollow and meaningless; only the man who has survived a death of the self has the right to exhort others to follow him. That view is somewhat like the panorama seen by a drowning man, who is able to look back over the whole course of his life and to see its totality precisely because that life is about to be concluded. We know from the existence of the poem that the pilgrim has in fact managed to cross the river, just as we can know about the panoramic vision in the instant before death only because by some accident a few victims of drowning have survived it. Dante's story seems as gratuitous as that of a man who has survived his own death. The death of his former self is almost an epistemological necessity for the existence of the story, and at the same time this miraculous event is the story itself. The traditional name for this death and rebirth is conversion, a burial of the "old man" so that the "new man" might be born. The destruction of the former self in preparation for the reception of sanctifying grace was known in Pauline terms as the "baptism unto death," the descent into the tomb before the ascent to grace, made possible by Christ's own death and resurrection. In figural terms, it takes place in the "river" before which the pilgrim is standing when he comes to the attention of Lucy. His failure to overcome the wolf is a failure to "come over" the *fiumana* into the promised land. Since Lucy is speaking to Beatrice, a fellow citizen of the heavenly Jerusalem, she refers to the last stage of his conversion in terms of the last river, known to all of the elect as Jordan, which must be crossed before the exodus is accomplished.

The narrative of the Book of Exodus may be broken down into three parts: first there is Egypt, from which the children of Israel escape into the desert by a miraculous crossing of the Red Sea which opens for them and closes over Pharaoh's soldiers. The crossing of the desert is accomplished next under the guidance of Moses, with the help of heaven. Moses does not, however, fulfill his mission; he dies and is taken by the Lord before Israel arrives at its goal. It remains for Joshua to take command and to lead his people into Jerusalem. Once more, an act of God is required before this can occur, for the river Jordan is flooded and must be parted by another miracle before Israel can cross. Thus there are three crucial stages along the way: the Red Sea, the desert, and the River Jordan, and the journey cannot be said to be complete until the last step has been taken. Unfortunately, however, the last stage on the way to perfection is the most difficult to take, for, to return to the language of the doctrine which underlies the figure, it is the work of sanctifying grace.

Three physical areas in the prologue scene correspond to these three figural areas in the drama of exodus.[6] Immediately after leaving the dark wood, the poet implicitly relates the wood to the crossing of a sea: "as he who with laboring breath has escaped from the deep to the shore . . . turns back to gaze upon the pass that never left anyone alive"(*Inf.* I, 22–27). The word *passo* associates the open sea with a crossing and thus foreshadows the first stage of the drama of exodus, which awaits the first scenes of the *Purgatorio* to reach its fulfillment. Again, the mountain slope is first called a *piaggia diserta,* and then a *gran diserto;* we therefore have little difficulty associating the desert slope with the second area of our exodus *manqué.* The problem seems to be only to distinguish the third moment of the prologue from the final "crossing" that is presented to us in the figure of exodus. That final moment, which proves the pilgrim's undoing, is identified by Lucy when she refers to the pilgrim as weeping on the banks of a *fiumana,* a swollen river, unable to cross without the help of Beatrice. Dante's contemporaries would have had no trouble in identifying it by its figural name: the River Jordan flooded before the Israelites.[7]

Within a Christian context, to speak of a "river over which the sea cannot boast" is necessarily to speak of the Jordan. The early commentators of this verse were inclined to take it literally, as a reference to a stream running at the foot of the mountain or else to the River Acheron itself. The dramatic and poetic difficulties entailed by such an identification appear to be insuperable and for this reason many modern commentators have abandoned it, choosing instead to understand the river as purely metaphorical.[8] The difficulty here is that whatever the ontological status of the river, that status is shared by the sea. *La fiumana* and *il mare* seem to have equivalent modes of existence. It therefore seems unsatisfactory to suggest that the river is superior to the sea because the former has a purely spiritual significance. A totally satisfying explanation would have to account for both the river and the sea on the same plane of reality. Even an uncompromisingly "aesthetic" commentator has insisted that the river is to be understood in the same way as we understand the *pelago* or "open sea" of the simile in Canto I, quoted above.[9] There remains the question of why, on any level of reality, this river should be superior to the sea.

In antiquity, there was one river considered to be superior to any sea: Oceanos, the father of all waters.[10] Homer describes it in the *Iliad:*

> . . . the deep and powerful Stream
> of Oceanos, the source of all rivers,
> every sea, and all the springs and
> deep wells that there are. (XXI, 196)

In the mythological cosmology of Homeric Greece, the river was thought to be the boundary of all reality. For this reason, the shield of Achilles had for its rim "the mighty Stream of Oceanos" (XVIII, 607). Beyond the boundary formed by the river lay the world of the dead, into which the river carried those who crossed it. Circe sends Odysseus to "the deep-flowing River of Oceanos and the boundaries of the world" (*Odyssey* XI, 21) in order to arrive at the kingdom of Hades. Eventually, the river was personified as a kindly old god and came to represent water itself.[11]

An analogous theme concerning the cosmological waters of the kingdom of the dead seems to have existed among the Jews. The waters of Tehom were the realm of the dead, sometimes appearing above the earth but more often beneath it as the black waters of chaos.[12] In the Book of Enoch, the prophet in his journey reaches the great river and the darkness of the west.[13] It therefore comes as no surprise to cultural historians to find such ideas prevalent among Christians too. Their great river was the Jordan. In the Gnosis, the Jordan was a cosmic river, the frontier between the world of the senses and the spiritual world.[14] In orthodox Christianity, the Jordan was associated with the rivers of paradise and came to represent all waters, purified by the baptism of Christ.[15] It was perhaps inevitable that Christian ideas about the "sacramental" and "cosmic" character of the Jordan should come to be associated with the mythology of Oceanos, the source of all waters, the boundary between life and death and hence the entrance to the other world.[16] By a logical extension of these associations, the name of Oceanos was also evoked within the context of exodus. The earliest such evocation seems to be in a report by St. Hippolytus on the teaching of the Nassenes:

> The Ocean is the birthplace of the Gods and of men: ever flowing backwards and forwards, now upwards, now downwards. When the Ocean flows downwards, then men are born; when it flows upwards, then are the gods born. . . . All that is born below is mortal: all that is born above is immortal, for it is begotten spiritual, of water and the spirit. . . . This is said of the great Jordan, whose current, when it flowed downwards, prevented the children of Israel when they left the land of Egypt from entering, was arrested and made by Jesus-Joshua to flow the other way.[17]

Thereafter, the association between Oceanos and Jordan became a commonplace. The theme of the flux and reflux of the river, inherent in the folklore of the cosmic river, was reinterpreted in terms of the figure of exodus.

This early mythological association will perhaps help to explain why the River Jordan is often personified by a thoroughly pagan river god throughout the history of baptismal iconography, at least until the Carolingian period and somewhat beyond it.[18] It also helps to explain why it should have been the object of fanciful geographic speculation in the Middle Ages—it was thought by some geographers that the river continued its course underground to reappear later at its own source.[19] Some commentators on Dante's poem, notably Grandgent, have suggested that the characteristic of not flowing into the sea was enough to qualify a river as "la fiumana ove 'l mar non ha vanto." If this were the case, then the Jordan would qualify as well as the Acheron, Grandgent's identification.[20] The spiritual importance of the Jordan in the baptismal liturgy led very early to statements about its geographic "transcendence" in terms reminiscent of the descriptions of Oceanos in antiquity. Gregory of Nyssa, for example, speaking of the Jordan, insists upon its cosmic importance: "For indeed the river of grace flows everywhere. It does not rise in Palestine to disappear in some nearby sea: it spreads over the whole earth and flows into Paradise, flowing in the opposite direction to those four rivers which come from Paradise, and bringing in things far more precious than those which come forth."[21] In this passage, there can scarcely be any doubt that the mythology of Oceanos is operative. The Jordan qualifies as a Christian Oceanos and is for this reason superior to any other body of water.

Of particular interest to the student of Dante in this admittedly remote conflation of mythological ideas is the association of these rivers, not only with death, but also with the *descensus ad inferos*. We have seen that in Homer the great river was considered a gateway to the other world. This was also the case with the "Great Jordan" in early Christianity. Per Lundberg has demonstrated that the descent into the river was traditionally seen as a victory over death and the devil and therefore was analogous to Christ's victory in the harrowing of hell.[22] The victory took place between Christ's death and Resurrection. Indeed, it might be said that the descent into hell is a dramatization of what was in fact accomplished by the Redemption. Similarly, the descent into the river and the ascent from it, commemorated by the liturgy of baptism in the primitive church, was read as a baptism "unto death" of the new convert; in effect, a Christian *descensus*. When we consider that the entrance into grace of the newly baptized soul is completely analogous to the restoral to grace of the fallen sinner in later Christianity, we come to see that it is precisely as a "Jordan" that we are to read the barrier in Dante's poem: the *fiumana* is a death which is a prelude to authentic life, but before the barrier is surmounted, a descent in humility, into hell itself, will be required.

All of this was thought to be contained in the name of the river. In an exegetical tradition that extends from Philo Judaeus to Thomas Aquinas, the etymology of the name "Jordan" was said to be *katabasis autōn, descensus eorum,* "their descent."[23] Aquinas explains the meaning of the name in terms that precisely recall the "descent into humility" that Charles Singleton[24] has shown to be the tropological meaning of Dante's journey through hell: "It should be said that in Baptism there is an ascent to the perfection of grace, which requires a descent in humility, according to James 4:6: 'To the humble He gives grace.' And the name of Jordan is to be referred to that type of descent."[25] That type of descent will be required of Dante's pilgrim before he can make his ascent to grace.

These ancient ideas constitute, at best, remote sources of the complex of motifs represented by Dante's *fiumana.* Except for the passage from Aquinas, none of the authors we have quoted was known directly to the poet. One expression of some of these ideas, however, may well be a more proximate source; it appears in Virgil. Indeed, it is so strikingly like Dante's poetic representation that, were it from a more familiar work, we might be tempted to suggest a direct influence. It is, however, from the *Georgics,*[26] which Dante never quotes and which is seldom mentioned in the Middle Ages. In the fourth book, Virgil presents us with the fable of Aristaeus, the shepherd and demigod, who attempted to violate Eurydice and so indirectly caused her death by the "solitary shore" of a river. The fable tells of the punishment of Aristaeus and his subsequent expiation. All his bees are killed, and he must descend to the abode of the gods and wrestle with Proteus in order to discover what sacrifices must be made before his bees can be restored to him. The story begins with the shepherd's complaint by the "holy spring of the riverhead" to his mother Cyrene, "who dwellest here deep beneath the flood": "why hast thou borne me in the gods' illustrious line—if indeed my father is . . . Apollo of Thymbra—to be the scorn of doom? or whither is thy love for me swept away?" From her chamber "in the river depths" Cyrene hears his cry. Another sea-nymph, Arethusa, hears his lament and calls it to the attention of his mother:

> O not vainly startled by so heavy a moan, Cyrene sister, he thine own, thy chiefest care, mourning Aristaeus stands in tears by

> Peneus' ancestral wave, and calls thee *cruel*. . . . To her the mother, stricken in soul with fresh alarm: Lead him, quick, lead him to us; he, she cries, may unforbidden tread the threshold of the gods. With that she bids the deep streams retire, leaving a broad path for his steps to enter in. *But round him the mountain-wave stood curving* and clasped him in its mighty fold, and sped him beneath the river.[27]

When they are finally reunited, son and mother together drink a libation to Oceanos, "Father of all things" and ruler of this "sisterhood of nymphs."

Dramatically speaking, the elements here bear a striking resemblance to what we have seen of the situation in Canto II: the hero, about to undertake a *descensus* in expiation for a sin, is heard weeping on the banks of a river associated with the other world. His cry is heard in a court of godly "sisters" who undertake a kind of relay in order to bring him to the threshold of the gods. The most important difference between the two dramatic representations is that in Virgil's fable, the shepherd actually crosses the river. This detail of the story is precisely what attracted some Christians to it and caused them to interpret it according to a much more familiar crossing. Lactantius, for example, when discussing the crossing of the Red Sea by the Jews, quotes Virgil, and specifically the lines I have italicized, to describe the parting of the waters: "Curvata in montis faciem circumstetit unda."[28] Even in the Renaissance, commentators on these verses recall that something similar occurred "in exitu Israel de Aegypto."[29] Whether or not Dante knew Virgil's verses and the Christian gloss directly, they certainly are paralleled in a striking way by his own poetic representation.

Thus far we have shown the reasons for the Jordan's superiority to any body of water. We have yet to explain specifically why it should be compared to a sea or indeed why the sea should be mentioned at all. But if we keep in mind the fact that river and sea should both exist on the same level of reality, then the answer begins to become apparent. The only sea that can be compared to the Jordan is the Red Sea, and it happens that they exist on precisely the same levels of reality, liturgically and literally, as stages in the drama of exodus. An examination of their relationship to each other will bring us closer to a clear understanding of Dante's verse.

We have asserted that the figure for baptism was the Israelites' crossing of the River Jordan under the leadership of Joshua. This contradicts, however, no less an authority than St. Paul. In a famous passage which enunciated the principle of figural interpretation, St. Paul suggested that it was the crossing of the Red Sea that constituted the figure: "I would not have you ignorant, brethern, that our fathers [the Israelites] were all under the cloud and passed through the sea. And all in Moses were baptized in the cloud and the sea. . . . Now all these things were done in a figure for us" (I Cor. 10:1). Thereafter, the great majority of exegetes asserted that the crossing of the Red Sea was the type of baptism. According to Jean Daniélou, Origen was the innovator who established the crossing of Jordan as a more suitable figure of baptism since it represented a later stage in the journey to grace. In his commentary on John, he sought to establish a relationship between the progress of the Jews and the progress of the convert to God, thus initiating the tropological reading of exodus upon which the structure of Dante's poem depends. Origen may well be also the first to claim the river's superiority over the sea:

> And even if those Paul speaks of were baptized in the cloud and in the sea, there is something harsh and bitter in their baptism. They are still in the fear of their enemies, crying out to the Lord and to Moses. *But the baptism in Joshua which takes place in sweet and drinkable water is in many ways superior to the earlier one.*[30]

Again, in a homily, he makes the classic division of the soul's progress to grace in terms of the stages of exodus:

> And you who have just abandoned the darkness of idolatry . . . then it is that you begin first to leave Egypt. When you have been included in the number of the catechumens . . . you have passed over the Red Sea. And if you come to the sacred font of Baptism . . . you shall enter into the land of promise.[31]

Daniélou has remarked that the "general tradition of the Church, which saw in the crossing of the Red Sea the type of baptism, was too strong to allow this other symbolism."[32] Nevertheless, the symbolism of Jordan as baptism and therefore as "superior" to the Red Sea persisted at least until Thomas Aquinas, who believed he had biblical authority for this interpretation. This authority was strong enough to influence Dante's poetic representation of the drama of salvation.

In the New Testament, Christ baptized his followers in the River Jordan, not in the Red Sea. However, the Gospels mention not one but two types of baptism: the baptism of the precursor, who for this very reason is known as John the Baptist, and the baptism of Christ, which is the true baptism. John says: "I indeed baptize you with water unto repentance; but he that cometh after me is mightier than I, whose shoes I am not worthy to bear: he shall baptize you with the Holy Ghost and with fire."[33] Medieval exegetes and philosophers saw in the two types of baptism an opportunity to distinguish the preparation for grace from grace itself, which is to say, the repentance of the sinner from the forgiveness of sin.[34] The baptism of John came to represent repentance for a former way of life and the preparation for a new—the new life that was sacramentally represented by the baptism of Christ. Every soul therefore required a baptism of water, repentance, as well as a baptism of the Holy Ghost, that is, justification, and the principle was supported by Christ's words from the Gospel according to St. John: "Verily, verily I say unto thee, except a man be born of water *and* of the Spirit, he cannot enter into the kingdom of God." The figure of baptism in general was indeed the Red Sea; baptism in the special sense, however, as a sacrament which brought with it grace, came to be figured by the River Jordan. Aquinas distinguishes between the two types:

> It should be said that the crossing of the Red Sea prefigures baptism insofar as that baptism takes away sin. But the crossing of the River Jordan insofar as it opens the gates of heaven, which is a more important effect of baptism, can be fulfilled only by Christ. It was more fitting then that Christ should be baptized in the Jordan rather than in the Sea.[35]

Again describing the figure, he insists on the supereminence of Jordan: "The River Jordan was the means whereby the children of Israel entered into the promised land. This the baptism of Christ has above all other baptisms, that it leads into the Kingdom of God which is signified by the promised land."[36] It is precisely because the River Jordan is a figure for the baptism of Christ that it is a river unlike all other rivers, superior to the sea, which figures only the baptism of John the Baptist. It stands to the sea as Christ stands to the Baptist; John the Baptist is said by Christ to be the greatest man born of woman, yet he is less than the least of the angels. Not even John could be considered greater than Christ. Similarly, the Jordan is a river over which not even the Red Sea can boast. In the figure of baptism, it is a "fiumana ove 'l mar non ha vanto."

Finally, in order to show how the poet's contemporaries would read both the Red Sea and the River Jordan together in a figure representing the justification of sinners, we have only to turn to St. Bonaventure. His remarks on the subject constitute a reinterpretation of Origen's exegesis not in terms of the typology of baptism, but according to the figure of conversion. Writing about the correspondence of the Jewish Passover to its Christian fulfillment, Easter, the liturgical time of Dante's poem, he notices that the word *pascha* signifies *transitus,* a crossing:

> There are three crossings, that is, the crossing that is a beginning *(incipientium)* and the crossing that is in the making *(proficientium)* and the crossing that is an arrival *(pervenientium)* . . . this then is the threefold paschal crossing, of which the first is through the *sea* of contrition, the second through the *desert* of religion, the third through the *Jordan* of death; and thus we arrive at the promised land.[37]

The great Franciscan Doctor then goes on to show how these three stages on the way to sanctifying (or *pervenient*) grace were foreshadowed by the three paschal feasts celebrated by the Jews, according to the account of the twelfth chapter of Exodus:

> it is written that first they ate the *pasch* of the Lord and this was the crossing of the beginning, for after this feast, having left Egypt, they crossed the Red Sea. And the children of Israel also had a paschal supper in the desert . . . at the mountain of Sinai, and that signified the crossing that was in the making, for it was while the children of Israel were progressing through the desert. They had the third paschal supper at their entry into the promised land . . . and this was the crossing of arrival for it was held in the promised land after the Jordan had been crossed.[38]

It is clear from the words describing these crossings *(incipientium, proficientium, pervenientium)* that Bonaventure has the moral sense of exodus in mind, accoring to which, in Dante's words, the soul is "brought out of the state of misery and grief into the state of grace," which is to say, sanctifying or "pervenient" grace. Furthermore, this conception of the stages of moral development corresponds to the drama of the *Purgatorio,* from the emergence on the shore, to the ascent of the mountain, to the crossing of the river to Beatrice. Here in the prologue scene, the figural landscape prefigures the successful journey that is to come.

Bonaventure tells us that Jordan signifies death (we hear in the background the plea of Lucy—"Non vedi tu la morte che 'l combatte?") and we understand now that he refers to the death which is a prerequisite to life in the Pauline sense: "Know ye not that so many of us as were baptized unto Jesus Christ were baptized unto his death? Therefore we are buried with him by baptism into death: that like as Christ was raised up from the dead by the glory of the Father, even so we also should walk in newness of life" (Romans 6:3–4). On his own, Dante has survived the perils of the dark wood and thus, from the perspective of heaven, the dangerous waters of everyman's Red Sea. Again he has made some progress on the desert slope. It is the wolf that finally stops him, short of the final crossing which is death and at the same time life. He will be introduced to that *vita nuova* when he is immersed in the River Lethe at the top of purgatory. Now, in the prologue scene, he is blocked on the shores of a *fiumana* which he cannot cross until, like Christ, he descends to the depths of the earth. The implication seems to be that the preparation for grace lies within the competence of man, in the purely natural order. However, only Beatrice can bring the pilgrim the grace that is needed to accomplish a death and resurrection. This is to state in theological terms what we have known all along: were it not for Beatrice, neither the journey nor the poem could have come into existence.

It has perhaps not occurred to Dante commentators to identify the *fiumana* with Christianity's river because Dante's river is so clearly terrifying, while the Jordan was traditionally a river of salvation. As we have said, however, this is to read the river entirely from the pilgrim's perspective and to forget that the purpose of the journey is to correct that perspective. In a Christian context, all salvation is a consequence of the death of the self. In a literary context, the poem, the triumph of the author, entails a death of the protagonist, a detachment of the self that was from the self that is. Unless one understands the death of the self involved in Dante's experience (as pilgrim and author), there is no way of appreciating the drama of the *Inferno.* The fears expressed by the pilgrim along the way constitute the very *askesis* that makes rebirth possible; if this were not so, they would have to be dismissed as an example of dramatic coyness on the part of a man who knows from the beginning that everything will turn out all right. It would be as if we refused to believe that the Dostoevskian hero is really frightened by the firing squad, because we know from the existence of the story that the reprieve from the Czar came through. Dante's river of death represents exactly the same sort of limit-situation. Short of the barrier, progress is impossible; beyond it, there seems to be only extinction. The story is testimony of the fact that this extinction of a false self in an inverted world is a necessary step before authentic life, and the story, can be born.

As readers of the story, we cannot know the experience of a death and resurrection. It is for this reason that the story was written: as a confession of faith for other men. The best we can do is to accept the *exemplum,* the story itself, in good faith and as part of our own experience, much as Dante accepted Virgil's story as a preparation for a synthesis of which his author could know nothing at all. If, in the twentieth century, it seems unlikely that a Beatrice will come or, were she to come, that we should call her Sanctifying Grace, the fault is neither ours nor Dante's; we shall at least have walked together to the river.

4. Pilgrim in a Gyre

When Dante speaks of the "way of our life" in the first line of his poem, he is using a figure that was familiar in his day and has become a banality in ours. It is especially important in the *Divine Comedy,* however, for it helps set off that great work from the bizarre travel literature which preceded it in the Middle Ages, and which we have come to call the literature of "oltretomba." Dante's journey is different, for it is not a dream and it is not his alone. It is an allegorical representation of a spiritual development: the *cammino* of man in this life. Dante's literary ancestor is Plato, and not Tnugdalus, and his *Inferno,* like Plato's cave, is the place where all men come to know themselves. St. Bonaventure was the medieval theorist who worked out the metaphor of the *itinerarium mentis* in great detail, but it remained for Dante to write the work which gave the metaphor substance and made great poetry from a figure of speech.

Few Dantists would quarrel with these generalities. Debates arise, however, when an attempt is made to show that the analogy between the pilgrim's progress through the other world and the mind's journey to God is seriously intended and therefore consistently maintained throughout the poem.[1] Given the basic metaphor, it remains to be explained why "the mind" should first descend "to the left" in a spiral, turn upside-down, then climb spirally "to the right" until it ends by spinning in a circle.

Furthermore, any attempt at explanation is impossible as long as the directions the poet gives us remain unclear on the purely literal level. It appears from the text, and particularly from the flight of Geryon in Canto XVII of the *Inferno,* that the descent into hell is accomplished by a clockwise spiral,[2] and there seems to be no doubt that the ascent of the Mount of Purgatory is counter-clockwise.[3] Curiously enough, Dante uses the phrase "a sinistra" to describe the first and "a destra" the second, expressions usually reserved for linear reference, which are meaningless in circular motion without established points of departure and arrival. Moreover, in modern usage, when such imprecise directions are applied to circular motion, they seem to suggest the contrary of Dante's apparent meaning. According to H. D. Austin, clockwise motion is usually designated movement "a destra" in modern Italian, and not "a sinistra" as in the *Inferno.*[4] Nothing appears to explain this discrepancy satisfactorily, and a doubt therefore remains concerning the text's literal meaning, precluding further investigation.

Finally, the search for tropological significance in the gyrations of the pilgrim seems doomed by inconsistencies in the general rule about the pilgrim's descent. In the circle of the heretics, for instance, Dante and Virgil turn "a la man destra" (IX, 132), rather than to the left as is normally the case in their *circular* movement throughout hell.[5] There is no literal reason for this deviation, and its gratuitous nature is underscored when Dante addresses Virgil: "O virtù somma che per li empi giri/mi volvi . . . com' a te piace" (X, 4–5). (O supreme virtue, who lead me round as you will through the impious circles). If Virgil has his reasons, they are clear neither to the pilgrim nor to the modern commentators of the poem.[6] Again, the pilgrim seems to approach the usurers by moving "to the right" in Canto XVII (71), and although there is this time an excellent literal reason for the turn (to avoid recrossing the river of boiling blood), this seems nevertheless another inconsistency.[7] Were it not for these violations of the general rule, the leftward turns in hell might be (and indeed have been) explained by a dichotomy as old as western thought: left-hand turns for *sinister* descent, right-hand turns for the righteous climb. Unfortunately, the exceptions prove fatal to any such theory.

In spite of all these objections, we must assume the existence of a coherent pattern and abandon our hypothesis only when our resources, or those of the poem, are exhausted. Only then may we conclude either that the significance of these details escapes us, or that the poem is unintelligible in this respect. Knowing Dante as we do, the latter conclusion seems rash in the extreme. If Dante chose to make pointed remarks concerning the pilgrim's path and did so with what seems a persistent lack of clarity, we must begin by assuming that the confusion is ours, and not his.[8] As it happens, a careful examination of the poet's terminology reveals not only that this is the case, but also that a complete understanding of the literal meaning of these directions at the same time points toward an explanation of their deeper significance.

We said that expressions such as "to the right" and "to the left" are ambiguous when used to describe circular or spiral motion, precisely because we do not know the points of reference. It will not help to say simply that these points are the pilgrim's own left and right, for he could then use the expression "to the left" to describe his motion through hell only while facing the central abyss, whereas in fact he sometimes uses the expression while he is actually turning clockwise, that is, when his left shoulder is closest to hell's wall and his right is toward the center. If this is motion "pur a sinistra," it is difficult to see whose *sinistra* and *destra* are the measure of such movement.

The answer is very surprising at first, for we are accustomed to thinking of "left" and "right" as completely relative directions. For Dante, however, an absolute right and left existed: the "right" and "left" of the closed Aristotelian cosmos. In the second book of *De caelo,* Aristotle flatly stated that "right" is the place whence motion through space begins. Rightward motion in the universe is that motion which begins in the east (the "right" of the world's body), moves to the west (left), and continues around the other hemisphere to return *to the right,* its point of origin. In other words, the diurnal motion of the heavens around the motionless earth is circular motion *(epi dexia)* to the right,[9] and when Dante says that the pilgrim moves "a destra," he is using the Italian equivalent of the phrase used in the ancient world to describe the movement of the heavens.

Nevertheless, the problem still remains, for even assuming that Dante employed the Aristotelian convention in describing a movement analogous to the circling of the heavens as motion "a destra" and its contrary as "a sinistra," we are unable to visualize the movement unless we are given an established vantage point from which to view celestial movement as Aristotle and Dante understood it. Briefly, to know which is the "right" is not enough; it is essential to know which is front and which is back, or which is up and which is down. It is as if we were told that the pilgrim moves in the direction of the hands on a transparent clock, and yet were not told whether to view the clock from before or behind. It is true that from incidental details in the poem we know that the pilgrim's path is generally clockwise throughout hell and counter-clockwise throughout purgatory. The question is, are the poet's specific directions enough, given their traditional meanings, to be self-explanatory? If not, they are at best superfluous and at worst misleading.

The Aristotelian convention was quite clear with respect to the point of view from which celestial motion was to be observed. When Aristotle assumed that east was "the right" and that the heavens moved "to the right" he was merely following an established tradition. He was more logically consistent than the Pythagoreans, however, for he was willing to draw the astounding conclusion from this assumption that south is "up" in the cosmos and north "down," and that we live in the northern, or upside-down hemisphere. If the cosmos is a living thing and the east is its right, then the south must be its head.[10]

Aristotle's reasoning is far from clear,[11] but for our purposes, it is enough to know how it was interpreted in the Middle Ages. St. Thomas, who appears to have taken it quite seriously, explained the curious deduction with the image of the cosmological man. If we suppose a man to be lying on his back along the earth's axis, looking up at the stars, with his feet toward the south and his head toward the north, the skies seem to him to rise on his left (east), move to his right (west), to return after twelve hours to his left.[12] This clockwise motion Aristotle would call movement *to the left.* By definition, however, the heavens move to the right. If the place whence motion begins (i.e., the point where the heavens rise) is the right, and if it nevertheless seems to correspond to such a man's left side, this can only mean that the man is upside-down with respect to the absolute directions of the closed Aristotelian cosmos. If his head were to the south and his feet toward the north, then indeed the sun and all the other stars would move *counter*-clockwise, rising on the right and setting on the left, to return once more to the *right.* It therefore follows that true "up" in the cosmos is to the south, and east is the right hand of the world's body. Consequently, we live in the lower hemisphere of a motionless earth.

From this argument, absurd to us, but nevertheless authoritative for Dante, it is clear that the pilgrim is traveling upwards, even during his descent into hell, for true "up" in the cosmos is "down" to us;

this is the literal justification of the moral truth which Augustine expressed with the exhortation: "Descend, so that you may ascend."[13] In the spiritual life, one must descend in humility before one can begin the ascent to truth, and in the physical world, according to both Dante and Aristotle, one must travel downward with respect to our hemisphere in order to rise. The analogy between the mind's journey to God and the pilgrim's journey to the Empyrean is in this respect, as so often, perfectly exact. Furthermore, the Aristotelian convention helps explain why Satan, embedded in the center of the earth, should have fallen *down* from the southern part of the heavens, and why he should appear right-side up in this world, of which he is prince.[14] Finally, the Aristotelian analysis of the movement of the heavens explains the convention used by Dante to describe the circular motion of his pilgrim. Just as we use a clock in our post-Copernican world for spatial reference in the words "clockwise" and "counter-clockwise," so celestial movement not only gives the pilgrim his time references in the poem, but also provides him with a means of "telling" circular direction. As the heavens following the same inexorable course move clockwise or "to the left" to the cosmological man in our hemisphere and "to the right" when viewed from the southern perspective, so the traveler moves in one absolute spiral direction which is to the left as he descends and to the right as he ascends, after having turned upside-down at the earth's center. When he called his clockwise descent "a sinistra" and his counter-clockwise ascent "a destra," Dante was evoking a tradition as old as Pythagoras and as authoritative as Aristotle. The apparent ambiguity of the text is the work of history, and not of the poet.

The analogy between celestial motion and that of the pilgrim is less vague when we press it further. The diurnal motion of the heavens is a uniform circle, whereas the pilgrim moves spirally. The diurnal motion, in Aristotle's view, is the simple circling of the sphere of the fixed stars around the earth as center. This is the movement "to the right" which carries along all other lower circles with it,[15] but they seem to struggle against this movement, in varying degrees, with a movement to the left along the Zodiac. In the case of the sun and the planets, the path formed by the resolution of these two forces is a slow-moving spiral, composed of the daily turns of the celestial equator and the yearly contrary circuit along the ecliptic, from west to east.[16] In other words, the sun appears to be traveling in a spiral, as the result of what we know to be the two movements of the earth: rotation, which causes the apparent east-west circling of the heavens each day, and revolution, which causes the apparent contrary circuit accomplished annually. To medieval men, far more accustomed to watching the heavens than we, the sun seemed to follow a spiral path, geometrically similar to the pilgrim's in the poem.

The first apparent circling, that of the fixed stars and of the other heavenly bodies in diurnal motion, moves "to the right," and with respect to this movement, we live in the lower, or upside-down hemisphere, for it seems to us to move "to the left." The second motion, that of the planets and of the sun in their yearly circuit, moves "to the left," and with respect to this movement, according to Aristotle, it may be said that we live in the upper hemisphere, for it seems to us to move "to the right."[17] When it came to accounting for two contrary motions in the cosmos, Aristotle explained that, since every function must have purpose, the uniformity of the first movement was attributable to the divine nature of the heaven's body, "which by nature moves forever in a circle." The second motion, and particularly the movement of the planets along the ecliptic, accounts for coming-to-be and passing-away.[18] Ours is the hemisphere dominated by generation and corruption, while the southern hemisphere is eternity's locus. The sun, "che mena dritto altrui per ogni calle" (that leads men aright by every path), moves in its composite way, for it ministers to the world below and at the same time circles with the divine motion of the first movement. So the pilgrim's journey through hell, upward (although a descent in humility), and to the right (when it seems to the left), is a composite movement, dominated throughout by the divine movement of the heavens, and, at the same time, partaking of the order of generation and corruption. The Aristotelian physics coincides in an extraordinarily precise way with mystical theology.

Thus far, we have seen only the literal implication of the language used by the poet to describe the gyre of his *persona.* His directions become all the more meaningful, however, when we consider the significance of the analogy between the movement of the heavens and the movement of the mind to God. The identity between the movement of the pilgrim and that of "il sole e l'altre stelle" (the sun and the other stars) is suggested explicitly in the poem's last *terzina* as the goal toward which poem and pilgrim alike have been moving, for the way has been prepared from the beginning to bring Dante step by step from erratic wandering to the perfect circularity of beatitude, "come rota ch'igualmente è mossa," (like a wheel that is evenly moved),[19] and the long path is precisely the literal manifestation of this transition. It is not fortuitous that we can make sense of that gyre only in terms of cosmic movement, for the movement of the universe is by analogy the archetype of all intellectual movement:[20]

e 'l ciel cui tanti lumi fanno bello,
de la mente profonda che lui volve
prende l'image e fassene suggello.
E come l'alma dentro a vostra polve
per differenti membra e conformate
a diverse potenze si risolve,
così l'intelligenza sua bontate
multiplicata per le stelle spiega,
girando sé sovra sua unitate. (*Par.* II, 130–138)

and the heaven which so many lights make beautiful takes its stamp from the profound mind that turns it, and of that stamp makes itself the seal. And as the soul within your dust is diffused through different members and conformed to different potencies, so does the Intelligence deploy its goodness, multiplied through the stars, itself circling upon its own unity.

Just as the sphere of the fixed stars derives its motion from the angelic intelligence which moves it, so too the soul imparts motion to the body which it animates. The various spheres are "organi del mondo"[21] arranged hierarchically, and subject to the daily turning of the outermost, just as the "membra" and "potenze" of the human composite are subject to the human soul. The soul "vive e sente e sé in sé rigira" (lives and feels and circles on itself),[22] which is to say that it is one soul, composed of vegetative, sensitive, and intellective faculties. Exactly as the intelligence of the sphere turns itself upon itself in the perfect circle of contemplation, and at the same time distributes its goodness to the orders below, the rational animal is above all reflective, "sé in sé rigira," and yet informs the whole human composite. The soul of the universe corresponds exactly to the soul of man, who is indeed a microcosm.

The ultimate source of this type of microcosmic theory of the soul is Plato's *Timaeus*.[23] There we read of the creation of the world-soul by the Demiurge, who takes a length of "soul-stuff" and cuts it in two, then places one piece upon the other, forming the letter "X." He then bends up the ends to form two hoops on the same axis, like the circular strips on a celestial sphere:

> comprehending them in a uniform revolution upon the same axis, he made the one the outer and the other the inner circle. Now the motion of the outer circle he called the motion of the Same, and the motion of the inner circle the motion of the Other, or diverse. The motion of the Same he carried round by the side *to the right,* and the motion of the diverse diagonally *to the left.* And he gave dominion to the motion of the Same and like, for that he left single and undivided; but he divided the inner motion in six places and made seven unequal circles . . . and bade the [planetary] orbits proceed in a direction opposite to one another.

The human soul has the same revolutions, Plato tells us, and is made from the same material. The highest part of the soul, its intelligence or speculative reason, moves as the circle of the Same. It can arrive at the perfection of knowledge, for it contemplates only eternal things, and yet at the same time it dominates all the other powers of the soul. The soul's revolutions according to the circle of the Other are contrary motions, which represent the soul's other powers in their relationship to the temporal world.[24] In Chalcidius' commentary on Plato's passage, the matter is summed up for us very briefly: "The sphere of the fixed stars [the motion of the Same] in the soul is reason, [the spheres] of the planets, *iracundia* and *cupiditas* and other movements of this sort."[25]

Timaeus' myth depends, in the first place, upon the analogy which exists between the shape of the human head and the circularity of the firmament,[26] and in the second place, upon the analogy between physical movement and movement of the mind: circular motion is perfection in the celestial order, and suggests reflection, which is perfection in the intellectual order; rectilinear motion, characteristic of matter, suggests irrational behavior; spiral motion, as of the planets, suggests the movement which is a combination of the other two, and therefore is characteristic of the soul incarnate. When the star-soul receives its body, it suffers a trauma that violently shakes its "courses" and completely stops the revolution of the circle of the Same:

> the circles were broken and disordered in every possible manner, so that when they moved they were tumbling to pieces, and moved irrationally, at one time in a reverse direction, and then again obliquely, and then upside-down, as you might imagine a person who is upside-down and has his head leaning upon the ground and his feet up against something in the air; and when he is in such a position, both he and the spectator fancy that the right of either is his left, and the left right.

When the child becomes a man, the disturbances in the soul's courses are quieted, and return to their natural orbits, and their possessor becomes a rational being. If the man neglects education, however, "he walks lame to the end of his life and returns imperfect and good for nothing to the world below."[27]

The suggestiveness of the *Timaeus'* myth of education as a gloss on Dante's journey of the mind is quite obvious. In the prologue scene of the *Inferno* we are presented with the figure of a man whose "circles" are surely disrupted. He undertakes a longer journey to set them right, and this is accomplished, in human terms, at the summit of the Mount of Purgatory. Thereafter, he transcends the human by achieving perfect circularity in paradise, far beyond the spiral path of the planets, like one of the Platonic race of stellar gods. Moreover, the symptoms of the soul's lack of order are strikingly alike in both the *Timaeus* and the *Inferno:* first, Dante's pilgrim, as I argue elsewhere (see chap. 2 of this book), drags his "piè fermo," or left foot, just as Plato's man who neglects education limps throughout his life.[28] Secondly, to Plato's youthful soul, as to Dante's pilgrim in hell, the left seems right and the right left, as to a man upside-down. To overlook the differences between the two allegories, however, would be to do violence to the poem and to the history of ideas. In spite of the striking similarity between the two works with respect to the transition from lameness to circularity as a physical sign of spiritual education, the difference between them is the difference between a classical theory of education and the Christian theology of grace.

It is not incarnation which disrupts the soul of Dante's pilgrim, for the soul did not pre-exist as far as Christians were concerned. Man's calamity in a Christian context was not therefore a fall from the heavens, but rather the fall from grace. The Platonic life cycle is recapitulated in a single moment of the Christian's moral existence, for at any time after the stain of original sin has been removed, the soul may fall from grace, and through grace be reborn. Moreover, the pilgrim is not a child who has yet to acquire the power of ratiocination; his affliction is more deep-seated than ignorance. The latter can be overcome by human effort, for man's reason can be taught to recognize the good. The overwhelming problem, however, is how o apply that vision of the good to moral action, and the solution of he problem lies only partially with man himself. To correct his deformity entirely, Dante's pilgrim needs help from heaven. In short, f we would know more about the meaning of the pilgrim's path, we had best return to the Middle Ages, and leave Plato, to see what became of the *Timaeus* analogy between man and the heavens in the Christian perspective. To do this is no more than to return to Dante's ext, for to read the pilgrim's directions, "a destra" and "a sinistra," without a firm knowledge of their symbolic implications in Dante's day is to misread the poem as surely as if we did not understand heir literal meaning in terms of astronomical convention.

The microcosmic myth was taken quite seriously in the ancient world.[29] Philo Judaeus, for instance, phrased it succinctly in terms which are very close to Dante's own: "I regard the soul as being in man what the heaven is in the universe."[30] This kind of statement became a commonplace in the Middle Ages through the translation nd commentary of the *Timaeus* by Chalcidius, which was echoed by writers of the School of Chartres and later scholastics.[31] Orthodox Christians among the latter thinkers perforce interpreted the idea of he *anima mundi* metaphorically, but the analogy between the movement of the heavens and the movement of the mind remained an ssential part of microcosmic speculation throughout the Middle Ages and well into the Renaissance.[32] Alanus ab Insulis gave the idea one of its clearest formulations in the *De planctu naturae:* "As the orces of the planets battle against the turning of the firmament by heir contrary movements, so a continual struggle goes on between man's sensuality and his reason.[33]

The most influential statement of the *Timaeus* analogy, however, occurs in the third book of Boethius' *Consolation of Philosophy.* The *nima mundi* is described in the famous ninth meter:

> You release the world-soul throughout the harmonious parts of the universe as your surrogate, three-fold in its operations, to

> give motion to all things. That soul, thus divided, pursues its revolving course in two circles, and, returning to itself, embraces the profound mind and transforms heaven to its own image.[34]

Dante virtually paraphrases this meter in *Paradiso* II, 130 ff., quoted above. It may therefore be assumed that Boethius was one of Dante's primary sources for his microcosmic theory, although Dante made the mandatory Christian adjustment by applying Boethius' description of the *anima mundi* directly to the soul of man.[35] We may add parenthetically that any doubt about the ability of the poet's contemporaries to recognize Boethius' (and ultimately Plato's) two circles in the expressions "a destra" and "a sinistra" is dispelled when we examine an Italian translation of the *Consolation* written in the second decade of the fourteenth century. The passage of the ninth meter which we have been discussing is there rendered with a crucial additional line to fill out the verse:

> [l'anima] con la potenza tua divina
> Il ciel con doppio movimento regge,
> Sì ch'a *sinistro e a destro* gli china.[36]

> with your divine power you govern the heaven with double motion so that you incline it *to the left and to the right.*

There seem to be good reasons to suppose that any reader in Dante's day sophisticated enough to see in the pilgrim's journey the journey of the mind would have recognized in his movements "a destra" and "a sinistra" precisely the composite movement of the by then metaphoric world-soul.[37]

The three movements of the universe discussed by Plato, circular, spiral, and rectilinear, corresponding to the movements of the stellar gods, planetary souls, and brute matter, are perhaps suggested in Boethius' statement that the world-soul is "three-fold in its operations."[38] This does not of course contradict the statement that the heavens move in two ways, because in celestial movement there is no linear course. The latter is a characteristic of the sublunary world. It is precisely because circular movement was not considered characteristic of matter that Plato had to assume the existence of a world-soul and Aristotle the existence of heavenly intelligences behind the celestial revolutions. In the Christian adaptation of this cosmologic doctrine, the angels took the places of the intelligences, as far as some thinkers were concerned, and the symbolic suggestion of these movements was quite naturally applied to the angels by such an eminent neoplatonist as the pseudo-Dionysius.[39] He tells us that the angelic intelligence moves in three ways: circular, when it adores God; rectilinear, when it ministers to man; spiral, for even though it ministers to the world below, it never ceases adoring God. Man, who is at least in part an intelligence, and in the great scale is a little less than the angels, is capable of three intellectual movements as well: circular, when the human mind enters within itself and contemplates the Supreme Being; linear, when the human mind concentrates on external things; spiral, when "the knowledge of divine things illuminates it, not by way of intuition or in unity, but thanks to discursive reasons and, so to speak, by complex and progressive steps."[40] One could hardly find a better gloss than this for the meaning of the spiral path in the itinerary of the mind to God.

By virtue of the analogy between the movements of the macrocosm and the interior movements of the microcosm, we may say that the three cosmic movements perceived by the ancients were the ultimate source of the medieval and neoplatonic doctrine of the three movements of the mind, the most famous expression of which is to be found in St. Bonaventure's *Itinerarium mentis:* conversion *extra nos* (linear), *intra nos* (spiral), and *supra nos* (circular).[41] Man, like a planet which stands at the border between earth and stars, or between time and eternity,[42] moves in a composite way on his journey to God, for his spiral path is formed by the resolution of forces between his interior motion according to the circle of the Same (to the right) and his motion according to the circle of the Other (to the left). So it is with Dante's pilgrim. In terms of the moral allegory, no progress can be made in the prologue scene, for this is erratic wandering *extra nos*; Augustine had warned that Truth was not to be found in this way. Once the pilgrim undertakes the other journey, in a sense a journey within, *intra nos,* he begins a spiral movement which is long at first, and gradually becomes more and more circular until it reaches perfect circularity, *supra nos,* in the Empyrean. Thus, his path represents a refinement of his love from human to supernatural.[43]

We must now examine the spiral path more closely. For Plato, the composite movement of the planets represented the resultant of the opposing forces of reason and sensuality. The theme had a subsequent history apart from the Platonic tradition, however, and we had best postpone our interpretation of the pilgrim's gyre until we know more about the *Timaeus* theme in the Aristotelian, rather than the Platonic, psychology. Aristotle, who did not believe in the existence of a world-soul, nevertheless used a version of Plato's analogy in his psychological speculations. In the *De anima,* he suggested that the powers of the soul stand in relationship to each other as do the spheres of the cosmos:

> Appetite sometimes overcomes and moves deliberation. But sometimes the latter moves the former, like a heavenly sphere; one appetition governing another, as in continence. Naturally the higher principle always holds priority, and originates motion, so that movement occurs on three courses.[44]

This idea was naturally picked up by virtually every commentator on Aristotle's text, from the earliest Greeks to Averroes and finally Albertus Magnus and Thomas Aquinas.[45] It would be well to quote the last at length on Aristotle's passage, so that we may fully appreciate how the Aristotelians, with their customary delight in precision, identified the spheres of the heavens according to the philosopher's classification of the soul's powers:

> Next, at "Appetite sometimes," he explains how rational deliberation may yield to the lower desire . . . Again, conversely, the superior appetite that follows rational deliberation sometimes sways the lower one that follows sensuous images (as a higher heavenly body may impel a lower). This happens in the case of "continence"; for the continent are those in whom deliberation gets the better of passion. Note that it is according to nature that the higher appetite should sway the lower. We see this in the heavenly bodies; the higher sphere gives the first impetus, moving the lower which, in turn, has a three-fold local movement. For the sphere, e.g., of Saturn moves first in diurnal motion turning about the poles of the Universe; then in the contrary zodiacal motion; and thirdly in its own proper motion. Likewise, the lower appetite, retaining something of its own proper movement, is also moved by another, and this naturally, following the impulse of the higher appetite and of rational deliberation. If the converse takes place, and the higher is in fact moved by the lower, this is contrary to the natural order of things.[46]

For Aquinas, the soul had three basic faculties: the vegetative, sensitive, and intellective. The first of these man shares with all living organisms, the second with animals, and the third only with his fellow men. Dante alludes to this tripartite division when he says that the soul "vive e sente e sé in sé rigira." The sensitive and the intellective faculties are further subdivided, however, into appetitive and apprehensive, so that the sensitive power consists of both a sensitive appetite and the imagination, while the intellective is composed of a rational appetite (i.e., the will, properly speaking) and the reason. In the comparison to Saturn, the movement of the soul may then be interpreted in this way: the sensitive appetite is subject to the rational appetite (or the will), just as the latter is subject to the reason. The sensitive appetite may be swayed out of its orbit by sensual images, just as the planet may have its own retrograde (or epicyclic) motion. In the soul, this irrational movement was known as the *primus motus* of the sensitive appetite, which was not considered in itself to be within man's control. Nevertheless, in the continent man, this movement is overcome by the *imperium* of the will, the movement from west to east along the Zodiac, according to the "circle of the Other." Finally, both these movements are governed by the reason, which moves all the heavenly bodies. In the incontinent soul, however, if we may recall Plato's words in an Aristotelian context, "the circles [are] broken and disordered in every possible manner," so that the right seems left and the left right.

The heavens, impelled by God, mark all creation with His circular sign: "la circular natura, ch'è suggello a la cera mortal."[47] In celestial motion, the rightward movement of the outermost spheres takes precedence over all others, and the resultant harmony is called Justice.[48] Similarly in human motion, which according to the Aristotelians begins with the circular motion of the spirits in the heart, the movement of the right side of the body takes precedence over the movement of the left. The analogue in the soul of this physical harmony is also called Justice. Moral action, a concatenation of alternate apprehensive and appetitive movements, is harmonious when the reason (like the right foot) moves out first and leads the way.[49]

Justice is achieved in the pilgrim's soul when he reaches the earthly paradise and his will is at last enabled to follow his reason's discernment. Virgil dismisses his charge with a circular blessing:

> Non aspettar mio dir più né mio cenno;
> libero, dritto e sano è tuo arbitrio,
> e fallo fora non fare a suo senno:
> per ch'io te sovra te corono e mitrio. (*Purg.* XXVII, 139–142)

> No longer expect word or sign from me. Free, upright, and whole is your will, and it would be wrong not to act according to its pleasure; wherefore I crown and miter you over yourself.

At the same time the interior condition of moral justice matches a similar condition in the heavens, cosmic justice, a harmony of the spheres arising from the resolution of all contrary motions in an instant of equilibrium. As the pilgrim is about to leave Eden, Dante draws our attention to the fact that the sun is rising near the vernal equinox:

> Surge ai mortali per diverse foci
>   la lucerna del mondo; ma da quella
>   che quattro cerchi giugne con tre croci,
> con miglior corso e con migliore stella
>   esce congiunta, e la mondana cera
>   più a suo modo tempera e suggella. (*Par.* I, 37–42)

> The lamp of the world rises to mortals through different passages; but through that which joins four circles with three crosses it issues with a better course and conjoined with better stars, and tempers and stamps the wax of the world more after its own fashion.

The sun has been near this point throughout the journey, but it is only here that we are told *why*. Commentators have interpreted this passage as an allusion to the four cardinal virtues *(quattro cerchi)* and the three theological *(tre croci),*[50] but they have not sensed its aptness here, at the summit. The sun is rising, Dante tells us, near the intersection of the equinoctial colure, the ecliptic, the celestial equator, and the horizon; this is the vernal equinox, "dove l'un moto e l'altro si percuote" (where the one motion strikes the other),[51] or, in Platonic terms, the point of cosmic balance where the circle of the Same meets the circle of the Other. The sun at this balance point, *Sol iustitiae,* appears to the man whose appetites (the motion "to the left") and reason (the motion "to the right") are in near-perfect balance. We must turn now to see how they arrived at that balance point.

The pilgrim in the prologue scene is a man left to himself, unable to order his appetites to his reason. This spiritual disorder, which Aristotle called "incontinence," is represented by the pilgrim's inability to move his feet consecutively, just as Plato represented disorder in the soul by the figure of a limping man.[52] Unfortunately for man in his fallen state, the soul's powers are not equal to the task of moving toward God, for the intellect is stronger in knowing than is the will in loving, or to state the matter in another way, "l'affetto l'intelletto lega" (the affections bind the intellect).[53] The Christian does not begin from a zero-point on his journey, but rather from the world of generation and corruption, a topsy-turvy world of inflated pride where directions and values are both inverted. Although the fall from grace left the natural light intact, it involved the will in a conversion to lower things, and the consequent distortion can be cured only by a descent in humility and an ascent to grace. Before the soul can make progress, the twisted course of the will must first be unwound. A passage attributed to St. Augustine expresses the situation in terms that are much the same:

> The love of earthly things extinguished in me the delectation of the heavenly: the habit of vice emptied in me the sense of the true gifts. From those gifts am I removed, in these evils am I occupied; secluded from them included in these; from those am I unwound *(devolutus)*, in these wound up *(obvolutus)*. Here is that prison and here are those chains, here is weight and darkness.[54]

Dante chose to be more philosophically precise. Sin is an aversion from God and a conversion to lower things; hence it is primarily of the will, and is punished in hell. To move against the governing force in our confused hemisphere is to move against the will's involvement. The descent is literally necessary to reach the hemisphere which is true "up," and tropologically necessary, for it profits a man to know moral truth only if he is able to will it,[55] and he is able to will it only after he has plumbed the depths and recognized sin for what it is.

In Aristotelian terms, our world is the world of generation and corruption ruled by the planets' movement along the ecliptic, "l'oblico cerchio che i pianeti porta, / per sodisfare al mondo che li chiama" (the oblique circle which bears the planets to satisfy the world which calls on them).[56] This movement is actually leftward, although it seems "to the right" to us. The equivalent of this movement in the microcosm is that of the appetites, sensitive and rational, and in an upside-down world, this motion seems to have dominion over the reason. To set the will right is to move "to the left" in our hemisphere, and to counter the disorder by placing first things first. After the will has accepted Divine Justice by its journey through hell, it clings unswervingly to God, for south of the point "al quale ogni gravezza si rauna" (to which all heaviness is gathered), sin ceases to exist and the soul is partially healed. There remains the painful work of purgation, with the soul's powers in their proper order. When the pilgrim reaches the end of his leftward spiral at the bottom of hell, he turns upside-down, "converts," and sees things from the other perspective. He then finds himself in the cave, a "natural burella," from which he may begin his climb. Plato, in the famous myth of the *Republic,* assumed that man began there; for him knowledge and virtue were synonymous, and therefore the journey to human perfection was half as long. For Dante, however, the arrival at that humble zero-point was already a triumph over a human defect.

In the other hemisphere, the world is righted, and the soul can follow its ordained course, governed by the first movement, with all powers in spiral harmony. It is then that we realize that from God's perspective the spiral direction has never changed, for to move through hell against corruption, to the left in our hemisphere, is to move with the sun itself, "to the right" under the aspect of eternity, as does Virgil in the *Purgatorio:*

Poi fisamente al sole li occhi porse;
   fece del destro lato a muover centro,
   e la sinistra parte di sé torse.
"O dolce lume a cui fidanza i' entro
   per lo novo cammin, tu ne conduci,"
   dicea, "come condur si vuol quinc' entro.
Tu scaldi il mondo, tu sovr' esso luci;
   s'altra ragione in contrario non ponta,
   esser dien sempre li tuoi raggi duci."   (*Purg.* XIII, 13–21)

Then he set his eyes fixedly on the sun, made of his right side a center for his movement, and brought round his left. "O sweet light, by trust in which I enter on this new road, do you guide us," he said, "with the guidance that is needful in this place. You warm the world,

you shed light upon it: if other reason urge
not to the contrary, your beams must ever be
our guide."

The sun, with its ardor and its light, is the exemplar of love and knowledge, the perfections respectively of will and reason.[57] To achieve the harmony the sun represents, the pilgrim moves in a solar spiral on his journey to the summit.

We noticed earlier that the pilgrim and his guide make two significant departures from their spiral path in the *Inferno.* The first deviation occurs in Canto IX just before the entry into the circle of the heretics. Dante there writes a line which seems to destroy the leftward pattern of the spiral through hell: "E poi ch'a la man destra si fu vòlto," (there, after he had turned to the right hand). This apparent exception to Dante's rule will help in reality to prove it. Heresy, unlike all other sins in hell, attacks the True, and not the Good; which is to say, in the words of St. Thomas, that its *subiectum* is not *voluntas* but rather *intellectus.*[58] Here is the only instance in Dante's moral system where an error of the speculative intellect is punished in hell, a fact which no pagan, neither Cicero, nor Aristotle, nor Virgil would have been able to understand.[59] It is for this reason that the pilgrim must perform his retrograde movement to the right, in order to deal with an aberration of the intellect in the realm of perverted will.

The intellect is not purely speculative, however, but has its practical function as well. What is more, man is capable of sinning in the exercise of the practical reason, for there exists an *art* the practice of which is in itself reprehensible.[60] The presence of this second aberration of the intellect, in Dante's moral system, the sin of usury, serves to explain the second deviation in the pilgrim's path.

In the eleventh canto of the *Inferno,* Virgil discusses the nature of the sin of usury with an introductory exposition of the analogy which exists between Divine creativity and human industry:

"Filosofia," mi disse, "a chi la 'ntende,
  nota, non pure in una sola parte,
  come natura lo suo corso prende
dal divino 'ntelletto e da sua arte;
  e se tu ben la tua Fisica note,
  tu troverai, non dopo molte carte,

che l'arte vostra quella, quanto pote,
  segue, come 'l maestro fa 'l discente;
  sì che vostr' arte a Dio quasi è nepote. (XI, 97–105)

> "Philosophy, for one who understands it," he said to me, "points out, not in one place alone, how Nature takes her course from divine Intellect and from Its art; and if you note well your *Physics,* you will find, after not many pages, that your art, as far as it can, follows her, as the pupil does his master; so that your art is as it were grandchild of God."

Art imitates nature, for like nature it works toward a specific end. Nature itself (*anima mundi,* to give it a neoplatonic name) imitates divine intellect, for it is the minister of God's Providence, and presides over all change in the world below. To phrase the matter metaphorically, in accordance with the tradition we have been exploring, the divine circularity is mirrored by the circling of the heavens "to the right." To be sure, there is some irregularity, caused by the movement contrary to the first movement in each of the separate spheres, but harmony reigns in the universe when the *primum mobile* "tutto quanto rape . . . seco" with the diurnal movement. So it is with the art of man, which in its proper functioning, as a virtue of the practical intellect, moves with the course of the heavens, "to the right." This is true of all the arts from the highest to the lowest, although there exists among them a hierarchy of excellence. In the famous enumeration of the liberal arts in the *Convivio,* Dante assimilates them precisely to the heavenly spheres, with theology and moral philosophy at the highest point.[61] Even the mechanical arts mirror the process of divine creativity, however, as we know from a simile of the *Paradiso* which compares the movement of the heavens to the art of a humble workman: "Lo moto e la virtù d'i santi giri, / *come dal fabbro l'arte del martello,* / da' beati motor convien che spiri . . ."(*Par.* II, 127) (the motion and the virtue of the holy spheres, even as the hammer's art by the smith, must needs be inspired by the blessed movers). Since all art by definition resides in the intellect, that "parte de l'anima che è deitade," it must be dominated in some measure by the diurnal movement, if it is to follow the path of nature and of God.

As heresy is the perversion of the intellect's higher function, the speculative activity of theology and moral philosophy, so usury is a sin of its lower activity: human industry, or art. Usury for this reason is also a sin against nature and God Himself:

> e perché l'usuriere altra via tene,
>   per sé natura e per la sua seguace
>   dispregia, poi ch'in altro pon la spene. (*Inf.* XI, 109–111)

> But because the usurer takes another way, he contemns Nature in herself and in her follower, for he puts his hope elsewhere.

This is the only sin in Dante's *Inferno* which the poet specifically tells us is against human industry, for it is the only sin which methodically and systematically reproduces the materials it began with in a parody of productivity which is in fact sterile. It is to counter this perversion of the practical reason that the poet retrogresses for the second time "to the right."

Finally, something must be said, however briefly and inadequately, about the last *cantica* of the poem. The harmony in the spheres arises from the resolution of all contrary motions of the universe, while harmony in the soul, Justice, arises from the reason's perfect control over all the soul's lesser powers. Continence is a suppression of lower powers by the higher, the tense victory of humanity over sensuality. As the victory becomes more and more secure, continence gives way to temperance, and finally, with sanctifying grace, temperance becomes rooted in the supernatural life. It is only with perfection in the supernatural order, however, that contrary motions cease to exist and spiral harmony gives way to circular unity.[62]

The pilgrim follows the heavens in ever increasing arcs, and follows the spiral path of each of the heavenly bodies in each of their respective spheres. In the Heaven of the Sun, Dante writes:

> Lo ministro maggior de la natura,
>   che del valor del ciel lo mondo imprenta
>   e col suo lume il tempo ne misura,
> con quella parte che sù si rammenta
>   congiunto, si girava per le spire
>   in che più tosto ognora s'appresenta;

e io era con lui; ma del salire
  non m'accors' io, (*Par.* X, 28–35)

> The greatest minister of nature, which imprints the world with heavenly worth and with its light measures time for us, being in conjunction with the part I have noted, was wheeling through the spirals in which it presents itself earlier every day. And I was with him, but of my ascent I was no more aware . . .

The part of the heavens to which the sun is here conjoined is the balance point of the sky's two movements, the vernal equinox, symbolic of the harmony in the pilgrim's soul. So he continues on his upward journey:

E come, per sentir più dilettanza
  bene operando, l'uom di giorno in giorno
  s'accorge che la sua virtute avanza,
sì m'accors' io che 'l mio girare intorno
  col cielo insieme avea cresciuto l'arco, (*Par.* XVIII, 58–62)

> And as from feeling more delight in doing well, a man from day to day becomes aware that his virtue makes advance, so did I perceive that my circling round with the heaven had inceased its arc.

In this passage, the analogy between the pilgrim's journey and his spiritual development is expressed in terms of the ever increasing circularity of his arc, much as the pseudo-Dionysius had expressed it before.

Nevertheless, there is still a deficiency in the operation of the soul's powers. It has yet to reach the fulfillment of its intellectual desire, and its love, thanks to sanctifying grace, outdistances the ability to understand. It is the will's nature to remain forever unsatisfied until it reaches God, and it cannot reach Him until He is seen face to face. Dante says to Cacciaguida, in the fifth heaven:

. . . L'affetto e 'l senno,
  come la prima equalità v'apparse,
  d'un peso per ciascun di voi si fenno,

però che 'l sol che v'allumò e arse,
  col caldo e con la luce è sì iguali,
  che tutte simiglianze sono scarse. (*Par.* XV, 73–78)

. . . Love and intelligence, as soon as the first Equality became visible to you, became of one weight for each of you, because the Sun which illumined you and warmed you is of such equality in its heat and light that all comparisons fall short.

In the blessed, who have seen God ("la prima equalità"), will *(affetto)* and intellect *(senno)* are perfectly equal, for God has transmitted His equality to them by the ardor of charity and the light of illumination. This is not yet the case with the voyager:

Ma voglia e argomento ne' mortali,
  per la cagion ch'a voi è manifesta,
  diversamente son pennuti in ali; (*Par.* XV, 79–81)

But will and faculty in mortals, for the reason that is plain to you, are not equally feathered in their wings.

The twin powers of the soul, represented fittingly by the Platonic wings here in the *Paradiso,* whereas throughout the terrestrial voyage they had been represented by the two feet of the body, are not yet perfectly matched, for the soul has more to learn. It is only in the last sphere, with the fulfillment of all desire, that they will become equal and identical.

The intricacies and the profundity of the last cantos cannot be covered here. We may say simply that as the *primum mobile* moves with a desire for the Empyrean, so the will revolves around God, and seeks to resemble Him as closely as it can. God, the circumference or Empyrean, causes the outermost sphere in the physical world to spin with love for Himself, as God, the center of the spiritual world, causes the will to turn about Him in eternal joy. At the supreme moment, the will's revolution is exactly equal to the mind's internal vision and resultant rotation, and the soul's powers are fused into a spinning unity, by the exalted and "equal" nature of their Object.

No image can convey this identity of movement, for to the intermediate power between the sensible world and the mind, *fantasia,* "qui mancò possa" (here power failed). The sensible world's nearest equivalent would be the compound movement of the stars, which for Plato was caused by the twofold movement of the stellar gods: "one uniform and in the same place as each always thinks the same thoughts about the same things; the other a forward motion, as each is subjected to the revolution of the same and uniform."[63] Here, however, rotation and revolution are the same, for God, center and circumference of the wheel of the soul, moves both from within and without[64]:

> ma già volgeva il mio disio e 'l *velle,*
> sì come rota ch'igualmente è mossa,
> l'amor che move il sole e l'altre stelle.
> (*Par.* XXXIII, 143–145)

> but already my desire and my will were revolved, like a wheel that is evenly moved, by the Love which moves the sun and the other stars.

As Plato knew nothing about a sphere beyond that of the fixed stars, so he knew nothing of the supernatural movement of the soul. To explain stellar irregularities which his predecessors had not perceived, Ptolemy posited the existence of a starless *primum mobile* beyond the other spheres, moving at the fastest rate and whirling all the other cirlces around with it. So in a Christian context, there is a dimension of the soul which transcends the human, and is touched directly by the hand of God.

5. Infernal Irony: The Gates of Hell

TO SPEAK OF VISION IN THE MIDdle Ages was to evoke the experience of St. Paul who, in his letter to the Corinthians, claimed to have been "rapt to the third heaven," where he saw things that it is not lawful for a man to reveal. It was universally assumed that this meant Paul had seen God directly and that this had been his unique privilege. The mystery surrounding the experience was enhanced by the enigmatic phrase, "the third heaven." From the earliest days of Christianity to the Renaissance,[1] exegetes wondered what was meant by those words.

In his commentary on the literal meaning of Genesis, St. Augustine provided the most authoritative gloss on the question, identifying the third heaven in psychological rather than cosmological terms by distinguishing three distinct modes of vision: the corporeal, the spiritual, and the intellectual. Corporeal vision was vision in the ordinary sense through the organs of the body. By spiritual vision, Augustine meant imaginative vision, whether stimulated directly by the senses or indirectly by writing, memory, or dreams. Finally, intellectual vision was of the highest order, bringing total understanding with it. It is called "vision" only figuratively, for it transcends sense perception and the workings of the imagination. Paul was presumed to have seen God in a direct intuition of the Truth, "face to face." The three modes of vision correspond to the stages of human understanding, from sense data, to the imagination, to the mind. Paul's privilege was to see God without mediation or accommodation.

In a difficult passage at the end of the *Vita Nuova,* Dante also claimed to have had a vision—a *mirabile visione*—after which he vowed to write about Beatrice things that had never been written of any other Woman. We know nothing more about that vision (although eminent Dantists have speculated about it), except that it inspired an alternate title for the *Divine Comedy.* The first translation of the poem into English, by Francis Cary, in fact bears the title of *The Vision.*[2] Moreover, the *Paradiso* implicitly compares itself to Pauline vision. It was perhaps inevitable that some critics of the *Divine Comedy* should associate Dante's vision with the Pauline tradition, claiming to have found in Augustine's analysis the basis for the tripartite division of Dante's poem.[3]

The vision represented in the *Inferno* is clearly corporeal; the souls of sinners are to be seen and even touched by the pilgrim. The representational power of Dante's verses enables us to sense our surroundings as though we were there. The sights and sounds and even smells of hell bombard the pilgrim and, with the immediacy for which Dante continues to be celebrated, the reader seems to share that experience. The *Purgatorio,* on the other hand, is the realm of *fantasia.* The focus of our attention is not on the pilgrim's surroundings, but rather on his mental state—it may be described, in Francis Fergusson's words, as "Dante's Drama of the Mind." The journey is punctuated by dreams and his imagination is moved by visions. Meditations throughout the *Purgatorio* might well have been taken directly from Augustine's text, even if the intricacies of later psychology (about which of course Dante was perfectly knowledgeable) profoundly transformed Augustinian doctrines. Canto XVII in particular contains an apostrophe to the imagination and a question concerning how the imagination can be moved directly without the intervention of the senses. Finally, the *Paradiso* is presented as what Marguerite Chiarenza has called "an imageless vision."[4] In many ways it is the most modern of the *cantiche,* for it announces its subject matter from the beginning as an impossibility: transcending the human cannot be signified in words. The human form is no longer to be seen in this realm and the stages of the pilgrim's progress are marked by a geometric refinement and a gradual dissipation of shadows, approaching pure light and silence as a limit, which is at once the culmination of the poem and its extinction.

There can be little doubt that Augustine's analysis is a source for certain thematic changes that are brought about in each of the successive parts of Dante's poem; yet an important nuance is overlooked in most critical discussions. *Vision* is the province of the prophet, but the task of the poet is *representation.* It is one thing to state discursively a change of theme from corporeal to imaginative to intellectual; to represent the change in poetry is another, more difficult matter. One might say that poetry is itself imaginative representation. Like all writing, it transcends purely corporeal vision, inviting us to see images not perceptible to the senses. "Looking at a text," Augustine writes, "is not like looking at a painting:"

> When you see a painting or a picture, you have seen everything there is to see and therefore praise the artist. If you observe a text, however, it is not enough to look, because the text invites you to read. When you look at a page of writing that you do not understand, do you not ask someone: "what is written here?" That is, you ask what it means; seeing is not enough.[5]

In terms of the Augustinian division, we might say that writing belongs in the second realm, a sense experience requiring interpretation. In the *Purgatorio* the focus is also on the interpretation of sensation: images move and speak, the souls are said to be composed of the aerial substance which they share with images and dreams, poets meet to discuss their craft. The goal of the journey is not only a terrestrial paradise, but also a kind of Parnassus. There is no difficulty in representing the imaginative vision in a medium that resembles it so closely.

The difficulty in reconciling the tripartite division with Dante's poetic representation resides in the first and third modes: corporeal vision falls short of the imagination, while intellectual vision transcends it. How can writing appear to be less or more than it is? Presence must be counterfeited in the *Inferno;* the mediation of poetry must be masked in order to represent a physical world as though it were *there.* In the *Paradiso,* on the other hand, the task is to represent a realm of pure yearning, lost even to memory and therefore beyond representation. For both of these realms, a different rhetorical strategy is required.

In her study Chiarenza has dealt with the poetics of the *Paradiso,* but so far as I know, no one has discussed the *Inferno* in terms of the Augustinian distinction, perhaps because the "realism" of the *cantica* seems to convey corporeal vision so precisely. Erich Auerbach[6] uses the word "mimesis" to describe this power and Charles Singleton speaks of Dante's "substance of things seen."[7] The examples adduced by both scholars are largely from the *Inferno,* although neither restricts his terms to apply to that realm. Here I should like to suggest on the contrary that mimesis is peculiarly infernal and represents Dante's effort to render corporeal vision. I shall also suggest that Dante's realism is not nearly so benign as Auerbach and Singleton would seem to suggest.

According to a tradition that goes back to the fourteenth century, the first canto of the *Divine Comedy* was intended as prologue to the entire poem, while the second was intended as prologue to the *Inferno* proper. On this reading, the journey of the poem may be said to begin with Canto III, when the pilgrim and his guide actually enter the gates of hell.

This division of the poem seems to assert nothing more than the obvious: the *Inferno* may be said to begin with the descent into hell. It is useful, however, for drawing our attention to the fact that the entrance into hell signals the beginning of a distinctive mode of poetic representation, radically different from the didactic allegorism of the first two cantos as well as from the modes of representation of both the *Purgatorio* and the *Paradiso.* The descent begins when the pilgrim sees the inscription and wonders about its meaning. His uncertainty is much like that of Augustine's hypothetical reader who asks, "What is written here?" In other words, the descent begins by calling attention to the fact that vision is not interpretation, precisely the fact that is passed over in silence in discussions of Dante's realism. An analysis of the first moment of the descent will help us to define more sharply how Dante represents vision in a medium that transcends it.

Until we come to the entrance of hell, things seem to exist in a double focus, suffused with moral and allegorical intent so that their substantiality seems totally compromised. Benedetto Croce had the self-confidence to express what many readers of those two cantos have often felt; that is, an impatience with a mountain, beasts, and woods that are clearly unreal.[8] With the beginning of Canto III, the inscription which Virgil will later describe as "scritta morta," Dante's mimetic fiction begins:

PER ME SI VA NE LA CITTÀ DOLENTE,
 PER ME SI VA NE L'ETTERNO DOLORE,
 PER ME SI VA TRA LA PERDUTA GENTE.

GIUSTIZIA MOSSE IL MIO ALTO FATTORE;
FECEMI LA DIVINA PODESTATE,
LA SOMMA SAPÏENZA E 'L PRIMO AMORE.
DINANZI A ME NON FUOR COSE CREATE
SE NON ETTERNE, E IO ETTERNO DURO.
LASCIATE OGNE SPERANZA, VOI CH'INTRATE. (III, 1–9)

Through me you enter the woeful city, through me you enter eternal grief, through me you enter among the lost. Justice moved my high maker: the divine power made me, the supreme wisdom, and the primal love. Before me nothing was created if not eternal, and eternal I endure. Abandon every hope, you who enter.

The bewilderment of the pilgrim upon seeing these words ("di colore oscuro") is not shared by the commentators—indeed, what has seemed puzzling is his confusion before the words whose ominous import is all too obvious. Yet the pilgrim's descent begins with an opacity that we would do well to consider. For one thing, this depiction of his state of mind insists on the difference between vision and understanding. For another, the opacity is expressed in terms that recall a hermeneutic failure of great importance in the New Testament. The pilgrim's first words in his descent, "Maestro, il senso lor m'è duro," recall the disciples' words in the Gospel of John (6:60) when they cannot understand Christ's eucharistic offer: "Durus est hic sermo" (this is a hard saying). Finally, the pilgrim's bewilderment brings to mind an episode in the Old Testament that is an analogue, if not the source, of the dramatic action. In the fifth chapter of the Book of Daniel, the interpretive power of the prophet is contrasted with the incomprehension of sinners who see the handwriting on the wall.

At the feast of King Belshazar, the orgy is interrupted when the guests see a hand which writes the mysterious words on the wall: *Mene Mene Tekel Epharsin.* The words remain impressed on the mind of the King, although he and his men cannot interpret them and so seek the help of Daniel. Daniel takes the words to be a condemnation of Belshazar: "Thou hast been weighed in the scales and hath been found wanting." That night, the king dies and Daniel's prophecy is fulfilled.

Although the sense of the handwriting and that of the inscription are similar, the resemblance between them might be taken as purely generic, were it not that Augustine chooses precisely this episode in his *De Genesi ad Litteram* to illustrate what he means by "corporeal vision."[9] His point is that the king and his sinful guests were able to see the handwriting, but that it required the prophet to interpret it. By beginning his descent with an analogous interpretive difficulty, Dante alludes not only to the biblical episode, but probably also to Augustine's text. Of all of the ways in which Augustine might have exemplified corporeal vision, he chose the most literary, by contrasting it with reading. Similarly, in a *cantica* whose theme is supposed to be *seeing,* Dante begins with a *reading* of an inscription. If this is not an allusion to the Augustinian tradition, it is at least an extraordinary convergence of mind.

Perhaps the reason that not much attention has been paid to its interpretive difficulty is that the inscription is one of the most familiar passages in Western literature; it presents itself as a text already read, even for the reader who knows nothing else about Dante's poem. If it were possible, however, to imagine ourselves reading these lines for the first time, without benefit of any received knowledge of what to expect, we might well share the pilgrim's perplexity, at least for a few moments. After the blank space separating the end of Canto II from this opening, there follow nine lines of verse in the first person without the slightest indication of who is speaking and who is being addressed. Only when the pilgrim expresses his incomprehension do we learn, retrospectively, what has happened.

In modern editions of this passage, some effort is made to set off the inscription from the rest of the text with quotation marks, block letters or italics, as if to warn the reader to suspend interpretation until the passage is concluded. In a medieval text, however, devoid of such visual clues to interpretation, our hypothetical first-time reader would be obliged to wait until the fourth tercet in order to realize that the pilgrim has been thrust in front of the infernal portals and *sees* the text that we have read. The extraordinary quality of this beginning has been masked by its very familiarity. The journey through hell begins with an interruption that serves to establish the fiction of immediacy: for the first and only time in this poem, perhaps in any poem, we directly share the protagonist's experience. That is to say, we read a text and imagine a gate on which we *see* the text we have read. In terms of C. S. Peirce's theory of signs, we might say that the words on the page cease to be symbols and become *icons,* signs that resemble their own significance.[10] They have been used in that way in the history of illustrations of the *Divine Comedy.* When artists of the fifteenth and sixteenth century wished to depict this moment in the poem, they had no choice but to represent the gate by the text itself, as though God had written in hendecasyllables.

The poetic strategy of the opening scene is to pretend that there is no poetic strategy, to represent the inscription with an implied replication of the text. The pilgrim's difficulty resides in the interpretation of what he sees, comparable to the confusion of our supposed naive reader who comes upon these words for the first time, without benefit of quotation marks. It is only retrospectively, in a second moment, that we are drawn into the fiction that would have us see the words that we in fact have read. Of the two processes, the interpretive trajectory of the first moment is in fact the normal movement from sense impression to conceptualization, while in the second moment we are drawn in the other direction, from the understanding of the text back to the visualization of the text, as though it were not written, but inscribed. Thus, mediation is turned back upon itself and reified in the letter of the text. The first words spoken by the pilgrim in this descent also suggest a reversal of the normal interpretive process: "Maestro mio, il senso lor m'è duro," is something of a pun, since it conflates signifier and signified. The *sign* is literally "hard," since it is written on impenetrable stone. To use that adjective of the *sense* is to turn reference back on itself. The same may be said of the world, "di colore oscuro." The uncertainty of the commentators about whether the dark color is a physical description or a characterization of the meaning of the phrase, its *rhetorical* color, suggests that they cannot decide whether the pilgrim is *seeing* or *reading* the inscription.

As if to echo faintly the repetition of the handwriting on the wall *(Mene, Mene . . .),* Canto III begins with the rhetorical figure of *repetitio,* or *anaphora:* "per me si va . . ." repeated three times. Its rhetorical function is clear, for it prepares the way for the allusion to the Trinity in the next *terzina,* that affirms unity in three-fold difference. Yet there is an obsessive quality in the repetition, especially since it occurs at the very beginning of our text. It is as if the figure contradicted the ease of passage implied both by the words themselves and the tradition concerning the portals of hell. Repetition seems to ensure that the reader, like the pilgrim, will sense an interpretive impediment at the beginning of this journey. If we think of the writing as the record of an absent voice, analogous to the tomb of Pope Anastasius in Canto XI, then it must be said that this voice is stammering.

Some of the early commentators did regard the representation of the gates as *conformatio* or *prosopopoeia,* the figure that attributes voice to inanimate objects. This medieval understanding adds an uncanny echo to the vertiginous specularity of the inscription. Our text is silent until we read it aloud, at which point we understand that there is another "text" to be read aloud; the voice projected from the gate echoes back as our own. The feedback and specularity constitute for the reader a suspension of the reading requiring an authorial intervention in order to be overcome.

For the modern reader, familiar with the funerary inscriptions of romantic poetry, the beginning of Canto III is not unlike an epitaph, written in the first person and marking with a presence in stone an absence of the spirit.[11] Like a Piranesi view of ancient Rome, it is in ruins ever since its invincibility was challenged by Christ's descent. It represents the abandonment of all hope by the abandonment of all reference in its marmoreal self-containment. Dante refers to it as a "scritta morta," which would seem to evoke St. Paul's "Letter that kills . . . engraven in stone" as opposed to the "Spirit that gives life . . . written in the fleshy tablets of the heart" (II Cor. 3:3–6).

The Pauline opposition associates many of the themes of his preaching with an implicit theory of signs. Hope, vitality, and the spirit are all compared with the referentiality of signs, while despair, death, and the body are described as reifications, signs that no longer signify. What is implicit in Paul became explicit in Augustine. In his *De Doctrina Christiana,* the movement of the mind from sign to significance is equated with the movement of the heart from desire to fulfillment. There is no such movement among the damned. Despair, like death, is like a sign emptied of its significance and is therefore mute. It remained for Dante to find a way to *represent* the abandonment of all hope in a medium which both Paul and Augustine took to be the very exemplar of reference and expectation. The iconicity of the inscription, its representation of non-representation, dramatizes the abandonment of hope by thwarting reference. It masks the mediation of words in order to present the gate as though it were *there.* In an effort to defend his theory of "substantial vision," Singleton once remarked that "Dante's fiction is that his fiction is not a fiction."[12] The rhetorical reduplication in the formula suggests that it might be used to describe the inscription as well, but it is Singleton's tone that helps us to identify the representational process for what it is: irony.

The representation of hell involves the negation of fiction's implicit negation of the real. This double negation affirms presence, but it renders it, so to speak, in quotation marks. Instead of beginning with a landscape that, however familiar, might at least have announced in a conventional way the difference between a text and the infernal reality it was meant to represent, the descent into hell begins *ex abrupto* with the representation of a representation, words on the page representing words inscribed in stone identical to the words on the page. This re-representation counterfeits presentation by refusing to acknowledge the obvious difference between the text and the inscription; or rather, it simultaneously affirms and denies that difference. This is perhaps the source of its uncanny effect.

Commentators have frequently pointed out that the words of the inscription apply not only to the gate but to all of hell as well. The same may be said of the representational process which we have observed in the description of the gate. The turning back of reference which we have seen to be operative at the semiotic level in the words of the inscription is operative as well thematically, in the representation of the damned. Just as the signs of the text indicate significances which are identical with those signs, so the souls of the damned, "significances," as it were, are represented as though they were the bodies from which they originated. The body is associated in the Pauline tradition with the "letter," while the soul is associated with significance. In the *Inferno,* dead souls are ironically represented as though they were living bodies. The iconicity of the inscription has its counterpart in the iconicity of the damned. Borrowing a phrase from the prologue of the *Purgatorio* ("qui la morta poesì resurga"), we may refer to this representational process as a poetics of death thoroughly analogous to the "scritta morta" of the inscription.

I have pointed out that the pilgrim's words about the opacity of the inscription, "il senso lor m'è duro," echo words from the Gospel of John that have to do with the presence of Christ's body. The disciples cannot understand Christ's offer of his flesh: "This is a hard saying; who can hear it?" In his commentary on this Gospel, St. Augustine explains that they understand it literally, as though Christ were offering His dead body to be divided up among them, rather than the living Word:

> The flesh was as a receptacle: consider what it contained, rather than what it was. . . . Whence comes to us the sound of a word, if not from the voice of the flesh? How could His words have come to us unless they had been written down? All of these are the work of the flesh, but thanks to the Spirit which uses it as though it were an instrument.[13]

For our purposes, this passage is remarkable in associating semiotic referentiality with the relationship of the body to the soul. Authentic life is the union of sign and significance, while death is their dissolution. A second death, the death of the soul, is non-significance. Representing the second death means representing the soul as though it were the body whose "significance" it was in the first place. This ironic replication is a form of "mimesis," to be sure, but because it is charged with the horror that accompanies all reification, it is mimesis with a vengeance.

Thus far I have spoken of letter and spirit, body and soul, as though the polarities were separable. In fact, however, they are no more separable than is the text of the first lines of Canto III from the inscription it is meant to represent. What is more, their inseparability leads to a dizzying reversibility. In the case of Canto III, the signs of our text refer to a meaning that is its significance, yet its significance is indistinguishable from the signs that signified it, which would in turn call for the interpretive circuit to begin again. Similarly, the body may be thought of as the visible manifestation of the soul—its signifier. At the same time, the soul was defined as *forma corporis,* the animating principle of the body—its "signified," as it were. Their inseparability at the doctrinal level is matched by their reversibility at the level of representation: if one wishes to represent a soul, one has no choice but to represent it as a body, while a body, if it is alive, must be represented by some principle of animation which is indistinguishable from what we mean by the soul. A dead soul is one whose vital trajectory has been turned back on itself so that it is indistinguishable from the body which it animated. Like the text which represents an inscription only by replicating itself, the replication of the living represents the damned.

The replication of reality is by no means the benign esthetic representation described by Auerbach, but is rather a fierce calling into question of the very foundation of that reality. The fiction of the *Inferno* unmasks reality's polite fictions and so is quintessentially real. Like all ironic imitation, it undercuts its own representation by negating what it affirms. Rather than transmitting reality, it brackets it, viewing it from the context of eternity, with all the animus of the exile who identifies his perspective with that of Divine Justice. Left to itself, this irony is unstable because of its reversibility; an ironic text can be momentarily neutralized by ignoring one of its polarities. So, for example, although the "humanity" of the damned and the implacable judgment to which they are subjected are no more separable than body and soul, or text and context, still the history of Dante criticism is filled with debates between partisans of "Divine Justice" on one hand and of "humanity" on the other. The debates are confined to the *Inferno,* because of the ironic mode of the representation, a consistent contradiction of the perspective of the pilgrim by the perspective of the poet. Were it not for the temporal distance introduced between those two perspectives by the allegory, they too would be reversible and therefore as inseparable as conflicting states of consciousness for which they are the dramatic figure. The story line, the trajectory of Virgil's guidance and the various hermeneutic interventions *en route* privilege the ending, the perspective of the author, and transform what threatened to become repetition into dialectic.

Yet that allegorical privilege of the ending can always be called into question, especially by a critical tradition such as the *lectura dantis,* that encourages episodic examination of the text and thereby invites ironic impasse. Auerbach himself, to whom we owe a masterful statement of Dante's figural allegory, chose in his later essay on Canto X to favor "immediacy," or purely human emotion over transcendent significance. Assuming that Dante meant the individuals in hell not only to *be,* but to *mean,* he suggested that Dante's power of characterization was so great as to overwhelm whatever figural or representative function the souls were meant to have in favor of their irreducible individuality. Their significances were obscured in the subsequent history of literature by their presence and historicity, so that the sympathy and immediacy with which Dante treated the characters who were meant to reveal the divine order, end up by subverting that order and portraying individuals in their own tragic autonomy. To the objection that might be raised against such an interpretation, that this is after all an infernal context, which colors every utterance of the damned, Auerbach might well reply that Dante is above all poet of the *secular* world and that hell is simply a device for heightening the human tragedy. *Mimesis* turns out to be much like the inscription on the gates of hell: signification turned back upon itself in order to render presence.

It would not be difficult to reintroduce signification into the examples adduced by Auerbach and thereby ironize his assertion in order to show that his insistence on the human autonomy of the characters at the expense of the divine order is a function of his own mystification. Negating the negation of secular values that is the function of the infernal context inevitably yields a positive portrayal. So Auerbach pictures Cavalcante Cavalcanti in all of his spontaneous grief, as though it were God or destiny, rather than the poet, subjecting him to his torment. In fact, the phrase in Canto X that Auerbach takes as the most immediate and "heart-rending," "non fiere li occhi suoi 'l dolce lume" (does the sweet light not strike his eyes?), not only evokes a warning from Ecclesiastes (11:7), but is also a cutting allusion to Guido's own verses in "Donna me prega," precisely when Dante's former friend seems to deny the possibility of transcendence. It would be difficult to find a more ironically contrived verse in the canto, but Auerbach is as blind to its citationality as Cavalcante is blind to the sweet light of allegory when, as Singleton has shown,[14] the old man sees Virgil and fails to understand the allegory he represents.

To dispel the unexamined assumption, encouraged by the fiction, of an innocent author describing an infernal reality rather than constructing it, we need only turn to the representation of the punishments. In these, the reification of irony is applied with an artistry that masks its ferocity. The general rule of the representation is that metaphorical heaviness increases as one descends into hell, approaching Satan as the "degree-zero" of form and of intelligibility. The relative gravity of sin is materialized on a scale of specific gravity established by the metaphor of the weight of love: "pondus meum amor meus." The metaphor enabled Augustine to give at least figurative authority to a Platonic or dualistic theory of good and evil. Since love is the soul's referentiality, it follows that turning it back to materiality is tantamount to semiotic reification.

The specifics of the representation follow the same rule of reification, except that the reification is rhetorical. The punishments in hell have little to do with moral theology and almost nothing with the physiology of pain. It is not clear, for example, why even a fictive body would be any better off being roasted alive than being frozen in a lake of ice, although the former represents a far less severe punishment in terms of the scale of culpability than the latter. I would like to suggest rather that the punishments are a clear example of what was later to be called "poetical justice," with all of the irony that the phrase implies. The punishments *fit* the crimes, provided we understand "fittingness" as an esthetic category. Whatever the moral theology of *contrapasso,* at the level of representation it is above all ironic wit.

The intention of hell is summed up in the second *terzina* of the inscription: "Justice moved my high maker." In a tradition that is Platonic in origin, Justice is a form of harmony, an ordering of parts within the whole. So St. Augustine could assert, in his *Confessions,* that God's Justice is revealed in history like a poem:

> When I composed verses, I could not fit any foot in any position that I pleased. Each meter was differently scanned and I could not put the same foot in every position in the same line. And yet the art of poetry, by which I composed, does not vary from one line to the other: it is the same for all alike. But I did not discern that justice . . . in a far more sublime way than poetry contains in itself at one and the same time all the principles which it prescribes and apportions them, not all at once, but according to the needs of the times.[15]

From God's perspective, therefore, Justice is an esthetic matter of the relationship of parts to the whole. Since the cosmos, God's supreme creation, is the exemplar of beauty and proportion, it follows that the order of Justice imitates the order of nature the way a poem imitates reality. Augustine's assertion is readily reversible: as the inscription on the gate of hell is inevitably in *terza rima,* so Divine Justice is a projection of Dante's hand. Its coherence is esthetic, but this does not mitigate the terror, any more than fictionality mitigates the terror of torture in the works of the Marquis de Sade. Whatever else the two writers have in common (and there is more than one might wish), it has nothing to do with "mimesis."

The punishments strike us as revolting, particularly since we no longer consider physical punishment to be an appropriate form of secular justice. Michel Foucault has shown that with incarceration as the universally accepted form of judicial punishment, the object of chastisement is no longer the body, but rather the metaphoric soul of the criminal. Nowadays, as he puts it, jurisprudence makes the soul the prison of the body.[16]

In the Middle Ages, however, it was the body which functioned as the sign of the criminal act and torture was the exemplary emblem, at once the retribution and a warning to those who would follow the criminal's behavior. Torture became a sign-system and its intricacies of representation constituted the rhetoric of the state's revenge. Four hundred years after Dante, Vico could refer to the ancient law as a serious poem and to ancient jurisprudence as a severe poetry.[17] I should like to suggest that Dante's poem represents the severest form of jurisprudence and represents a rhetoric of God's revenge. Once again, the principle is that of literalization. If Dante's irony turns words into icons, souls into bodies and the spirit into the letter, it also turns rhetorical figures into things.

Abstractions are turned into bodies virtually everywhere in the *Inferno:* the composite monsters of the circle of violence; the scaly back of Geryon, which seems substantial in spite of its ironic nature as the "image of fraud"; Satan and the Giants, who are pure spirit, yet appear to be grossly material. The same may be said of the punishments. Bertrand de Born, for example, split apart a father from his son, a metaphoric "head" from an equally metaphoric "body politic." He therefore carries his head cut off from his body. In Canto XIX, Pope Nicholas says of himself: "su l'avere e qui me misi in borsa." The chiastic construction of the verse, "money in the world above and here myself I have put into a purse," neatly juxtaposes a figure for simony with the infernal reality. Francesca was buffeted by the winds of passion, Ciacco wallowed in the mire of his gluttony, even the pilgrim risked being tarred with the accusation of barratry in the world above. Each of these cases is a concretized form of the sin itself, a literary conceit, an etymology (as in the circle of hypocrites), an emblem travestied (the avaricious and the prodigal), an hyperbole (the tyrants steeped in blood). In each of these cases the ordinary dynamism of language is turned back on itself, immobilized in literalisms that are ironically irreducible.

If the bodies in hell are really souls, then it follows that their physical attitudes, contortions and punishments are really *spiritual* attitudes and states of mind, sins made manifest in the form of physical punishment. It is therefore correct to say that the punishments *are* the sins; sin bears the same relationship to punishment as the souls in hell bear to their fictive bodies. They are significances become icons. The rhetoric of revenge works like the inscription of the gate, turning signification back against itself. To "read" these punishments, as one would the signs that go to make up a figure, is to give them back their figurality.

I have been suggesting that Dante's descent is a journey of interpretation, an itinerary of the mind seeking understanding. In a sense, then, it parallels our own reading; the trajectory of the pilgrim *is* the intentionality of the text. It begins with an opacity, an obstacle, somehow suspended from the journey itself. It continues through what Dante's irony has represented as a linguistic graveyard, ruins both architectural and human: the crumbling bridges and landslides as well as the dismembered bodies. Life comes back to the *Inferno* thanks to the pilgrim's journey, which is interpretation itelf.

According to Dante's own definition in the *Purgatorio,* love is a spiritual motion of the mind as it moves to God. This provides us with the allegorical significance of the pilgrim's journey and identifies it as interpretive. It begins in terms that are in fact hermeneutic: speaking of Virgil's guidance, Dante says: "mi mise dentro a le segrete cose"—"he introduced me to hidden things." In the ancient world, this descent in search of understanding was known as a *katabasis.* The analogy between a literal journey and interpretation is of course not original with Dante, but exists even in the etymology of some rhetorical terms. To mention just one, *digression* means "a stepping aside." It happens that the word in Greek to indicate such a stepping aside, "parekbasis," is the word used by Friedrich Schlegel in the nineteenth century and revived by Paul de Man in our own time to define the figure of *irony.*[18] In the *Inferno,* moments of *parekbasis* continually threaten the completion of *katabasis.*

I have used the word "irony" repeatedly without offering a definition principally because there is little general agreement among literary theorists about what it is. Since antiquity, it has been thought of as an unexpressed negation of what is expressly affirmed, sometimes extended over an entire discourse simply by a gesture or tone of voice. Context is all important in evaluating the negation, but it is precisely in defining context that difficulties in interpretation arise. Ironic discourse is set off from context—in quotation marks, as it were—and constitutes a kind of citationality of some other discourse.

A pragmatist such as Dan Sperber uses the philosophical distinction between "use" and "mention" in order to describe this setting-off. In irony, words are *mentioned* (cited) as though they were being *used*.[19]

The felicity of this distinction for our arguments here is that the word "use" corresponds precisely to an Augustinian theory of reference, whether of signs or of love. Reference, allegory, is the rhetorical analogue of the journey. All things are to be used *(uti)*, that is, treated as though they were signs, God only to be enjoyed *(frui)*, as the ultimate signification. To enjoy that which should be used is reification, or idolatry. The representation of reification, of immobility and stasis, is a turning back of reference to what Marianne Shapiro calls "iconicity." This is the movement of irony.[20]

The play of irony is apparent in the succession of negations that establishes a fragile and specular affirmation at every other moment of its oscillation and it is this mimicry of the "real" that has been called "mimesis." Perhaps every imitation of the real carries with it the potentiality of irony because representation can never be presentation; its very existence denies its identity with its object. It is timeless, with repetition rather than sequence as its only rationale. In this, it is much like the temporality of Farinata and Cavalcante in the passage studied by Auerbach and would constitute a permanent *parekbasis*, were it not for the temporality of the pilgrim, which is dramatized in his journey.

De Man has argued that irony is the figure of self-consciousness, since it involves the kind of division familiar to us in every act whereby we alternately become aware of ourselves or cease to be aware. Whatever the possibility of escape from irony in the real world, in literature such an escape is possible by translating irony into a narrative structure, especially an autobiographical structure, where the alternating phases of the ironic predicament are translated into an ideal temporality that separates the self as character from the self as narrator. Autobiography is a tautology—"I am I"—into which a negative is introduced in order to generate a narrative—"I am I, but I was not always so." Such a narrative transforms irony into an allegory of conversion.

These rhetorical exigencies fit in admirably with the theme, inasmuch as the journey that Dante depicts is both a critique of human society and of his own "illusory" former self. The imitation of the real world that takes place in Dante's poem is a hostile, critical imitation because it takes place in hell. One might even turn the formula around and suggest that it is hell *because* it imitates the real world—a world seen from the perspective of death (the source of the negation), comparable to the prison camp or the cancer ward in modern versions of the genre. Every dramatic encounter with the pilgrim is undercut by the framework of the journey and gives rise to interpretive debates that swing back and forth depending upon whether the critics choose to ignore the substance of the words or the infernal framework that undercuts them. By the time that the descent is concluded, virtually every purely human value that one would care to affirm has been undermined. The master negation, however, is of Dante himself. Many of his encounters are with his own most cherished opinions; every self-citation is a parody. This auto-destruction is thematized by the theology of death and resurrection. Conversion is a metamorphosis, which implies the destruction of an anterior form, the goal of the first part of the journey.

Paradoxically, then, mimetic representation has for its principal strategy the calling into question of the real. "Things seen" are like the shadows in Plato's cave; it is only irony, "la morta poesì," that gives them substance.

6. The Neutral Angels

IN THE FIRST MOMENT OF ANGELIC existence, as St. Augustine imagined it, the most perfect of God's creatures turned inward and discovered both itself and its Creator. For the angel, to know itself was to perceive within its being a dim reflection of God, mirrored darkly in His handiwork, and this obscure perception, which the tradition called the "twilight vision," was testimony of the link that bound the angel to its Maker. Thereafter, some of the angels turned to the reality above them, to await the eternal morning of vision face-to-face, while others remained within themselves, and sank into eternal night. In those two moments, angelic destiny was fulfilled, and the light was separated from the darkness.[1]

This separation left no room for a middle ground. Twilight, like indecision, is a temporal condition, and ceases to exist at the moment of choice. The human being may struggle throughout life in the hazy province of neither/nor, but the angels had only a moment in which to deliberate, and, once committed, were fixed for eternity. Angelic neutrality was unthinkable in orthodox medieval theology, precisely because the balance sheet of merits and transgressions had but a single entry.

It would appear, then, that Dante departed from the tradition when he created the angels of hell's vestibule, for the description of their sin implies a third alternative open to angelic choice. By considering that alternative from a purely theological standpoint, this essay uncovers some of its complexities and significance.

In the third canto of the *Inferno,* Virgil tells Dante of a special group of spirits mixed up with the souls of the vestibule:

> Mischiate sono a quel cattivo coro
> de li angeli che non furon ribelli
> né fur fedeli a Dio, ma per sè fuoro. (vv. 37–39)

At first glance we seem to be dealing with three types of dedication. The presence of the preposition *per* tempts us to stray from the verse, and to substitute an apparently equivalent statement: they were not for God, nor were they for Satan (for surely he is the archetype of the rebel), but rather were they for themselves.

John Ciardi, in his translation of the *Inferno,* succumbed to such a temptation:

> that despicable corps of angels who were neither for God nor Satan, but only for themselves . . .[2]

Dorothy Sayers, although not equating rebellion with allegiance to the Devil, nevertheless translated "per sè" as "to self only true,"[3] Charles Eliot Norton translated "for themselves,"[4] as did John A. Carlyle,[5] and Henry F. Cary.[6] A shade of meaning is lost, inevitably, in these translations. In the situation presented by the verses, there are just two poles specifying a spiritual movement: God and the *sè* of this group of angels. There is no third. They were neither rebellious nor faithful to God. They were "per sè."

It cannot be that "per sè" means simply "for themselves." If that were so, how could being for oneself be different from being rebellious from God? Satan, "il primo superbo" (*Par.* XIX, 46), was precisely for himself rather than for his Maker.

The faithful angels were those who

> furon modesti
> a riconoscer sé da la bontate
> che li avea fatti a tanto intender presti . . .
> (*Par.* XXIX, 58–60)

> were modest to recognize their being as from the Goodness which had made them apt for intelligence so great . . .

If the rebellious angels sinned by pride, this could only mean that they did not recognize their source and cause, but rather imagined themselves to be independent. One might almost say they struck off for themselves, as indeed did every sinner relegated to hell. The "per sè" angels represent the angelic nature depraved as surely as if it had sinned with Lucifer and his followers, for between love of God and love of self, there can be no middle ground. Some of the angels were for God, the others against Him and for themselves. Of the latter group, however, some stood apart and were by themselves.[7]

Part of the meaning of that preposition is the sense of separation. This is the *per sè* of the scholastic philosophers and the *da sè* of modern Italian. Dante himself gives us the ultimate authority for affirming that as a possible meaning, for he has Cacciaguida tell him later on in the poem: "a te fia bello/averti fatta parte *per te* stesso" (*Par.* XVII, 68–69) (it will be for your fair fame to have made you a party by yourself). This is more than analogous syntax, for here Cacciaguida tells Dante that it will be to the poet's credit to be off by himself, rejecting identification not only with the Neri, who were to exile him, but even with the Bianchi, "la malvagia compagnia" with whom he would be exiled. Dante "per sè" is distinguished as standing apart from the "malvagia compagnia," just as the vestibule angels are set apart from all others. Thus, by an irony which was undoubtedly part of the gall of exile, Dante will find himself in a position politically analogous to that of the neutral, outside the entire framework. The enormity of the distance between the two members of the analogy, however, is the measure of the meaning of fidelity.

The "per sè" angels, then, are the lukewarm, the afterlife's equivalent of the Laodiceans of the Apocalypse, who were neither hot nor cold but tepid, and therefore more contemptible than the worst of sinners.[8] The souls and angels in the vestibule find themselves outside of heaven and hell, excluded at once from the region whose apex is encircled by the seraphic ardor of charity, and from that whose dead center is locked in the ice of treachery. Lukewarm indeed; the correspondence seems almost exact.

On closer inspection, a difficulty arises. The admonition of the Apocalypse has a strictly temporal reference. Only in this life, while there is yet hope of conversion, can the sinner be considered somehow better than the Laodicean. Sin implies a capacity for love, no matter how perverted, and the coldness of blasphemy is closer to belief than the tepidity of indifference. Once the trial period is over however, and the cosmos is divided for all time, how is the lukewarm different from all other sinners?

Confronted with this difficulty, some commentators have fel

compelled to explain the surd quality of the vestibule situation in terms of a supposed personal judgment, expressing Dante's contempt for these souls without reference to the objective framework of the poem. This hardly seems likely, since Virgil as guide shares the pilgrim's contempt.[9] Others, particularly in the Renaissance, ignored the element of exclusion, and took the elevated position of the lukewarm on the infernal scale as indicative of a correspondingly low degree of culpability, as though the souls of the vestibule were the least guilty of all hell's inhabitants. Neither of these interpretations satisfies, for they violate either the poetic context or the structure of the poem as whole.[10]

Both the rebel and the lukewarm angels were for themselves in that they put love of self before love of God. This is the essence of mortal sin, it would seem, for both groups are included within the gates of hell, among the spirits who have for eternity "perduto il ben dell'intelletto." But the vestibule angels are not within the circular boundary of the River Acheron, and are entirely cut off and isolated even from limbo. To adopt the reading "for themselves," is to ignore the obvious exclusion suggested by the opposition rebellion/fidelity. To adopt the reading "by themselves," is to drop the category of moral value in the absolute sense. If "per sè" means *by themselves,* then we may no longer ask whether they are "good or evil." Two spiritual movements are implied: to move toward God in fidelity, or to rebel and move away. Between these movements there is stasis, or better, isolation. To maintain both readings is to reconcile the dyadic "either/or" of Christian ethics with a triadic notion of movement.

This movement is the movement of love, for fidelity and rebellion are the height and depth to which love can reach: "Però ti prego, dolce padre caro,/che mi dimostri amore a cui reduci/ogne buono operare e'l suo contraro" (*Purg.* XVIII, 13–15) (Wherefore, dear and gentle father, I pray that you expound love to me, to which you reduce every good action and its opposite). Fidelity is the perfection of that love, as rebellion is its perversion, and to be unmoved by love is to be a surd element in Dante's system. The "per sè" angels are creatures which have somehow managed to break the bond of divine love without thereby embracing its contrary, the parody of love symbolized in Giudecca's winds. Far from belaboring the obvious in seeking to explore these verses fully, we are in fact examining the axis of Dante's cosmos.

The interpretive problem presented by these verses is a reflection of a more general problem in the moral theology of Dante's day: how can one reconcile the "either/or" of Christian ethics with the "natural" love of self? On one hand, Augustine saw the choice of the angels as either the love of self, or the love of God:

> The true cause therefore of the bliss of the good angels is their adherence to Him who supremely *is*. When we ask the cause of the evil angels' misery, we find that it is the just result of their turning away from Him who supremely is, and their turning towards themselves, who do not exist in that supreme degree.[11]

On the other hand, the Greco-Thomistic[12] theoreticians of love maintained that it was in the rational creature's nature to love itself, and that only grace made possible love of God exclusively. There were two ways in which the creature could love itself, however, sinfully or justly, depending upon whether its love of self were founded in right reason, or upon *cupiditas*. The three choices might then be restated as the love of God in the supernatural order of charity, the love of self in conformity with reason and nature, or finally the love of inferior objects through the disordered love of self which is cupidity, the contrary of charity. Natural love would then be indifferent to the opposition of supernatural *caritas* and sinful *cupiditas*. The indifferent quality of natural love is affirmed in one of the objections the pseudo-Alexander poses against his own formulation of angelic love. The question is whether natural love is compatible with supernatural love:

> The states of punishment and of glory are opposed to one another, but the state of nature is indifferent to both. It is therefore not to be destroyed by the advent of glory. Nothing, then, prohibits us from having a love of nature and of glory at the same time. Thus the good angels, although they have a love of glory, do not give up the love of nature.[13]

He refutes this objection effectively, however:

> The state of punishment is directly opposed to the state of glory, but the state of nature is not opposed to that of glory in the simple sense, but rather by reason of a certain imperfection attached to it which is removed even if that nature remains.[14]

The point is that once the opportunity of beatitude is presented, nature is no longer indifferent, but rather presents a certain imperfection with regard to the state of glory. The choice to remain in the state of nature is at the same time a refusal to ascend. Such a refusal would constitute the very core of sinful action.

The objection raised against the anonymous Franciscan's contention that the supernatural love of the angels supersedes their natural love began by maintaining that the *status naturae* is indifferent both to the state of glory and to that of misery. This is of course true in a logical sense only, and it is by ignoring the successive or temporal element of choice that the objection derives all its cogency. In the first moment, there is no standard by which to judge natural love; it simply is, and there can be no merit or blame attached to its exercise. In the second moment, however, when the supernatural vocation is presented, and the necessary grace supplied, then clearly the state of nature falls short of the creature's capability, which has received a new dimension. As far as the individual is concerned, once the opportunity to attain beatitude is presented, then the state of nature is imperfect, for it has received a potentiality which remains to be actualized—the potentiality to be elevated supernaturally. In short, one can be either for God or for oneself, and anything else that one is "for" is simply a further commitment after the decision to be for oneself. Action may be logically three-fold, but the relationship of creature to God is always "either/or."

In Dante's verses, there are likewise three possibilities: *fedeli, ribelli,* and *per sè,* analogous respectively to the conversions "ad eum qui supra eds est," "ad inferiora," and "ad se." The opposition is specified in quite a different way, however, for in the verses, the *ribelli* and the *fedeli* are on the same side of the polarity, mutually opposed to *per sè.* Here there is no question of moral choices but rather of choices of action. The *per sè* can be regarded as morally neutral only if the temporal element in choice is overlooked, since the choice for or against God is logically prior to the movement incarnating that choice in an *act* of rebellion or fidelity.

For Dante, the angels were created in grace. If they confirmed that natural commitment by opening their hearts to acknowledge God's grace, that merit predisposed them to the gift of illuminating grace, which in turn elevated them to the state of beatitude in God's presence.[15] If the angel did not wait for the light of glory, then it fell "acerbo" with respect to the supernatural end for which it had been created.[16] There are just these two possibilities:

> sì tosto, come de li angeli *parte*
> turbò il suggetto d'i vostri alimenti.

> *L'altra* rimase, e cominciò quest' arte
> che tu discerni, con tanto diletto,
> che mai da circüir non si diparte. (*Par.* XXIX, 50–54)

> a part of the Angels disturbed the substrate of your elements. The rest remained and with such great delight began this art which you behold that they never cease from circling.

Those who fell broke faith, those who remained faithful perfected that faith in Love, or rather, Charity. There was no third group.

This initial division was only the first movement in the act of choice, the establishment of a predisposition for or against God, eternally separating the evil angels from the good. In this moment, the *fedeli* are logically opposed to both the *per sè* and the *ribelli.* In the second movement of choice, the *per sè* stand in logical opposition to both the *ribelli* and the *fedeli.* Those who had accepted the gift of grace moved toward God, while among those who rejected it, some rebelled and others remained within themselves, in a state of aversion. The latter were as the zero point in a scale of action extending from the highest angel to Satan himself. It is for this reason that they too "mai non fur vivi," having failed to complete the first act of their existence.[17] *"Per sè"* is logically the midpoint between two opposed movements, but morally speaking, such a position merits only damnation, for as St. Bernard expressed it, he who stands still on the road to God has already fallen back.[18]

In both of the logical movements of choice, predisposition and act, the angel of the vestibule was on the negative side of the polarities. To use the language of the scholastics in a way that Dante himself used it, the first opposition was in the genus of moral good, while the second was in the genus of action.[19] The first negation, privation of good, won for the rebellious and the *per sè* angels eternal damnation. The second, privation of action, won for the *per sè* angels complete isolation in Dante's cosmos.

All of these considerations seem somewhat superfluous until we recall that in scholastic thought, both aversion from God and *act* were required for the commission of sin. "Malum est defectus, peccatum est actus" was the formula used by Thomas and his contemporaries to distinguish between simple evil and sinful action.[20] In order to be adjudged a sinner, a rational being had both to turn away from God and somehow do evil. Thus choice was thought to consist of two elements. In the first moment, a position is taken up with respect to God. In the second, the rational creature acts within the framework of that position. The anterior stand, the aversion from God or the conversion to Him, establishes two moral universes, one of salvation and the other of damnation. The next moment, the election of one of the myriad objects of choice, determines the grade of culpability or grace within each of those universes. In the case of man, if he preserves the bond uniting him to God, and nevertheless acts incorrectly, all is not lost, for God's order provides for purgation. On the other hand, after an aversion of the heart from God, each moral act within that frame will of necessity be vitiated, regardless of the apparent, exterior worth of the action.

Ever since Augustine, evil was defined as privation of good, an existential absence. Sin, on the other hand, was action, and hence could not be termed non-being. In order for a positive act to be considered evil, it had to be founded upon a previous negation—*defectus*—the lack of consideration of a principle which should be considered. This negative predisposition was not a movement; rather was it the taking up of a stand, the establishment of an intent, and it colored as evil every subsequent action based upon it. Sin is the incarnation, so to speak, of nothingness.[21]

The angels of the vestibule underwent no such incarnation. They simply did not act, but remained frozen in a state of aversion from God. It is pointless to ask whether they were better or worse than the lowest of sinners, for they do not fit into any category, after the initial division of heavenly light from infernal dark. With the aversion from God, the bond of charity was smashed; with the abstention from action, they deprived themselves of the one positive element that could win them a place in the cosmos. They are as close to nothing as creatures can be and still exist, for by their double negation, they have all but totally removed themselves from the picture.[22] To be deprived of action is to be deprived of love, and love is the law of Dante's cosmos, determining all classifications. There remains nothing for them but the vaguely defined vestibule of hell, and they merit no more than a glance from the pilgrim before he passes on to the realm of love perverted.

For the angel, to avert from the vision of God is to ignore not only Him, but the self that depends upon Him. The rebellious angel will act on the basis of that aversion, but the "per sè" angel, having turned from the roots of its own being, refuses even this negative affirmation. It remains, locked tightly in the self, an irreducible negation, meriting not even classification among the damned, having done nothing to distinguish itself from the void out of which it was created. In the first moment of its existence, it saw God at the center of its being, and in the second moment, the moment of choice, it averted from that vision. It looked above itself to the angels who were elevated, below it to those who rebelled, and stood, undecided, as if it could really forge a destiny for itself, somehow different from the one God intended, and from the only other one the angel could elect in spite of its Maker. That hesitation was not so much an inability to choose as it was the result of a proto-choice, the choice for nothing, and because of it, the "per sè" angel was spewed forth from the supernatural cosmos.

7. Medusa: The Letter and the Spirit

SEVERAL TIMES IN THE COURSE OF his poem Dante insists that his verses be read allegorically, but nowhere is his insistence more peremptory or more baffling than in Canto IX of the *Inferno,* after Virgil covers the pilgrim's eyes to protect him from the sight of the Medusa:

> O voi ch'avete li 'ntelletti sani,
> mirate la dottrina che s'asconde
> sotto 'l velame de li versi strani. (vv. 61–63)

> O you who have sound understanding, mark the doctrine that is hidden under the veil of the strange verses!

These lines have always represented something of a scandal in the interpretation of Dante's allegory, primarily because they seem to fail in ther didactic intent: the *dottrina* referred to here remains as veiled to us as it was to the poet's contemporaries. More than that, however, the *dottrina,* whatever it is, seems scarcely worth the effort. The verses suggest a personification allegory—Medusa as moral abstraction—very different from the theological allegory that, since the work of Charles Singleton,[1] we have taken to be uniquely Dantesque. The allegory of the episode would seem to be no different from the "allegory of poets," described in the *Convivio* as a *menzogna* hiding a moral truth, so that we are tempted to conclude either that Dante's allegory, though obscure, is no different from that of other poets, or that this first explicit reference to it in the poem is somehow atypical.

My argument is that neither of these alternatives is correct and that this passage, when property understood, can supply a model for understanding Dante's allegory throughout the poem. I hope to show that the allegory is essentially theological and, far from being of purely antiquarian interest as a bizarre exegetical theory irrelevant to poetic practice, it is actually indistinguishable from the poem's narrative structure. Christian allegory, I will argue, is identical with the phenomenology of confession, for both involve a comprehension of the self in history within a retrospective literary structure.

Perhaps the principal difficulty with the address to the reader in the episode of the Medusa has arisen from our tendency to read it as though it were dramatically unrelated to its context, a generic recall to a moral code exterior to the text. In fact, however, this passage, like all of the addresses to the reader, is exterior to the fiction, but central to the text. The authorial voice is at once the creation of the journey and its creator, an *alter Dantes* who knows, but does not as yet exist, dialectically related to the pilgrim, who exists but does not as yet know. The addresses to the reader create the author as much as they create his audience; they compose the paradigm of the entire narrative, ensuring the presence of the goal at each step along the way. It is Dante's fiction that the author's existence precedes that of the poem, as though the experience had been concluded before the poem were begun. In reality, however, the experience of the pilgrim and the creation of the authorial voice take place at the same time, in the writing of the poem. The progress of the pilgrim and the addresses to the reader are dramatic representations of the dialectic that is the process of the poem. Journey's end, the vision of the Incarnation, is at the same time the incarnation of the story, when pilgrim and author, being and knowing, become one.

In precisely the same way that the pilgrim and the authorial voice are dialectically related to each other, the dramatic action involving the Medusa is related to the address to the reader immediately following it. This is suggested by a certain inverse symmetry: the *covering* of the pilgrim's eyes calls forth a command to *uncover* and see (*mirate*) the doctrine hidden beneath the verses, as if the command were consequent to the action rather than simply the interruption that it is usually taken to be. As readers of the poem, we ordinarily assume that the dramatic action is stopped from time to time for an authorial gloss, as if the poet were arbitrarily intruding upon a rerun of his own past in order to guide us in our interpretation. Here, however, the symmetry between the action and the gloss suggests a more intimate, even *necessary,* relationship. The antithetical actions (covering/uncovering) suggest that we look for antithetical objects (Medusa/*dottrina*) in two analogous or parallel realms: the progress of the pilgrim and the progress of the poem. The threat of the Medusa lends a certain moral force to the command to *see* beneath the strange verses, just as the address to the reader lends to the Medusa a certain hermeneutic resonance. It is *because* the pilgrim averted his eyes from the Medusa that there is a truth to be seen beneath the veil; because seeing it is a way of understanding a text, however, the implication seems to be that the Medusa is an interpretive as well as a moral threat. In other words, the aversion from the Medusa and the *conversion* to the text are related temporally, as the *before* and *after* of the same poetic event. Between those two moments, there extends the experience of the pilgrim, who has himself seen the *dottrina* and has returned as poet to reveal it to us.

A passage in the *Purgatorio* lends considerable weight to our suggestion that petrification is an interpretive as well as a moral threat and that the act of interpretation depends on a moral condition. At the end of the second *cantica*, on the occasion of Dante's own revelation, Beatrice chides him for his "pensier vani" and for the delight he has taken in them:

io veggio te ne lo 'ntelletto
fatto di pietra e, impetrato, tinto,
sì che t'abbaglia il lume del mio detto . . . (XXXIII, 73–75)

I see you turned to stone in your mind, and
stonelike, such in hue that the light of my word
dazes you . . .

If we apply this imagery to the episode of Canto IX, then it is clear that petrification can mean the inability to see the light of truth in an interpretive glance. Thus, the threat of the Medusa may in a sense be a danger to be averted by the reader as well as the pilgrim: an "intelletto sano," as Dante tells us in the *Convivio,* is a mind that is not obscured by ignorance or *malizia,* a mind that is not petrified.[2]

The dialectic of blindness and vision, aversion and conversion in the interpretation of the text, is central to biblical hermeneutics and is discussed by St. Paul with the figure of the veil. The use of the word "velame" in Dante's verses would seem to be an allusion to the Pauline tradition. To speak of a truth hidden beneath a veil was of course a banality in Dante's day, as it is in ours, but its familiarity derived from its biblical origin, where the veil was literally a covering for the radiant face of Moses and figuratively the relationship of the Old Testament to the New. Paul, in II Corinthians, extends his discussion of the "letter that kills" and of the "spirit that gives life" by blending the words of Jeremiah about God writing his law in the hearts of his people with those of Ezekiel about the people of God having hearts of flesh instead of hearts of stone.[3] In St. Paul's New Testament perspective, the hearts of stone become the inscribed tablets of the law of Moses, contrasted with the inscribed hearts of the faithful. He then discusses the meaning of the veil:

> Having therefore such hope, we show great boldness. We do not act as Moses did, who used to put a veil over his face that the Israelites might not observe the glory of his countenance, which was to pass away. But their minds were darkened (*obtusi sunt sensus eorum*); for to this day, when the Old Testament is read to them, the selfsame veil remains, not being lifted (*non revelatum*) to disclose the Christ in whom it is made void. Yes, down to this very day, when Moses is read, the veil covers their hearts; but when they turn in repentance to God, the veil shall be taken away (*Cum autem conversus fuerit ad Dominum, auferetur velamen*). (II Cor 3:12–16)

Paul here contrasts the letter of the Old Testament, written on tablets of stone, with the spirit of the New, who is Christ, the "unveiling" or *re-velation*. The significance of the letter is in its final term, Christ, who was present all along, but revealed as the spirit only at the end, the conversion of the Old Testament to the New. Understanding the truth is not then a question of critical intelligence applied here and there, but rather of a retrospective illumination by faith from the standpoint of the ending, a conversion. In the original Greek, the term used to describe the darkening of the minds of the Jews, *pōrōsis*, petrification,[4] is rendered in the Vulgate as *obtusio,* but the sense of hardness remains alive in the exegetical tradition, where the condition is glossed as *duritia cordis.*[5]

After the Revelation, the inability to see beneath the veil is attributable to the "God of this world," who strikes the unbeliever senseless. It is this God, which later tradition was to identify with the devil, that provides a generic biblical meaning for the Medusa:

> But if our gospel also is veiled, it is veiled only to those who are perishing. In their case, the God of this world has blinded their unbelieving minds, that they should not see the light . . . while we look not at the things that are seen, but at the things that are not seen. For the things that are seen are temporal, but the things that are not seen are eternal. (II Cor. 4:3 ff.)

The familiar dialectic of blindness and vision, as old as Sophocles, assumes a special poignancy in the life of Paul, who was at successive moments blind: first to the truth of Christ and then, on the road to Damascus, to the things of this world. Conversion is for him, much as it was for Plato, a turning away from the false light of temporal things, seen with the eyes of the body, to the light of eternity, seen with the eyes of the soul. Above all, blindness and vision are in the Pauline text metaphors for interpretation, the obtuse reading of faithless literalists transformed, by unveiling, into a reading of the same text in a new light.

I should like to propose that the episode of the Medusa is an application of this dialectic to both the pilgrim and the reader. The "before" and the "after" of the conversion experience are rendered sequentially and dramatically by the threat to the pilgrim, on one hand, and the authorial voice on the other. Between the aversion from a temporal threat and the conversion to the Christian truth, the *dottrina,* there is the Christ event in the experience of the pilgrim, the moment that marks the coming together of pilgrim and poet. From that ideal moment, Dante fulfills the role of a Virgil to the reader, sufficient to the task of averting his pupil's glance from the "God of this world," the temptation of *temporalia,* yet not sufficient for the task of *re-velation.* The threat to the pilgrim, petrification, seems to correspond to the various conditions of unbelief suggested by the Pauline text: blindness, hardness of heart, darkening of the mind, senselessness; while vision (presumably accomplished by the pilgrim/author and now proffered to the reader) corresponds to the eternity of "things that are not seen." Literalists are blind to spiritual truth precisely because they see temporal things, while the things of this world are invisible to those who see the spirit within. The Christ event in history, as described by St. Paul, is applied to the *now* of the pilgrim's journey in his meeting with Beatrice and is left as testament to the reader, who is exhorted to follow in his own way. En route, however, both must avert their glance from the God of this world.

Whatever the merit of this dramatic outline, it still leaves us in the realm of poetic fiction. Several difficulties immediately present themselves, which can be resolved only by exploring more deeply the relationship between the Pauline text and the verses of Canto IX. In the first place, the Pauline dialectic is built upon the fundamental opposition of two terms that are a unity in the Bible: the letter and the spirit, figuratively translated into visual terms by the opposition "veil"/"face of Moses" (Christ). Dante's use of the word "velame" also suggests a translation into visual terms of the interpretive act required of the reader at this point; what is not as yet clear is the sense in which the threat of the Medusa is in Dante's text, as petrification is in Paul's, the corresponding threat of the "letter that kills." In other words, how is the face of Medusa the opposite of the face of Moses? Secondly, once the opposition between the threat of the Medusa and the *dottrina* is established, there remains the problem of their relationship, for letter and spirit, though opposed, are still one, as the Old Testament, written on tablets of stone or engraved on the stony hearts of unbelievers, is still one with its New Testament interpretation, written upon the "fleshly tablets of the heart" (II Cor. 3:3). The same is true of the figure of the veil: it is under the same veil, perceived by believers and unbelievers alike, that the truth is hidden. Paul attributes interpretive blindness to the "God of this world" but in Dante's text it is the diabolic threat that must somehow lead beyond itself. In what sense might it be said that the threat of the Medusa masks a *dottrina* that is nowhere to be found on the printed page? The resolution of both difficulties will become clear when we decide which, precisely, are the *versi strani* referred to in the text.

Our solution must begin with some interpretive and historical remarks about the Medusa herself. Her story in antiquity seems a perfect counterpart to the story of the veiling of Moses' face. Dante was doubtless aware of the false etymology of her name concocted by the mythographers: *mē idōsan, quod videre non possit.* [6] To see her was death; to protect himself Perseus required the shield of Minerva, just as we, according to the allegorization of Albertus Magnus, require the shield of wisdom to protect us against *delectationes concupiscentiae.*[7] On the other hand, the face of Moses is a figure for the glory of Christ, *illuminatio Evangelii gloriae Christi* (II Cor. 4:4), requiring nothing less than a conversion in order to be unveiled (*revelatio*). It remained for Dante to associate the two stories, recasting the Pauline dialectic of blindness and vision into the figure of the Medusa (corresponding to St. Paul's "God of this world") and contrasting it with the admonition, immediately following, to gaze at the truth beneath the veil. The two stories serve as excellent dramatizations of the two moments of conversion: aversion from the self and the things of this world, conversion to God. Separating those two moments at that point extends the whole of the journey.

A closer look at the tradition surrounding the Medusa suggests a more than dramatic aptness in the choice of this figure for the representation of a diabolic threat. The most startling thing about traditional efforts to discuss this episode is that they have missed what to a modern reader is most obvious: whatever the horror the Medusa represents to the male imagination, it is in some sense a female horror. In mythology, the Medusa was said to be powerless against women, for it was her feminine *beauty* that constituted the mortal threat to her admirers. From the ancient *Physiologus* through the mythographers to Boccaccio, the Medusa represented a sensual fascination, a *pulchritudo* so excessive that it turned men to stone.[8] In Dante's text the theme of fascination survives; otherwise it would be difficult to imagine why Virgil does not trust the pilgrim's ability to shield his own eyes if the image were not an entrapment.

Fascination, in this context, suggests above all the sensual fascination celebrated in the literature of love. Whatever the significance of the Medusa motif to Freud and Ferenczi, we are dealing here with a highly self-conscious poetry and a kind of love poetry at that. An explicit reference in the text helps to identify the subject matter as specifically erotic and literary, rather than abstractly moral. When the Furies scream out for the Medusa, they recall the assault of Theseus: "Mal non vengiammo in Tesëo l'assalto" (IX, 54). This would seem to be an allusion to Theseus' descent into the underworld with his friend Pirithoüs, a disastrous enterprise from which he, unlike his hapless companion, was rescued by Hercules, but the point is that the descent had for its objective the abduction of Persephone; it was therefore an erotic, not to say sexual, assault.

The presence of the theme here is not merely anecdotal; Dante is himself in a sense searching for a prelapsarian Persephone, an erotic innocence which he recaptures, at one remove, in his encounter with Matelda at the top of the Mountain of Purgatory:

Tu mi fai rimembrar dove e qual era
  Proserpina nel tempo che perdette
  la madre lei, ed ella primavera. (*Purg.*, XXVIII, 49–51)

You make me recall where and what Proserpine was at the time her mother lost her, and she the spring.

These two references to Persephone in the poem, the first implied and the second clearly stated, suggest that the figure of the Medusa is somehow coordinate to that of Matelda. Whatever else she may represent, the pastoral landscape and the erotic feelings of the pilgrim would indicate the recapture, or near recapture, of a pastoral (and therefore *poetic*) innocence, a return to Eden after a long *askesis*. For the moment, it might be argued that the Medusa represents precisely the impediment to such a recapture: her association with Persephone goes back to the *Odyssey,* where Odysseus in the underworld fears that Persephone will send the gorgon to prevent him from leaving.[9] Whatever Dante's sources for making the same association,[10] the point is that, short of Eden, there is no erotic—or *poetic*—innocence.

A generation later, Geoffrey Chaucer was to use the Furies in a way that is quite consistent with my hypothesis about the passage in Canto IX. The invocation of *Troilus and Creseyde,* that bookish tale of woe, addresses the Furies, rather than the Muses, as the proper inspirers of the dark passion that is the subject of the romance. Indeed, the insistence on the Furies foreshadows the "anti-romance" quality of Chaucer's poem, a deliberate undercutting of a genre that had been the poet's own. The *Troilus* is in many ways a palinodic autocritique: the language with which it begins, with its address to "Thesiphone . . . cruwel Furie sorynge," may even be an allusion to the passage under discussion here, as well as to Statius.[11] At any rate, it would seem to support our hypothesis: the threat of the Medusa proffered by the Furies represents, in the pilgrim's *askesis*, a sensual fascination and potential entrapment precluding all further progress.

Of all the texts that might support the hypothesis, one seems to me to give to the Medusa a specificity that is lacking in most moralizing interpretations: the *Roman de la Rose.* A passage from that work will establish the sense in which Dante's Medusa exists as a dark counter-statement to the celebration of a poetic eros for which the *Roman* was the quintessential type. It offers us a precise, if inverted, parallel of the action of Canto IX, an illusion, in Dante's view, of which the Medusa is the disillusioning reality. At the ending of Jean de Meun's poem, as the lover is about to besiege the castle, an image is presented to him from a tower, a sculptured image far surpassing in beauty the image of Pygmalion, fired by Venus' arrow. Of interest to us is that in some versions of the poem that might have been available to Dante, the image is contrasted for some fifty lines with the image of the Medusa:

> Tel ymage n'ot mais en tour;
> Plus avienent miracle entour
> Qu'onc n'avint entour Medusa . . .
> Mais l'ymage dont ci vous conte
> Les vertux Medusa seurmonte,
> Qu'el ne sert pas de genz tuer,
> Ne d'eus faire en roche muet.[12]

> Such an image was never in a tower; more miracles happen around it than ever occurred around Medusa . . . But the image I'm telling you about here goes beyond the powers of Medusa. For it doesn't seem to kill people or to change them into stone.

The passage goes on to draw an extraordinary parallel to the drama of Canto IX, an ironically optimistic view of the power of eros, of which Dante's Medusa seems the dark and reversed counter-image. The presence of mock-epic machinery in this erotomachia is matched by the pointedly non-Christian fortifications of Dante's infernal city. The Medusa does not appear in the *Roman,* any more than she does in the *Inferno,* but exists only as an antitype to Venus' idol. Dante's Medusa, on the other hand, *is* Venus' idol, stripped of its charm and seen, or almost seen, under the aspect of death. Recent study suggests that, as a youth, Dante had written a poetic paraphrase of the *Roman;* hence this episode constitutes his final judgment on the dark eros celebrated in that work.

The figure of the Medusa is a perfect vehicle for conveying this kind of retrospective judgment because it is inherently diachronic, stressing historicity and change: before and after, then and now, the beauty of the lady changed to ugliness, fascination turned to horror. In ancient mythology she was said to be a kind of siren,[13] and in this temporal respect she resembles Dante's siren, the stinking hag of the *Purgatorio* whom the pilgrim, under the influence of song, takes to be a ravishing beauty.

A simple abstraction of personification allegory is least able to account for this temporal dimension of meaning, for the temporality is derived not from the gap that separates the poetic statement from some abstract moral code, but rather from the temporality of the beholder.[14] I should like to suggest that the temporality we sense in the threat of the Medusa is a representation of the temporality of retrospection, of a danger narrowly averted, of a former illusion seen for what it is. Such a temporality is the essence of the descent into hell, the past seen under the aspect of death. The traditional threat on all such journeys is the threat of nostalgia, a retrospective glance that evades the imperative to accept an authentically temporal destiny. Moreover, the threat is not merely a petrification, but also a *no return:* "Nulla sarebbe del tornar mai suso." The Gospel of Luke (17:32) warns of such a danger with an Old Testament figure that seems peculiarly appropriate here: "Remember Lot's wife."

The threat of the past faces St. Augustine just before his conversion, when his former mistresses seem to appear behind him, tempting him to turn and look at them, *respicere,* as they pluck at his "fleshly garment."[15] In the medieval allegorization of the journey of Orpheus to the underworld, a similar significance is given to the irreparable loss of Eurydice. According to Guillaume de Conches, Orpheus' descent represents the sage's effort to find himself, his Eurydice, and he is defeated by his nostalgia for his own former sin.[16] At this point in his descent, the pilgrim faces a similar temptation: the Furies, a traditional representation of guilt and remorse, urge him to confront what is, in effect, his own past as poet. Dante did not have to read the *Roman de la Rose* in order to learn of a lady who turned her lovers to stone, for he had in fact celebrated such a lady in his *Rime Petrose,* the stony rhymes, written for the mysterious *Donna Pietra.*

The *Rime Petrose,* the dazzling virtuoso pieces of Dante's youth, celebrate a violent passion for the "Stony Lady" whose hardness turns the poet, her lover, into a man of stone. In the survey of the progress of Dante's love and of his poetry from the *Vita Nuova* to the *Commedia,* the *Rime Petrose* constitute a surd element, radically fragmentary, Contini has called them,[17] finding no clearly identifiable place in the poet's development. At one point in the *Purgatorio* when Beatrice castigates the pilgrim for his infidelity, she accuses him of a love for "vanità," a "pargoletta," or little girl, using precisely the same word that the poet had used somewhat disparagingly of his *Donna Pietra* in one of the *rime.* The recall in the *Purgatorio* of this word has given rise to endless speculation about the identity of the woman whom Dante denoted with the code name of "Donna Pietra." Critics have been right, I think, to wish to see biography in the poem, but they have been incorrect to imagine that the words of the poem were simply vehicles for communicating true confessions. We have learned from Contini that the biography of a poet, as poet, is his poetry,[18] and it is in a quite literal sense that the *Rime Petrose* are present and relevant here. In the same poem that has given rise to speculation about the "pargoletta," there appear some verses of potentially greater significance. They paint a wintry scene described by a despairing lover. They should be compared with the *versi strani* of Canto IX:

Versan le vene le fummifere acque
per li vapor che la terra ha nel ventre,
che d'abisso li tira suso in *alto*;
onde cammino al bel giorno mi piacque
che ora è fatto rivo, e sarà mentre
che durerà del verno il grande *assalto*;
la terra fa un suol che par di *smalto*,
e l'acqua morta si converte in vetro. (*Rime* 43c, 53–60)

Con l'unghie si fendea ciascuna il petto;
battiensi a palme e gridavan sì *alto*,
ch'i' mi strinsi al poeta per sospetto.
"Vegna Medusa: sì 'l farem di *smalto*,"
dicevan tutte riguardando in giuso;
"mal non vengiammo in Tesëo l'*assalto*."
(*Inf.* IX, 49–54)

The springs spew forth fumy waters because the earth draws the gases that are in its bowels upwards from the abyss; a path that pleased me in fine weather is now a stream, and so will remain as long as winter's great onslaught endures; the earth has formed a crust like rock and the dead waters turn into glass.[19]

Each was tearing her breast with her nails; and they were beating themselves with their hands, and crying out so loudly that in fear I pressed close to the poet.

"Let Medusa come and we'll turn him to stone," they all cried, looking downward. "Poorly did we avenge the assault of Theseus."

The description of a world without love, matching the poet's winter of the soul, contains exactly the rhyme words from Dante's description of the Medusa, sibilants that might qualify as *versi strani* in the address to the reader. Thus a passage that threatens petrification recalls, in a reified, concrete way, precisely the poem that described such a reification at the hands of a kind of Medusa. The words themselves reflect each other in such a way that they constitute a short-circuit across the temporal distance that separates the two moments of poetic history, a block that threatens to make further progress impossible. For the reader, the parallel threat is to refuse to see the allegory through the letter, to ignore the double focus of the *versi strani.* The echo of the *Rime Petrose* is an invitation to the reader to measure the distance that separates the *now* of the poet from the *then* of his *persona;* in the fiction of the poem, the Medusa is, like the lady of stone, no historic character at all, but the poet's own creation. Its threat is the threat of idolatry. In terms of mythological *exempla,* petrification by the Medusa is the real consequence of Pygmalion's folly.

The point is worth stressing. Ever since Augustine, the Middle Ages insisted upon the link between eros and language, between the reaching out in desire for what mortals can never possess and the reaching out of language toward the significance of silence. To refuse to see in human desire an incompleteness that urges the soul on to transcendence is to remain within the realm of creatures, worshipping them as only the Creator was to be worshipped. Similarly, to refuse to see language and poetry as continual *askesis,* pointing beyond themselves, is to remain within the letter, treating it as an absolute devoid of the spirit which gives meaning to human discourse. The subject matter of love poetry is *poetry,* as much as it is love, and the reification of love is at the same time a reification of the words that celebrate it.

The search for the self which is the quest of the poet can only be accomplished through the mediation of the imagination, the Narcissus image which is at once an image of the self and all that the self is not.[20] For a medieval poet steeped in the Augustinian tradition, the search for the self in the mirror of creatures, the beloved, ends with a false image of the self which is either rejected in favor of God, the light which casts the reflection, or accepted as a true image, an image which is totally other. Seeing the self in otherness and accepting the vision as true reduces the spirit to something alienated from itself, like a rock or a tree, deprived of consciousness. Like language itself, the image can only represent by pointing beyond itself, by beckoning the beholder to pierce through it to its ultimate significance. Idolatry in this context is a refusal to go beyond, a self-petrification.

Virgil is the mediator between Dante's former dark passion and verbal virtuosity on one hand and the restless striving of the pilgrim on the other, at least until his guidance gives way to the guidance of Beatrice. It may seem strange to think of Virgil at all in the context of love poetry, except insofar as every poet is a poet of desire. Yet Virgil's portrait of Aeneas was a portrait of passion overcome. At the opening of the fifth book, as Aeneas sails away from Carthage, he looks back at its burning walls and leaves Dido forever behind him. The chaotic force of *folle amore*—mad passion—was epitomized for Dante by the figure of Dido and of Cupid, who sat in her lap. Further, it is under the sign of Dido that Paolo and Francesca bewail their adulterous love in hell. In the struggle between individual desire and providential destiny, Virgil's Aeneas is the man who renounces self in the name of his mission. It is for this reason that he helps the pilgrim avert his glance, until Beatrice shows the way to a reconciliation of human love with the divine plan. Just as the historic Virgil, in Dante's reading, had pointed the way out of the erotic impasse toward *lo bello stilo,* so in the poem it is Virgil who helps him to avoid the pitfall facing all poets of love. It is perhaps in this sense, specifically, that his help was spurned by Guido Cavalcanti (*Inf.* x, 63). In any case, Dante's encounter with Beatrice is the moment at which the poem transcends the Virgilian view of human love. Dante marks his beloved's return with the words "conosco i segni dell'antica fiamma" (*Purg.* xxx, 48), echoing the despairing words of Dido, while the angels sing "*Manibus, oh, date lilia plenis*" (give lilies with full hands), echoing the funereal gesture of Anchises in the underworld, but transforming the purple lilies of mourning into the white lilies of the Resurrection. At that point Virgil definitively disappears, when death, before which even he and his Rome had to bow, gives way to transcendent love (*Canticum Cant.* viii, 6).

There is some evidence that our suggested reading of the Medusa episode may have been anticipated by a near contemporary of the poet, or at least that the problematic was recognized and radically transformed by him. I refer of course to Petrarch, whose very name was for him an occasion for stony puns. In the course of his *Canzoniere,* he provides us with a definitive gloss of Dante's Medusa. Like Pygmalion, Petrarch falls in love with his own creation and is in turn created by her: the pun *Lauro/Laura* points to this self-contained process which is the essence of his creation. He creates with his poetry the Lady Laura who in turn creates his reputation as poet laureate. She is therefore not a mediatrix, pointing beyond herself, but is rather enclosed within the confines of his own being as poet, which is to say, the poem. This is precisely what Petrarch acknowledges when he confesses in his final prayer to the sin of idolatry, adoration of the work of his own hands. Speaking of Laura no longer as the infinitely beloved, he calls her a Medusa: "Medusa e l'error mio m'han fatto un sasso." For all of his tears of repentance, however, there seems to be a consolation for a more secular age. Petrarch's enduring fame as the weeping lover suggests that if he was turned to stone because of idolatry, at least a stone lasts forever. If it is devoid of the spirit linking it to reality and to the life of the poet, it is nevertheless immune to the ravages of time, a monumental portrait of the artist. In the same poem, he sees the problem of reification and idolatry as inherent in all poetry, including that of his illustrious predecessor. This, I take it, is the point of his address to the Virgin as the only true mediatrix and "bringer-of-blessings"; *vera beatrice,* where the absence of capitalization drives the point home more forcefully. For Petrarch, precursor of Romanticism, there can be no middle ground, not even that occupied by Dante.

We are now in a position to answer some of the fundamental questions concerning Dante's allegory raised by the episode of the Medusa. Doubtless, the Pauline "God of this world" provides an appropriate and abstract moral meaning in the dramatization that might lead us to classify it as an example of the allegory of poets. At the same time, however, we have seen that the passage is charged with the temporality of the poet's own career, the Dante who is, looking back at the Dante who was, through the medium of words. This retrospective illumination is the very essence of biblical allegory, what Dante called the "allegory of theologians." The Christ event was the end term of an historical process, the "fullness of time," from the perspective of which the history of the world might be read and judged according to a meaning which perhaps even the participants in that history could not perceive. The "then" and "now," the Old Testament and the New, were at once the continuity and discontinuity of universal history, the letter and the spirit respectively of God's revelation. Christian autobiography is the application of this diachronicity to one's own life for the purpose of witness, "confession," of the continual unfolding of the Word.

Both confession and Christian allegory have their roots in the mystery of language. As language is unfolded along a syntagmatic axis, governed at each moment of its articulation by a paradigm present in the mind of the speaker and made manifest at the ending of the sentence, so the authorial voice in the text is the paradigm of the entire narrative, of which the evolution of the pilgrim is, as it were, the syntax. When this dialectic is translated into dramatic terms that purport to be autobiographical, we are presented with a narrative which seems to demand both continuity and discontinuity: an organic continuity, so that it may make a claim to authenticity, yet with the definitive detachment of the author who makes a claim to finality. For the pilgrim and the author to be one and the same requires nothing short of death and resurrection: death, so that the story may be definitive and final: resurrection, so that it may be told. This narrative translation of the dialectic of language may in turn be translated into theological terms: conversion, the burial of the old man and the birth of the new, the essence of Pauline allegory. Christ, the ending of the story, is simply the manifestation of its subject, paradoxically present as the paradigm, the Logos, from the beginning. The final manifestation of the paradigm is the presence of the Logos made flesh. Just as history required an Archimedean point from which Christians could judge it to have been concluded, so the literature of confession needs a point outside of itself from which its truth can be measured, a point that is at once a beginning and an end, an Alpha and an Omega. "Conversion" was the name that Christians applied to such a moment in history and in the soul. In this sense, biblical allegory, conversion, and narrative all share the same linguistic nature.

When St. Paul refers to the relationship of the Old Testament to the New, he is in fact applying this linguistic metaphor to the Christ event, the spirit inseparable from the letter of the Bible whereby it is made manifest. Without the letter, the spirit is the eternal Logos, with no point of tangency to history; God's intentionality without relation to man. Without the spirit, the letter is utterly devoid of significance, as dead as the mute stones upon which it was written. God's utterance to man is the Word incarnate.

Paul goes on to suggest that the Word of God interprets the hearts of men, the stony tablets turning to stone the hearts of unbelievers, while the spirit writes upon the fleshly tablets of the faithful. So too, in Dante's text, it is the power of the letter to enthrall the beholder that makes of it a Medusa, an expression of desire that turns back to entrap its subject in an immobility which is the very opposite of the dynamism of language and of desire.[21] To see beyond it, however, is to see in the spiritual sense, to transform the eros of the Medusa into the transcendent Eros of Caritas. This is Dante's whole achievement as a love poet: a refusal of the poetics of reification, sensual and verbal, for the poetics of "translation," as scribe of the spirit which is written on "the fleshly tablets of the heart":

"I' mi son un che, quando
Amor mi spira, noto, e a quel modo
ch'e' ditta dentro vo significando." (*Purg.* XXIV, 52–54)

"I am one who, when Love inspires me, takes
note, and goes setting it forth after the fashion
which he dictates within me."

The book of memory has as its author God Himself. In this sense, Dante's poem is neither a copy nor an imitation of the Bible. It *is* the allegory of theologians in his own life.

Nonetheless, the passage from the events of Dante's life to the words and images he uses to signify them is one that we cannot make. This is why it is impossible to guess at the identity of the *Donna Pietra,* just as it is impossible to see in the Medusa some event of the poet's life. We must be content with words on words, the double focus on a poetic expression, beyond which it would take an act of faith equal to Dante's to go; beyond which, indeed, there is no Dante we can ever know.

The address to the reader is thus not a stage direction, but an exhortation to conversion, a command to await the celestial messenger so that we, like the pilgrim, may "trapassare dentro.[22] Beneath the veil of Moses, we behold the light of the Gospel; beneath the veil of Dante's verses, the *dottrina* is derived from that, or it is nothing at all.

8. Dante's Ulysses: From Epic to Novel

In antiquity, history seemed to follow a biological pattern. Civilizations, like men, succeeded one another according to the life cycle: a coming-to-be and a passing away to which all things were forever subject. Time moved in an eternal circle, with repetition as its only rationale. In the face of inexorable destiny, man's only hope for permanence, or at least for its pale reflection, resided in his aspiration to worldly glory and human renown.

For St. Augustine, the advent of Christ changed all of this by introducing into history an absolutely new event. In the twelfth book of the *City of God* he asserts that the "circles have been shattered" for all time. The coming of the Redeemer cut through the circle of time and established a fixed point, making of the circular flux a linear progression toward that new and eternal event. Time seemed at last to have been moving toward its consummation, the fullness of time, which in retrospect gave to all of history a meaning, as a target gives meaning to the flight of the arrow. The coming of Christ wrought a change not only in universal history, but in the history of the individual soul as well, whose story could no longer be reduced to the curve extending from birth through maturity to death, but was rather a continuous trajectory toward the target: a death that would give meaning to life. It was this new linear conception of time that some have claimed as the ancestor of our own idea of progress.

Whatever the accuracy of such a dichotomy, the circle and the straight line, time as continued repetition and time as a progression toward an apocalyptic goal, these are logically opposite poles of historiography. They are at the same time logically opposite poles of the narrative art, insofar as that art gives a picture, however idealized, of human existence. Homer's *Odyssey,* for example, seems to reflect in the spatial circularity of the journey's trajectory a temporal circularity as well. The gem-like episodes are strung together as on a necklace, one set of events succeeding another quite independently while the strand measures ten years of the hero's life—Ulysses leaves Ithaca, has his adventures, and to Ithaca he returns. What gives meaning to the adventure is the portrait of the hero in an epic world where there are great dangers and great challenges, but scarcely ever any doubts. The hero may not know what fate has in store for him, but he has no illusions about fate itself or about the limits of his own mortality in dealing with it. Whether the gods are benevolent or malign, their behavior is predictable and the punishment for offending them is equally clear. There can be misfortunes or disasters, monsters and sirens, but from beginning to end the game is fixed and both the reader and the protagonist, confident by tradition about the eventual outcome of the adventure, are more concerned with the "how" of it than with the "why" of the universe in which it is enclosed.

Ulysses' journey was widely read in antiquity as the spatial allegorization of circular human time; Ulysses' return to his homeland served as an admirable vehicle for Platonic and gnostic allegories about the soul's triumph over material existence, its gradual refinement back to its pristine spirituality. The return of Ulysses to Ithaca by force of his own wits, the most important element of the story, was taken to represent the most important event of man's spiritual odyssey: the return of the soul to its heavenly *patria* by the exercise of philosophical wisdom. All of human existence seemed to be strung out between the point of departure and the point of return, the homeland of philosophers as well as heroes.

Nothing could be further from the modern form of narrative, the novel, in which linear temporality is of the essence. In any linear narrative, there arises one fundamental doubt that is enough to call the whole world of the novel into question: assuming that there is a goal, will it be reached or not? and the question cannot be answered until the story is fully told. It becomes desperately important to know the outcome because the rules of the game are no longer fixed simply by the character of the protagonist. At any stage along the way, the freedom of the protagonist or the inscrutability of the laws to which he is subject can combine to stop the evolution for reasons which seem not at all to spring from any inner exigency. The reader is often tempted to skip ahead, to ignore the incidental excursions which are the stuff of epic, in order to arrive at the conclusion, awaited with anxiety and suspense. To be sure, a faith in God and the supernatural limited the anxiety that concerned the exterior events, but this had the effect simply of shifting the suspense to a different plane, not of eliminating it: death ceases to be the end of the trajectory and is replaced by the question of the meaning of death—salvation or damnation in medieval language—the definitive ending of any story. Death within a Christian context is threatening, not because it is the end of life, but because it enters the sphere of human responsibility as the most important moment in life. Like the syntactic silence that ends the sentence and gives meaning retrospectively to all that went before, it is the moment of significance. The irreversible linearity of time is perceived even in the absence of that significance, when its terminal points are shrouded in obscurity.

György Lukacs suggested that Dante wrote the last epic and the first novel, so that in the matter of literary genre, as well as in the history of western culture, he bridges the gap between the Middle Ages and the modern world. On one hand, we know from the beginning that Dante's story will have a reassuring ending. In the first sentence, the narrator says "I," an unmistakable sign that he has returned from his adventure in order to tell us his story. At the same time, however, the pilgrim's terror en route, his bewilderment in the world of the beyond, cannot be dismissed simply as dramatic coyness. The terror of the pilgrim is gradually refined away until it becomes the confidence of the author who has been with us from the beginning. To understand the *Divine Comedy* simply as a religious epic is to dismiss the transformation of the pilgrim as unimportant. To call it a novel, on the other hand, is to miss the confidence of the poet's voice, one of the narrative's most distinctive characteristics. Epic and novel exist, side by side, linearity with circularity, in this poetic synthesis which has always been considered a genre apart.

As in Homer's epic, so in Dante's story the journey of Ulysses stands as an emblem of human time, but the Homeric story is glossed from a linear, Christian viewpoint, from the perspective of death. It is for this reason that Dante's Ulysses ends as a shipwreck rather than at home with Penelope. In spite of the fact that, as Benvenuto da Imola tells us, even unlearned people in Dante's day knew that Homer's hero returned safely to Ithaca, Dante has him die within sight of the Mount of Purgatory. This startling transformation of one of the world's most famous stories is the mandatory Christian corrective of the ancient view of human destiny. It is as if the poet had accepted the ancients' allegorical reading of Ulysses' trajectory as a spatialization of human temporality and then had transformed the circularity of the literal journey in order to have it correspond to a linear reading of human time. The transformation of Ulysses' circular journey into linear disaster is a Christian critique of epic categories, a critique of earthly heroism from beyond the grave.

Because it provides us with an antitype of Dante's experience, the Ulysses episode is one in which Dante is intimately involved, for all of the pilgrim's silence. Ulysses' itinerary is clearly set forth as an ancient analogue of Dante's adventure: it is for this reason both an episode in the *Inferno* and, unlike any other, a constant thematic motif referred to several times throughout *Purgatorio* and even at the last stage of the journey in *Paradiso.*

The metaphoric shipwreck at the foot of a mountain with which Dante begins his poem ("and as he who with laboring breath has escaped from the deep to the shore") is followed by a reference to the sea as a "pass that never left anyone alive"; and when the pilgrim at last reaches the mountain in sight of which Ulysses drowned, he refers to the shore as a

> . . . lito deserto,
> che mai non vide navicar sue acque
> omo, che di tornar sia poscia esperto. (*Purg.* I, 130–32)

> . . . desert shore, that never saw any man navigate its waters who afterwards had experience of return.

The waters are finally crossed by the angel's bark, bringing the souls of those who are saved to the mountain of their purgation. The implications of this dramatic theme would seem to be that one can indeed return home from such an exploration, provided that one can experience a death and resurrection. Exactly the same point was made by Augustine, in the same terms, in the *De beata vita* (see Chap. 1 in this book). The point I wish to make here is that the tragic death of Ulysses seems to have as its counterpart the survival of Dante's hero. The poem is in this sense the view of his own life grasped by a drowning man who somehow survives to tell his life story. In other words, the *morphosis* of the soul, the circular return to the truth read into Ulysses' ancient, trajectory, becomes a *metamorphosis,* a death and resurrection, in Dante's poem. What separates Ulysses' definitive death by water from Dante's baptism unto death and subsequent resurrection is the Christ event in history, or grace, the Christ event in the individual soul.

In Dante's story, as well as in literary tradition, Virgil's Aeneas mediates between Homer's Ulysses and Dante's pilgrim. The pilgrim begins his journey with a metaphoric survival of shipwreck within sight of the mountain in the first canto of the *Inferno,* at a point, that is, where Ulysses met his death. It happens that Aeneas too begins his journey with a quite literal near-shipwreck. It must have been clear to Dante that his readers would assume that only a providential stroke, "com' Altrui piacque," separated the fate of Dante's Ulysses from the landing of Aeneas in Book I of the *Aeneid.* Recently Robert Hollander has examined the first scenes of the *Inferno* with this book in mind and has come up with some remarkable parallels, although he acknowledges a great difference in tone between the two episodes.[1] The providential stroke, of course, was the election of Aeneas and his men for the foundation of Rome. Virgilian providence does not, however, extend to the fate of individuals, who die as everyone must, finding whatever solace they can in the collective survival of Rome. To return to the dichotomy with which we began, we may say that Virgil seems to exempt only Rome from the circular epic destiny. Aeneas' trajectory is linear, but his descent into hell ends not in survival, but in Anchises' funereal reminder of the fate that still awaits individual men:

> manibus date lilia plenis,
> purpureos spargam flores animamque nepotis
> his saltem accumulem donis, et fungar inani
> munere. (*Aen.* VI, 883–886)

> Give lilies with full hands; let me scatter bright flowers and let me at least heap these gifts for my descendant's soul and perform an empty tribute.

Aeneas' descent into hell was the model for Dante's. The difference is in the kind of hell presented in each poem. The descent into the underworld is signaled by the most famous of classical similes indicating a cyclic view of human destiny. As Aeneas and his guide prepare to cross the River Styx, the gathering of souls on the bank recalls to the poet the Homeric comparison of generations of men to falling leaves:

huc omnis turba ad ripas effusa ruebat,
matres atque viri defunctaque corpora vita
magnanimum heroum, pueri innuptaeque puellae,
impositique rogis iuvenes ante ora parentum:
quam multa in silvis autumni frigore primo
lapsa cadunt folia, aut ad terram gurgite ab alto
quam multae glomerantur aves, ubi frigidus annus
trans pontum fugat et terris immittit apricis.
(*Aen.* VI, 305–312)

Hither all crowded and rushed streaming to the bank, matrons and men and high-hearted heroes dead and done with life, boys and unwedded girls, and children laid young on the bier before their parents' eyes, multitudinous as leaves fall dropping in the forests of autumn's earliest frost, or birds swarm landward from the deep gulf, when the chill of the year routs them overseas and drives them to sunny lands.

The use of this simile suggests that, whatever the difference between the linear nature of Aeneas' journey and that of his ancient rival, the two views of individual destiny are the same. For all the eternity of Rome, death remains the common goal for all men, including the poet himself. This elegiac note in Virgil sets the poet off for a brief poignant moment before he too must enter into the cycle which is the extinction of the individual for the sake of the species—a pathos tempered, perhaps, by a collective survival. It finds its exact dramatic counterpart in the pathos of the figure of Virgil in the *Divine Comedy,* lighting the way for others, yet unable to help himself. As Rome was the *praeparatio* for Christianity, so Virgil was Dante's poetic *praeparatio,* and his own reward, in the fiction of the poem, is simply the respite from Limbo for the duration of the journey, just as the historic Virgil, presumably, found a respite from the circle of time for the duration of his authorial voice in the poem.

In the poem, Virgil stands between Ulysses and Dante above all as poet and it is as a poet that he addresses Ulysses. The two ancient figures speak the same language, right from the beginning of their encounter. Dante wishes to question the flames of Ulysses and Diomed, but his guide says:

> Lascia parlare a me, ch'i' ho concetto
> ciò che tu vuoi; ch'ei sarebbero schivi,
> perch' e' fuor greci, forse del tuo detto. (*Inf.* XXVI, 73–74)

> Leave speech to me, for I have understood
> what you wish—and perhaps, since they were
> Greeks, they would be disdainful of your words.

"Speech" in this context is by no means "language"—naive commentators in the past have attempted to gloss this passage by saying that it means simply that Virgil could understand Greek, while the poet could not—but Dante's text shows that such a reading is a misunderstanding, for in the next canto, the soul of Guido da Montefeltro, who, we presume, has overheard Virgil dismissing Ulysses, not only has understood their language, but claims to identify a Lombard dialect:

> . . . O tu a cu' io drizzo
> la voce e che parlavi mo lombardo,
> dicendo 'Istra ten va, più non t'adizzo' (*Inf.* XXVII, 19–21)

> O you to whom I direct my voice and who
> just now spoke Lombard, saying, 'Now go your
> way, I do not urge you more' . . .

In other words, the language that Virgil and Ulysses share is a common style, the high style of ancient epic, whose qualities are unappreciated in the vulgar company of hell, where the language is the *sermo humilis* of Christian *comedìa.* Virgil implies as much when he turns to the pilgrim, disdaining to answer Guido, and says: "Parla tu, questi è latino" (You speak, this one is Italian) (*Inf.* XXVII, 33).

In part, Virgil's disdain for this sinner, who is guilty of the same sin as Ulysses, is a biting commentary on false counselors in Dante's world, and particularly in the papal court. The suggestion of the episode is that at least in antiquity, when men were evil counselors they were still capable of a certain heroic stature and magnanimity, whereas the meanness and base quality of this thirteenth-century evil counselor puts him beneath Virgil's contempt. At the same time, Dante meant to draw the parallel between Guido and Ulysses as closely as possible, even to the navigational figure. As Guido recounts his attempted false conversion to make up for a sinful life, he describes his approaching old age in terms of that figure:

> Quando mi vidi giunto in quella parte
> di mia etade ove ciascun dovrebbe
> calar le vele e raccoglier le sarte,
> ciò che pria mi piacëa, allor m'increbbe,
> e pentuto e confesso mi rendei;
> ahi miser lasso! e giovato sarebbe. (*Inf.* XXVII, 79–84)

> When I saw myself come to that part of my life when every man should lower the sails and coil up the ropes, that which before had pleased me grieved me then, and with repentance and confession I turned friar, and—woe is me!—it would have availed.

The major difference between Ulysses and Guido da Montefeltro, therefore, is neither in their material guilt nor in their language, but quite simply in their style.

Virgil's style in his conversation with Ulysses is elevated and rhetorical, beginning with the traditional *apostrophe,* containing at least one antithesis, and passing quickly to a *captatio benevolentiae* (S' io meritai di voi assai o poco) (*Inf.* XXVI, 81). Ulysses' tongue of flame flickers with equal oratorical and tragic fervor, and when he addresses his men, he too begins with the traditional *captatio* and manages at least one famous Virgilian figure as well as several lesser oratorical flourishes. Ulysses' speech to his men is of course modeled on Aeneas' speech to his men in the first book of the *Aeneid,* beginning "O Socii" (*Aen.* I, 198–207), and it is even conceivable that Dante might have known from a remark in Macrobius that the "O Socii" speech was itself modeled on a Homeric original, as David Thompson has suggested,[2] so that Dante came as close to recapturing Ulysses' original speech as anyone could come who had never seen

Homer's text. There would seem to be no difference between the rhetoric used by the character of Virgil and that of Ulysses.

At the same time, Ulysses is portrayed as an anti-Aeneas, who is mentioned in passing, for he lacks the essential quality of *pietas:*

> né dolcezza di figlio, né la pieta
> del vecchio padre, né 'l debito amore
> lo qual dovea Penelopè far lieta,
> vincer potero dentro a me l'ardore . . . (*Inf.* XXVI, 94–96)

> neither fondness for my son, nor reverence for my aged father, nor the due love which would have made Penelope glad, could conquer in me the longing . . .

The essential characteristic of Ulysses' rhetoric is that it is completely self-serving, dedicated to a heroic enterprise, without any sense of moral duty. In his speech to his men, the comfort he offers them is their own manhood and stature:

> Considerate la vostra semenza:
> fatti non foste a viver come bruti,
> ma per suguir virtute e canoscenza. (*Inf.* XXVI, 118–120)

> Consider your origin: you were not made to live as brutes, but to pursue virtue and knowledge.

By contrast, the comfort that Aeneas offers his men is the foundatio of Rome, the eternal consolation for individual suffering. Aeneas i portrayed in the *Divine Comedy,* as he is in the *Aeneid,* as the ma who is constantly receptive to his providential destiny, who is electe to greatness by God. His descent into hell was, like Dante's, wille in heaven, and is not simply a consequence of his heroic stature.

The contrast between Aeneas' humility and Ulysses' pride is a least in part the contrast between Greek and Roman ideas of the us of rhetoric. In a passage in the *De Inventione,* Cicero describes th corrupt orator in terms that serve very well to describe the figure o Ulysses:

> Postquam vero commoditas quaedam, parva virtutis imatrix, sin ratione offici, dicendi copia consecuta est, tum ingenio fret malitia pervertere urbes et vitas hominum labefactare as suevit. (I, 2.3)

> When a certain agreeableness of manner—a depraved imitation of virtue—acquired the power of eloquence unaccompanied by any consideration of moral duty, then low cunning supported by talent grew accustomed to corrupting cities and undermining the lives of men.

Dante seems to accept Cicero's judgment about the social function of eloquence when he condemns Ulysses by showing that his objective was to find virtue and understanding outside of himself, in a world without people ("il mondo sanza gente").

The providential course of history is represented in the *Divine Comedy,* as it is in the *Aeneid,* by the trajectory of the sun from east to west. Once it is established that this is the linear course of history, then the proud man who, in his excess, would outstrip history, or grace, dies a shipwreck even if enfolded in the arms of Penelope. In other words, Ulysses' journey in the *Divine Comedy* exists on exactly the same plane of reality as does Dante's: a journey of the body which stands for a journey of the soul. If it were otherwise, then it would be difficult to understand why Dante would use the figure as a moral *exemplum* as he does in the very beginning of the canto:

> Allor mi dolsi, e ora mi ridoglio
> quando drizzo la mente a ciò ch'io vidi,
> più lo 'ngegno affreno ch'i' non soglio,
> perché non corra che virtù nol guidi; (*Inf.* XXVI, 19–22)
>
> I sorrowed then, and sorrow now again, when I turn my mind to what I saw; and I curb my genius more than I am wont, lest it run where virtue does not guide it.

It cannot be coincidental that in the previous canto Dante's poetry has reached the heights of virtuosity with the double metamorphosis of the thieves, a display of his poetic powers that led him first to challenge Ovid and Lucan and then finally to repent for letting his pen run away with him. The episode of Ulysses thus provides a moral *exemplum* metalinguistically as well, as a poetic representation of such gravity that it both warns against and atones for a poetic excess beyond the poem's didactic needs. Dante's warning to himself at the same time furnishes one more indication of the way in which Ulysses stands for a kind of writing as well as for a habit of mind.

The navigational image serves admirably as a metaphor both for the journey of the mind and the progress of the poem. The metaphoric use of the image is what accounts for the close analogy that we feel between the figure of Ulysses and Dante himself. We have already seen several examples of its use as a figure for the pilgrim's journey, but equally obvious is the use of the figure in the *exordia* of the *Purgatorio* and the *Paradiso,* Dante's adaptations of an epic topos studied in detail by Curtius.[3] The "bark of genius" ("navicella del mio ingegno"; *Purg.* I, 2) sets sail in purgatory just as the pilgrim reaches the shore of the mountain. The use of the word "ingegno" associates the journey with the poem—both are in a sense itineraries of the mind. At a deeper level, the journey is the poem, for the ultimate objective of the pilgrim is to become the poet. In the beginning of the canto of Ulysses, it is as an admonition to his *ingegno* that Dante introduces the episode: "E più lo 'ngegno affreno ch'i non soglio" (*Inf.* XXVI, 21) (I curb my genius more than I am wont).

For this and other reasons, it seems safe to presume that the figure of Ulysses, for all of its apparent historicity, is at the same time a palinodic moment in the *Divine Comedy.* As Bruno Nardi once suggested, it implies a retrospective view of Dante himself both as poet and as man, when with confidence and *ingegno* he embarked upon the writing of the *Convivio,* a work never completed, which began by stating that all men desire to know and that ultimate happiness resides in the pursuit of knowledge. Ulysses would then stand for a moment in the pilgrim's life. In the recapitulation of salvation history, that is, the history of the Christian soul, Ulysses' story would stand for the disastrous prelude to the preparation for grace, a misleading guide before the encounter with Virgil. Whatever the validity of the suggestion, it goes a long way toward explaining at once the greatness of the figure and the harsh judgment upon him implied by his position in hell.

The distance that separates Ulysses' point of shipwreck from the pilgrim's survival, or, for that matter, the *Convivio* from the *Purgatorio*, is measured by the descent into hell. This is literally true, according to the geography of the poem, and figuratively true as well, as the descent into the self, *intra nos*, is the prerequisite for the kind of transcendent knowledge that all men desire. It is a journey that cannot be undertaken without a guide and here, too, Virgil spans the gap that separates Dante from the pre-Christian or pre-conversion time represented by Ulysses.

I have said that the contrast between Virgil and Ulysses in the poem is not one of language, but rather of the uses to which an almost identical rhetoric is put. In literary terms, Ulysses is the man whose greatness determines epic history, while Aeneas is the man whose greatness is determined by the providential destiny thrust upon him. Both history and the individual follow a circular course in the *Odyssey,* while the pathos of Virgilian epic seems to lie in the discrepancy between the linear destiny of Rome and the cyclical turn of the seasons, to which individual men remain forever subject. Christian time shattered both circles, however, and insisted on the perfect congruence, in the geometric sense, between history and the soul. I should like to turn now to Dante's transformation of that inner circularity, the life of man as seen by the ancients. In dramatic terms, we have seen how the figure of Ulysses is undercut by the *pietas* of Aeneas. We must now examine briefly how Aeneas is in turn superseded by the new alter-Aeneas in Dante's poem.

Earlier I described Virgilian pathos with a reference to the simile of falling leaves, borrowed from Homer (*Il.* VI, 146), with which Virgil described the beginning of Aeneas' journey across the River Styx. It happens that Dante imitates that simile as the pilgrim is about to cross the River Acheron, thereby inviting the sophisticated reader to make an important structural comparison of Dante's poem with Virgil's:

> Come d'autunno si levan le foglie
>   l'una appresso de l'altra, fin che 'l ramo
>   vede a la terra tutte le sue spoglie,
> similemente il mal seme d'Adamo
>   gittansi di quel lito ad una ad una,
>   per cenni come augel per suo richiamo. (*Inf.* III, 112–117)

> As the leaves fall away in autumn, one after another, till the bough sees all its spoils upon the ground, so there the evil seed of Adam: one by one they cast themselves from that shore at signals, like a bird to its lure.

The purpose of the simile in both Homer and Virgil was to render some idea of the vast numbers of men who have fallen before the inexorable law of nature. Generations come and go, multitudinous as leaves which succeed one another. This purpose seems to be directly undercut by Dante's adverbial modifiers "l'una appresso dell' altra," (*Inf.* III, 113) and "ad una ad una" (*Inf.* III, 116) in both tercets. If the point of the original simile is in the vast numbers of men who die, then the point is blunted when the poet invites us to follow the fall of each individual leaf from the bough to the ground. Dante's simile seems to insist on the fact that this fall is a collective phenomenon which is at the same time very much an individual destiny, leading to a grammatically decisive conclusion: "fin che 'l ramo/vede a la terra tutte le sue spoglie" (*Inf.* III, 113–14; till the bough sees all its spoils on the ground). The verb personifies the bough in a daring way and substitutes its perspective for that of the detached epic poet. The word *spoglie* (spoils), moreover, suggests a wanton loss that is far from the inevitability of an autumnal fall. If this branch can look at its own spoils, presumably with sadness, then the implication is that this need not have happened: in short, that God's tree was meant to be evergreen.

The reflexive verbs in Dante's Virgilian imitation, "si levano," "gittansi," seem particularly appropriate, for the point of Dante's verses is that if this fall from God's tree is a destiny, then it is one deliberately chosen. Just as tragedy is out of place in a Christian context, so is Virgil's elegiac tone—these leaves chose to separate themselves from the tree of life. This would seem to be the difference between Virgil's introduction to the world of the dead and Dante's introduction to the world of the damned. Two different deaths are represented by these two similes: Dante would have referred to the Virgilian death as the first death, a death of the body. His own simile, however, refers to "la seconda morte"—a death of the soul (*Inf.* I, 117). The death of the *Inferno* is a decision and not a fate. It is also irreversible. For these leaves, there is not even the biological comfort of a collective spring to come.

We should note in passing that this distinction between the two kinds of death is useful in explaining the difference between the natural death of Ulysses, largely irrelevant to Dante, and the death by shipwreck which he devised. The first is an organic fact of the body, but the second is a shipwreck of the soul, which can happen at any time and which, while there is life and grace, can be survived.

This probably explains why Virgil asks Ulysses about his death in a curiously tortuous sentence:

> . . . ma l' un di voi dica
> dove, per lui, perduto a morir gissi. (*Inf.* XXVI, 83–84)
>
> . . . but let the one of you tell where he went,
> lost, to die.

The strange passive construction was also used by Virgil in the first canto, when he said that the Emperor of Heaven did not will that "per me si vegna," that heaven be arrived at *by* me (*Inf.* I, 126), the passive construction in both cases indicating divine predestination. Furthermore, *perduto* (lost) would be a redundancy if this were simply a question of physical death. As it is, Virgil's question, "how, when you were lost, did you arrive at death," most likely refers to Ulysses' damnation, of which drowning is merely the figure, as it was for the fathers of the Church ever since St. Ambrose.

To return to Dante's transformation of the Virgilian simile, it would seem to be emblematic of the shift in time, from the cyclical time of organic nature to the linear time of the soul. The perspective is shifted as well, from the elegiac to the theocentric, from history viewed with the momentary and poignant detachment of a poetic sensibility to history viewed from the transcendent aspect of eternity. The basis of the comparison is changed as well: the point of Virgil's simile is to compare the almost infinite number of souls to falling leaves: "quam multa." Here, however, the comparison is in the manner of the fall—"come." By a distortion that would probably be considered a poetic violence in the hands of a lesser poet, a horizontal motion, the crossing of a river, is compared to the downward motion of falling leaves in order to indicate that this crossing is in fact a "fall" in the spiritual sense of the word.

The last part of the simile once more stresses personal choice, in a daring and original way. Turning back to the Virgilian original, the phenomenon of the migration of birds serves to elaborate the theme of the cyclical turn of the seasons: "as birds swarm landward from the deep gulf, when the chill of the year routs them overseas and drives them to sunny lands." Dante accepts the comparison of the flight of birds as an emblem for the flight of the soul—indeed, some of the most exquisite figures of the poem derive from this comparison—but their flight is no longer an instinctive response that changes with the seasons: "Like a bird," writes Dante, "to its lure" (*Inf.* III, 117). The terms borrowed from medieval falconry seem particularly apt for describing a motion that is at once instinctive and a conditioned response to the falconer's deception, a natural inclination toward a totally alien goal. In terms of this figure, all of the souls in hell arrived there as did Ulysses, at the end of a "folle volo," a mad flight.

At the very beginning of Virgil's tutelage, the sharp distinctions between the poetry of the *Aeneid* and that of the *Divine Comedy* are perceptible in the most minute details. At the end of Virgil's guidance, the transformation is dramatic and definitive. At the end of the sixth book of the *Aeneid,* the famous *tu Marcellus eris* (*Aen.* VI, 883) passage is perhaps the high point of Virgilian pathos, where human grief for precocious death can derive almost no consolation from the eternity of Rome. Virgil's providential history might redeem, or at least pacify the world, but the poet is powerless before death and can do nothing more than offer purple funereal lilies in mourning: "Manibus date lilia plenis" (*Aen.* VI, 883). It happens that this is the only line quoted from the original in Dante's *Divine Comedy*, but it appears, not at the ending of the underworld voyage, as one might expect, but at the ending of the *Purgatorio,* where the angels sing precisely those words to greet Beatrice's return from a precocious death with the white lilies of the Resurrection.

At the beginning of this essay, I suggested a distinction between the circular and the linear forms of human time and of narrative structure and said that Dante's poem could be characterized by neither figure because it partook of both. The problematic, tentative view of the pilgrim is a novelistic striving toward a kind of finality which can be described as a linear goal: the death of the pilgrim and the end of his story. At the same time, this ending is a new beginning, for it marks the birth of the poet, who has been with us from the start. There is a circularity to the adventure as well: the voice of the poet which ends as it began. The central mystery of Christianity is at the same time the resolution of the epic and novelistic duality, or would be if it could adequately be represented. Representing that synthesis of linearity and circularity is as out of reach, however, as is the squaring of the circle:

Qual è 'l geomètra che tutto s'affige
  per misurar lo cerchio, e non ritrova,
  pensando, quel principio ond' elli indige,
tal era io a quella vista nova. (*Par.* XXXIII, 133–36)

As is the geometer who wholly applies himself to measure the circle, and finds not, in pondering, the principle of which he is in need, such was I at that new sight.

9. Bestial Sign and Bread of Angels: *Inferno* XXXII and XXXIII

THE EPISODE OF CONTE UGOLINO, virtually the last in the *Inferno,* has been considered through the centuries as one of the most moving accounts of human suffering and, by some readers, as one of the most grotesque. From the Renaissance to the time of Shelley, it has been read as an attempt to understand the most unfathomable of evils. The suffering of the children, like the slaughter of the innocents, represents the most radical instance of the irreducibility of evil, just as the mystery of salvation is represented, at a structurally corresponding place in the *Paradiso,* by the joy of the children in the celestial rose. This formal correspondence dramatizes the limits of salvation history, limits more familiar to modern readers, perhaps, in the form given to them by Dostoevsky. In *The Brothers Karamazov,* Ivan asks: "What of the *children,* Alyosha?" and, as if in answer, the novel ends with the anticipation of the Resurrection in the form of a love-feast, with the children gathered around the table recalling the former life. In the *Inferno,* Dante confronts both the stumbling block of children's suffering and, as we shall see, the traditional Christian answer. The episode is thus neither merely anecdotal nor simply another infernal monstrosity; it is rather a paradigm of death and salvation, stripped of comforting illusions and conventions, and so epitomizes the theme of the entire poem.

At the same time the episode is a paradigm of political understanding, representing a model of what civic life has become within a purely secular order. Seen from the perspective of the *Inferno,*

Dante's own political philosophy, expressed in his treatise *On Monarchy,* seems an optimistic dream. It may be said that Ugolino's condemnation to the circle of political traitors functions as a political palinode, an Augustinian and very nearly despairing view of the possibilities for social peace in the political order. Augustine defined the city as a group of human beings joined together by the love of the same object. Since there were for him only two ultimate objects of love, God and the "self" (however illusory), it followed that there were only two cities: the City of God and the city of man. Similarly, I will suggest, in the episode of Ugolino the alternatives are narrowed down to two in man's relationship to his fellow man: communion or cannibalism.

Finally, the episode has been something of a scandal in the history of Dante criticism, for Ugolino's story ends with a verse whose meaning has been the subject of much debate. Unlike other interpretive problems in the text, however, this crux is part of its own theme, rather than the accidental product of semantic history. The critical stumbling block of Ugolino's last words marks the intersection of Dante's theme with his poetics and so constitutes one of those interpretive moments that the attentive reader comes to expect in a poem whose story, at one level, is its own genesis. Like virtually all of the sinners in hell, Ugolino does not grasp the import of his own words and so demands, on our part, an ironic reading, a *mystificatio* that permits us to see Dante's eschatological hope in Ugolino's eternal despair. The succession of such ironic moments in the characterizations of the *Inferno* adds up to the allegory of that *cantica.* At the same time, the debates of the critics in this and in other cantos reproduce its ironic tensions, translating them into an allegory of interpretation. We shall see that the significance of Ugolino's story is revealed by the struggle of his critics to arrive at that significance.

To begin with the theme itself, there are several indications that Dante intends it to be read, not only as a human and familial horror, but also as political tragedy. In the first place, we are in lowest hell, in the circle of treachery, where Ugolino is specifically identified as a traitor to his city, Pisa. He begins his story by explaining (XXXIII, 15) why he is such a neighbor, "tal vicino," to Ruggieri. Ugolino's dream, in which he is cast as a wolf and his children as whelps, is politically emblematic—we recognize in the animal an emblem for the Guelf party. This allusion to contemporary

Italian factionalism is reinforced by the identity of the traitors. Ugolino thinks of himself as a man who *was* a count: "i' fui conte Ugolino" (v. 13). His bitter enemy is and remains forever Archbishop Ruggieri: "questi è l'arcivescovo Ruggieri" (v. 14). Ugolino's eternal hatred seems to be as much directed against the office as against the person who held it. The two men stand for enemy institutions in Dante's day: the Church, in the person of the archbishop, and the Empire, in the person of the count. Finally, Ugolino's story evokes the narrator's invective against the city of Pisa, calling it a "New Thebes" (v. 89). The ancient city, raised from dragon's teeth and nurtured in parricide and fratricide, is Dante's model for the city of man throughout the *Inferno,* the crystallization of the disease that afflicts all of mankind.

Confirmation of a political dimension of meaning in the episode is provided for us in the sixth canto of the *Purgatorio,* when Sordello and Virgil embrace at the mention of their city, Mantova. The embrace occasions the narrator's bitter tirade in a passage which has become a set-piece for Italian political rhetoric to the present day. It pictures the body politic as wracked by the disease of violence and compares the city of Florence to a sick woman, unable to find relief from her pain as she tosses and turns in a featherbed. The image that Dante uses to describe the illness recalls the infernal situation:

> e ora in te non stanno sanza guerra
> li vivi tuoi, e l'un l'altro si rode
> di quei ch'un muro e una fossa serra. (vv. 82–84)

> and now in you your living abide not without
> war, and of those whom one wall and one moat
> shut in, one gnaws at the other!

Thus, the savage hatred Ugolino expresses for his eternal enemy is not only a reenactment of Tydeus' hatred for Menalippus in the story of Thebes, but is also a dramatization of the disease that affects contemporary society. Ugolino and Ruggieri are enclosed in a single ditch; the passage from the *Purgatorio* serves in retrospect to give that situation a universal dimension of meaning, making of it an emblem of the Italian political order.

In the tangle of violence for which Ugolino and Ruggieri are the paradigm, vengeance is the law. Where every person is a god unto himself, the existence of another is perceived as a menace to be combated to the death. At the same time, this precarious uniqueness or individuality is continually threatened by the increasing resemblance of each to each. The social consequence of this struggle is a generalized violence, a parody of the city, such as is represented in the *Inferno.* Virtually every episode of the *cantica* reveals this alienation in physical proximity. This may explain why so many of the souls in hell are represented in pairs or groups, even when only one speaks to the pilgrim or to his guide. It is as if the heroic uniqueness of Ulysses, for example, were deliberately undercut by the silent presence of Diomede, who is physically indistinguishable from him, just as the thieves, for all of their individual virtuosity, are literally interchangeable. So too, in the episode under consideration, even the syntax seems to stress reciprocity, in spite of the fact that Ugolino's claim to justice rests on the distinction between himself and his enemy.

Reciprocity seems to govern phrases such as "l'un capo a l'altro era cappello" (XXXII, 126) (the head of the one was a hood for the other), while phrases such as "io vidi *due* ghiacciati in *una* buca" (125) (I saw two frozen in one hole) underscore the political irony, a unity in multiplicity. At the same time, the horrible isolation of Ugolino is reinforced by reflexive verbs that serve to distance him from his reified enemy: "si rose" (130) and "tu . . . ti mangi" (134). As in the Augustinian description of sin, to assert one's subjectivity is to treat the other as object, reified as though he were a piece of bread, and the consummation is literal: "come 'l pan per fame si manduca" (127) (as bread is devoured for hunger). Ugolino and Ruggieri are alone together, with their master-slave roles, "maestro e donno" (XXXIII, 28), symmetrically reversed. In his dream, Ugolino was hounded by Ruggieri; in infernal reality, he is a dog to Ruggieri's flesh. The rule of reciprocity finds its counterpart in the attitude of the pilgrim, who says that he will repay Ugolino for what he has suffered (XXXII, 136). The implication is that Ugolino's portrait in the *Inferno* is what he deserves, despite his protestations. The horror alluded to in the ending of XXXII builds up the suspense and carries us to the next canto; it is literally occasioned by the ghastly scene which the pilgrim witnesses, but perhaps also contains an allusion to the greater horror recounted in the tale: the suffering and death of innocent children. Ugolino and Ruggieri are damned for the same crime, of which the children are the innocent victims:

Che se 'l conte Ugolino aveva voce
  d'aver tradita te de le castella,
  non dovei tu i figliuoi porre a tal croce.
Innocenti facea l'età novella,
  novella Tebe, Uguiccione e 'l Brigata
  e li altri due che 'l canto suso appella. (vv. 85–90)

For if Count Ugolino had the name of betraying you of your castles, you ought not to have put his children to such torture. Their youthful years, you modern Thebes, made Uguiccione and Brigata innocent, and the other two that my song names above.

The phrase "tal croce" is more than a figure of speech here. The innocent victim placed on a cross by an act of treachery cannot but recall in this, of all poems, the archetypal Victim and the Crucifixion.

Although critics have not noticed it until recently,[1] the Christological language that is used to describe the children seems the most salient feature of the story. Apart from the word *croce* in the passage just cited, perhaps the clearest allusion to the passion of Christ is in verse 69: "Padre mio, che non m'aiuti?" echoing the words of Christ on the cross: "My God, my God, why has thou forsaken me?" The children's words are the last words spoken by the Savior before his death. The Christological suggestion is equally strong in verse 61 where the children, with devastating naiveté, offer themselves to their father:

  "Padre, assai ci fia men doglia
se tu mangi di noi: tu ne vestisti
queste misere carni, e tu le spoglia." (vv. 61–63)

"Father, it will be far less painful to us if you eat of us; you did clothe us with this wretched flesh, and do you strip us of it!"

They echo at once the eucharistic sacrifice and the words of Job: "The Lord giveth and the Lord taketh away. Blessed be the Name of the Lord." It must not be supposed that the allusions to Christ's passion are merely pietistic embellishments to contrast with the infernal horror story; they are in fact the key for the whole dramatic interpretation. The point of the language here is that the suffering of the children is of a sacred order, carrying with it a redemptive possibility. To accept such suffering with total selflessness and no thought of vengeance is to put an end to the otherwise eternal series of violent acts, making possible a communion that was not possible before. The spirit of their words offers the hope of a shared grief and a reconciliation to their father, but he sees in their death only a spur to his infernal retribution, thereby repeating in hell the pattern set forth in his dream. His tragedy is a failure of interpretation, as well as an inability to accept the suffering of his children.

The Christological pattern is not only linguistic, but narrative as well, for anyone with an acquaintance with biblical typology. To speak of a sacrifice of a son in the presence of a father who only half understands the gesture is inevitably to recall, if only by contrast, the moment of the foundation of Israel in the story of Abraham and Isaac. To a Christian interpreter, that story is the foreshadowing of the Redemption; the sacrificial animal substituted at the last moment for Isaac is the prefiguration of the *Agnus Dei.* The language of Ugolino's children recalls at once the naive obedience of Isaac and the resignation of the Savior. As so often in the poem, Dante seems to have collapsed both the figure and its fulfillment into a single historical event which is both itself and part of the pattern of salvation history. The generational struggle of fathers and sons, resolved in the covenant that founded Israel in the story of Abraham and Isaac, finds a new representation in contemporary Pisa, where it ends in Theban failure.

Because Ugolino's story ends as an emblem of political as well as human failure, Dante refers to Pisa as a new Thebes. Every city, every covenant has its foundational myth, cast in terms of the smallest social unit, the family. Israel has its Abrahamic sacrifice and Thebes, by contrast, has the story of Oedipus. Dante's "*novella* Tebe" may be said to be Theban tragedy in a New Testament perspective, where the Christological promise is no longer a messianic dream but is rather a bitter and despairing memory. The story of Abraham and Isaac represented an alternative to the repeated succession of fathers and sons in the Theban story, where the temporary survival of one generation seemed to demand the destruction of the other. Abraham is prepared to give up his lineage in the sacrifice of his son, and Isaac is ready to give up his life. In this mutual surrender to the will of God, a compact is formed, a third term that founds the new nation.

The Christ event was believed by Christians to represent a new and eternal covenant, replacing the Abrahamic for all time and making communion possible.

In this perspective, the story of Ugolino is a sign of a second, perhaps definitive failure of men to live in peace according to a covenant. Insofar as the Abrahamic typology is evoked in violent contrast, the story is reminiscent of the Jewish legend of the woman who was forced to sacrifice her seven sons during the Roman persecution: "Go and tell Father Abraham: Let not your heart swell with pride! You built one altar, but I have built seven. . . . What is more, yours was a trial; mine was an accomplished fact."[2] The bitterness in Dante's story is reserved, however, not for a messianic promise unfulfilled, but rather for the failure to understand the promise implicit in Abraham's words: "The Lord will provide."

For all the sympathy that the portrayal of Ugolino has aroused in readers of the poem, beginning with De Sanctis in the nineteenth century, there can be little doubt that he is condemned by Dante not only as a traitor but also for his inability to grasp the spiritual meaning in the letter of his children's words. In another context, he says of himself that he turned to stone at the sound of the nailing of the door—that *duritia cordis,* as well as his subsequent blindness, both Pauline signs of the interpretive obtuseness of non-believers, blind him equally to the spiritual significance of his children's words. He begins by not taking their offer seriously and ends, if we are to trust the traditional and unsophisticated reading of his last words, with a bestial literalism. That unspeakable ending transforms the potentially Abrahamic situation into Theban horror, suggesting quite literally that no matter how great is Ugolino's love for his children, the father's survival, for however brief a time, depends on the destruction of his sons, whose bodies he treats as he does that of his enemy. In the absence of a covenant, it is every man for himself and a man for himself is a beast.

Ugolino's failure is an inability to interpret the Christian hope contained in the words of his children. In the episode, he is portrayed primarily as an interpreter, first of his dream and then his life, but the meaning he reads is always death. His dream seems to foreshadow his capture and ends with a grim prophecy: "con l'agute scane / mi parea lor veder fender li fianchi" (35–36) (and it seemed to me I saw their flanks ripped by the sharp fangs). He infers from this incident in his dream no more than can be learned from any of the prophecies in hell: that is, that he and his children will die. Finally, when the children beg him for help, he is struck silent in incomprehension.

Ugolino's inability to understand his children's words is matched by the inability of Dante critics to understand his last words: "Poscia, più che 'l dolor, potè il digiuno" (v. 75) (then, hunger was stronger than grief). A traditional reading sees in the verse an allusion to cannibalism, confirming a legend that surrounded the death of the historical Ugolino and the children. Another group of critics rejects that reading, preferring instead to interpret the verse as an allusion to Ugolino's death, construing it as follows: "Hunger succeeded in killing me, whereas grief did not."[3] In other words, they interpret Ugolino exactly as *he* interpreted his own dream—the ripping of flanks by teeth as simply a prophecy of death. However interesting the theme of death may be as literary motif, it is a banality in the afterlife; something more is contained in Ugolino's words although it is *unspeakable.* In the same way, we can see that something more was contained in Ugolino's dream than he realized upon his awakening—not simply a message of death, but an inverted drama of damnation.

The point of Ugolino's story in hell is not simply that he died. He tells us specifically that it is the *how* of his death that is significant:

> Che per l'effetto de' suo' mai pensieri,
> fidandomi di lui, io fossi preso
> e poscia morto, dir non è mestieri;
> però quel che non puoi avere inteso,
> cioè *come* la morte mia fu cruda,
> udirai. . . (vv. 16–20)

> How, by effect of his ill devising, I, trusting in him, was taken and thereafter put to death, there is no need to tell; but what you cannot have heard, that is, how cruel my death was, you shall hear.

The specific nature of his grief is, however, unspeakable. When Ugolino says, at the beginning of his story, "tu vuo' ch'io rinovelli disperato dolor" (v. 5), he is echoing Aeneas' words to Dido in the second book of the *Aeneid,* with the first and most important word omitted, precisely the word "unspeakable": "*Infandum,* Regina, iubes renovare dolorem."[4] The omission of that word in Dante's allusion seems to underscore its import in this even more terrible context. Nevertheless, as we shall see, the absence of this sign is itself significant. On closer inspection, the whole of the episode seems very much concerned with signs and their interpretation. As it begins, in Canto XXXII, the pilgrim sees Ugolino gnawing his enemy as if he were eating bread, but recognizes that his eating has a significance, as a *sign* of hatred: "O tu che mostri per sì bestial segno / odio sovra colui che tu ti mangi" (v. 133–34) (O you who by so bestial a sign show hatred against him whom you devour). The bestiality of the gesture is somewhat tempered by the fact that it appears to be a dramatization of a Pauline figure describing the absence of charity: "But if you bite and devour one another, take heed or you will be consumed by one another" (Gal. 5:15). It is important to notice that in this introduction, the contrast between "hunger" and "hatred" is tantamount to the difference between eating and speaking, between bestial reflex and paralanguage. The action, whether reflex or sign, remains the same, and Dante underscores the ambivalence of the gesture with a paradoxical description: *bestiale,* because eating is natural to beasts; *segno,* because in this case, eating has human significance. The binary opposition between hatred and hunger is thus the opposition between significance and non-significance, between language and nature.

This opposition reappears in Ugolino's dream as does the "bestial segno." The dream, on the surface of it, seems an action of beasts, the wolf and the whelps ripped apart by the fangs of the dogs. On interpretation, however, the dream has the meaning of a sign that prefigures both death and, in the symmetrical inversion characteristic of the thematics of vengeance, the form of damnation. Ugolino says of his dream that "del futuro mi squarciò il velame" (XXXIII, 27). The "rending of the veil" echoes the rending of the veil of the temple at the Crucifixion and so constitutes one more recall to Christ's Passion, yet it should be noticed that the specifically prophetic quality of the dream could be perceived only after death; that is, after it was too late. At his awakening, Ugolino understood only its most generic meaning: he and his children would die. In this respect, the dream resembles all of the infernal prophecies. Like the ancient oracles, they are accurate in detail to an extent that can be appreciated only after the future has come to pass, at which point they cannot help.

The specific significance of Ugolino's dream is that it prefigures the form of his damnation, but that is something he can know only in hell. The ironic distance between his earthly reading of his dream and the infernal reality, between the generic message of death and the specific form of infernal cannibalism, corresponds exactly to the critical dispute about the meaning of his last words in the text. Ugolino's dream, as we shall see, is Dante's allegory for the reading of his own text.

Most significantly, the gesture of biting human flesh reappears when Ugolino sees himself mirrored in the faces of his children and bites his hand in a gesture of desperation: *dolore.* The children apparently misunderstand its nature as a sign and take it to be instead an attempt to eat himself:

> ambo le man per lo dolor mi morsi;
> ed ei, pensando ch'io 'l fessi per voglia
> di manicar, di sùbito levorsi . . . (vv. 58–60)

> I bit both my hands for grief. And they, think-
> ing I did it for hunger, suddenly rose up . . .

Once more, the opposition is between significance and non-significance, between *dolore* and hunger. The action is ambivalent in exactly the same sense as the *bestial segno,* for the children interpret it as a natural desire for food, while their father means it to express his grief. It is at this point that they offer themselves and, by their surrender and innocence, offer as well a redemptive hope. Unlike their father's pain, their *dolore* would be assuaged by their offer. Because their father is a literalist, however, he cannot understand the spiritual significance of their apparently literal statement.

There is a certain condescension implied in Ugolino's suppression of the sign of his grief: "Queta' mi allor per non farli più tristi" (v. 64) (then I calmed myself in order not to make them sadder). The irony, if I am correct in my reading, is that in the passage that follows, he exercises the same discretion, this time to spare the feelings of the pilgrim, by suppressing all mention of what must be assumed to have been the very same action: the biting of flesh that was symbolically, but no less really, his own: "then, hunger was stronger than grief." Although the gesture has been suppressed, the same binary opposition is involved between significance and non-significance, but this time it is clear that we have moved into the realm of the purely biological, not *grief* but *hunger* motivated the reappearance of the same action. We are spared the details by the particular form of ellipsis known as *reticentia,* used in rhetoric to avoid mentioning horrible or obscene details. Perhaps the most famous Dantesque use of the same figure occurs in the words of Francesca: "Quel giorno più non vi leggemmo avante." At the thematic level, there is no point in suppressing the fact of death here in the afterlife; it is something worse than death that is suppressed by Ugolino. The absence of the sign, in this series of oppositions, must be construed as a sign. There is a very strong implication that in the last moment, he accepts quite literally the offer of his children and simultaneously moves into bestial muteness or, perhaps, noise:

> Quand' ebbe detto ciò, con li occhi torti
> riprese 'l teschio misero co' denti,
> che furo a l'osso, come d'un can, forti. (vv. 76–78)

> When he had said this, with eyes askance he again took hold of the wretched skull with his teeth, which were strong on the bone like a dog's.

Moving away from the purely thematic, we may say that both Ugolino and Francesca exist only as exemplars of their own stories; in short, as literature. The passage from literature to life, from significance to biology, is the functional equivalent, in both stories, to the disappearance of the character.

The movement from *dolore* to *digiuno* in the last lines of Ugolino's story marks the waning of his consciousness and his humanity. It is at this point that language is extinguished and that nature takes over. Ugolino ceases to exist as a speaker and thus as a character. Yet that mute unconsciousness is not the same as death: it is animality. Throughout the canto, the opposition has been between significance and non-significance, between the human and the bestial. Ugolino's last words do indeed report the triumph of biology over language and, in the long run, that triumph is indeed physical death, as the earthbound significance of his dream was death. In the context of hell, however, such a statement would be pure redundancy—in the long run, death is *always* the end term of life. Much more significant is the fact that the intermediate stage of the final entropy in terms of the oppositions set forth in the canto is *bestiality,* the midpoint between humanity and reification, as hunger is the intermediate stage between *disperato dolore* and death. To say that hunger overcame grief is to say that Ugolino moved one step from humanity and one step closer to death by becoming a beast to the flesh of his children. Thereafter, the final step, far from being dreaded, would seem precisely the relief that Ugolino has himself previously sought: "ahi dura terra, perché non t'apristi?" (66) (Ah, hard earth! why did you not open?). Whatever the sensibilities of the modern critic, in hell at least, there are some things worse than death.

The words of the children, we recall, held out a redemptive possibility—their literalism is of a different order. To discover it, we have simply to oppose and recombine the terms of the oppositions that we have established: the "savage repast," "fiero pasto," has its counterpart in the sacred feast, the *agape.* If the first is a sign of despair and hatred, then the second is a sign of hope and love: the Eucharist is the eating of a living body, *come 'l pane per fame si manduca.* As the Eucharist is the opposite of the corpse, so communion is the opposite of cannibalism and the bread is not only the "bread of angels," but also of peace in the human community, *panis concordiae.* Eating food is an action in the biological order, whether the food is bread or human flesh. When it becomes significant behavior in hell, Dante calls it a "bestiale segno." The opposite of that phrase would in fact be "divine food," or, to use the phrase that Dante uses elsewhere, the "pane degli angeli." What seemed at first to be simply an oxymoric phrase invented by Dante to describe the lowest degradation of the highest powers turns out to be the logical opposite of the central mystery of Christianity: not bestial, but angelic; not simply a sign, but a presence. The children's offer is sacramental, a sign that presents what it represents. To Ugolino, as to the reader, a literal reading of their words suggests cannibalism.

I have suggested that throughout Ugolino's narrative, the action is the same, alternately ascribed to the realm of biology or to the realm of signification. The same dichotomy is expressed in medieval terms by Dante's text in the opposition of physical hunger to spiritual hunger. The offer of the children to their father is the same as Christ's offer to his disciples: a spiritual eating of the *living* bread, which absorbs the recipient into the mystical body of Christ. In the seventh book of the *Confessions,* the voice of God says to Augustine, "I am the food of grown men; grow, and thou shalt feed upon me; nor shalt thou convert me, like the food of thy flesh into thee, but thou shalt be converted into me."[5] Ugolino's children, whether they understand it or not (the understanding of the children whose words lead to the conversion of Augustine in the eighth book, for instance, is irrelevant to the efficacy of their words), offer their father their suffering as an example, the promise of ultimate deliverance and the eschatological hope for the unity of the human community. The Eucharist, the central mystery of Christianity, is the message that Ugolino cannot understand. His death by starvation is a dramatic reenactment of the interpretive failure as it is represented in the New Testament.

In the sixth chapter of the Gospel of John, Christ offers the Jews two kinds of bread, the letter and the spirit. They come not for a sign, but for bread. They associate the miracle of the loaves and fishes with the manna that came down from heaven to assuage the hunger of the Jews in the desert, but Jesus says, "Moses did not give you the bread from heaven, but my Father gives you the true bread, which gives life to the world . . . so that if anyone eat of it he will not die. I am the living bread." The Jews ask the same question that might be asked of Ugolino's children: "How can this man give us his flesh to eat?" He replies, "He who eats my flesh and drinks my blood has life everlasting and I will raise him up on the last day." The Jews are left in perplexity: "This is a hard saying. Who can listen to it?" The "scandal," as Jesus calls it, the stumbling block of the cross, is the same as the crux in our text. Christ's words retrospectively gloss the natural hunger of the Jews in their exodus as a figure for the spiritual hunger for the Christian comfort, just as the children gloss Ugolino's grief, as he bites his own hand, as a figure for his spiritual hunger. Ugolino's "sensible" reading of their offer, like the "sensible" reading of Jesus' words (or Freud's reading in *Totem and Taboo*), interprets it as though it were an invitation to cannibalism. It is this literalism, this *letter* that, in the end, "kills" Ugolino spiritually. Once more, Dante glosses the Bible's words with a historical situation, substituting literal starvation for the metaphoric hunger of the Jews. Without that background text, the episode seems merely a grotesque anecdote.

The meaning of this chapter of the Gospel of John has occasioned centuries of debate, but on one point medieval thought was unanimous: the foundation of the Eucharist was at the same time the foundation of the Church, the mystical body of Christ. Henri de Lubac has shown that the phrase "mystical body" was in fact first used to describe the presence of Christ in the sacrament, in an age when there was no contradiction between "mystical" and "real," and only later applied to the Church.[6] For our purposes, the important point is the association between the Eucharist and what might be called its "political" dimension of meaning. It suggests that the political overtones in the story of Ugolino are likewise intrinsic to its theme. When Ugolino bites his own hand from grief and subsequently turns on the flesh of his children, the analogy between the members of his body and the "members" of the mystical body makes the same point as the eucharistic sacrifice. Moreover, it provides us with the necessary link between his behavior toward his enemy in hell and his behavior on earth: gnawing the head of his neighbor is analogous to gnawing his own hand, for both he and Ruggieri were members of the human community.

At the same time, the mystery of the Eucharist is a mystery of interpretation. The word *mysterion* itself, in one of its acceptances, in fact refers to the hidden relationship between the sign and its significance in the indissoluble unity of the sacrament. It is in this sense that the word comes to be synonymous with the word "allegory," the search for the "mystic" sense. In a tradition that goes back to St. Augustine, the indissoluble unity of the letter and the spirit is what Christ offers his disciples when He calls himself the *living bread.* For the Jews who do not understand Jesus' words, like Ugolino who does not understand his children's words, the flesh is dead. Augustine says: "They understand it in the sense of dead bodies that are torn apart or that are sold by butchers, not in the sense of bodies quickened by the spirit." In the same paragraph, he makes it clear that the analogy holds in the realm of signs as well: "Whence comes to us the sound of words, if not from the voice of the flesh? How could Jesus' words have come to us had they not been written down? And these are works of the flesh, thanks to the spirit that causes it to move as an instrument."[7]

Ugolino and his children are at opposite ends of the drama of salvation and, at the same time, at the opposite ends of signification. The children, in their apparent naive literalism, offer themselves as food and in so doing, present themselves as a sign for which the text offers no explicit signification. In symmetrical opposition, the last words of Ugolino offer us a signification for which there is no apparent sign. Critics who refuse to see in this *reticentia* anything but death are forced to read it as pure tautology and are at the same time blind to the eucharistic meaning of the children's offer. They are undoubtedly correct for any *literal* reading of the episode, but that is the point: a literalist who refuses to acknowledge the spirit that animates the text reifies it as a cannibal reifies the human body. The letter alone is dead.

The central interpretive problem of the canto of Ugolino turns out to be its theme: Ugolino's critics dramatize the difficulty they seek to resolve. Put most simply, the problem is the allegorical problem of the relationship of the spirit and the letter, of the Word and the flesh. To read only death in Ugolino's words is at the same time to misunderstand his children's offer. Just as Ugolino misreads his own dream and then acts out his misreading, so the critics continue to trope the text itself. The resolution of the difficulty lies beyond the limits of signification, however, for it implies the search for a sign which presents its own representation. Between that Incarnation and the noise of teeth against bone, there is only the constant referentiality of the poem, pointing continually beyond itself.

10. The Sign of Satan

THE LAST CANTO OF THE *Inferno* seems at once the most medieval and, to the modern sensibility, the least satisfactory in the poem. T. S. Eliot[1] found it so grotesque that he advised the student reading the *Inferno* for the first time "to omit the last canto and return to the beginning" or "to wait until he has read and lived for years with the last canto of the *Paradiso.*" The problem seems to be that the infernal emperor is hardly the threat we had been expecting; he himself appears to be suffering as helplessly as the rest of the damned. Moreover, far from the attractive, "curly-haired Byronic hero of Milton," he is repellent in his bestiality and not touching in his tears. Faced with the revolting spectacle, the reader finds himself forced either to agree with Eliot that Dante "made the best of a bad job" or to conclude that we do not understand precisely what "job" the poet had in mind.

It is because we have taken Eliot's advice rather more seriously than he intended that we must reject his conclusion. Since he wrote his famous essay, we have learned to look back to the prologue and ahead to the *Paradiso* as we read the poem and we have come to see that the infernal center is no less than the beginning of a journey which this time is bound to succeed. Satan is a point of departure, the zero-point in the *askesis* of a pilgrim who began from a topsy-turvy world of negative transcendence and is now ready to ascend to the light. The fallen angel is therefore not merely an epic spectacle, but also a stage along the pilgrim's way. It is the pilgrim, not the reader, who sees him as an immobile brute. The implication is that the pilgrim's descent into hell makes this vision possible and constitutes a victory over sin; the figure remains unrecognizable to the reader, who has not gone through hell. The discrepancy between our vision and that of the pilgrim is as great as the abyss separating the first canto of the *Inferno* from the last, which is to say, as great as the distance separating the pilgrim of the *selva oscura* from the pilgrim who is now ready to emerge to the light. To view Dante's infernal portrait as we would Milton's and therefore to find it wanting is to read the poem as though it were an epic of creation rather than a novel of the self. Milton's Satan seems rational and comprehensible because the intention of the poet is apologetic: a justification of the ways of God to men. Dante's Satan seems absurd because it is an exemplum of an experience which is not yet ours: God's justification of this man's way. It will not do to confuse the perspectives.

The justification[2] of the pilgrim, like Plato's *paideia,* begins with a conversion in a cave. What makes Dante's conversion distinctively Christian is the acknowledgment that a man must go through hell in order to arrive at the point of departure. In spite of Dante's efforts to rationalize the process of justification in philosophical terms, it remains mysterious to the non-believer because both its point of arrival and its point of departure are in themselves unintelligible. Vice is more than a matter of ignorance and virtue is more than a matter of knowledge. The pilgrim's journey to justice, the transition from one polarity to the other, differs from its classical antecedents in that it cannot be effected by human effort alone. The movement from vice to virtue, conversion, was accomplished in antiquity by a turning of the soul. The same process in a Christian context called for no less than a death and resurrection, made possible by the event that seemed to rationalists as grotesque as the crossing of Satan does to us—the Crucifixion. Here I intend to show that the grotesque quality of the last canto of the *Inferno* derives precisely from the presence there of reason's traditional stumbling block, the cross, the grotesque absurdity which transformed Plato's *paideia* into *imitatio Christi.*

The pattern for justification was established by Christ's descent in humility, his death on the cross, and his ascent to glory, the Resurrection. The event took place in Jerusalem, the navel of the earth, according to Ezechiel (38:12), or, according to Jeremiah (5:5), the center of the world. Because of this belief in the central location of Jerusalem, the exegetes had no difficulty in associating the arms of the cross with the coordinates of all earthly measurement. The cross became the vantage point from which the Christian was enabled "to comprehend with all the saints what is the breadth, and length, and depth, and height" (Eph. 3:18).[3] But the Crucifixion was an event which had even more profound repercussions; between his death and Resurrection, Christ "also descended into the lower parts of the earth" (Eph. 4:9), in the harrowing of hell. Thus, the descent into hell was correlative with Christ's death on the cross and his ascent with the Resurrection. It follows that the cross of Calvary had its counterpart at the rock-bottom of the universe, the transitional point where descent meets ascent and death meets Resurrection. St. Bonaventure meditates on what the *verus mathematicus,* the spiritual astronomer, sees when he considers the center of the universe with the eye of the soul. The passage provides us with an excellent gloss on the meaning of the Ptolemaic center in Dante's symbolic cosmography:

> The astronomer *(mathematicus)* considers this [central point] not only because he is concerned with the measure of the earth but also because he is concerned with the movement of the higher bodies, which dispose inferior things according to their influence. This central point was Christ in his crucifixion, according to the Psalms: *Rex noster ante saecula operatus est salutem in medio terrae* (Ps. 73:12). Now the earth is obviously the center and therefore the lowest and the least . . . So also the Son of God, the lowest, the poorest and the least, putting on our dust, made of dust, not only came to the surface of the earth but also to the depths of the center, that is, "he brought about our salvation at the center of the earth," for after the crucifixion his soul descended into Hell and restored the heavenly places. That midpoint is our salvation, from which he who withdraws is damned, that is, from the midpoint of humility . . . In that midpoint our salvation is achieved, which is to say, in the humility of the cross.[4]

If we reread the first line of *Inferno* XXXIV with this passage in mind, we begin to see that the parody of the hymn to the cross, *Vexilla regis prodeunt inferni* (the banners of the king of hell go forth), is no mere irony but is rather a signal of the inversion, the crucial turning, about to take place. Satan is fixed at the center in the attitude of parody; nevertheless, he still has a role to play in the regeneration of the pilgrim. The first line of the hymn that is generally recited on the day before Passion Sunday is parodied here in hell, at the same liturgical time, in order to indicate what that role is: the figure of Satan exorcised is in fact an instrument of the pilgrim's salvation. Our shock at the violent juxtaposition of the polar opposites in the drama of Redemption, Christ and the devil, is the reflection of the absurdity of the cross, the point at which the highest meets the lowest and death meets resurrection. The apparently blasphemous parody underscores the parodox of conversion.

The verbal parody of the opening of the canto is matched by the visual parody in the portrait of its central figure. The three heads issuing from a single trunk suggested to Charles Singleton the primitive *patibulum* which is mentioned as a synonym of the cross in the hymn by Venantius Fortunatus.[8] At first glance, then, Satan's outline is somewhat like that of a cross. The impression is reinforced by the comparison of the figure to a windmill, "un molin che 'l vento gira," with its four rectangular arms. These visual impressions of parody are confirmed by a comparison of Dante's description of Satan with a pietistic meditation on the cross that was written in the poet's day. In a passage of Ubertino da Casale's *Arbor Vitae,* which Dante may have read, the original *vexilla* are colored precisely as are the three heads of Satan: "Reflect on your beloved Jesus, oh soul smitten by the dart of compassion, and see him as the three-colored standard *(vexillum)* of your pilgrimage. For the whiteness of his virgin flesh and the livid blackness of the scourges and the redness of the blood that pours forth reveal him to you tri-colored."[6] One might be tempted to propose a direct influence; as a matter of fact, however, the tradition to which Ubertino here alludes is at least as old as St. Augustine. A brief investigation of it will help us to explain not only the relationship of Christ's cross to Satan's in the exegetical tradition, but also the significance of the three colors as they are used in the *Inferno.*

In the seventeenth chapter of Luke (v. 6), Christ speaks to his disciples about faith in terms of the famous mustard seed:

> If you had faith as a mustard seed, you might say to this mulberry tree, 'Be thou plucked up by the root, and be thou planted in the sea'; and it should obey you.

The more familiar version of Christ's words about the mustard seed is the one reported by Matthew (17:20), where faith moves mountains rather than mulberries. The passage from Luke had an altogether independent history, however, thanks in part to St. Ambrose, who helped establish the exegetical tradition for the meaning of the mulberry. He identifies the tree with Satan, planted in the hearts of men, precisely because of its three-colored fruit:

> For the fruit of this tree is white when in flower, then turns red when formed, and black when mature *(nam fructus eius primo albet in flore, deinde iam formatus inrutilat, maturitate nigrescit).* So the devil, deprived by his transgression of the white flower and red power of angelic nature, bristled with the black odor of sin.[7]

Ambrose's colors identify the tree as Satan and at the same time provide Satan with a history that captures in an instant the dynamism of decay. There can be scarcely any doubt of the influence of the gloss on Dante's description of the devil.

But an equally authoritative and contemporary exegete, St. Augustine, gave the mulberry tree a reading totally different from the one just quoted. Commenting upon the same passage, he insists that the mulberry tree represents the gospel of the cross of Christ, *Evangelium crucis Christi,* because of its bloody fruit, *tanquam vulnera in ligno pendentia* (like wounds hanging from the tree).[8] These two glosses by Ambrose and Augustine, respectively, on the passage in Luke entered into the *Glossa Ordinaria* and became traditional allegorizations of the mulberry tree, to be repeated by virtually every important commentator throughout the Middle Ages and well into the Renaissance, either as alternate meanings of Christ's words, *in bono* and *in malo,* or as the tropological and allegorical meaning of the verses.[9] Thus the mulberry tree was associated with both the devil and the cross and its three colors were therefore applied indifferently to either of the two poles in the drama of man's redemption.

The paradox that Dante chose to represent at the center of his symbolic cosmos was already implicit in the exegetical tradition and was available to almost any literate man who could take the hint of the canto's first verse and who knew enough to approach the figure of Satan, not as spectacle, but as figure of the poem's dramatic action. Dante chose this brilliant gloss because it captured a process, a becoming, and was no mere static juxtaposition of "this for that." His colors do not stand for the moral abstractions which the critics have since invented.[10] They are rather a portrait of Satan in all of his awful historicity—a synoptic view of all gradations of the process of corruption. The poet's own survey of the history of Satan serves as a device for the infernal emblem:

> S'el fu sì bel com' elli è ora brutto,
> e contra 'l suo fattore alzò le ciglia,
> ben dee da lui procedere ogne lutto. (vv. 34–36)

> If he was once as beautiful [white] as he is ugly [black] now, and lifted up his brows [red] against his Maker, well may all sorrow proceed from him.

Nowhere is Dante's teleological view of moral history more obvious and nowhere in his allegory is his distaste for the arbitrary more profound.

Just as the exegetes would have recognized in Satan's symbolic colors the process of moral corruption, so the natural philosopher would have recognized in the colors themselves the process of physical decay. This becomes apparent from the poet's retouching of the infernal portrait. The right head of Satan is not white, the first stage of his history, but is waxen instead: "tra bianca e gialla." This realistic touch—it happens that the first fruit of the mulberry is indeed waxen and not white—tells us unmistakably that the irreversible process whose history is painted on Satan's frozen figure is analogous to the physical process of decay that begins from the moment of birth. The colors stand for moral process rather than moral abstractions for the simple reason that the colors themselves are not arbitrarily chosen but are the colors of process in the natural world. The shift to off-white indicates unmistakably that the history which we read in retrospect ended in blackness, the end of the medieval spectrum.

According to some medieval theories of color, changes in heat or humidity are materially responsible for changes in color, while light is merely the occasion that makes the colors perceptible. Black is usually associated with coldness and white with heat. When they operate together "normally," on material that is disposed "normally" *(mediocriter)* the resultant color is red. Bartholomeus Anglicus says precisely this in his authoritative *De rerum proprietatibus:* "black and white, in equal proportions, come together to form a medial color, and thus the color will be equidistant between the extremes, like red."[11] When white is withdrawn from a mixture of whatever color, by a removal of heat, it tends to be replaced by black. The first stage of its fading is toward either the colors *glaucus* and *flavus,* in the case of plants which change color in the fall, or the color *pallidus* in the case of man.[12] Thus the color "tra bianco e giallo" is the moment of the blackening process, the first perceptible indication of the deprivation of light and warmth. The pictorial history of Satan which Dante presents to us begins from the moment of decay, when that angelic creature "per non aspettar lume / cadde acerbo" (through not awaiting light, fell unripe).

The analogy between physical and spiritual processes, such as we have described in the figure of Satan, was neither a poetic parallelism nor Dante's original idea. Scholastics of the thirteenth century saw all change, whether physical or spiritual, in terms of metaphysical principles. In their search to give the theology of grace a basis in natural philosophy, they turned to the teachings of Aristotle for a rationalization of the process of justification. Sanctifying grace was interpreted as an accidental form of the soul; justification was therefore a real change, a generation of a new form—*generatio ad formam.* Charles Singleton[13] has shown the relevance of the Aristotelian philosophy of becoming, *generatio et corruptio,* to Dante's drama of justification, the *Purgatorio.* We need only review some of the principles established by Singleton's essay in order to show the dramatic link between the retrospective panorama of Satan's history, as reflected in his three colors, and the change that the pilgrim is about to undergo. Using the pictorial language of the portrait, it may be said that in the tropological sense the pilgrim is about to move away from the blackness of sin, corresponding to Egypt in the figure of exodus (to which the poet himself alludes: "tal quali / vegnon di là onde 'l Nilo s'avvalla"; *Inf.* XXXIV, 44–45) (such as those who came from whence the Nile descends), toward the red of grace, before his final ascent to the light.

Sanctifying grace was recognized as a form of the soul and the movement to sanctifying grace was therefore a movement to form: *motus ad formam.* No substance, however, may have more than one form at the same time. If in the process of justification there is indeed, as Thomas maintained, the generation of a new form, it is necessary that there be a *corruptio* of the old form before the new one can take its place. The *motus* to a new form may be a continuous linear change; logically, however, it implies two mutations.[14] First, there must be the *mutatio* that is corruption of the old form; this is followed by the second *mutatio,* the generation of the new. To use the spatial language that the scholastics so often employed, we may say that every movement from place to place is logically a departure from one *terminus* and an arrival at another. To phrase the matter differently, in terms of the opposites that Aristotle used abstractly and Dante used in concrete detail, the change from one form to another requires first a mutation from black to non-black, *corruptio* of the old, and then a mutation from non-white to white, *generatio* of the new.[15] The zero point is neither black nor white: "Io non mori', e non rimasi vivo" (*Inf.* XXXIV, 25).

The pilgrim is approaching the central point where descent meets ascent and death meets Resurrection. Singleton has demonstrated that the continuous movement of the pilgrim from sin to justification is a *motus ad formam.* We need only add that such a movement implies two mutations: the leaving behind of sin, *terminus a quo,* and the movement to grace, *terminus ad quem.* Satan is the zero point where corruption meets generation, which is to say, the pilgrim's *re*generation. The colors of Satan's retrospective portrait recapitulate the history of the fall from a pristine whiteness. In order to see the reverse history in the making, an as yet incomplete counterpart of the infernal process, one need only read as far as the gates of purgatory. The three steps leading to the angel of God in the ninth canto of the *Purgatorio* (vv. 95–103) are, in order, white, black and red. The first is of pristine whiteness, the second is *perso,* the color of hell itself (cf. *Inf.* V, 89), while the last is porphyry, "come sangue che fuor di vena spiccia." (*Purg.* IX, 102) (as blood that spurts from a vein). We know by this time whose blood was shed so that man could take the final step of regeneration. We know too that when that step is completed it will be white.

We have remarked that, for all of Dante's rationalizations, justification remains mysterious because it is founded on the absurdity of the cross. It is to the cross that we must return if we are finally to come to grips with the drama at the center of the universe. The first problem is how the "rational" stages of the Aristotelian drama of justification fit in with biblical tradition concerning the cross. In short, how has the poet managed to reconcile the twofold mutation of *motus ad formam* with the cross of Christ?

The emblem of Satan is ultimately derived from a blending of two separate and parallel exegetical traditions concerning the mulberry tree of Luke 17:6. Ubertino da Casale seems to have taken the colors of the mulberry tree from the Ambrosian tradition, according to which the tree is the devil, and applied them instead to Christ on the cross, whereas Dante seems to have taken the cross of the Augustinian tradition and applied it to his Ambrosian devil. This neat interchange might easily be explained by the venerable (and indeed biblical) association of the tree and the cross on the one hand and of the tree and the devil on the other.[16] We might then understand Dante's peculiar association of the devil with the cross as a simple analogical leap. Such a hypothesis seems confirmed by the parody of the hymn which begins the canto, for if in the original version the cross, *vexilla regis,* is said to be an *arbor decora et fulgida,* then Satan's tree, the mulberry of Ambrose, is quite appropriately referred to as the *Vexilla regis inferni.* To rest content at this stage, however, is to explain Dante's careful staging of doctrine in terms of poetic caprice.

The exegetes, beginning most probably with Origen, were quite familiar with the *crux diaboli.*[17] They read St. Paul as alluding to it in Colossians 2:18:

> [Christ] quickened [you] together with him . . . blotting out the handwriting of ordinances that was against us, which was contrary to us, and took it out of the way, nailing it to his cross; and having spoiled principalities and powers, he made a show of them openly, triumphing over them in it.

For Origen, this meant that Christ's triumph on the "exterior cross" was at the same time the crucifixion of the demons, and specifically the devil, on the metaphoric or "interior cross." The "crux diaboli" was the symbol of Christ's triumph over sin and death; it became an inconspicuous element in the voluminous exegetical literature devoted to the cross.

The tradition of the cross of the devil also survived in another context. When the exegetes glossed the passion itself, they noted that there were three crosses involved: that of the bad thief, that of the good thief, and that of Christ. It seemed natural to gloss these as signifying tropologically the cross of the devil, the cross of the penitent *(cuiuslibet iusti),* and finally the cross of Christ. A passage from the *Claustrum Animae* of Hugo de Folieto will serve to illustrate the point:

> The first cross is the cross of the devil, the second of whichever just man, the third of Christ. The first of malice, the second of

penance, the third of justice . . . On the first cross do I suffer, toward the second I go, and for the third do I yearn. The first I fear, for the second I search, and the third I desire. The first is of punishment alone, to the cross of penance pertains forgiveness, to the cross of justice pertains glory. I therefore fear punishment, search for forgiveness, and desire glory.[18]

A more sophisticated theologian, Alanus ab Insulis, summed up the three stages on the way to glory precisely in terms of the three crosses:

> Let us therefore ascend the threefold cross: the cross of penance, whereby we are liberated from sin; the cross of compassion, whereby we reign with our neighbor; the cross of the passion whereby we are glorified in Christ.[19]

These three stages of spiritual ascent bear a certain resemblance to the three stages on the pilgrim's way: the preparation for grace in the natural order, the state of grace itself, and, finally, the state of glory. It is not unlikely that Dante marked each of his stages with the sign of the cross at the end of each of his *cantiche:* here in hell with the cross of Satan, in purgatory with the tree of the cross of *cuiuslibet iusti,* and in paradise the cross of Christ, our image circumscribed by the circle of divinity, an emblem of the Incarnation. This would explain the recurrence of the motif of the mulberry tree both immediately before the pilgrim's entry into Eden and immediately after Beatrice's description of the tree and the *narrazion buia.* Both allusions are Ovidian and refer to the history of Pyramus and Thisbe (*Purg.* XXVII, 37 and XXXIII, 69), but anyone acquainted with the tradition of the *Ovidius moralizatus* would have known that the famous love-story was interpreted exactly as Augustine interpreted Luke 17:6—that is, with Pyramus as Christ, who stained the tree with his blood. These are, however, speculations which must be left for another time. For the moment, what Dante tells us in the *Inferno* seems enough to permit the identification of Satan's sign as the *crux diaboli.*

It should be observed that our interpretation leaves the obvious trinitarian imagery of the canto undisturbed. If anything, it reinforces it, for the three points of the cross were traditionally taken to indicate the three persons of the Trinity.[20] Furthermore, when once we see in the figure of Satan the outlines of the venerable instrument of torture, the punishment of the three arch-sinners seems less capricious than before. The most convincing evidence that can be adduced in support of the interpretation, however, is the meaning of the action here. Virgil specifically tells the pilgrim what Satan represents to spiritual progress: "per cotali scale . . . conviensi dipartir da tanto male" (v. 82) (for by such stairs as these we must depart from so much evil).

Dante twice refers to Satan as a *scala* (vv. 82 and 119) and we are meant to think of the ladder of ascent and descent, Jacob's ladder, which for the Middle Ages was *figura crucis*. Before we demonstrate this, however, it will at least be granted that if we conceive of Satan as a cross, the ladder whereby man may ascend to justice, then Dante's climb (and his descent is a climb, *sub specie aeternitatis*) on the side of Satan seems less bizarre than it may have before. Dante is simply a man who climbs a tree on the road to salvation. As it happens, just such a man appears in the Gospels as the type of the humble man who is converted: Zachaeus, *id est, iustificandus,* and the tree he climbs is very like the mulberry. In fact its name was interpreted by some to mean *sicut morus*.

The Italian word for mulberry, *gelso,* is not derived from *morus* but rather from *celsa,* a word which usually refers to a quite different tree in late Latin: the sycamore. No doubt the transfer can ultimately be explained by the fact that the names of the two trees look very much alike, at least in Greek: *sūkamīnos,* mulberry, and *sūkomoros,* sycamore. Where the Vulgate has the word "mulberry" in Luke 17:6, the King James version reads "sycamine." Some medieval scholars, more familiar perhaps with words than with trees, tried to reflect the at least verbal similarity in their etymology: *sycomorus, idest, sicut morus.*[21] The exegetes certainly had no trouble associating the two trees allegorically, for it seemed to them that their common root, again verbally, was *mōros,* meaning "foolish" in precisely the same sense that St. Paul spoke of the cross as foolish: "unto the Jews a stumbling block and unto the Greeks foolishness" (I Cor. 1:23). The association of a passage discussing the mulberry with another passage discussing the sycamore would not have surprised exegetes as much as it does us. At any rate, it seems that Dante had such an assimilation in mind when he climbed his infernal tree.

In the nineteenth chapter of Luke that deals with the entry of Christ into Jericho, the writer tells an anecdote which was destined to become allegorized as a drama of conversion (v. 2 ff.):

> And behold, there was a man named Zachaeus, which was the chief among the publicans, and he was rich. And he sought to see Jesus . . . and could not for the press, because he was little of stature. And he ran before, and climbed up into a sycamore tree to see him: for he was to pass that way. And when Jesus came to the place, he looked up, and saw him, and said unto him, Zachaeus, make haste, and come down; for today I must abide at thy house.

Commentators on this passage saw in it every detail of conversion, the miraculous change which made of a rich oppressor the figure of the *iustificandus*.[22] Albertus Magnus wrote a lengthy but entirely commonplace gloss on the passage which will serve to represent the traditional interpretation.[23] He first observes that Zachaeus signifies the man who comes to God *ut iustificaretur.* The fact that he is small signifies that he is humble, a disposition which is required on this journey, for Christ *humilibus dat gratiam.* The climbing of the tree is laudable both as an ascent of the cross and as a descent in humility. Following the climbing of the tree, Christ's entry into the house of Zachaeus is tantamount to the harrowing of hell:

> So did he enter into the house of Zachaeus as he entered into hell, the house of the devil. He drew out from it those who were gathered there . . . The house of Zachaeus was the jaws of the devil . . . so did Jesus enter into the house that, having ejected the devil, he might . . . consecrate it to himself as his abode.[24]

Finally, the conversion of Zachaeus is a miracle which is no less than a death and resurrection: "For it took no less power and mercy to call Lazarus back to life, from hell to the upper world, than to call Zachaeus back from the abyss of vice to the grace of repentance and justification."[25] It seems very likely that Dante's *crux diaboli* is just such a tree and that Zachaeus might very well serve us as a *figura dantis.* Like the sign of Satan, the sycamore brings about a *transitus* out of this world, or as Hugo de Sancto Caro phrased it, "from the world to the Father, through the medium of the cross of penitence. . . . This is the ladder that Jacob saw."[26] We may add that this too is the *scala* that the pilgrim climbed.

There is a good deal more to be said about Satan's sign, of course; we have at best merely indicated what may be its broad biblical, or at least exegetical significance. If it seemed much more strange to us before, it was perhaps because we had forgotten that it was a banner, therefore a sign, a *vexillum,* and we must look beyond it. To be properly read, moreover, it must be taken as a sign for the pilgrim, not for us. Dante can see the devil as immobile and impotent because he has been through hell and so exorcised the demon before crossing into another world. Here, as in paradise, the pilgrim affects what he sees by the fact that he is seeing it. The prince of this world (no less than the souls in heaven) takes part in a command performance for the benefit of this man. The best that we can do is to gauge the significance of the action from the dramatic interplay of the pilgrim and his world. To lament the loss of the Satan we had been expecting, made in our own image and likeness, is to ignore the objective which the poet had before him from the beginning: to show *how* paradise is regained.

11. Infernal Inversion and Christian Conversion: *Inferno* XXXIV

IN HIS INTRODUCTION TO A NOW famous collection of essays dedicated to an understanding of Dante's philosophical culture, Bruno Nardi characterized the tradition in which Dante wrote his poem with a principle that has not yet been sufficiently applied to our reading of the poem:

> In the poetic representation of the ascent of the soul beyond the heavens celebrated in the second discourse of Socrates (in the *Phaedrus*), as in the vision of Er at the conclusion of the *Republic,* rather than in the impoverished medieval visions, one truly discovers the fecund germ of the philosophy and poetry of the *Commedia.* To those who claim that the Florentine poet had no knowledge of the two works of the Athenian philosopher, it is easy to answer that Platonic thought, propagated through thousands of streams, informed a vast literature which was at least in part well known to Dante.[1]

It follows that any reading of Dante's poem which fails to take account of its tropological significance disregards history as well as the text, for it is precisely the poet's effort to capture the dynamism of spiritual development in figurative terms that enables us to place his poem in the tradition to which it most properly belongs. Just as Plato sought in his allegories to give poetic expression to his conception of human *morphosis, paideia,* so Dante chose to represent the Christian *metamorphosis, deificatio,* in terms of a journey to the absolute. As an example of how a knowledge of the tradition can help illuminate an important passage in the poem, I hope to demonstrate that a puzzling detail at the center of Dante's cosmos, the pilgrim's turning upside-down on the hide of Satan, in fact derives from the blending of a passage in Plato's *Timaeus,* the one Platonic work that Dante might have known directly, with a commonplace Christian motif.

In its general outlines, the historical transformation of the Greek ideal of education into what has been termed Christian humanism was traced by Werner Jaeger in his last work: *Early Christianity and Greek Paideia.*[2] The late historian proposed to study the Christian texts which seemed to him to mark a critical point in the dialectic between antiquity and Christianity before the Augustinian synthesis. For all of the vast difference between ancient and early Christian ideas of education, Jaeger perceived the two traditions had in common their concern for process, *formation* in the etymological sense, with the pedagogical reference that the word still conveys in French and Italian. The Christianity of Gregory of Nyssa, for example, was not simply a static doctrine to be possessed by the faithful, it was rather a development of the human personality through grace and a new type of education founded upon the reading of the Bible. The goal was the restoration of the image of God in man. In order to give verbal expression to this process, Gregory had need of a poetic language capable of capturing in words a spiritual becoming without betraying either abstract doctrine or vital flow. He found an appropriate language of process already prepared for him in the Platonic tradition. Insofar as Dante also sought to give a dynamic incarnation to an abstract theory of education with the corporeal metaphor of an *itinerarium,* a "cammino di nostra vita," he placed himself within a literary tradition which, whether the poet knew it or not, extended as far back as Gregory's divine *anabasis* or even as far back as Plato himself.

Christianity added one element to the Platonic ideal of education, however, which sufficed to undermine completely its rational bases: the doctrine of the crucifixion. Before *paideia* could become *imitatio Christi,* provision had to be made in the divine *anabasis* for "the stumbling block," the central Christian absurdity of the cross. The darkness of error was to Christians not merely ignorance, as it was to Socrates, nor was virtue merely knowledge. The transition from one polarity to the other required not only human effort, but a death and resurrection as well. In the previous essay I have tried to show that the pilgrim's transition in the last canto of the *Inferno* depends precisely on the help which Christians believed was provided them by Christ's death on the cross and Resurrection. Satan is in fact Satan crucified, exorcised from the pilgrim and thus become an instrument of his salvation. Here I should like briefly to discuss how Platonic, as well as Christian, conceptions of spiritual change are represented by the pilgrim's turning upside-down on the side of the *crux diaboli.*

By turning upside down at the center of the universe, the pilgrim and his guide right the topsy-turvy world of negative transcendence from which they began. Satan, the prince of this world, seems right side up from the perspective of hell; after crossing the cosmic starting-point, however, Dante sees him from God's perspective, planted head downward with respect to the celestial abode from which the angel fell. Moreover, the pilgrim will ascend the mountain in the same absolute direction that characterized his spiral descent into hell. Because of his inversion, however, the direction can no longer be described as a descent "a sinistra," but is rather an ascent "a destra." In short, one of the symptoms of the pilgrim's spiritual disorder in the first part of the poem is that up seems down and left seems right. As it happens, this is precisely a symptom of the disorder of the newly incarnate soul in Plato's *Timaeus.* The "circles" of reason and passion in the soul are disrupted when it is yoked to a mortal body. The circles "barely held together, and though they moved, their motion was unregulated, now reversed, now side-long, now inverted. It was as when a man stands on his head, resting it on the earth, and holds his feet aloft by thrusting them against something: in such a case right and left both of the man and of the spectators appear reversed to the other party."[3] In Chalcidius' gloss on this passage, we learn that these random motions are *concupiscentia* and other passions of this kind. Education will set the "circles" right once more. If the human being neglects education, however, "he journeys through a life halt and maimed and comes back to Hades uninitiate and without understanding."[4]

The historian of ideas will recognize here the "germe fecondo" of the problem besetting Dante's pilgrim in the *Inferno,* even to the detail of the wound to the "piè fermo." The disorder of the soul is represented in the *Divine Comedy* by the soul's disorientation. For Plato, spiritual disorder was represented in an imaginative context by physical inversion, whereas for Aristotle, speaking in natural terms, the cosmos had an up and down, a right and left, just as did the human body and these directions were reversed in our hemisphere. The question is, how were these cosmological directions associated with the cross?

In an important study of the use of Platonic motifs by the early Christians, Wilhelm Bousset has shown that the arms of the cross were associated with the Platonic cosmic dimensions: up and down, right and left.[5] For our purposes, the most interesting text he cites is from the apocryphal Acts of St. Peter. It was of course a banality that St. Peter chose to be crucified head downward out of a sense of humility. The specific wording of his speech has more to tell us, however. Explaining to his audience and to his executioners why his head must be downward, he says:

> For the first man, whose image I bear, thrown downward with the head . . . who cast his origin upon the earth . . . showed the right as the left and the left as the right, and changed all signs of nature, to behold the ugly as beautiful and the really bad as good. On this the Lord says in a mystery: "Unless ye make the right as the left and the left as the right, and the top as the bottom and the front as the backward, ye shall not know the Kingdom [of heaven].[6]

It is clear from this text that Peter's decision to be crucified, not like Christ, but like "the first man" who fell "head downward," may well be Christian; its expression, however, with its allusion to the fall of *Anthropos,* is clearly gnostic. And if the Lord is indeed quoted correctly, we can be sure that he is a Platonic Lord. The significance of the passage for our purposes is that it represents a startling blend of the Platonic motif of *paideia* with a clear, albeit bizarre, suggestion of *imitatio Christi.* Education consists of righting the inverted world and distinguishing right from left; such a conversion, however, is accomplished on the cross of Christ.

It must not be imagined that this is an isolated example of the curious blending of the Platonic topos with the theology of the cross. By an involved historical process, the words of Peter in this curious text were transmitted throughout the Middle Ages and even to modern times by the single most important pietistic collection of lives of the saints that has come down to us: Jacopo da Voragine's *Legenda Aurea,* which Dante undoubtedly knew. In his section on St. Peter, Jacopo quotes the Apostle: "Because my Lord descended from heaven to earth, and was raised up on an upright cross, the cross used for me, whom He deems fit to call from earth to heaven, ought to show my head at the ground and direct my feet towards heaven. Therefore, because I am not worthy to be raised on the cross in the same way as my Lord was, turn over my cross and crucify me with my head pointing downwards."[7] Thus far, the passage is perfectly traditional and would by itself provide a generally satisfactory gloss on the significance of turning upside-down on the cross. The following lines make it quite clear, however, that for all of its ostensible orthodoxy, the *Legenda* is here dependent on the apocryphal Acts of Peter, which compare Peter's position to that of the *Anthropos,* whose inversion the gnostic original described in terms of the Platonic inversion and subsequent confusion of left and right. Peter continues his speech in the *Legenda:*

> I chose to imitate you, Lord, but I did not usurp [your right to] be crucified upright. You are always upright, lofty and high, [but] we are the sons of the first man, who buried his head in the earth, [and] whose fall the species of human generation signifies: for we are born so that we seem to be inclined down towards the ground. Our condition is also changed, so that the world thinks that which is agreed to be left is right *(sic enim nascimur, ut proni in terram videamur effundi. Mutata quoque conditio est, ut hoc putet mundus dextrum, quod constat esse sinistrum).*[8]

Whether or not the author was aware of it, and he probably was not, the last lines of this speech in the widely diffused pietistic legend are a paraphrase of the passage in Plato's *Timaeus* describing the condition of the newborn soul and of the *mutatio* brought about by *paideia.* The only innovation, and it is most significant for the historian of ideas, is that the turning upside-down is accomplished on the cross.

In the poem, the poet and his guide turn upside-down on the *crux diaboli* and Virgil tells us specifically what it is that is accomplished by the turning:

> "Attienti ben, ché per cotali scale,"
> disse 'l maestro, ansando com' uom lasso,
> "conviensi dipartir da tanto male." (vv. 82–84)

"Cling fast," said the master, panting like a man

> forspent, "for by such stairs as these we must
> depart from so much evil."

The use of the word *scale* of course suggests the cross, the *Vexilla regis*. Because it is the *vexilla regis inferni,* the cross is the *crux diaboli.* It marks the transition from sin to penance, through a first "conversion." The point we make here, however, is that the pilgrim and his guide turn upside-down, not only as a sign of humility (the goal of this first part of the poem), but also as a sign to other men, so that they may know up from down and left from right. The malaise was first diagnosed by Plato: the treatment, however, was, for Christians, the work of the Great Physician.

12. Casella's Song: *Purgatorio* II, 112

WHEN DANTE QUOTES HIS EARlier poetry in the *Commedia,* we are meant to perceive a distance, perhaps even an ironic distance, between a former poetic self and the poem that we read. The same can probably be said of any writer who refers to his former work within a confessional structure, but it is especially true of Dante, whose whole poetic career was a continual *askesis* in preparation for his last work. In such a linear evolution, a glance backward to a previous poetic achievement is more likely to be a sign of transcendence rather than of return, of self-critique rather than self-satisfaction.[1]

Like the spiritual evolution of his protagonist, Dante's poetic history derives its significance retrospectively from its ending. The *Commedia* provides a new framework within which the total poetic experience of its creator is ordered toward an ending that could not have been foreseen at any single moment of the evolution, while appearing to be its inevitable outcome. An allusion to a former work within such a context is inevitably palinodic, for it invests the poetry itself with the dramatic double focus that is part of the story: the conversion of the Dante who *was* into the poet whose work we read.

The clearest example of such a palinodic moment is also the earliest instance in the poem recalling Dante's previous poetry. There is scarcely any need to point out that Francesca's description of love, "Amor, ch'al cor gentil ratto s'apprende" (*Inf.* V, 100) (Love, which is quickly kindled in the gentle heart), no longer reflects the author's view, even though her words echo those of Dante's youth and of

Guido Guinizelli before him. The rejection of Francesca's theory of love is implicit in her damnation; if her words echo Dante's own, she is their refutation. Like Flaubert's heroine, Emma Bovary, she stands as a surrogate for her creator, both the sign and the vehicle of his transcendence.

An analogous moment occurs in the second canto of the *Purgatorio* when Casella sings the second *canzone* of the *Convivio,* "Amor che ne la mente mi ragiona" (Love that discourses in my mind), to the delight of the new company of souls. Once more the subject is love and the vehicle is Dante's former work. Here too, the dramatic situation implies a criticism: Cato's scolding is severe enough to embarrass Virgil as well as the pilgrim. Finally, the canto closes with a simile comparing the souls to doves, as in *Inferno* V:

Come quando, cogliendo biado o loglio,
  li colombi adunati a la pastura,
  queti, sanza mostrar l'usato orgoglio,
se cosa appare ond' elli abbian paura,
  subitamente lasciano star l'esca,
  perch' assaliti son da maggior cura; (*Purg.* II, 124–129)

As doves, when gathering wheat or tares, assembled all at their repast and quiet, without their usual show of pride, if something appears that frightens them, suddenly leave their food because they are assailed by a greater care . . .

In spite of these resemblances, however, no consensus exists among the critics as to whether the episode of the *Purgatorio* carries the same palinodic force that is borne by Francesca's words. The purpose of this discussion is to suggest that this is indeed the case, and that the episode constitutes a partial correction of an important thesis of the *Convivio.*

The principal difficulty is that Casella is made to choose a relatively abstruse, doctrinal, and therefore inappropriate *canzone.* The Anonimo fiorentino defines the difficulty succinctly: "per le canzoni morali, come fu questa, non suole essere usanza d'intonarle" (for moral canzoni such as this were not normally sung).[2] The critical assumption has always been that Casella's song is a recreational interlude, which would seem to call for a less weighty theme: either this song is not the very famous *canzone* of the same name (as the

Anonimo goes on to argue), or Casella's *canzone* is somehow not intended to have the philosophical meaning that the original indisputably bears. I should like to argue that, on the contrary, this is the very same poem and we are meant to understand its full philosophical force. The "Amore" celebrated here marks an advance over the "Amore" of Francesca's verses in the same measure that the *Convivio* marked an advance over the *Vita Nuova.* Casella's song is not simply light relief, but is rather a signal for the poem's entrance into a new area of concern.

First of all, there is no way that the *canzone* of the *Convivio* can be interpreted as a simple love song of the type that we would suppose Casella to have sung, even if he were the innovative composer that some historians have imagined him to have been.[3] The lady of "Amor che ne la mente mi ragiona" is clearly Lady Philosophy and not a mortal woman, not even at the literal level, as even a cursory reading of the *canzone* will demonstrate. Some of its philosophical detail might conceivably be read as erotic hyperbole, but it would be difficult on those grounds to explain away verses such as "Ogni Intelletto di là su la mira" (v. 23) (Every Intelligence on high gazes on her), or "Costei pensò Chi mosse l'universo" (v. 72) (She was in the mind of Him who set the universe into motion), alluding to the biblical Wisdom (Proverbs 8:27). Because of the poet's uncertainty about his lady in the first *canzone* of the *Convivio,* there may be some slight grounds for arguing that that poem be read as a secular love poem which was interpreted allegorically as an afterthought; in "Amor che ne la mente mi ragiona," however, the poet seems completely caught up in his newfound love for philosophy. We scarcely need his commentary to recognize in his beloved the same Lady that appeared to Boethius in *The Consolation of Philosophy.*

Dante was explicit about the importance of the *Consolation* for an understanding of the *Convivio.* So linked are the two works that Dante's citation of his own brings with it several allusions to that of Boethius even here in the *Purgatorio,* thus making it clear that the verse of the *canzone* is to be read in its original context:

> . . . "Se nuova legge non ti toglie
> memoria o uso a l'amoroso canto
> che mi solea quetar tutte mie voglie,
> di ciò ti piaccia consolare alquanto
> l'anima mia . . .   (II, 106–110)

> "If a new law does not take from you memory or practice of the songs of love which used to quiet in me all my longings, may it please you therewith to comfort ["console"] my soul somewhat . . .

Given the subject-matter and the provenance of the song, the use of the word "consolare" seems particularly meaningful, for it recalls the function of the *Donna Gentile* in the *Convivio* and of Lady Philosophy for Boethius. It seems reasonable to assume that Casella offers the same kind of consolation by celebrating the love of Wisdom, *Philosophia,* rather than passionate love. If we have trouble thinking of this as an "amoroso canto," it is because the meaning of the word "amore" has narrowed since Dante's time.[4] We shall see that the definition of this love, transcending the erotic and falling short of the divine, is part of the significance of this episode.

It may be objected that the comfort offered by Casella is in his music rather than in his words. Apart from the problem of explaining why Dante would have chosen *these* words to be ignored, this objection would make of the episode a distraction rather than a consolation. Instead, it must be interpreted in its context, a context in which the comfort of philosophy is accompanied by song, rather than the reverse. Such was the case with Boethius: "It is time, then, for you to take a little mild and pleasant nourishment which by being absorbed into your body will prepare the way for something stronger. Let us bring to bear the persuasive powers of sweet-tongued Rhetoric and . . . let us have as well Music, the maid-servant of my house, to sing us melodies of varying mood."[5] In Casella's song, our attention must be fixed on the words, for we have nothing else. The unheard melody is a fiction and must be understood as part of a literary tradition in which the consolation of philosophy is set to music as a sign of its all-absorbing power.[6] Dante's choice of a historical person to provide the accompaniment, rather than an allegorical abstraction such as Lady Philosophy, serves to reinforce at the stylistic level what is, after all, the significance of Cato's reproof: we are a long way, both in style and in substance, from the philosophical allegories of the *Consolation* and the *Convivio.* In a single episode, Dante's figural realism transcends both philosophy and the allegories that celebrated it, including his own.

A recurrent figure in Boethius' text (as in our language) is of philosophy as "food" for thought, the same figure from which the *Convivio* derives its title as well as its central theme. In the *Purgatorio,* the rapt attention of the souls to Casella's song is compared to the total absorption of birds feeding on wheat or tares. The simile might be explained by the association of the flight of birds with the ascent of the soul, in Plato as well as in Dante, or with a retrospective glance at the canto of Francesca, where the subject was also "amore." With such literary resonances, the feeding of birds might be considered a fitting emblem for the momentary satisfaction of desire that the souls in fact experience here, feeding on the *esca* of Casella's song. These speculations would remain only that, were it not for the fact that the simile was probably drawn from the second meter of Book III of the *Consolation.* The subject there is the natural desire for happiness; its treatment is very like Dante's in the first canto of the *Paradiso,* but one of the examples of innate desire is reminiscent of our passage. Caged birds will scorn the sweet food set forth for them by their captors and will yearn instead for their home:

> Si tamen arto saliens texto
> Nemorum gratas viderit umbras,
> Sparsas pedibus proterit escas,
> Silvas tantum maesta requirit . . .[7]

> Yet when within her prison fluttering
> The pleasing shadows of the groves she spies,
> Her hated food she scatters with her feet,
> In yearning spirit to the woods she flies . . .

The resemblance of this simile to Dante's is evident in such a context. If Dante is actually alluding to it, then it is not without a certain irony, for Boethius' point is that philosophy is the means to satisfy the natural desire for happiness, a thesis not unlike that of the opening lines of the *Convivio.* In the *Purgatorio,* however, the goal is *supernatural* happiness, for which philosophy is definitely not sufficient. Just as Boethius' *Philosophia* had cast out the Muses of secular poetry,[8] she in turn is "cast out" in Dante's text by Cato's rebuke. With the simile of the birds feeding, Boethius' figure is used against his own thesis.

These birds are doves, symbols of human desire, as they were in the canto of Paolo and Francesca:

Quali colombe dal disio chiamate
  con l'ali alzate e ferme al dolce nido
  vegnon per l'aere, dal voler portate;   (*Inf.* V, 82–84)

As doves called by desire, with wings raised and steady, come through the air, borne by their will to their sweet nest . . .

Among the many texts that might be cited as background for this simile, the poignant cry of Psalm 54 deserves special attention:

Quis dabit mihi pennas sicut colombae
et volabo et requiescam?   (Psalm 54:6)

Who will give me wings like a dove, and I will fly and be at rest?

Because wings are specifically mentioned in this text, as well as the yearning for peace reminiscent of Francesca, it would seem to be at least as apt as the Virgilian passages usually adduced by commentators in their glosses to *Inferno* V.[9] It is also fitting as background for the simile of *Purgatorio* II, where the doves have found, momentarily at least, a certain peace: "colombi . . . queti." For all of their anecdotal charm, the two similes represent coherent statements regarding Dante's theory of human desire.

For Francesca, peace means the end of a desire that is in human terms insatiable. Even the virtuous pagans, Virgil tells us, can never hope for that final *quies:* "sanza speme vivemo in disio" (*Inf.* IV, 42) (without hope we live in desire). The "bufera infernale" to which Paolo and Francesca are condemned represents the restlessness of what St. Augustine called "the unquiet heart,"[10] at once the sin and its punishment. The simile of the doves in Canto V represents the insatiability of human desire quite accurately, by placing the will and the apparent object of its desire at opposite poles. The pilgrim calls the souls in the name of the "amore" which impels them (v. 78) and they respond: "dal disio chiamate . . . dal voler portate" (called by desire . . . borne by their will). The flight of the doves, then, is literally "amore," the attempt to bridge the gap between the will *(velle)* and its object *(disio)*. Francesca's fate is evidence enough that concupiscence cannot bring the fulfillment of desire, while Virgil's fate is evidence that the higher love of reason is equally powerless, through no fault of its own, however. Virgil's embarrassed reaction to Cato's reproof is a belated recognition of an order of reality undreamt of in antiquity. The problem is, quite simply, that although the desire for God is innate and natural in man, the satisfaction of that desire is supernatural. Only in the beatific vision is Christian happiness possible, when the will and its object are one in eternal fruition: "il mio disio e il velle" (*Par.* XXXIII, 143).[11] The human heart is unquiet, "until it rest in Thee."

In such a dynamism, which is at once the poem and its story, the sudden flight of doves which were temporarily "queti" cannot fail to signify the momentary peace to be found in this life through philosophical study ("quetar tutte mie voglie," v. 108) and the subsequent realization of a further, transcendent goal. In his scolding, Cato defines that goal in terms of *vision:*

> Correte al monte a spogliarvi lo scoglio
> ch'esser non lascia a voi Dio manifesto. (*Purg.* II, 122–123)

> Haste to the mountain to strip off the slough
> that lets not God be manifest to you.

The poignancy of man's fate in the natural order resides in the fact that he cannot know his own goal.[12] When the souls hurry up the mountainside, they go "com'om che va, nè sa dove rïesca" (v. 132) (like one who goes, but knows not where he may come forth), an unmistakeable indication that they go toward an objective that transcends human reason and therefore the limits of philosophy. The "nuova legge" (v. 106) to which Casella's song is subject is the new law, the supernatural order to which nature must ultimately give way. It requires that a new song be sung unto the Lord, the song with which the canto opens: *In Exitu Israel de Aegypto.*

The first lines of the *Convivio* set forth the Aristotelian doctrine of the natural desire to know and of knowledge as man's *ultima felicitade:*

> Sì come dice lo Filosofo nel principio de la Prima Filosofia, tutti li uomini naturalmente desiderano di sapere. La ragione di che puote essere ed è che ciascuna cosa, da providenza di propria natura impinta, è inclinabile a la sua propria perfezione; onde, acciò che la scienza è ultima perfezione de la nostra anima, ne la quale sta la nostra ultima felicitade, tutti naturalmente al suo desiderio semo subietti.

> As the Philosopher says in the beginning of the First Philosophy, all men naturally desire to know. The reason for which can be and is that each thing, impelled by a providence that is proper to its own nature, inclines to its proper perfection; wherefore, since knowledge is the ultimate perfection of our soul, in which our ultimate happiness lies, all of us are naturally subject to desiring it.

This view, which places man's desire to know in a providential context, is readily assimilable to the doctrine of Book III of the *Consolation* and especially to the second meter mentioned above, although Boethius seems to be using a more Platonic vocabulary. Both of these views are assimilable to Christian ideas of beatitude as long as the qualifying phrase, "in this life," be understood to apply to the philosophical definitions. Here in the *Purgatorio,* however, we have gone beyond the limits of "this life," whether the phrase be understood literally or tropologically: Virgil is a pilgrim here, as is everyone else (v. 63), and Ulysses' attempt to reach a philosophical truth without supernatural guidance is a faint memory (*Purg.* I, 132). In such a setting, the *otium* traditionally required for philosophy is *negligenza* (v. 121) and philosophical pride (cf. "usato orgoglio," v. 126) must give way to Christian humility.

A last word should be said about the relevance of what I have called the "dynamism of desire" for poetry. In the similes we have examined, the images of doves have been associated with poetry, as well as desire. The association of language and desire is at least as old as the *Phaedrus* and is documented in Dante's poem by the story of Francesca. The transfer of the virtual image of desire from the written text to the human heart and back again is part of the history of all erotic literature, but especially of Dante's writing, where Love's progress is identical with the movement of poetry toward the silence of the ending. The doves in the story of Francesca contribute to the literary dimension of the episode's significance, for in their flight they suggest the imagery with which Guido Guinizelli's *canzone* began: "Al cor gentil reimpara sempre amore / come l'ausello in selva a la verdura" (Love always seeks the gentle heart, like a bird the green of the forest). In a sense, then, the imagery of the *dolce stil novo* is used to undercut its theory of love, just as Boethius' bird simile is used against him in the *Purgatorio.* Throughout the poem, the association of poetry with desire is signaled by such imagery: in the canto of Guido Guinzelli most notably, where the subject is also poetry and love, and in the canto of Bonagiunta,[13] where Dante gives his definition of the *dolce stil novo:*

> Io veggio ben come le vostre penne
> di retro al dittator sen vanno strette
> che de le nostre certo non avvenne;

> Clearly I see how your pens follow close after him who dictates, which certainly befell not with ours—

> Come li augei che vernan lungo 'l Nilo,
> (*Purg.* XXIV, 58–60, 64)

> As the birds that winter along the Nile sometimes make a flock in the air . . .

The imagery possibly derives from a topos used by Guinizelli[14] in his own poetry comparing the variety of poets to various birds. In this passage, however, the proximity of the word "penne" to the simile of birds in flight and the suggestion of motion in pursuit of the *dittatore,* Love, invite us to reflect on the sense in which eros and poetry are inseparable on a journey that strains both to their limit: "ma non eran da ciò le proprie penne" (*Par.* XXXIII, 139) (but my own wings were not sufficient for that). Casella's song was a respite, as was the *Convivio;* both had to be interrupted for the long journey that lay ahead.

13. Manfred's Wounds and the Poetics of the *Purgatorio*

IN THE THIRD CANTO OF THE *Purgatorio,* one of the excommunicants calls out asking if the pilgrim recognizes him:

> biondo era e bello e di gentile aspetto,
> ma l'un de' cigli un colpo avea diviso. (vv. 107–108)

> blond he was, and handsome, and of noble mien, but a blow had cloven one of his eyebrows.

The mark is not enough to identify him, so that the spirit names himself:

> "Or vedi";
> e mostrommi una piaga a sommo 'l petto.
> Poi sorridendo disse: "Io son Manfredi,
> nepote di Costanza imperadrice; (vv. 110–113)

> "Look now," and showed me a wound high on his breast, then said smiling, "I am Manfred, grandson of the Empress Constance.

The episode marks one of the most famous moments of the *Purgatorio:* a generic description of masculine beauty, slightly skewed by rhetorical distortion, is interrupted by the adversative "but" that suffices to mar the ideal with what appears to be an accident of history. That cleft brow helped to make Manfred a Romantic hero in the nineteenth century and still serves as testimony of Dante's prodigious power of representation.

At first glance, the representation might appear to be an example of what Erich Auerbach called mimesis; indeed, his classic work on the subject began with a chapter entitled "Odysseus' Scar." Manfred's wounds are equally unforgettable and perhaps for some of the same reasons, but they serve a deeper purpose than Dante's desire to hold up a mirror to reality. In fact, the wounds are an anomaly in the representation, a flaw that seems to undermine the bases of Dante's fiction: we learn, later on in the *Purgatorio,* that the souls wending their way up the mountain have aerial bodies, fictive replicas of their real bodies and exact reflections of the soul itself. Wounds are inexplicable on such bodies, because they seem to be accidental intrusions into the ideal corporeity of the afterlife. If Manfred's wounds are reminiscent of Odysseus' scar, it cannot be at the level of descriptive detail. Odysseus' scar, Auerbach tells us, is an example of Homeric realism, described by the poet because it is there; Manfred's wounds, on the other hand, demand an interpretation. They are there, on a body made of thin air, and ought not to be.

The basis for associating the two texts is mythic, rather than mimetic, and becomes clear when we challenge Auerbach's reading of Odysseus' scar. The thesis of Auerbach's essay seems undermined by its title. The purpose of the essay was to reveal "the need of the Homeric style to leave nothing which it mentions half in darkness and unexternalized."[1] In the style that "knows only a foreground, only a uniformly illuminative, uniformly objective present . . . never is there a form left fragmentary or half-illuminated, never a lacuna, never a gap, never a glimpse of unplumbed depths."[2] Yet Odysseus' scar is itself precisely all of those things: an indelible mark of the past within the present, an opaque sign healed over a hidden depth. The scar is the mark of Odysseus' identity and manhood, or there could be no recognition. In a passage whose significance Auerbach does not discuss, Homer tells us that the hero, when hunting as a boy, was gored in the thigh by a wild boar which he then killed with his lance. Almost seventy lines are devoted to describing the nobility of his lineage and his youthful courage, so that the scar remaining from the hunting accident takes upon itself a meaning never hinted at by Auerbach: it is a sign of Odysseus' coming-of-age, almost a ritual scar, and it identifies him in the eyes of his former nurse, not fortuitously, but rather as the sign at once relating him to his ancestors and distinguishing him from them. In the succession of fathers and sons, Odysseus' scar marks his place precisely, bracketing him between his ancestors and Telemachus, his son, who is about to undergo his own baptism of blood.

At some level, of course, Auerbach knew that the primordial drama of male identity was hidden beneath the apparently innocuous and realistic detail. When he turned for contrast in the same essay to an equally ancient epic in a totally different tradition, he chose the story of Abraham and Isaac, the foundation story for Israel and a foreshadowing of the circumcision. Odysseus' scar is also a kind of circumcision. It bears the same relationship to Adonis' fatal wound (in Northrop Frye's masterful reading of the myth)[3] that circumcision bears to castration. For all of the irreducible differences between the two epics, they are united by a common theme: the rites of violence that have traditionally been used by males to mark their identity and manhood.

Manfred's wounds hide a similar story, for they signify his relationship to his father, yet, by an ironic reversal of earthly values that is one of the functions of Dante's otherworldly perspective, they mark his passage away from patrilinear succession toward the mother. Critics have noticed that Manfred identifies himself only as the grandson of the Empress Constance; in fact, he was the son of Frederick II Hohenstaufen, known in Dante's day as *Stupor Mundi.*[4] This pointed reticence has been explained in various ways: psychologizing critics have suggested that Manfred, although Frederick's favorite, was a natural son and not the legitimate heir of the mighty emperor. It is indelicate, according to this line of reasoning, for a bastard to name his father. A slightly more sophisticated view, the thematic interpretation, insists that Frederick is in hell, with the rest of the Epicureans, and thus is erased from the memory of his son. The contrast between Manfred's radiant smile and his ghastly wound serves as a contrast between the vicissitudes of history and the power of grace for the late repentant.

A more interesting thematic reading of the passage involves Dante's own political ideals. Frederick was the founder of the Ghibelline imperial dream, but was by Dante's time totally discredited as a heretic and an excommunicant. The fictive salvation of his son, mortally wounded at the battle of Benevento, might then represent a survival of the Ghibelline ideal, to which Dante clung against all the evidence of his senses. On this reading, Manfred's insistence on grace, "mentre che la speranza ha fior del verde" (as long as hope keeps aught of green) might then mask a much more specific hope for Dante's own political dream. In the *Purgatorio,* Manfred remembers his daughter, "la mia buona Costanza," the "mother of the honor of Sicily and Aragon," and asks the pilgrim to tell her that he has been saved, in spite of his excommunication. Manfred is therefore bracketed between the two Constances, his grandmother in paradise and his daughter on earth. The ideal of Empire lives on, but in matrilinear succession, outside the city of man, and reconciled at last to *Mater Ecclesia.* Manfred's message to his daughter repeats, yet transforms, the popular oracle that was said to have kept Germany dreaming imperial ideals for centuries after the death of Frederick II: "He lives not; yet he lives."[5] The body of the father is entombed in porphyry, the monument to imperial aspirations in Palermo or, for that matter, in Paris, but Manfred's bones are scattered to the four winds:

> Or le bagna la pioggia e move il vento
> di *fuor dal regno,* quasi lungo 'l Verde,
> dov' e' le trasmutò a lume spento. (vv. 130–132)

> Now the rain washes them and the wind stirs them, *beyond the Kingdom,* hard by the Verde, whither he transported them with tapers quenched.

The dispersion of Manfred's corpse suggests that, insofar as he is still a hero of a realm, the kingdom is not of this world.

Manfred's wounds are the scars of history, but his smile is a revisionist smile, belying the official versions of his fate. Although the young man was excommunicated by the Church, Dante places him among the late repentant, who will ultimately reach paradise. Manfred tells us that the bishop who had his body disinterred had misread that page in God's book; the implication seems to be that the poet, unlike the Church, has read God's book correctly. Manfred's salvation therefore represents an interpretation of the brute details of history, an allegorical reading of those wounds that belies the horror that they literally imply. As Manfred survived extinction, so Dante's political ideal survives historical contradiction by assimilation into the unity of his vision.

If Manfred's real body is dispersed, then it is clear that his fictive body is a representation, bearing symbolic wounds, diacritical marks slashed across the face of his father. Frederick's beauty won for him the title of *Sol invictus:* the adjectives *biondo, bello e di gentile aspetto* might have been taken from contemporary chronicles describing the Emperor.[6] At the same time, Frederick's *persona* is the mystical body of Empire, the head of state, as we still say, whose heart is the law. The dazzling incongruity of Manfred's smile serves to affirm the triumph of the ideal in spite of the apparently mortal wounds to both the head and heart. Like the scar of Odysseus, the adversative "ma" serves to affirm sameness with a profound difference—that is to say, the syntax performs the function of ritual scarring. The wounds incurred in his father's name win for him his own: "Io son Manfredi"—so that the mortal wounds are in fact a baptism, a rebirth into a new order, with what St. Paul called "a circumcision of the heart" (Romans 2:2).

For all of the apparently mimetic power of Dante's verses, there can be no doubt that corporeal representation in the poem is self-consciously symbolic. In this respect the *Purgatorio* does not differ greatly from the *Inferno.* The recognition of Manfred has its infernal counterpart in Mohammed among the schismatics, who bares his cloven chest as an emblem of theological schism and is introduced by similar syntax—"vedi com'io mi dilacco" (see how I rend myself). In the same canto (XXVIII), Bertrand de Born's decapitated body suggests the schism in the political order. The clinical horror—Bertrand carrying his head like a lantern—lends horror to the more abstract political enormity. Bertrand is said to have set father against son:

> Perch' io parti' così giunte persone,
> partito porto il mio cerebro, lasso!,
> dal suo principio ch'è in questo troncone.
> Così s'osserva in me lo contrapasso. (vv. 139–142)

> Because I parted persons thus united, I carry my brain parted from its source, alas! which is in this trunk. Thus is the retribution observed in me.

Applying the same figure, we may say that the marks on Manfred's fictive body also stand for his relationship to a wounded theological and political order which he has survived and, in a sense, redeemed.

The representation of Manfred is meant to bear witness of this redemption within the fiction of Dante's purgatorial journey. His wounds, apparently accidental, are in fact signs of his identity and distinction. They are like the marks of history, which cannot be accommodated by the abstract mimetic claim of a one-to-one correspondence between the aerial bodies of purgatory and the souls which produce them. At some level, the disfiguring marks of history mark the soul as well. Like writing itself, they deface in the name of significance. Their presence in the *Purgatorio* is at the same time the poet's mark, his intervention in the fiction that otherwise purports to be an unmediated representation of the other world. As wounds are inexplicable on an aerial body, so writing is inexplicable on what is claimed to be an exact representation of an otherworldly vision. Paradoxically, the text "mirrors" the other world only by virtue of its cracks.

Lest the parallel between Manfred's wounds and the text itself seem too ingenious for a medieval text, it should be pointed out that such an analogy is implied in what is probably the most famous and most solemn of recognition scenes. The newly risen Christ shows his wounds to Thomas so that he may believe what he has seen: "Thomas, because thou hast seen me, thou hast believed: blessed are they that have not seen, and yet have believed." Christ's wounds, made manifest to Thomas, bear witness to the Resurrection. The solemnity of that moment lends to the representation of Manfred a theological force that serves to underscore the strength of Dante's imperial faith.

It is, however, the passage immediately following Thomas' recognition in the gospel of John that I wish especially to recall in this context. The narrative of Jesus' works ends with his remark to Thomas and almost as if to end his work, John adds these words: "And many other signs truly did Jesus in the presence of his disciples, which are not written in this book, but these are written, that ye might believe that Jesus is the Christ, the Son of God, and that believing, ye might have life through his name." The writer of the gospel thereby establishes a parallel between the wounds of Christ's body and his own text, filled with signs that demand of the reader the same assent that is demanded of the doubting Thomas. As Christ's scarred body is seen by the disciples, so John's text is read by the faithful. That analogy is operative in Dante's poem. Manfred's wounds, slashed across a body made of thin air, stand for Dante's own intrusion into the course of history. They are, as it were, writing itself, Dante's own markings introduced across the page of history as testimony of a truth which otherwise might not be perceived. It is this parallelism between the text and the aerial body of the *Purgatoio* that establishes the fiction of the *Purgatorio,* the vision of the pilgrim translated by the writing of the poet, scars of history erased and assimilated into God's book, where the truth is finally conveyed, according to Saint Augustine, without letters and without words.

The analogy between the aerial body and the poem itself is consistently developed throughout the *Purgatorio.* It underlies the apparently gratuitous account that Dante gives us in Canto XXV of the formation of the body in the afterlife. The question is how the souls in this circle can speak of nourishment or grow thinner in their *askesis* when there is no need of food. Virgil answers with generic theories of mimesis and poetic representation: the bodies of the *Purgatorio* are related to real bodies as the torch was related to the life span of Meleager in the eighth book of the *Metamorphoses* or as an image in a mirror is related to what it reflects. This statement of the relation of the aerial bodies to nature—like a mirror or like a lamp—establishes the context as unmistakably aesthetic, with ancient figures for doctrines of poetic inspiration that have become particularly familiar to us since they were studied by M. H. Abrams.[7] If the bodies of purgatory are related to nature as either mirror or lamp, then the poem itself is either a mimetic or metaphoric representation of nature. This is as far as Virgil will go in his explanation, asserting that a complete understanding of the process transcends human understanding. He then defers to Statius for a fuller explanation than he can provide.

At this point, Dante enters upon a digression that has been something of a scandal in the history of Dante criticism, not only because of its apparent irrelevance, but also because of its reputed technical aridity. In the midst of six cantos of the *Purgatorio* that deal more or less explicitly with poetry, Dante now embarks upon what amounts to a lesson in medieval embryology. This occurs when Statius chooses to answer the question about the fictive bodies of purgatory with a discussion of the general relationship of body and soul, on earth as well as in the afterlife. As we shall see, the lesson has at least as much to do with poetics as it has with embryology. Like an analogously technical discussion in the *Paradiso* on the nature of moon spots, this scientific disquisition can be skipped over by the general reader only at the risk of missing something essential about the nature of Dante's poetic theory.

To anticipate somewhat, I should like to suggest that Statius' discussion about conception and reproduction in Canto XXV also serves as a gloss on Canto XXIV, where the subject is literary creation and conception. More than that, it seems to suggest strongly an analogy between the act of writing and the act of procreation. Dante begins with the clinically obvious and proceeds to explain its metaphysical significance. Sexuality is, for Dante, nature's expression of creativity, rather than the repressed subject-matter of literary expression. This is one important sense in which it may be said that art imitates nature. As the soul is inspired in the fetus, so the inspiration of the poet comes from God. The body, however, is the work of parenthood. In the same way, the poetic corpus is sired by the poet, who provides the vehicle for God's message.

Statius begins by telling us how the seed is formed. A small portion of blood is stored and purified in the heart of the male and is eventually transformed into the male seed, which contains within it an informing power, *virtute informativa,* that will gradually mold the blood of the female into a human body, with all of its organs. When this power is released into the female, the two bloods unite and the fetus is formed. The fetus then naturally grows into a vegetative and then into a sensitive soul. As yet, there is no human life at all, strictly speaking; it is not until the brain is completely formed, in about the sixth month of pregnancy, that God directly inspires the intellective soul into the embryo:

> sì tosto come al feto
> l'articular del cerebro è perfetto,
> lo motor primo a lui si volge lieto
> *sovra tant' arte di natura, e spira*
> *spirito novo, di vertù repleto,*
> che ciò che trova attivo quivi, tira
> in sua sustanzia, e fassi un'alma sola,
> che vive e sente e sé in sé rigira. (*Purg.* XXV, 68–75)

so soon as in the fetus the articulation of the brain is perfect, the First Mover turns to it with joy *over such art of nature, and breathes into it a new spirit replete with virtue,* which

> absorbs that which is active there into its own substance, and makes one single soul which lives and feels and circles on itself.

Statius then moves directly to a discussion of the formation of the fictive body in the afterlife. At the moment of death, the soul falls to the shore to which it is destined and there the informing virtue which it possesses irradiates the surrounding air, as a ray of light irradiates moist air to form a rainbow, in order to form its aerial body. The soul *imprints,* "suggella," the surrounding air with its own form and so creates the ghostly body that the pilgrim sees.

Except for a passing reference in Hugh of Saint Victor, there does not seem to be a precedent in specifically Christian thought of the Middle Ages for the belief that the soul could unite with the air in order to form an aerial body, although that demons had such power was a commonplace of popular and learned belief. Neoplatonic thought might well admit such a possibility, but the Christian emphasis on the indissoluble unity of the human composite and the Aristotelian theory of hylomorphism to which Dante subscribed rule out the possibility that Dante means us to take the fiction seriously as metaphysics.[8] It does not require a great deal of the reader's imagination to see in this fiction a disguised poetic claim. The seal of reality is stamped upon the dreamlike medium of the *Purgatorio* as the seal of the soul is affixed to the wax of the body. Dante's poem seems to make a claim for a kind of mimetic essentialism—realism in the medieval sense of the word.

The "realistic" quality of the *Purgatorio* is the central theme of this portion of the poem. It has often been remarked that the second realm of the poem is the most lifelike, the most modern part of the vision. Here souls are on the move, on pilgrimage as they were on earth, possessed of a temporality that is measured by the imagination of the pilgrim. His subjectivity is the stage of the action here. Unlike the claim of objective presence in the *Inferno* or the ethereal non-representation of the *Paradiso,* the surrounding world is here filtered through the pilgrim's *fantasia,* which is itself the power that creates images in the form of dreams, out of thin air. The action of *fantasia* is exactly analogous to the process of the afterlife as Dante imagines it. The bodies of the *Purgatorio* are of the same order of reality as the bodies of the imagination, quite literally the "stuff that dreams are made on." The pilgrim's initial question about the mode of existence of the bodies here amounts to a question about the relationship of his poem to the real world.

With this hypothesis in mind, Statius' discussion of conception takes on a new dimension of meaning. There are echoes, in Statius' speech, of Dante's doctrine of poetic inspiration contained in the canto immediately preceding this. In Canto XXIV, Bonagiunta da Lucca asks the pilgrim if he is the man who drew forth, "trasse fore," the new rhymes of the sweet new style. The verb unmistakably suggests childbirth and the adjective "new," repeated several times, prepares the way for the discussion of the infusion of the intellective soul by God: "spirito novo, di vertù repleto." Most interesting, however, is the pilgrim's reply, which for centuries has been taken as Dante's definition of his own art:

> "I' mi son un che, quando
> Amor mi spira, noto, e a quel modo
> ch'e' ditta dentro vo significando." (vv. 52–54)

> "I am one who, when Love inspires me, takes
> note, and goes setting it forth after the fashion
> which he dictates within me."

The moment of poetic inspiration exactly matches the moment of inspiration of the new soul: "sovra tant' arte di natura . . . spira spirito novo." The work of art is not nature's art but that of the poet, although the source of inspiration, *spirito novo,* is the same. The forcefulness and syntactic isolation of the verb "noto," etymologically, "I mark," seems to highlight the moment of inscription; given the analogy with procreation, it would seem to correspond with the moment of conception, recalling Jean de Meun's playful references to "nature's stylus" in the sexual act.[9] Dante's emphasis is, however, on the unitary source of spiritual inspiration, the soul of the fetus or the spirit of the text. At the same time, the gerund "vo significando" suggests that literary creation is not a moment but a process, a constant approximation approaching but never quite reaching God's inner text as its limit. The construction used in that sense has since been hallowed by literary tradition. When the Romantic Leopardi wrote his own lyric on the subject of literary inspiration, invoking the wind rather than God's spirit, he used a similar construction to describe his own effort: in "L'Infinito," the act of writing is rendered "vo comparando"—"I am comparing"—presumably the present text with nature's own. For Dante, the gerund depicts the process of writing, the *askesis* that will bring the "body" of the text closer and closer to the spirit which informs it. The words suggest that the poem, like the pilgrim, is still en route in the *Purgatorio.*

Manfred's wounds constitute the marks that must be expunged in order for history to be brought into conformity with God's will, just as sin must be purged in order for the soul to be made "puro e disposto a salire alle stelle," (pure and ready to rise to the stars). At the same time, the wounds have served a providential purpose, in much the same way that sin can prepare the way for conversion. In this respect, both history and sin are analogues for writing itself. As history disfigures the face of Manfred with apparently accidental marks that in fact give him his significance under the aspect of eternity, so writing progressively disfigures the page ("vo significando") in order paradoxically to make it clear. The process of interpretation, like the process of purgation, is an assimilation and a gradual *effacement* of the marks, like melting footprints in the snow: "così la neve al sol si disigilla." The phrase from the *Paradiso* signals the ending of the poet's work and the vision of God's Book, "legato con Amore in un volume, ciò che per l'universo si squaderna," (bound by love in one single volume that which is dispersed in leaves throughout the universe).

Readers of the *Purgatorio* will remember that its central action, for the pilgrim, is the erasing of his sins, sins that are at once wounds and letters. The instrument is not nature's stylus, nor that of the poet, but history's pen. The angel guardian of purgatory draws seven letter P's on the forehead of the pilgrim with his sword, as a representation of his history:

> Sette P ne la fronte mi descrisse
> col punton de la spada, e "Fa che lavi,
> quando se' dentro, queste *piaghe*" disse. (IX, 112–114)

> Seven P's he traced on my forehead with the
> point of his sword and said, "See that you wash
> away these *wounds* when you are within."

The penitential process for the pilgrim consists in the eradication of wounds inflicted by a sword. We may imagine this also to be the case with Manfred's wound, eternally there in the space of Canto III but effaced in the process of refinement toward the resurrected body.

Later on, Statius describes the whole penitential process in this way: "Con tal cura conviene e con tai pasti, / che la piaga da sezzo si ricucia" (With such care and with such a cure will the wound be completely healed). Underlying these images is the affirmation that the poem we read has its counterpart in Manfred's face.

In God's book, Manfred's brow is clear. This is implied by a verse that has always presented a certain difficulty for commentators. Speaking of the bishop who had his body disinterred and thrown into the river, Manfred says that had the pastor realized that Manfred was saved, he would have spared his body. The difficult sentence reads: "Se 'l pastor di Cosenza . . . avesse in Dio ben letta questa faccia," and the difficulty resides in the translation of the word "faccia," which means either "face" or, as Charles Singleton has translated it, "page." (Had the pastor of Cosenza well read that page of God.) Our discussion thus far suggests, however, that one might equally well have translated the word "faccia" as "face," thereby giving more force to the bishop's misreading and more concreteness to the demonstrative adjective "questa": "Had the pastor of Consenza well read this face in God." God's book has no marks that are subject to misinterpretation; Manfred's wounds, however, might have been taken as signs of his damnation when read from a purely human perspective, without benefit of their radiant smile.

Finally an additional nuance of meaning can be derived from comparing this passage with what is undoubtedly its source. There is a culminating moment at the end of Book VI of the *Aeneid,* when Anchises points out to his son the shadow of a soul who might have been a hero of Rome equal to Aeneas had he not died prematurely. Scholars tell us that he was the adopted son of the Emperor and Octavia is said to have fainted with grief when Virgil first recited his lines. They describe the handsome boy in terms that recall, if only by contrast, the description of Manfred, even to the adversative *sed* which indicates not a wound, but an enveloping darkness suggestive of premature death:

> A man young, very handsome and clad in shining armor, *but* with face and eyes down cast and little joy on his brow . . . What a noble presence he has, *but* the night flits black about his head and shadows him with gloom . . . Alas his goodness, alas his ancient honor and right hand invincible in war! . . . Ah poor boy! If thou mayest break the grim bar of fate, thou shall be

Marcellus. Give me lilies with full hands . . .
Aeneid (VI, 860–85)

The foreboding darkness contrasts with the smile of Manfred in the same way that Virgilian pathos contrasts with the hope of the *Purgatorio;* even the eternity of Rome must bow before the death of this beautiful young man. He too is an Emperor's son, but the success of Empire cannot mitigate individual grief. We are left with Anchises' futile funereal gesture.

From Dante's standpoint, of course, this is the Virgilian misreading of death; Manfred's smile, with an imperial dream in shambles, is in a sense a smile at Virgil's expense. It happens that this passage contains the only verse from the *Aeneid* literally quoted, in the original Latin, in the *Divine Comedy:* "Manibus, Oh, date lilïa plenis!" As Beatrice approaches for the first time, the angels sing out for the lilies of the Resurrection and Anchises' funereal gesture is turned into a note of triumph.

This deliberate misreading of Virgil brings me to the final point I want to make concerning the effacement of heterogeneity in Dante's text. I have said that Dante's doctrine of poetic inspiration cannot account for what may be called the body of his text as opposed to its spirit. If the inspiration is claimed to be God-given, the poetic *corpus* is very much Dante's own. To extend the procreative image that Dante has established, we may say that the claim of inspiration does not account for the ancestry of the text, especially for the influence of Virgil, whom Dante refers to as his "dolcissimo patre" at precisely the moment when he quotes the *Aeneid* verbatim, thereby acknowledging Virgil's part in the genesis of his own poem. Once more, heterogeneity is assimilated by an effacement before our eyes. The foreignness of the Virgilian sentiment here at the top of the mountain, underscored by the foreignness of the original language, is neutralized by the otherwise seamless context; death is transformed into resurrrection, leaving behind the distinctive mark of the disappearing father, his text in Latin like a foreign element. Like Manfred's wound (or the scar of Odysseus), the sign of the father is most in evidence at the moment of the son's triumph; like Manfred's wound, however, it is about to be effaced.

After that quotation from Virgil's text, the pilgrim trembles at the approach of Beatrice and turns to tell Virgil, "Conosco i segni de l'antica fiamma,"—"I recognize the signs of the ancient flame"—

which is not a direct quotation this time, but a literal translation of Dido's words of foreboding when she first sees Aeneas and recalls her passion for her dead husband while she anticipates the funeral pyre on which she will die: "Agnosco veteris flammae vestigia" (*Aeneid* IV, 23). Dante transforms those words as well, for he uses them to celebrate the return of his beloved and a love stronger than death. He turns to Virgil for support and finds him gone. Calling to him three times, the text evokes the merest allusion to a Virgilian text, the disappearance of Eurydice in the fourth *Georgic:* "Eurydice, Eurydice, Eurydice":

> Ma Virgilio n'avea lasciati scemi
> dì sé, Virgilio dolcissimo patre,
> Virgilio a cui per mia salute die' mi . . . (XXX, 49–51)

> But Virgil had left us bereft of himself, Virgil
> sweetest father, Virgil to whom I gave myself
> for my salvation . . .

The calling out to Eurydice is the culmination of Virgilian pathos, lamenting death that is stronger than poetry, as it is stronger than love and even than Rome. Dante's adversative *ma* records the loss, yet transcends it with an affirmation. The progression from direct quotation to direct translation to merest allusion is an effacement, further and further away from the letter of Virgil's text, as Virgil fades away in the dramatic representation to make way for Beatrice. It is then, for the first time, that the poet is called by name: "Dante!" The intrusion of Virgil's words into Dante's text is at that point the mark of poetic maturity.

14. An Introduction to the *Paradiso*

DANTE'S CLAIM FOR THE *Paradiso,* the last *cantica* of his poem, is as daring as it is clear: "My course is set for an uncharted sea." History has in fact granted him the unique place that he claimed with that navigational metaphor, both to the pilgrim and to the poet. Just as, within the fiction of the poem, the pilgrim's course is privileged beyond the aspiration of ordinary men, so in its final course the poem accomplishes what no other poet had ever dared. Throughout the *Divine Comedy,* the metaphor of the ship serves to describe both the pilgrim's journey and the progress of the poem: on both counts, Dante can refer to himself as a new Jason, who returns with the Golden Fleece that is at once the vision of God and the poem that we read.

For the twentieth-century reader, the fiction of the story requires a great effort of the imagination—few of us still believe in a paradise in any form, much less in the possibility of reaching it in this life. The claim of the pilgrim to have reached the absolute seems to us even more fantastic than the fiction of the *Inferno,* where at least the characters, if not the landscape, are quite familiar. For this reason, the *Paradiso* is often thought of as the most "medieval" part of the poem. This reputation should not, however, obscure for us the sense in which, as poetry, it remains daring and even contemporary. By attempting to represent poetically that which is by definition beyond representation, this *cantica* achieves what had scarcely seemed possible before (even for the poet of the *Inferno* and the *Purgatorio*) and has remained the ultimate aspiration of poets ever since. The quest of Romantic poets and their successors for "pure poetry" has for its prototype the *Paradiso.*

The poetry of the *Paradiso* represents a radical departure from that of the *Purgatorio,* as the latter represented a departure from the poetry of the *Inferno.* The changes may be thought of as a gradual attenuation of the bond between poetry and representation, from the immediacy of the *Inferno* to the dreamlike mediation of the *Purgatorio* to the attempt to create a non-representational poetic world in the last *cantica.* This refinement of poetic representation perfectly matches the evolution of the pilgrim's understanding within the story: he learns first of all from his senses, from the sights and sounds of a hell that seems actually to exist, now and forever, thanks to the celebrated mimetic power of Dante's verses in the *Inferno.* As the pilgrim depends upon his senses in his travels, so the reader seems to be with him in a world which exists autonomously, almost as if it had not been created by an act of the imagination.

In the *Purgatorio,* on the other hand, the major revelations come to the pilgrim subjectively, as interior events in what Francis Ferguson has called a "drama of the mind." The dream-vision is the primary vehicle for this illumination; Dante refers to the power which receives it as the *imaginativa* (*Purg.* XV). According to medieval psychology, this is the same power that enables poets to create a totally new world from the fragments of sense experience and memory, so that in Dante's view, the poetic power that created the poem is the same that is ignited within the pilgrim during his ascent of the mountain. The poet's imagination, hidden by its own concreteness in the first part of his poem, becomes the focus of his attention and of ours in the *Purgatorio.* Thus, the landscape is suffused with mist, the tone is nostalgic, and the reader is called upon to respond with his imagination to both the sensory and the emotional suggestiveness, to imagine "visible speech" in the bas-reliefs, to hear the music of familiar hymns, to recall the lessons from the Sermon on the Mount. The substantiality of this part of the poem resides in the subjectivity of the pilgrim and in our reaction to it more than in an explicit architectonic creation of the poet.

In the last part of the poem, the pilgrim's vision is transformed until it no longer has need of any representational media whatever in its communication with the absolute. The technical problem involved in finding a stylistic correspondence to this transformation reaches insoluble proportions by the poem's ending, for it demands straining the representational value of poetry to the ultimate, approaching silence as its limit. Insofar as the *Paradiso* exists at all, therefore, it is an accommodation, a compromise short of silence, as Dante suggests in the first canto:

> Trasumanar significar *per verba*
> non si poria; però l'essemplo basti
> a cui esperïenza grazia serba. (vv. 70–72)

> The passing beyond humanity may not be set forth in words: therefore let the example suffice any for whom grace reserves that experience.

This sense of compromise, of poetic inadequacy for the ultimate experience, is what accounts for the poignancy of much of the *cantica,* but particularly of the last cantos, where both memory and *fantasia* fail the poet, who can describe only the sweetness distilled within his heart.

The prodigious achievement of the poet is that he manages, within the limits of this compromise, to represent non-representation without falling either into unintelligibility or into silence. Within the story, this accommodation takes the form of a "command performance" of all of the souls of the blessed for the exclusive benefit of the pilgrim. In the fourth canto, Beatrice tells him that all of what he sees in the heavenly spheres of the moon, the sun, and the planets is there only temporarily, until he is able to behold all of paradise without any such "condescension":

> Così parlar conviensi al vostro ingegno,
> però che solo da sensato apprende
> ciò che fa poscia d'intelletto degno. (vv. 40–42)

> It is needful to speak thus to your faculty, since only through sense perception does it apprehend that which it afterwards makes fit for the intellect.

The extraordinary implication of Beatrice's remark is that the whole of the *Paradiso,* at least until the crossing of the river of light toward the poem's ending, has no existence, even fictional, beyond the metaphoric. When the souls return to their home in the Empyrean, the last heaven beyond time and space, they leave the spheres, presumably forever, and no subsequent voyager will ever see them again as the pilgrim saw them. If the *Inferno* may be said to have a fictionally autonomous existence and the *Purgatorio* a subjective substantiality, paradise and the poem are co-extensive, like the terms of a metaphor and, even within the fiction of the story, neither can exist without the other.

The metaphoric quality of the story has a stylistic counterpart in some of the distinctive features of the poetry, the most startling of which may be referred to as anti-images. One of the most memorable occurs in the first heaven (III, 15), where spirits appear within the moon and are described as "a pearl on a white brow." The comparison is obviously self-defeating as far as its function to convey information is concerned: we are told simply that the poet saw white upon white. The point is of course the *difference,* which we are unable to see, yet within which all of the reality of the *Paradiso* is contained. The juxtaposition of the pearl and the brow, in their concreteness, serve in a negative way to block the attempt to leave the confines of the text, defying us, as it were, to find more than a shadow of reference to the real world.

It cannot be coincidence that the comparison is found in a section of the poem where the moon spots are discussed at great length in what at first seems to be a superfluous digression. Its point becomes apparent when we realize that for Dante the spots on the moon were visible only from the earth, while the heavenly body shone with a uniform radiance on the side closest to the sun. The spots are therefore also shadows, in a sense an accommodation of God's light to the eyes of mortal men below, gradations within a unity which might not otherwise be perceived. Finally, the literary significance of the complicated interplay becomes clear when one recalls the terms with which Dante had set forth his ambition in the prologue of Canto I:

O divina virtù, se mi ti presti
  tanto che l'ombra del beato regno
  segnata nel mio capo io manifesti . . . (vv. 22–24)

O divine Power, if you do so lend yourself to me that I may show forth the image of the blessed realm which is imprinted in my mind . . .

The experience of the pilgrim, like the experience of pure whiteness or, for that matter, the experience of the divine light, remain out of reach to mortal minds, which can proceed to unity only analogically. It is in difference that meaning is born, as when two phonetic sounds, unintelligible in themselves, constitute meaning when linked together. So with the poem, which manages to approach its conclusion and silence by the gradual dissipation of all difference between light and light, and yet remains as the shadow of all that the experience is not, as irreducibly literary as "a pearl on a white brow."

There was a whole corpus of writings in the Middle Ages which dealt with the subject of "light metaphysics," an adaptation of light imagery, considered literally as the connecting link between God and the cosmos. These writings are obviously of doctrinal relevance to the study of the *Divine Comedy;* the point I wish to make here, however, is the poetic function of the interplay of light and shadow as a figure for the poem itself. Dante's ascent through all of the heavenly spheres provides him with excellent occasions for modulating his poetic effects to suit the cosmic context. We have already seen the correspondence between poetic imagery and the specific nature of the moon. Mercury's proximity to the sun is an occasion for fugitive effects; Venus' shift in the sky suggests the dramatization of a didactic passage in terms of a solar "illumination" from behind and before the pilgrim; the heaven of the sun calls forth zodiacal imagery and a dance of the hours; Mars colors even Beatrice with its ruddy glow, and so on; in each of the successive spheres, astronomical imagery contributes its color and its geometry to lend to the poem such concreteness as it possesses.

Perhaps the most daring of all sequences in the poem, again at the stylistic level, occurs in the heaven of Jupiter. I have already described what I have called an anti-image in the sphere of the moon; Jupiter provides us with an anti-image which might almost be referred to as an anti-character: the figure of the eagle. In Canto XVIII, Dante sees the souls of the just and temperate rulers as so many lights that gradually arrange themselves in order to form the first sentence from the Book of Wisdom: *DILIGITE IUSTITIAM, QUI IUDICATIS TERRAM*—"Love righteousness, ye that are judges of the earth." The last letter of the Latin sentence, as it is spelled out, is gradually transformed into the shape of an eagle, the symbol of justice, which then speaks to Dante of its universal history. As image, it must have seemed unprecedented in Dante's time, while we, who are used to "spectaculars" and flashing billboards have no trouble imagining such a display. In terms that were set forth at the beginning of this essay, those of poetic representation, the figure is as astounding now as it ever was, for it seems to make a series of references beyond itself, yet the series is perfectly closed and self-contained, in effect leading nowhere beyond itself. In this dramatic sequence, there is no reality that is not a sign, pointing to another level of meaning: the words of the poem point to men of history, the men are lights that are the words of a text from the Bible, which in turn unfolds to its meaning, the eagle. But the eagle also points beyond itself to the words of the text we read, where the series began. Just as there is no concrete reality which may be distinguished in its own right as irreducible, not even the lives of men who serve as the signifiers of God's Providence, so there is no ultimate reality signified beyond the text itself. The eagle, as unlike an eagle as can be imagined, stands as a figure for the poem itself, a non-representation that is its own reality.

If the logical series of references in the episode turns back upon itself, giving the eagle a purely literary meaning, independent of the natural world or extant eagles, it is also true that at the farthest remove from the text in that logical series there is another text: *Diligite Iustitiam,* a biblical verse. The Bible was considered by the Middle Ages to be the exemplar of all books, possessed of a totality to which mortals could only aspire with their books, for God was taken to be its author. Moreover, it is this sense of the universe as a symbolic book, of which the Bible was the concrete manifestation, that gives to everything its quality of sign, pointing beyond itself to its maker. So it is in Dante's poem, where the ultimate reality is seen precisely as a book:

> Nel suo profondo vidi che s'interna,
> legato con amore in un volume,
> ciò che per l'universo si squaderna. (XXXIII, 85–87)

> In its depth I saw ingathered, bound by love
> in one single volume, that which is dispersed
> in leaves throughout the universe.

The aspiration of the pilgrim throughout the poem is to pick up the scattered leaves of God's book, but as he achieves that in the last canto of the *Paradiso* with his vision, the vision escapes him:

"thus on the wind, on the light leaves, the Sibyl's oracle was lost." His own book, the poem we read, is an attempt to reconstruct the archetypal book and it is in this sense that it may be said, in Charles Singleton's words, that Dante "imitates God's way of writing." For the twentieth-century reader, whatever his beliefs, the inference is that the written word represents the ultimate reality and coherence.

The observation about the ways in which Dante's poem is an imitation of God's book brings us to the substance of his revelation in the final *cantica.* Heretofore we have been concerned with the poet's stylistic daring, but the daring of Dante the theorist is no less. The entire poem, from the dark wood to the Empyrean, traces the gradually transcendent view of Dante on his own culture, his own country, and even his own family, from the isolated and alienated bewilderment of the pilgrim in the first scene to the soaring view of the eagle in the upper reaches of the universe. It is characteristic of Dante and of his faith that any such transcendence must begin with the self. Dante's own history occupies the central cantos of the *Paradiso* in the form of his meeting with his ancestor, Cacciaguida. The encounter is based on Aeneas' meeting with Anchises, his father, in the sixth book of the Aeneid and has for its principal function the clarification of all of the dark prophecies the pilgrim has received throughout his journey concerning the future course of his life. As early as the sixth canto of the *Inferno,* he had been warned about future exile and misery in ambiguous terms; in the canto of Cacciaguida it is spelled out for him "not in dark sayings . . . but in clear words":

> Tu proverai sì come sa di sale
>   lo pane altrui, e come è duro calle
>   lo scendere e 'l salir per l'altrui scale.   (XVII, 58–60)

> You shall come to know how salt is the taste
> of another's bread, and how hard the path to
> descend and mount by another man's stairs.

In spite of the formal resemblance to an ancient model, the mode of the revelation is distinctly biblical, as the phrase "dark sayings" and the context suggests. As the coming of Christ gave meaning retrospectively to all of history, so the revelation of Cacciaguida, a surrogate for the divine perspective in the poem, gives meaning to all of the prophecies in the poem.

The essential thing about an oracular utterance is that it contains the truth without revealing it; only in retrospect, after the fact, can its truth be appreciated. At the same time, when those ancient oracles deal with death, their truth can be tested only from beyond the grave, that is, when their truth is too late to be of value to humans. The coming of Christ changed all of this, for Christians, by providing a point of closure, an ending in time within time, an Archimedean place to stand, from which the truth in life and in world history might be judged. It was therefore a death-and-resurrection perspective on the oracular utterance, at once an understanding and a survival. This mode of structuring history according to the Christ event forms the basis of Dantesque revelation in the poem: to tell the story of one's life in retrospect with confidence in the truth and the completeness of the story is somehow to be outside of, or beyond, one's own life. It is to undergo a kind of death and resurrection, the process of conversion, a recapitulation of the Christ event in the history of the individual soul. The retrospective illumination of Dante's own life by Cacciaguida is the dramatization of the poet's self-transcendence, the achievement of a point from which the course of time, its trajectory, may be viewed as though it were completed.

It was St. Augustine in his *Confessions* who first drew the analogy between the unfolding of syntax and the flow of human time. As words move toward their conclusion in a sentence in order to arrive at meaning and as the sentences flow toward the poem's ending in order to give it meaning, so the days of a man's life flow toward his death, the moment of closure that gives meaning to his life. Meaning in history is revealed in the same way, from the standpoint of the ending of history or Apocalypse, to use the biblical term. The same analogy is operative in Dante's poem, which is why the *Paradiso* is inseparable from the earlier *cantiche.* As we approach the poem's ending (and, incidentally, the literal ending of the poet's life), the closure that gives meaning to the verses and to the life that they represent, so all of history is reviewed under the aspect of eternity, beginning with Adam and ending with an indeterminate triumph of justice on earth.

As the dark prophecies concerning the poet's life are given meaning by the revelation of Cacciaguida, so the dark political struggles which are a counterpoint to the pilgrim's story throughout his voyage are finally revealed, in a way that no historian today would consider historical. Indeed, the ultimate structure of history, from the perspective of paradise, would seem to be the very opposite of the history we learn from the chronicles. St. Peter's invective against the corruption of the Church, for example, insists three times on the sacredness of his chair in Rome, which from his perspective appears to be empty, when we know it to have been filled, during the fictional time of the poem, by Boniface VIII, perhaps the most secularly powerful Pope of the Middle Ages. Again, we know that Henry VII of Luxemburg, upon whose entry into Italy Dante had placed so much of his hope for the restoration of the Empire, died rather miserably in 1313, eight years before the poet's death and the conclusion of the poem. Yet Dante awards him the very highest place among contemporaries in the heavenly spheres. This is the implication of Beatrice's remark in Canto XXX as she points out an empty throne:

> E 'n quel gran seggio a che tu li occhi tieni
> per la corona che già v'è sù posta,
> prima che tu a queste nozze ceni,
> sederà l'alma, che fia giù agosta,
> de l'alto Arrigo, ch'a drizzare Italia
> verrà in prima ch'ella sia disposta. (vv. 133–138)

> And in that great chair whereon you fix your eyes because of the crown that already is set above it, before you sup at these nuptials shall sit the soul, which on earth will be imperial, of the lofty Henry, who will come to set Italy straight before she is ready.

In the last phrase, Dante almost casually points up the difference between fallen time and the fullness of time that is the Christian eternity. Henry's death seems the merest accident of history, in no way affecting its meaning, as the presence and continued existence of a powerful Pope, Dante's bitter enemy on earth, is inconsequential under the aspect of eternity.

One of the last figures used by Dante to describe his transcendent view of universal history and of his own life seems particularly contemporary in an age when the view from the stars is no longer a poetic dream but a reality. In the heaven of the fixed stars, as the poet looks down from his constellation, Gemini, he describes the entire terrestrial surface:

L'aiuola che ci fa tanto feroci,
   volgendom' io con li etterni Gemelli,
   tutta m'apparve da' colli a le foci;
poscia rivolsi li occhi a li occhi belli. (XXII, 151–154)

The little threshing-floor which makes us so fierce was all revealed to me from hills to river-mouths, as I circled with the eternal Twins. Then to the beauteous eyes I turned my eyes again.

The convulsions of war and cataclysm are contained and almost domesticated by the figure of the threshing floor on which the winnowing is a contained violence with a purpose: the separation of the wheat from the chaff, the traditional biblical figure for judgment. At the same time, the pronoun "us" strains to have it both ways: the pilgrim is elevated far enough beyond human concerns to give him a perspective that seems supernatural, but the pronoun involves him in the fate of the whole human community so that even in the starry heaven he is not alone. This integration of the pilgrim into the human family, after the isolation of the dark wood, points to an essential feature of this poem and to the central paradox of the faith to which it bears witness: the Incarnation.

The last stages of the poem prepare the way for the final resolution of all paradoxes in terms of the paradox of the Incarnation. First of all, it should be observed that the final revelation that comes to the pilgrim is not simply beatific vision, but a vision of the principle that renders intelligible the union of humanity and divinity in the person of Christ. This mystery forms the basis, in Dante's view, for all of the "concrete universals" involved in the story as well as in the poem itself. It explains (to the pilgrim, if not to us) how an individual man, Dante Alighieri, can at the same time be all men, without any compromise of his identity. It also helps to explain, retrospectively, how an apparently chance encounter of a boy and a girl in medieval Florence on an exactly specified day could at the same time contain within it the pattern of universal salvation, without any surrender of historicity to a vague realm of ideas. Finally, perhaps most importantly for the modern reader, the vision of the Incarnation coincides with the coming together in the poem of the pilgrim and the author and narrator who has been with us from the beginning of the poem.

It is as if the abstracted, confident voice of Dante-poet were an all-knowing principle of intelligibility and the figure of Dante-pilgrim were a flesh-and-blood reality, for that very reason struggling to understand his own meaning. When pilgrim and poet meet at the last stage of the journey, the circle is squared, to use Dante's figure, the poet's word joins the flesh of his experience and, in a sense that is at once paradoxical and exact, the poem is born.

At the beginning of this essay, I suggested that Dante could think of himself as a new Jason, returning with the Golden Fleece of his vision and of the poem that we read. In the last canto of the poem, this is in fact the figure that he uses:

Un punto solo m'è maggior letargo
   che venticinque secoli a la 'mpresa
   che fé Nettuno ammirar l'ombra d'Argo. (vv. 94–96)

A single moment makes for me greater oblivion than five and twenty centuries have wrought upon the enterprise that made Neptune wonder at the shadow of the Argo.

The perspective of Neptune, from the bottom of the ocean looking up to witness man's first navigation, is our perspective on the poet's journey, a celestial navigation, of which the "mad flight" of Ulysses' journey is the Promethean anti-type. The figure completes the navigational imagery with which the *Paradiso* began. At the same time, the perspective from the depths is the poet's as well, who, like all prophets worthy of the name, has returned to tell us all. This didactic intent is finally what separates Dante's vision from its Romantic successors or from its heroic predecessors. The final scene is not an apotheosis of the self in splendid isolation, but a return to the darkness of this world for its own good and a reintegration of poetry into society. There is a precise syntactic moment that marks his return in the final verses:

A l'alta fantasia qui mancò possa;
   ma già volgeva il mio disio e 'l *velle,*
   sì come rota ch'igualmente è mossa,
l'amor che move il sole e l'altre stelle. (vv. 142–145)

Here power failed the lofty phantasy; but already my desire and my will were revolved,

like a wheel that is evenly moved, by the Love
which moves the sun and the other stars.

The restless drive of Dante's verse reaches its climax and its repose with the word "Love" in the last verse, just as the desire that is in human terms insatiable finds its satisfaction in the love of God. What follows after the word represents a fall to earth, which is to say to us, after the ecstatic moment. Dante's personal fulfillment of his own most intimate desires is perfectly harmonized with the love that is the motive force of the entire universe, of the sun and the other stars. Spatially, to speak of the sun and stars is to return to our perspective, looking up at the heavenly bodies which had long been surpassed by the pilgrim's journey to the Empyrean. The word "Love" is therefore the link that binds heaven to earth and the poet to his audience, containing within it the substance of the poem.

15. The Dance of the Stars: *Paradiso* X

IN THE FOURTH CANTO OF THE *Paradiso,* Beatrice enunciates the principle upon which much of the metaphoric structure of the *cantica* depends. She tells the pilgrim that the display of souls distributed throughout the heavenly spheres is a celestial command performance in his honor, devised to enable him to perceive in spatial terms the spiritual gradations of blessedness:

> Così parlar conviensi al vostro ingegno,
>   però che solo da sensato apprende
>   ciò che fa poscia d'intelletto degno. (vv. 40–42)

> It is needful to speak thus to your faculty, since only through sense perception does it apprehend that which it afterwards makes fit for the intellect.

At the same time, it is clear by the inexorable logic of the story (whose principal theme is how the story came to be written) that what applies to the dramatic action applies to the poem itself; that is, heaven's condescension to the pilgrim is matched by the poet's condescension to us. In the poem, the descent of the divine to the human is for the benefit of a pilgrim whose ultimate goal is presumably to transcend the need for any such compromise, except of course (and the whole of the poem is contained in this exception) in order to tell others of his journey. Heaven's metaphor for the state of blessedness is in fact the poet's metaphor for a spiritual experience that transcends the human, an *exemplum* of what it means to *trasumanare:* "l'essemplo basti / a cui esperienza grazia serba" (Par. I, 70) (let the example suffice any for whom grace reserves that experience).

The extraordinary poetic implication of Beatrice's words is that, unlike any other part of the poem, the *Paradiso* at this point can claim no more than a purely *ad hoc* reality. When the pilgrim's ascent to the celestial rose is completed, the blessed return to their seats in the heavenly amphitheater and the heavenly bodies are left to travel in their respective spheres unaccompanied by the family of the elect—no Farinata strikes an attitude here for all eternity. This amounts to saying that the representation points to no reality, however fictive, beyond itself. The structure of the *cantica* depends, not upon a principle of *mimesis,* but rather upon metaphor: the creation of a totally new reality out of elements so disparate as to seem contradictory by any logic other than that of poetry. What is more, some of the elements represent fragments of world systems long since abandoned by Dante's time and fused together only long enough to attempt a rendering in images of what cannot be imagined. The concession of a command performance to the pilgrim within the fiction of the story stands for a poetic *tour de force* whereby Dante reconciles Christian images of heaven with a neoplatonic cosmic vision in a synthesis which, for all of its reputedly "medieval" flavor, seems almost baroque in its daring and fragility. It is the poignancy of the *Paradiso,* as it is of baroque poetry, that the synthesis is dissipated by the poem's ending:

> Così la neve al sol si disigilla;
> così al vento ne le foglie levi
> si perdea la sentenza di Sibilla. (XXXIII, 64–66)

> Thus is the snow unsealed by the sun; thus in the wind, on the light leaves, the Sibyl's oracle was lost.

Whether the reader is left, like Dante, with an ineffable sweetness in his heart, or with what a baroque theorist called "the taste of ashes"[1] is a question that transcends the limits of poetry.

We can, however, set out to identify the various elements that make up the kaleidoscopic structure of the *Paradiso* with a view to understanding not only how they fit together, but also their metaphoric relationship to the spiritual reality they were chosen to represent. It is my intention to examine a very small portion of the *Paradiso* with these ends in view. Specifically, I should like to identify some of the elements of symbolic cosmology contained in Dante's description of the Heaven of the Sun and to discuss some of the themes that make possible in these cantos the translation of beatitude into astronomical terms.

Before proceeding, however, it would be well to identify, in Dante's terms, the process whereby he pieces together his spatial metaphor for beatitude. It is characteristic of the poet that at the moment of his striking *tour de force* he should invoke the authority of the Bible for his accommodation of spiritual reality to human faculties. Immediately after telling Dante about the descent of the blessed to the planetary spheres, Beatrice says:

> Per questo la Scrittura condescende
> a vostra facultate, e piedi e mano
> attribuisce a Dio e altro intende . . . (IV, 43–45)

> For this reason Scripture condescends to your
> capacity, and attributes hands and feet to God,
> having other meaning . . .

We have already noted that the accommodation of heaven to the senses of the pilgrim stands for the accommodation of the poet's experience *per verba* to us, but the pattern for all such accommodation was established by the Bible, the eternal witness of God's accommodation—his Word—to man. Thus, at precisely the point in the *Paradiso* where Dante seems to depart most radically from the Christian tradition, he implies that his accomplishment is essentially an imitation of the Bible. This passage might well serve as confirmation (if confirmation were still required) of Singleton's thesis[2] that Dante consciously chose to write an allegory which he took to be biblical even in those passages where we are inclined to see more of Plato, Servius, and Macrobius than of the Holy Spirit.

Nevertheless, the Christian mystery underlying Dante's representation seems to be clothed in Platonic myth. Beatrice's words in the fourth canto are occasioned by what the pilgrim assumes to be a resemblance of the *Paradiso* to Plato's *Timaeus,* inasmuch as the blessed souls seem to dwell eternally in the stars, "secondo la sentenza di Platone" (v. 24). If Plato's text means what it says, Beatrice denies that the resemblance can be real. If, on the other hand,

> e forse sua sentenza è d'altra guisa
> che la voce non suona, ed esser puote
> con intenzion da non esser derisa. (IV, 55–57)

> But perhaps his opinion is other than his words sound, and may be of a meaning not to be derided.

The implication is that if Plato intends his account to be read as myth, then it may be taken to bear a resemblance to the representation of the *Paradiso.* Whatever this implied resemblance suggests for the interpretation of Plato, it certainly seems to reinforce the suggestion that the descent of the blessed to the heavenly spheres is in fact a dramatization of the process of myth-making and, as such, is an extended figure for what the poet is himself doing as he writes his poem. The relationship of the true home of the blessed in the Empyrean to the temporary positions they occupy in the celestial spheres is exactly the relationship between Plato's presumed meaning and his mythical account of it in the *Timaeus.* Paradoxically then, in this most theological of *cantiche,* Dante seems to fashion his representation according to what might be called the allegory of poets (for Plato is surely a poet in this respect); yet the paradox is compounded and thus, perhaps, resolved by the suggestion that, while the technique and the terms of the figure may be Platonic, the inspiration is essentially biblical. The biblical representation of divine reality in anthropomorphic terms would seem to be the exemplar of all such verbal accommodations, in which the letter says one thing "ed altro intende."

It should be noted in passing that Beatrice's theory about the possible meaning of the Platonic myth concerning the stellar origin and the stellar destiny of the human soul may indirectly shed some light on the question of how extensive was Dante's knowledge of the *Timaeus* tradition.[3] She suggests that the myth really refers to the doctrine of stellar influences:

> S'elli intende tornare a queste ruote
> l'onor de la influenza e 'l biasmo, forse
> in alcun vero suo arco percuote.

> Questo principio, male inteso, torse
> già tutto il mondo quasi, sì che Giove,
> Mercurio e Marte a nominar trascorse. (IV, 58–63)

> If he means that the honor of their influence and the blame returns to these wheels, perhaps his bow hits some truth. This principle, ill-understood, once misled almost the entire world, so that it ran astray in naming Jove and Mercury and Mars.

It happens that this explanation of the myth as an "integumentum"[4] for describing stellar influence occurs in twelfth-century apologetics for Plato associated with the School of Chartres.[5] In particular, Guillaume de Conches, in his glosses on the *Timaeus,* not only ascribes this kind of meaning to Plato, but immediately follows his interpretation with a qualification, lest he be accused of an heretical astrological determinism.[6] Similarly, in his glosses on the meter of Boethius which alludes to the Platonic myth, he puts forward the same interpretation and a similar qualification:

> God assigned the souls to the stars, that is, He made souls of such a nature that they have their bodily existence according to the influence of the stars. For heat comes from the stars, and without it there is no life, nor can the soul exist; not because, as they say, all things that come to pass come from the stars, but certain things, such as heat and cold, and certain infirmities and the like. And if someone should say, "Aren't these things created by God?" the response would be: they come into existence from God, but through the influence of the stars.[7]

Beatrice's similar interpretation of the passage from the *Timaeus,* with its corresponding qualification about the limits of astrological influence, implies a knowledge on the part of the poet that is more than casual of both the text and the interpretation, which made the theme acceptable to Christian philosophers.

It is quite clear that Beatrice's interpretation cannot provide us with a literary explanation of why Dante chose to structure his *ad hoc* poetical representation so as to resemble the Platonic myth. We have seen that the extended metaphor of the *Paradiso,* established by the command performance of the elect for the benefit of the pilgrim, is in fact a poetic reconciliation of the Platonic myth of the stellar souls with the Christian conception of heaven.[8] And, constructing his representation, Dante seemed to be imitating the technique of both Plato and the Bible. I should now like to discuss other facets of the significance attributed to the Platonic myth in the Middle Ages, not mentioned by Beatrice, but nonetheless crucial for understanding how this theme from the *Timaeus* functions within the extended metaphor of the paradisiac representation. This will lead us directly into an examination of the Heaven of the Sun, our example of metaphoric structure in the *Paradiso.*

In a number of other essays included here I have tried to show that the tradition established by the *Timaeus,* according to which the spiritual development of the soul was represented by corporeal movement, is the ultimate (although not necessarily proximate) source of Dante's own allegorical journey in the poem. For Plato, the most perfect of all corporeal motion was that exemplified by the regular, diurnal circulation of the stars. It follows, at least according to the logic of myth, that the most perfect movement of the mind, the microcosmic equivalent of the universe, could best be represented by the movement of the stars. The stars, that is, perfect rationality, represent at once the soul's birthright and its destiny; education is the process whereby the star-soul, fallen to earth, struggles to regain its celestial home. So in Dante's poem, the stars represent the goal of the itinerary of the mind: a goal barely glimpsed at the end of the *Inferno,* within reach by the end of the *Purgatorio,* and achieved at journey's end.[9]

This allegorical significance of stellar movement is probably implicit in the somewhat obscure etymology of the Latin word *consideratio* (*cum* plus *siderare,* to move with the stars?) which was given technical force in the mystical theology of St. Bernard. Such a resonance seems to come very close to the surface in the verse that Dante uses to describe the soul of Richard of St. Victor, "che a considerar fu più che viro" (*Par.* x, 132) (who in contemplation was more than man). Given the profusion of comparisons of the "spiriti sapienti" to the stars and the fact these blessed souls represent most particularly the intellectual perfection for which the pilgrim strives, it does not seem too much to suppose that Dante intended to give the word a Platonic force whether or not that force is demonstrably part of the semantic tradition.[10] At any rate, it is clear to the most casual reader of the *Paradiso* that the souls of the Heaven of the Sun, as well as those of Mars, Jupiter, and Saturn are repeatedly compared to the fixed stars.

On the face of it, this comparison of the souls to stars would seem to create a poetic difficulty somewhat analogous to the difficulty of reconciling the immaterial Christian paradise with the Platonic heavenly spheres, at least as far as the representation of the Heaven of the Sun is concerned. Put most simply, that representation raises the question of what stars are doing in the sphere of the sun. The blessed souls have achieved the spiritual perfection toward which the pilgrim strives by degrees; the fiction of their temporary descent to the heavenly spheres makes it possible for the pilgrim to see and talk with them while he is still short of his goal. In imagistic terms, the perfection toward which he strives and which they have achieved is expressed in terms of the fixed stars. Under what circumstances can stars be said to "descend" to the sun? The rules of physics or of logic admittedly do not apply to poetic representations; once having accepted the fact that Dante's representation is not meant to represent any recognizable material reality, we are inclined to accept without question a *stellar* display, the souls of the "spiriti sapienti," in the sphere of the *sun,* especially since we do not believe in a *sphere* of the sun and are inclined to take a post-Galilean view of astronomical imagery anyway. A contemporary of the poet with an equal amount of astronomical learning, however, would not have failed to see that there is in the Heaven of the Sun an image mediating between the solar and stellar elements of the poet's metaphor, thus binding them together into the kind of coherence that one would expect of a metaphor that seeks to establish a new reality.

The poet sets forth the controlling image of his representation by beginning the canto with one of his most imperious and most famous addresses to the reader, inviting him to look up, neither to the stars nor to the sun, but to a point on the Zodiac, the sun's apparent path through the stars:

> Leva dunque, lettore, a l'alte rote
> meco la vista, dritto a quella parte
> dove l'un moto e l'altro si percuote;
> e lì comincia a vagheggiar ne l'arte
> di quel maestro che dentro a sé l'ama,
> tanto che mai da lei l'occhio non parte. (X, 7–12)

> Lift then your sight with me, reader, to the lofty wheels, straight to that part where the one motion strikes the other; and amorously there begin to gaze upon that Master's art who within Himself so loves it that His eye never turns from it.

This mention of the Zodiac, which may at first seem somewhat irrelevant, in fact invites the reader to consider that part of the heavens which, because of traditional associations, probably suggested to the poet the scene that he describes in the rest of the canto.

In any other poet, a similar scene might strike us as bizarre or at least undignified. The twelve spirits form a circle around the poet and his guide and begin their dance:

> Poi, sì cantando, quelli ardenti soli
> si fuor girati intorno a noi tre volte,
> come stelle vicine a' fermi poli,
> donne mi parver, non da ballo sciolte,
> ma che s'arrestin tacite, ascoltando
> fin che le nove note hanno ricolte. (x, 76–81)

> When, so singing, those blazing suns had circled three times round about us, like stars neighboring the fixed poles, they seemed as ladies not released from the dance, but who stop silent, listening till they have caught the new notes.

The consummate artistry of these lines temporarily suppresses the astonishment that one experiences in retrospect when one realizes that these twelve stars are among the greatest heroes of Christian philosophy and theology. The masterstroke of the second terzina, the pause before the continuation of the dance, both sets the scene dramatically for the speech that is to follow and allows the reader the time to contemplate the *tour de force;* it is in fact a subtle underscoring of what I have been referring to as the "command performance" quality of the *cantica*—in the normal course of things, the circumpolar dance of the stars awaits no man.[11] In spite of the reader's sense of shock in reading these lines, however, it happens that they depend in part upon a very precise tradition, an examination of which may help us to see that the dance is in fact zodiacal.

The origins of the theme of what I shall call the "zodiacal dance" of wisemen are doubtless lost in antiquity and are at any rate not immediately relevant. For our purposes, the earliest and best text I am able to offer is gnostic in origin, was known to St. Augustine,[12] and was transmitted in the apocryphal Acts of John. On close inspection, it seems to reveal many of the elements present in the Dantesque scene. After recounting several incidents of his discipleship, the pseudo-John tells us that the Savior one day called the apostles together and commanded them to form a ring around him and to sing and dance:

> So He commanded us to make as it were a ring, holding one another's hands and Himself standing in the middle. He said, "Respond 'Amen' to me." He began, then, to sing a hymn and to say: "Glory to Thee, Father!" And we, going about in a ring, said: "Amen":
>
> Glory to Thee, Word! Glory to Thee, Grace!
> Amen . . .
> I would wash myself and I would wash. Amen.
> Grace is dancing.
> I would pipe, dance all of you! Amen.
> I would mourn, lament all of you! Amen.
> An Ogdoad is singing with us! Amen.
> The Twelfth number is dancing above. Amen.
> And the Whole that can dance. Amen . . .[13]

Nowhere is the astronomical imagery explicit in this hymn, but without it, the last three lines are incomprehensible. The "Ogdoad" is the number eight, the favorite of the Gnostics, standing for, among other things, the eight celestial spheres.[14] "The Whole that can dance" seems in fact to be a reference to the cosmos, whose rotation is the eternal dance to the "harmony of the spheres." Finally, the "twelfth number" that dances above, the emblem of these twelve disciples who dance below (and the ancestor of the twelve spirits who dance in the Heaven of the Sun), is the Zodiac, whose twelve constellations were represented, in a tradition that goes as far back as the Chaldeans,[15] surrounding the most important of all heavenly bodies (see illustration).[16] In short, the hymn depends upon one of the most ancient of Christian mysteries: Christ is the Sun.[17] As the twelve

Part of the pavement of the Baptistery of Florence.

constellations surround what Dante calls the "sole sensible," so the twelve disciples turn about Christ, whom Dante calls the "Sole de li Angeli" (*Par.* X, 53). It is one of the ironies of intellectual history that the cult of the sun, adapted eventually to the exigencies of Christian symbolism, should have reached its highest point within a Ptolemaic world-view, when its centrality was regarded as purely symbolic.[18]

The comparison of the twelve disciples to the twelve signs of the Zodiac is not simply an inference from an isolated text. The theme has been carefully documented by Jean Daniélou,[19] who has traced it from Judaeo-Hellenic antiquity (the comparison of the twelve tribes to the Zodiac) to fourth-century Christianity, although he does not mention the hymn quoted above. The persistence of the theme throughout the Middle Ages had been previously traced by F. Piper in the nineteenth century.[20] To sum up their findings, we may say that the association arose because of the importance of the number twelve in both the astronomical (twelve hours in the day, twelve months in the year, twelve signs of the Zodiac) and the biblical (twelve tribes of Israel, twelve gates of the temple, twelve apostles, etc.) traditions. Indeed, some historians of comparative religion trace the rise of the latter to the former.[21] The exegetical tradition centered the association on those biblical passages which seemed to identify Christ as the "Day of the Lord" (Ps. 117:24) and as the "Year of the Lord" (Is. 61:2).

It may seem like forcing the text to invoke this tradition for an explanation of the scene in the *Paradiso*. If twelve theologians and philosophers are easily assimilable to twelve apostles, can the same be said for the signifiers of the respective comparisons? That is, could Dante have assimilated a whole zodiacal sign or a whole constellation with a single star? A biblical passage which has little relevance for Daniélou's exposition but which is central to ours enables us to answer in the affirmative. In a passage from the Apocalypse which is probably of some importance for understanding the imagery of *Paradiso* XXIII (and such an understanding does seem to be required for all but the Crocean reading of the poem), there appear to be twelve stars which the exegetical tradition assimilated to the theme under discussion: "And there appeared a great wonder in heaven; a woman clothed with sun, and the moon under her feet, and upon her head a crown of twelve stars" (Apoc. 12:1). The sun in this portrait was invariably glossed as a reference to Christ and the twelve stars as his disciples.[22] The motif of the crown of stars is explicitly recalled in the tradition studied by Daniélou (Ps. 64:12: "Benedices coronae anni benignitatis tuae") as it is by Dante (*Par.* X, 65, 92; XIII, 13–15). The passage from the Apocalypse supplies the complement to the zodiacal theme required for an account of Dante's representation.

There is another passage in *Paradiso* X which, when interpreted in the light of this central theme, gains considerably in coherence. It is not in itself obscure, yet its presence in the poem is difficult to understand until we consider the central astronomical figure which binds it to the rest of the canto—an organizing principle, as it were, at the imagistic level. I refer to the exquisite image of the mechanical clock at the end of the canto. For all of its familiarity to us, it must have startled contemporaries, most of whom had undoubtedly never seen any such device.[23] It serves as an example of how radically juxtaposed elements, in this case the most ancient ideas of astronomic speculation and the most modern of mechanical inventions, are fused together in Dante's synthesis, much as Solomon and Siger of Brabant[24] both find a place in his cast of characters:

Indi, come orologio che ne chiami
  ne l'ora che la sposa di Dio surge
  a mattinar lo sposo perché l'ami,
che l'una parte e l'altra tira e urge,
  tin tin sonando . . .   (vv. 139–143)

Then, like a clock which calls us at the hour when the Bride of God rises to sing her matins to her Bridegroom, that he may love her, in which the one part draws or drives the other, sounding *ting! ting!*

Of the many themes alluded to in this dense and beautiful passage—the sun and the liturgy,[25] the Church and Christ as Bride and Bridegroom, the dawn song of lovers[26]—I should like to single out just one: the aptness of comparing the "spiriti sapienti" to an instrument for measuring the diurnal course of the sun. We have seen from the discussion of Daniélou's work that solar imagery applied to Christ in both of his symbolic roles, as both the Day and the Year of the Lord. Because the sun measures both the day and the year (it is for this reason "lo ministro maggior de la natura"—*Par.* X, 28), its path, the Zodiac, may be said to mark both the hours and the months. The manifestation of the number twelve would thus compress universal history—the span of history represented by the "spiriti sapienti," the hours and the years—into the eternal now of the "dance" in the Empyrean of which this is a foreshadowing. A text from St. Ambrose will serve as an example of the tradition: "If the whole duration of the world is like a single day, its hours mark off centuries: in other words, the centuries are its hours. Now there are twelve hours in the day. Therefore, in the mystic sense, the Day is indeed Christ. He has his twelve Apostles, who shone with the light of heaven, in which Grace has its distinct phases."[27] So in Dante's *Paradiso,* the souls of the blessed take in all of history by gazing into history's center: "mirando il punto / a cui tutti li tempi son presenti" (*Par.* XVII, 17–18).[28]

Because this is a foreshadowing of the movement of the blessed souls in the Empyrean, the center of this circular dance is not occupied by the *Sol salutis,*[29] but simply by the pilgrim and his guide. Beatrice clearly contrasts this representation with the paradisiac original when she juxtaposes this material sun with the "Sole de li Angeli." There is, however, one comparison that suggests Beatrice's role in the representation; her position in the center of the circular dance is very much like that of a heavenly body—not the sun, but the moon:

> Io vidi più folgór vivi e vincenti
> far di noi centro e di sé far corona,
> più dolci in voce che in vista lucenti:
> così cinger la figlia di Latona
> vedem talvolta, quando l'aere è pregno,
> sì che ritenga il fil che fa la zona. (X, 64–69)

> I saw many flashing lights of surpassing brightness make of us a center and of themselves a crown, more sweet in voice than shining in aspect. Thus girt we sometimes see Latona's daughter when the air is so impregnate that it holds the thread which makes her zone.

This passage cannot be dismissed as merely decorative or merely metaphoric, for the comparison it suggests between Beatrice and the pilgrim on one hand and the moon on the other has been rigorously prepared by the verses which immediately precede it. Beatrice tells the pilgrim to thank God, whom she describes as the Sun, for having given him the grace to ascend to the sphere of the material sun. He does so with such concentration that he forgets Beatrice for the moment: "E sì tutto il mio amore in lui si mise / che Beatrice eclissò ne l'oblio" (*Par.* X, 59–60) (and all my love was so set in Him that it eclipsed Beatrice in oblivion). The word "eclipse" here does not signify a darkening, but rather a blotting out by a greater light, as Benvenuto da Imola observed: "[Beatrix] eclipsata est, idest, nubilata in luce."[30] It is a commonplace of symbolic astronomy that the moon regularly endures such an "eclipse" as it approaches the light of the sun, which for this reason is thought of as a lover embracing his beloved.[31] This submerged significance of Beatrice's "eclipse" by God comes to the surface in the lines immediately following, when she is indirectly compared to the moon.

The phenomenon of the halo around the moon (sometimes referred to in the Middle Ages as *Iris,* like the rainbow to which Dante later compares the spirits in *Par.* XII, 10 ff.)[32] is a substitute for an astronomical spectacle, the sun surrounded by the stars, which no mortal eye can ever see. We may presume, then, that it stands to the sun as the human to the divine or, to use Dante's own language, as the "essemplo" to the "essemplare" (*Par.* XXVIII, 55–56). It is abundantly clear that the sun is here a symbol for divinity and that Beatrice is associated with the moon; it remains for us to establish the sense in which she may be said to substitute for the referent of the solar image whose history we have discussed. It will come as no surprise in the context of Hugo Rahner's "Christian Mystery"[33] of the sun and moon, if we suggest that Beatrice's role here is meant to be emblematic of the Church guiding the faithful. Put most simply, we may say that if the twelve apostles are the Zodiac of *Sol Christi,* then the twelve philosophers and theologians are the "corona" of *Luna Ecclesiae.*

From the earliest days of Christianity, as Rahner has shown, "it is as though Helios and Selene were only created in order—to quote Origen—'to carry out their stately dance for the salvation of the world.' "[34] The ancient world had already characterized the relationship between sun and moon as that of lovers; it remained only to apply the teaching of Paul about the heavenly Bridegroom and his Bride to that ancient image-complex in order to see in the *mysterium Lunae* the whole drama of the Church. The waxing and waning of the moon, the derivation of its light from the sun, its illumination in darkness and its fading in the light of day all seemed perfect allegories of the relationship of Christ to the Church. The woman "clothed with the sun" of Apoc. 12 (quoted above) became the *locus classicus* for discussions of this kind which, according to Rahner, were perfected in the writings of Augustine. Rahner ends his discussion by citing *Paradiso* XXIII, Dante's direct treatment of the theme:

Quale ne' plenilunïi serenii
 Trivïa ride tra le ninfe etterne

che dipingon lo ciel per tutti i seni,
vid' i' sopra migliaia di lucerne
un sol che tutte quante l'accendea,
come fa 'l nostro le viste superne . . . (vv. 25–30)

As in the clear skies at the full moon Trivia smiles among the eternal nymphs that deck heaven through all its depths, I saw, above thousands of lamps, a Sun which kindled each one of them as does our own the things we see above . . .

If, as a recent critic has suggested, the function of this metaphor is "purely emotional,"[35] then it must be said that the emotion is that of all of Christendom, occasioned by the fulfillment of universal history. This moment in the poem marks the shift in the metaphor we have been discussing and in many others as well—perhaps of all of the astronomical metaphors of the *Paradiso* up to this point. The contrast is still between the "Sole de li Angeli" ("Un Sole") and the "sole sensibile" ("il nostro") but this time their functions are reversed: for the first time in the poem, the *Sol Christi* may be beheld by the pilgrim, while the material sun is simply a memory of the sphere and the world below. If that transcendent sun is compared to the moon (Diana—Trivia) and the stars (*ninfe*) here in our world, it is because the *mysterium Lunae,* the Church, is all we have on this side of the frontiers of material reality to foreshadow the triumph of Christ; a contingent, provisional image, like those of *Paradiso* X, until the break of eternal Day.

I have tried to show that the traditional image of the apostles and the Zodiac may be taken as the background for the controlling theme of *Paradiso* X and that the shift from apostles to theologians and philosophers finds its counterpart in a shifting of the center from the sun to Beatrice and the pilgrim or, according to one of the comparisons, the moon. There are two additional reasons that can be adduced to support the hypothesis that this shift is implicitly from Christ to a traditional image for the Church. The first of these is that the comparison to the moon surrounded by water vapor (expressed in terms subtly suggestive of generation and maternity: *cingere, pregno, zona*), like the faint suggestion of flowers and fields noticed by Aldo Scaglione in the *Trivia* image ("le ninfe etterne / che dipingon lo ciel . . ."; cf. "le piante [di] questa ghirlanda," *Par.* X, 91)[36] underscores precisely the elements of moon imagery which enabled early exegetes to identify the heavenly body with the Church. Rahner makes the point:

> What causes the Sun's light to grow more mild is that Selene mingles the fire of Helios with the water of her own being, and I might as well at this stage tell you more about the rioting fancies of Greek thought on the subject of "heavenly moon-water." Poets and nature mystics produced an abundance of ideas about it, ideas which lingered on for a thousand years . . . Selene becomes a giver of water, dew is created which she causes to drip down . . . it is a begetter of life upon the earth; it brings about the growth of the grass and the growth of beasts and makes it possible for human mothers to bear their children . . . In view of what has been said, it is not surprising that in seeking to give expression to his own beliefs the Christian should have made use of this lunar imagery with which the whole Hellenistic world was familiar.[37]

He then goes on to demonstrate how this imagery seemed perfect for conveying ideas about spiritual rebirth and the water of baptism associated with the Church. The virgin goddess Diana (or "Trivia," to use Dante's name for her) was transformed by Christianity from moon mother into the *Mater Ecclesia.*

The second, much more obvious reason for thinking that the triumph of the theologians and philosophers is a triumph of the Church foreshadowing the triumph of *Sol Christi* has already been mentioned, although in passing. It is simply this: the harmonic song produced by the dance of the philosophers and theologians is compared by the poet at the culminating point of the canto to the liturgical song of the Church, the eternal present marked by the hours of the day.[38] By referring to this song in erotic terms ("la sposa di Dio surge / a mattinar lo sposo perchè l'ami") the poet binds into a single stunning unity not only Christ and his Church, sun and moon, apostles and theologians, but also his own longing relationship to God, through the mediation of Beatrice. It would be foolhardy to generalize this mediation into an identification. We may say only that the mediation on the personal level, this man's salvation, finds its counterpart in human society in the role of the Church and for this reason Dante chose to use the traditional imagery of mediation to describe her. It is in this sense, as the relationship of incarnate reality to salvation history, that Beatrice may be said in this canto to be a *figura Ecclesiae.*

The ending of the narrative and therefore of the canto calls our attention to Christ, the second person of the Trinity and the exemplar of all wisdom—*Somma Sapienza.* The propriety of such an ending in the canto of the "spiriti sapienti" is too obvious to require extensive commentary. What is equally obvious, however, is that the beginning of the canto seems to have little to do with this ending, for all of the didactic insistence of the involved address to the reader. The opening lines of the canto hint at some of the most complicated of all problems of medieval thought: the inner life of the Trinity, its role in the creation, the relationship of the heavens to generation and corruption on earth and, finally, the relationship of all of these problems to the moral life. After touching upon all of these themes, the poet somewhat impatiently dismisses his reader:

> Or ti riman, lettor, sovra 'l tuo banco,
> dietro pensando a ciò che si preliba,
> s'esser vuoi lieto assai prima che stanco.
> Messo t'ho innanzi; omai per te ti ciba;
> ché a sé torce tutta la mia cura
> quella materia ond' io son fatto scriba. (X, 22–27)

> Now remain, reader, upon your bench, reflecting on this of which you have a foretaste, if you would be glad far sooner than weary. I have set before you; now feed yourself, because that matter of which I am made the scribe wrests to itself all my care.

It would take more than a lifetime to complete the task set for us in these lines and certainly more than these pages to sketch out how this doctrinal passage serves to introduce not only the tenth canto, but the next four as well. To conclude, however, I should like simply to point to a few elements of the opening verses that relate to the translation of beatitude into astronomical terms. This will require first of all a return to our discussion of the relevance of the Platonic tradition to the canto's theme.

The theme of the circular dance of the stars is a familiar one in the *Timaeus.* The phrase "choreae stellarum" used in the translation of Chalcidius is already a figurative application of the word meaning "choral dance" to the exigencies of astronomical description. In the commentary of Guillaume de Conches a definition is offered of the movement of the starry spheres that might equally well describe the dance of the "spiriti sapienti";

> And the dance is a circular motion accompanied by harmonious sound. For this reason the philosophers say that the stars perform (*facere*) a dance, because they move in a circle, and from their motion they produce (*reddunt*) a harmonious sound.[39]

Elsewhere, Guillaume identifies the music specifically as *cantus*.[40] The song produced by the stellar dance is of course the music of the spheres, the music produced by the varying movements of the heavenly bodies, inaudible to mortal ears.[41] The music of the Heaven of the Sun, "voce a voce in tempra," seems to have the same transcendent quality, for the poet twice insists that it cannot be heard here below (vv. 75 and 146). Of more importance for the association of these ancient, admittedly generic themes with the tenth canto is the fact that it is the sun, according to the *Timaeus,* that sets the standard of motion for all of the heavens by measuring time:

> And in order that there might be a conspicuous measure for the relative speed and slowness with which they moved in their eight revolutions (*chorea*), the god kindled a light in the . . . Sun—in order that he might fill the whole heaven with his shining and that all living things for whom it was meet might possess number, learning it from the revolution of the same and uniform. Thus and for these reasons day and night came into being, the period of the single and most intelligent revolution.[42]

It should be observed that the sun has an equally regulatory function in Dante's metaphoric universe even down to the detail of the motion which it induces in the "spiriti sapienti." When their rank is doubled and the poet asks us to imagine two garlands circling about a center, the description he gives us of their motion, as if "l'uno andasse al prima e l'altro al poi" (*Par.* XIII, 18) (one went first and the other after), is part of the definition of time: "numero di movimento [celestiale] secondo prima e poi."[43] Time may have its roots in the *Primum Mobile,* but its measure in hours and years is determined by the sun.

The centrality of the sun and its essential role in the cosmos led very early, possibly with the Stoics, to the idea that it represented the location of the world-soul, the *anima mundi,* whose varied history in the Middle Ages, including identification with the Holy Spirit and then finally with the goddess Natura, has been traced by Tullio Gregory.[44] By Dante's time, of course, no Aristotelian could take the idea of a world soul seriously, but a poet was perfectly free to do so and survivals of the idea remain in Dante's poem (see chap. 4 above). In the present context, I should like simply to point out a poetic survival, not explicitly stated, in the form of an associative principle that binds together the introduction of the tenth canto with the narrative contained within it and relates both to the moral imperative of the journey. That associative principle finds its expression precisely in the address to the reader; when Dante asks the reader to look up at that critical point in the Zodiac he is in fact asking us to contemplate not only the image which underlies the narrative of the canto, as we have seen, but also the complex of themes traditionally associated with the Zodiac in the tradition of symbolic cosmology.[45] The Zodiac was traditionally believed to be the emblem of the Creator's mark on the world and the seal of rationality both on man and on the heavens. So in the tenth canto, it is the sign of "quanto per mente e per loco si gira" (v. 4).

The text that first associated the circular movement of rationality (*per mente*) and of the heavens (*per loco*) with the circularity of divinity was Plato's *Timaeus.* It was obvious to subsequent commentators on Plato's text that the motions of the world-soul, for all of their apparently mythical character, were in fact derived from the two motions observable in the heavens: the diurnal circling of the sun from east to west, marking the hours of the day, and the annual circling of the sun in the opposite direction along the Zodiac, marking the months of the year. When the sun crossed the equator at its point of intersection with the ecliptic, "dove l'un moto e l'altro si percuote," it was thought to mark the spot where the Platonic Demiurge had set into motion both the soul of the world and the soul of man.[46] Boethius' *Consolation of Philosophy* (III, 9) provided the Middle Ages with a most concise statement of the manner in which the universe bears the image of the *anima mundi:* "You release the World-Soul throughout the harmonious parts of the universe . . . to give motion to all things. That soul, thus divided, pursues its revolving course in two circles, and, returning to itself, embraces the profound mind and *transforms heaven to its own image."*[47] It remained only to identify the Demiurge with the Father, the profound mind with the Son and the world-soul with the Holy Spirit in order for Christians to see in both the heavens and the human mind the image of the Trinity,[48]

The history of the assimilation of the three persons of the Trinity to their Platonic counterparts is of course a substantial part of the history of Christian philosophy in the Middle Ages and especially in the twelfth century.[49] What is of more concern to us here, however, is the assimilation of Platonic imagery to the Christian revelation. From the earliest days of Christianity, the Platonic emblem of the Demiurge's creative act, the letter "chi" corresponding to the intersection of celestial movement that Dante asks his reader to contemplate, was associated with the emblem of Christ and of his redemptive act: the cross. Wilhelm Bousset has traced the history of that association.[50] Among the passages he cites, one is of particular interest to us, for it brings together the theme of wisdom in the person of Christ and the theme of celestial harmony. The passage comes from the apocryphal Acts of John, quoted above in relation to the dance of the disciples. The Lord appears to John and shows him a celestial "cross of light" specifically distinguished from the true cross:

> This cross of light . . . is the marking off of all things and the uplifting and the foundation of those things that are fixed and were unsettled, and the harmony of the wisdom—and indeed the wisdom of the harmony. . . . This, then, is the cross which fixed all things apart by the Word, and marked off the things from birth and below it, and then compacted all into one.[51]

In his commentary, Bousset has shown that this passage reflects a blending of the cosmological theme from the *Timaeus* with elements of the Gospel and of the sapiential books of the Old Testament. He goes on to document the diffusion of the idea throughout the Patristic era and we may add to his findings that it survived well into the Middle Ages, for the association of the Platonic "X" with the cross reappears in the works of Peter Abelard.[52] The general relevance of these Christian accommodations of Plato's text to a reading of the *Paradiso* is probably considerable—the cross of light in the Acts of John, for example, seems particularly suggestive for an interpretation of Dante's representation in the heaven of Mars. In the present context, however, the relevance is simply this: the history traced by Bousset provides an analogue to the opening verses of the tenth canto, wherein a glance up at the celestial "X" (the intersection of the equator and the ecliptic on the Zodiac) also serves to evoke the central mysteries of Christianity, through the mediation of Platonic myth.

If both the movement of mind (*per mente:* the "spiriti sapienti") and the vital principle of the universe (the heavens and the "mondo che li chiama"—v. 15) can be encompassed by the same astronomical motif (the sun and the Zodiac), it is by virtue of the Christianization of the Platonic theme of the *anima mundi.* The Platonic theme and its Christian elaboration, together with the glance up at the Zodiac which exemplifies the concepts they represent, provide us with a sufficient background for interpreting the entire introduction to the canto.

The opening of the canto sets forth the twofold movement of the threefold Deity:

> Guardando nel suo Figlio con l'Amore
> che l'uno e l'altro etternalmente spira,
> lo primo e ineffabile Valore
> quanto per mente e per loco si gira
> con tant' ordine fé ch'esser non puote
> sanza gustar di lui chi ciò rimira. (X, 1–6)

> Looking upon His Son with the love which the One and the Other eternally breathe forth, the primal and ineffable Power made everything that revolves through the mind or through space with such order that he who contemplates it cannot but taste of Him.

Were it not for the standard Christian effort to re-establish equality in the hierarchical relationship of the One, Mind and Soul in a neoplatonic system, this opening might well be a paraphrase of Macrobius.[53] At any rate, Dante intends here to set forth the two motions of the Trinity or, as he puts it in v. 51, "mostrando come *spira* e come *figlia.*" These two motions, intellectual generation and the spiration of love, volition, are the two motions in the Trinity which find their counterpart in the cosmos, "dove l'un moto e l'altro si percuote," insofar as the cosmos can reflect the inner life of the Trinity. Because of the way in which these two motions along the Zodiac affect all of creation, they are the instruments of God's Providence in the world (vv. 13–21).[54] More than that, however, because of the parallelism previously mentioned, the motions are the exemplar of all created mind as well: whatever rotates *per mente* or *per loco.* It is for this reason that all mind and all of the heavens offer a foretaste of the Trinity.

This, I take it, is the force of the word "dunque" in the address to the reader: "Leva *dunque,* lettor, a l'alte ruote / meco la vista" (vv. 7–8). The call to look up at the heavens to contemplate the wonders of the creation is of course a familiar religious theme,[55] but it is also a Platonic theme that fits in very well with the microcosmic-macrocosmic context of the opening lines. It is exactly in the context of the passage in Macrobius referred to above, reminiscent of the poet's trinitarian opening, that the significance of the motif is clearly enunciated:

> Human bodies . . . were found to be capable of sustaining, with difficulty, a small part of it [the divinity of Mind], and only they, since they alone seemed to be erect—reaching toward heaven and shunning earth, as it were—and since only the erect can always gaze with ease at the heavens; furthermore they alone have in their heads a likeness of a sphere . . . the only one capable of containing mind.[56]

The glance up at the heavens is in this sense the fulfillment of human rationality.

To conclude, and at the same time to show the ways in which my findings may be generalized to extend to the entire representation of the Heaven of the Sun, I should like for the last time to mention the circular dance of the star-souls. There are of course two motions described when all of the "spiriti sapienti" finally appear. We have discussed the twofold motion of the Trinity, whereby it *figlia* and *spira,* with intellect and volition. We have suggested its analogies with the twofold motion of the sun along the Zodiac. It seems reasonable to assume that the Trinity is also the exemplar upon which the movement of the heavenly garlands[57] is based. The repeatedly parallel syntax used to describe each pair of motions—"che l'uno e l'altro etternalmente spira," (X, 2), (the One and the Other eternally breathe forth); "dove l'un moto e l'altro si percuote" (X, 9) (where the one motion strikes the other); "e l'un ne l'altro aver li raggi suoi" (XIII, 16); (and one to have its rays within the other)—leads one to suspect that the poet intends to associate the movement of the "spiriti sapienti" with the twofold movement of the Trinity, comparing both to the two movements of the Zodiac. The suspicion is confirmed by the descriptions of the two wheels. The two movements of the Trinity (the generation of the word and the spiration of love) represent respectively an act of intelligence and an act of will. However else one divides the cast of characters in the Heaven of the Sun, there seems general agreement that the first circle represents intellectuals who shone with "cherubic splendor" and the second represents lovers who burned with "seraphic ardor,"[58] exemplifying respectively intelligence and will.

The evidence of the zodiacal nature of the imagery beyond the tenth canto is equally clear, although perhaps not as widely recognized. First of all, as soon as the second circle appears, Dante describes the movement as that of a "mola" (XII, 3), a millstone, the same word that he used in the *Convivio* in order specifically to distinguish zodiacal motion from generically circular motion.[59] Again, he refers to the song of the souls as more beautiful than that of "nostre muse / nostre serene" (XII, 7–8), the mythological goddesses who presided over the turning of the spheres.[60] We have seen that the phrase "l'uno andasse al prima e l'altro al poi" (XIII, 18) recalls the measurement of time by celestial motion. Most convincing of all, perhaps, is the fact that the two accounts of the lives of the saints, obviously constructed in parallel, make reference to the course of the sun at precisely the same verse—the "rising" of Francis is associated with the rising of the sun, while the "rising" of Dominic is associated with its setting. At verse 51 of *Paradiso* XI, Dante describes Francis' birth as a sun coming to the world, "come fa questo tal volta di Gange" (even as this [sun] is wont to rise from Ganges). At verse 51 of *Paradiso* XII, he describes the birth of Dominic as taking place near where "lo sol tal volta ad ogni uom si nasconde" (where the sun sometimes hides himself from every man). This evidence would seem to indicate that the twofold zodiacal motion constitutes the pattern even of the narrative portions of the succeeding cantos.

When the third light appears above the other two, the "vero sfavillar del Santo Spiro" (XIV, 76), we, like the pilgrim, are unable to make it out precisely. As the light appears, the poet's comparison is to twilight:

> E sì come al salir di prima sera
> comincian per lo ciel nove parvenze,
> sì che la vista pare e non par vera, (XIV, 70–72)

> And as, at rise of early evening, new lights

begin to show in heaven, so that the sight does,
and yet does not, seem real.

The pilgrim ascends almost immediately to the next heaven, as if he were not quite ready to see this celestial, but not yet paradisiac triune light. In this metaphoric area that is Dante's own creation, somewhere between the daylight of earth and the daylight of eternity, the sun with his two motions sets the scene for the revelation that is to follow. It is clear here, as it was in the *Convivio,* what that revelation will be, for, as Dante put it, "Nullo sensibile in tutto lo mondo è più degno di farsi essemplo di Dio che 'l sole" (No object of sense in all the world is more fit to be made the symbol of God than the sun).[61]

16. The Final Image: *Paradiso* XXXIII, 144

AT THE END OF THE POEM, WHEN the pilgrim's vision is complete, his powers fail him and he is touched directly by the hand of God:

A l'alta fantasia qui mancò possa;
  ma già volgeva il mio disio e 'l *velle,*
  sì come rota ch'igualmente è mossa,
l'amor che move il sole e l'altre stelle. (vv. 142–145)

Here power failed the lofty phantasy; but already my desire and my will were revolved, like a wheel that is evenly moved, by the Love which moves the sun and the other stars.

High fantasy failed Dante then, before the pilgrim became the poet whose account we have just finished reading. Now, however, he has a responsibiity to approximate that moment in his verses. His experience—perhaps all experience, ultimately—remains incommunicable. Nevertheless, a poet who would bear witness to the Light must make his peace with the limitations of the flesh. The final simile is Dante's compromise, here and now, the closest his art can come to what for us is out of reach.

To refuse to examine that simile too closely on the rather facile grounds that it transcends our understanding is to confuse the now of the poet with the then of his *persona.* If, as Natalino Sapegno suggests, the failure of *fantasia*[1] coincides with the failure of poetic representation, then it is no longer possible to distinguish the intricacy of the simile from the ineffable quality of the vision it seeks to approximate. But the failure here is ours, not Dante's, for while the final simile is profound, it is totally coherent; the mystical fervor it recalls remains a memory, indelible, to be sure, but not so overwhelming that the poet can forget either his learning or his art as he seeks to recapture it. Until the last stages of the pilgrim's journey, his was a faith seeking understanding: *fides quaerens intellectum*. Now that he has attained all that he sought, we must take the poetic fact on faith and seek an understanding of our own—which is to say that although we cannot follow the pilgrim to the heights, we can at least rise to the poet's compromise. To fall short is merely to approximate what is already an approximation.

For all its poetic immediacy, the final image makes considerable demands upon our learning. In the first place, although the vision itself transcended all human understanding, Dante does not hesitate to use a technical scholastic term, *velle,* as he describes its effect. There can be nothing vague about the word, for it is used in conjunction with *disio,* so close to it in meaning that unless we define both precisely, *velle* seems redundant and its use here pedantic. Secondly, although no image will suffice to recall that intensely personal experience, the poet nevertheless turns to a commonplace mystical theme, the circular turning of the stars, to describe the final integration. Moreover, because he has also used the word *stelle* at the close of both of the preceding *cantiche,* it seems clear that he has transformed the commonplace into a structural element of some importance in the poem and has therefore made of it something profoundly his own. Finally, the comparison of the wheel needs some clarification. The syntax of the preceding verse sets up a barrier to our visualization of it, for it is one image standing for two movements. The love that moves the sun and the other stars turned two powers, *disio* and *velle,* as a single wheel is moved. Either the final movement is not so simple as it appears to be, or *disio* and *velle* are not so distinct as poetic precision would seem to require.

There is more at stake here, in the precise understanding of the simile, than merely a formal principle. If, along with the majority of critics,[2] we take the final image to be that of a circle moving around a divine point, which is at once the source of the soul's motion and its most intimate possession, a point with which the soul coincides, we simplify, and therefore falsify, Dante's idea of the soul's ultimate relationship to God. The final movement of the soul is not simply the private fruition of a personal possession. In Dante's view, which is not the view of a solipsist, the complete fulfillment of the soul's desires is at the same time an integration with the rest of creation. The circular turning of the soul does not shut out external reality but rather joins with it in the majestic sweep of the final verse. If this were a purely subjective fulfillment, a Romantic apotheosis of the self to the exclusion of all others, there would be little need of a complex approximation—a closed circle or a Mallarméan *page blanche* would have done equally well. But precisely because that personal fulfillment was at the same time an objective commitment to the cosmic order, it entailed a responsibility to bear witness to the Light, as do the sun and the other stars—therein lies its complexity. The final simile, then, is not only a most intimate expression of self-fulfillment, but also public testimony of God's grace: "l'essemplo basti / a cui experienza grazia serba" (*Par.* I, 71–72). It is to the final *essemplo* that we must now turn.

Dante could hardly have been more explicit. The last image is not of a circle, but of a wheel: "sì come rota ch'igualmente è mossa." Yet, in spite of the apparent simplicity of the comparison, or perhaps because of it, it does not seem to have evoked any coherent image in the minds of its numerous commentators. Benedetto Croce,[3] for example, called into question the poetic worth of the last canto precisely on the grounds that Dante had surrendered poetic vision to abstract thought; and, while many have quarreled with the verdict,[4] few have debated the evidence. No one, so far as I know, has bothered to consider the difference between the circle, a geometric abstraction, and the concrete object that embodies it. Such an oversight is easy to understand. We are so accustomed to the symbol of the circle in the mystical tradition and in the works of Dante himself that we read it here, into the word *rota,* and explain the verbal discrepancy with more scholarship, this time of the exegetic variety: given a context such as this, a scholar might be reminded of the famous vision of another prophet—Ezekiel—and of the wheels he saw.[5] Because biblical exegetes often glossed the vision of the prophet in anagogic terms,[6] it seems logical enough to refer to Ezekiel's winged and fiery wheels here, in order to explain the presence of the word *rota* where our learning had led us to expect a circle, pure and simple.

If this were some other poet, such a reference would perhaps be enough. The static allegory of this for that, characteristic of the mainstream of medieval exegesis, ordinarily does quite well for the extraction of general meaning from particular statement, although in the process it usually reduces dialectic to juxtaposition and poetic experience to banality. For Dante, however, it will not do. The poet who sought to give dynamic incarnation to his experience began from the image and communicated meaning in it as well as through it. He could scarcely have been content with pointing vaguely in the direction of biblical tradition with an image that meant nothing in itself. It is with the image that we must therefore begin, and there Ezekiel's text helps us not at all. The biblical wheel, we are told, is, among other things, a wheel within a wheel, *rota in medio rotae,* a mysterious description that was taken by various exegetes to mean anything from celestial colures to fiery hubcaps.[7] To explain Dante's wheel by means of Ezekiel's, therefore, is to beg the question and to enter upon a logical circle of our own. The text of Ezekiel provides us with only the biblical resonance of Dante's verse. For the substance, however, we shall have to leave exegesis and turn to the dynamics of Christian neoplatonism.

The problem of understanding Dante's image of the wheel is probably identical with the problem of visualizing Ezekiel's wheel as Dante visualized it. The solution of both problems, I believe, begins to become apparent from a closer reading of a text that Dante scholars have known about for a long time. Bruno Nardi[8] has suggested that the commentary of pseudo-Dionysius on the wheels of Ezekiel was of some importance for the introduction of neoplatonic ideas into the scholastic doctrines of beatitude. Dionysius applies the figure of the wheel to the angels and attempts an anagogic reading of Ezek. 1:16 and 10:2:

> As for the winged wheels that advance unerringly without swerving, they signify the power to advance straight ahead, in a straight line, on the straight way unerringly, thanks to a perfect rotation, which is not of this world . . . These fiery wheels, which receive the divine form, have the power to turn upon themselves because they move perpetually around the highest good.[9]

Nardi's intention was to trace the struggle of the schoolmen to reconcile the Aristotelian idea of beatitude as eternal rest with the Platonic idea of eternal circulation, an idea which was transmitted to them through Dionysius the Areopagite in texts such as the one just quoted. The relevance of the discussion for the historical and philosophical background of Dante's verse was considerable, although it contributed little to our literal understanding of the verse itself. The point that Nardi failed to make is that the passage from the Areopagite describes not only circulation, but forward motion as well: a circle turns endlessly in the abstract and describes a single simple motion, and is for that very reason the traditional symbol of perfection or eternity. But when a wheel turns, it goes somewhere. So Dionysius mentions "perfect rotation," wheels turning "upon themselves," their perpetual movement "around the highest Good"; but at the same time he adds that the wheels "advance . . . straight ahead, in a straight line, on the straight way." Thus, the product of angelic rotation is a forward motion. A wheel is moved by its center, as is the circle of the mystics; simultaneously, however, the wheel's point of tangency with the ground gives it rectilinear thrust, and it moves forward as well as around. Like the movement of the pilgrim, the motion of the wheel itself is uniform (*igualmente mossa*) and yet logically twofold.

The distinction between the movement of a wheel and the movement of a circle was as obvious to Dante's contemporaries as it is to us. Thomas Aquinas, for example, unlike most commentators on the *Divine Comedy,* takes pains not to confuse the two. His commentary on Aristotle's definition of *circulatio* as the first and most perfect of motions introduces the distinction in an unexpected context. His point is that not all circularity can qualify as simple motion:

> He says, then, first of all, that "revolution," i.e. circular motion, means that which moves around a center. And we understand by this around the center of the *world;* for a *wheel,* which moves around *its own* center, does not move with true circularity. Its motion is composed of elevation and depression.[10]

The example of the turning wheel serves here as an illustration of circular motion that is not simple, but compound: a terrestrial wheel turns around its own center in a circle, but with respect to the earth it moves in a rectilinear fashion. So, in the passage from pseudo-Dionysius, the angelic wheels rotate, but at the same time ascend to heaven. Similarly, Dante's celestial wheel moves in two directions, and thus he calls it a wheel and not a circle. His personal fulfillment is represented by a perfect rotation around God, upon whom he is centered. At the same time, however, because he moves in harmony with the rest of creation, represented by the heavenly bodies, the forward motion is along the circular track that surrounds God. The pilgrim's motion is not only a rotation around the interior object of his desire, but also, because the contact with reality is never lost, a revolution around the spiritual center of the universe. The same revolution carries with it the angelic intelligences of the spheres; they in turn transmit the motive power of primal love to the sun and the other stars.

All of this is implicit in the literal image. In order to understand its tropologic implications more fully, we must turn now to examine the source of the image of the wheel, common both to Dionysius and to Dante. Without much doubt, we can affirm that if the wheel of beatitude is Ezekiel's, it is also Plato's. Here again, as throughout the poem, the tradition of the *Timaeus* furnished to Dante a poetic representation of a spiritual development.

For Plato, *paideia* was not simply a goal, but rather a development, a shaping or evolution of the human personality. To capture its dynamism, however, and to translate into static concepts what he believed to be spiritual becoming, he needed a poetic language that would encompass both the immutable truth of the goal and the vitality of the process. He chose a corporeal analogy so as to give poetic substance to his theory of education. To distinguish modes of knowledge, for example, he established a symbolic dichotomy between the eye of the body and the eye of the soul, while the dynamic itself was translated into its physical analogues: the journey or the flight. It was the Pythagorean system of the *Timaeus,* however, that inserted both the poetic substance and the dynamic of the Platonic allegory into a symbolic cosmology that gave to man a central place in the universe and at the same time gave to the physical laws of that universe a moral, which is to say a human, dimension. Werner Jaeger[11] has shown that when the *morphosis* of Plato changed its name to *deificatio,* the human *anabasis* became divine, and Plato's *paideia* was transmitted to posterity in a new form, as *imitatio Christi.*

This amalgam of Platonic imagery and Christian doctrine was precisely the compromise to which Dante turned in order to express his vision. In a number of essays I attempt to show how several themes in the *Divine Comedy* are ultimately dependent, if not on Plato's text, then at least on his influence (see especially chap. 4 in this book). What concerns us now is the final scene of the drama of human perfection as Plato stages it, for it is against that Platonic background that Dante's final verses are to be understood. Because of the analogy established by Plato between physical movement and spiritual development, perfection in the spiritual order was symbolized in the *Timaeus* by perfect motion in the universe: the diurnal movement of the fixed stars. The soul began its pre-existence in the stars, and it is to the stars that the perfect soul will return, when the perfect "circlings" of its mind will exactly match the circlings of the universe. The first movement of the heavens, the twenty-four-hour circling of all heavenly bodies, is a manifestation of the perfect intelligence of the world-soul, the *anima mundi,* which carries around with it all things, including the star-souls themselves. In this Platonic version of the microcosm-macrocosm analogy, the Demiurge created the star-souls according to the same pattern and with the same material that he used for the world-soul, so that each individual soul also moves as the world-soul, according to what Plato called "the motion of the same and uniform." As the world-soul rotates endlessly in a perfect circle (the diurnal turning of the heavens), so each individual soul rotates upon its own center. But the individual souls are also carried around by the perfect movement of the world-soul because of the universal symphony, *harmonia,* that reigns throughout the cosmos. Thus, the souls move with two motions, and the stars, which manifest the movement of those souls, rotate as well as revolve. In the following passage, Plato explains the meaning of the two motions that the Demiurge gives to the stellar gods:

> And he assigned to each two motions: one uniform in the same place, as each always thinks the same thoughts about the same things; the other a forward motion, as each is subjected to the revolution of the same and uniform [i.e., the diurnal motion]. . . . For this reason came into being all the unwandering stars, living beings divine and everlasting, which abide for ever revolving uniformly upon themselves.[12]

But assuming that the fixed stars not only revolve around the heavens but also rotate on their own axes, Plato provided himself with a perfect analogue of the twin aspect of intellectual perfection: perfect circling within, because of a fixity of knowledge and purpose, as well as perfect circling without, because of a perfect integration into a harmonious cosmic order. This representation of twofold perfection is the ancestor of Dante's celestial wheel. For confirmation of what at this point seems only likely, we have merely to turn to the Latin translation of this passage by Chalcidius. Describing the two movements, he says:

> The one always going around itself in the same orbit and in the same place, always deliberating about the same things; the other of the sort which, always desiring to proceed forward, maintains a wheel-like movement around its object through the coercion of the same and unchanging nature (*intra obiectum eius rotabundus teneretur*).[13]

The unusual adjective *rotabundus,* which does not appear in Latin before Chalcidius so far as I know, associates the twofold movement of the heavens with the word *rota,* so that the phrase *motus rotabundus* might well be translated into Italian by the words "come rota ch'igualmente è mossa." In a context such as this, combining a twofold human perfection with astronomical imagery, a sophisticated contemporary of Dante would associate the two expressions.

Because Plato's assertion that the stars rotate on their own axes was based upon an *a priori* metaphysical assumption rather than upon a desire to account for appearances, it was rejected by Aristotle in the *De caelo,* and therefore by most of his followers. It nevertheless remained as one of the alternative answers to an empirically insoluble question concerning the *motus proprius* of the fixed stars.[14] Of more interest to us than the history of the purely scientific question, however, is the survival of the metaphysical exigency, to which Plato hoped to respond with his stellar theory.[15] According to Plato, a star was a being with a soul, which is to say, a self-moving principle: *arché kinéseós.* It therefore had to have a movement proper to itself, independent of, but in harmony with, the movement of the same and uniform. Moreover, so perfect was such a soul that the movement it caused had to be the most perfect of all, a selfsame movement, which could be only a rotation in the same place. Thus, while the star revolves around the heaven with the diurnal motion because of its perfect subjugation to the dominion of the world-soul, it also rotates with a uniform circular motion because of its individual perfection.

Aristotle did not share Plato's theory of the soul and therefore had to account for celestial movement in terms of his own theory of motion.[16] He accomplished this by substituting for Plato's star-souls the intelligences of the spheres, which the Christians were much later to adopt into their own cosmologies by identifying them with the angels of revelation.[17] The symbolic mechanics of Plato's *Timaeus* was not, however, neglected by Christian thinkers; it entered into the angelology and mysticism of pseudo-Dionysius, who used the patterns of motion contained in the *Timaeus* to describe the spiritual movement of the angels.[18] Nardi[19] has demonstrated that Dante presented a reconciliation of Platonic and Aristotelian theories of motion when he staged the circular dance of the movers of the spheres around God—derived from Dionysius—in order to explain the movement of the spheres around the earth, according to the theories of Aristotle. It should also be noted that, thanks to the analogy between the human and the angelic or stellar soul, a key part of the doctrine of both Dionysius and Plato, the symbolic movements of the human soul, in this case of the pilgrim, are also analogous to the movement of the heavens, throughout the poem, but especially here at the final moment.[20] The angels are the analogical link between the perfect motion of the pilgrim and the motion of the stars. This explains the association of human perfection with the movement of "il sole e l'altre stelle." We may expect that a closer look at Dante's angelology will shed some further light on the specific meaning of the image of the wheel.

In the twenty-eighth canto of the *Paradiso,* Dante explains that the angels move like circles of fire around God, the point from which all light radiates. They are moved by the desire to "somigliarsi al punto quanto ponno / e posson quanto a veder son soblimi" (*Par.* XXVIII, 100–102) (liken themselves to the point as most they can, and they can in proportion as they are exalted in vision). The same is true of the pilgrim's final movement: he is moved by love to whirl around the Divine Essence, but his ability to do so is governed by his ability to see that essence. His final blinding vision is the fulfillment of his intellectual desire by the grace of God, to which his will subsequently responds with the revolution of love.

The precedence of vision over action, or of intellect over will, is a rationalistic principle derived from Aristotle to which Dante always remained faithful.[21] In his fallen state, according to Dante, man's ability to understand exceeds his ability to will, while in the faithful, "voglia e argomento . . . diversamente son pennuti in ali" (*Par.* XV, 79–81) (but will and faculty . . . are not equally feathered in their wings). While the will approaches perfection thanks to sanctifying grace, the reason is still dependent upon faith and must go on, *quaerens intellectum.* But the souls of the blessed are balanced, as the pilgrim says to Beatrice,

> L'affetto e 'l senno,
> come la prima equalità v'apparse,
> d'un peso per ciascun di voi si fenno,
> però che 'l sol che v'allumò e arse,
> col caldo e con la luce è sì iguali,
> che tutte simiglianze sono scarse. (vv. 73–78)

> Love and intelligence, as soon as the first Equality became visible to you, became of one weight for each of you, because the Sun which illumined you and warmed you is of such equality in its heat and light that all comparisons fall short.

The souls who have seen God enjoy a perfect equality of powers, for the twin powers of the soul reach their own specific perfection when the soul beholds *la prima equalità* in His essence. The intellect, which desires unceasingly to know, is at last satisfied, because in knowing God it knows all that it possibly can know. The will, the perfection of which is to love, celebrates the primal love in an eternal fruition.[22]

But the objects of these two powers are not, strictly speaking, the same, for, as Aristotle says in the *Metaphysics,*[23] the good is something exterior to us (*in rebus*), while the true, on the other hand, is always within (*in mente*). Therefore, the will, whose object is the good, always tends toward what is exterior to it and is contented only when it encircles its object in eternal fruition, while the intellect, whose object is the true, is contented only when it possesses the truth at the very center of its being, by a connaturality which is a mirror image of what it sees.[24] In the beatific vision, when the soul stands in the presence of the One, True, and Good, the "First Equality" is somehow both the center of an action, outside, and the center of a vision within. It is one point, which moves the soul uniformly, both from within and without, like a wheel whose forward revolution is constantly and exactly proportional to its rotation because of its uniform motion.[25]

If it is true that the reason and the will are logically distinct, it is also true that they are ontologically one, just as their object is ontologically one. The rotating and revolving wheel therefore symbolizes them perfectly, and its uniformity of motion perfectly represents the exact proportion that exists between the two spiritual motions of the soul. The divine point is perfectly reflected in the mind and coincides with the soul—but the force of the possessive pronoun in Dante's verse (*il mio disio*) is directed against the total absorption of personality into that identity. The intellect reaches its most profound desire and is therefore most perfectly itself, in all its individuality, when it coincides with God. Dante's doctrine concerning the mind's desire for God and the ultimate satisfaction of that desire is expressed in the fourth canto of the *Paradiso:*

> Io veggio ben che già mai non si sazia
> nostro intelletto, se 'l ver non lo illustra
> di fuor dal qual nessun vero si spazia.
> Posasi in esso come fera in lustra,
> tosto che giunto l'ha; e giugner puollo:
> se non, ciascun disio sarebbe *frustra.* (vv. 124–129)

> Well do I see that never can our intellect be wholly satisfied unless that Truth shine on it, beyond which no truth has range. Therein it rests, as a wild beast in his lair, so soon as it has reached it; and reach it it can, else every desire would be in vain.

It is in the last canto that the thirst of the intellect is satisfied and the pilgrim's *disio* fulfilled. As Dante uses the word *disio* in the verses we have just quoted, it can refer only to intellectual desire, as it does most of the time in the poem.[26] To understand why the word has this anagogic connotation, we have only to turn to the first words of the philosopher in the *Metaphysics:* "omnes homines natura scire desiderant" (All men by nature desire to know). Dante in turn quotes Aristotle in the first line of the *Convivio,* his "first" philosophy, and so begins the quest which will take him beyond philosophy to the vision of God.[27]

The center of the intellectual circle of the soul is the point that in turn traces the circumference of another circle, with a much wider sweep. This is the circle of *velle,* of the will, properly speaking. It symbolizes the perfect act of fruition, which is the necessary and natural end of the will. The word *velle* here denotes, as it does for Thomas Aquinas,[28] the unshakable adherence of the will to its natural end, which it loves in itself. As the angels whirl around God in the circular track that is moved by love, the *velle* of the pilgrim joins them and the rest of creation in a dance of glory. The rate and proximity of his orbit is governed, as is theirs, by the intensity of his vision at the center of his being, which, because of the mechanism of intellect, is both God and himself (see diagram below).[29]

Georges Poulet[30] has suggested that in the final cantos of Dante's poem, the attributes of God are in a sense shared by the pilgrim, inasmuch as the pilgrim's soul is a center which contains the infinite sphere of divinity. The movement by which the soul approaches God is thus a movement of "concentration" that is accomplished in the depths of the soul itself. But if the pilgrim's soul resembles God, then the mystical definition of God also applies to it: a *circumference* as well as a center.[31] Even in beatific vision, when God becomes the soul's most intimate possession, the external world of suns and stars never ceases to exist. The dialectic between the human soul and God was for Dante never to be dissolved into its two polarities, as it was

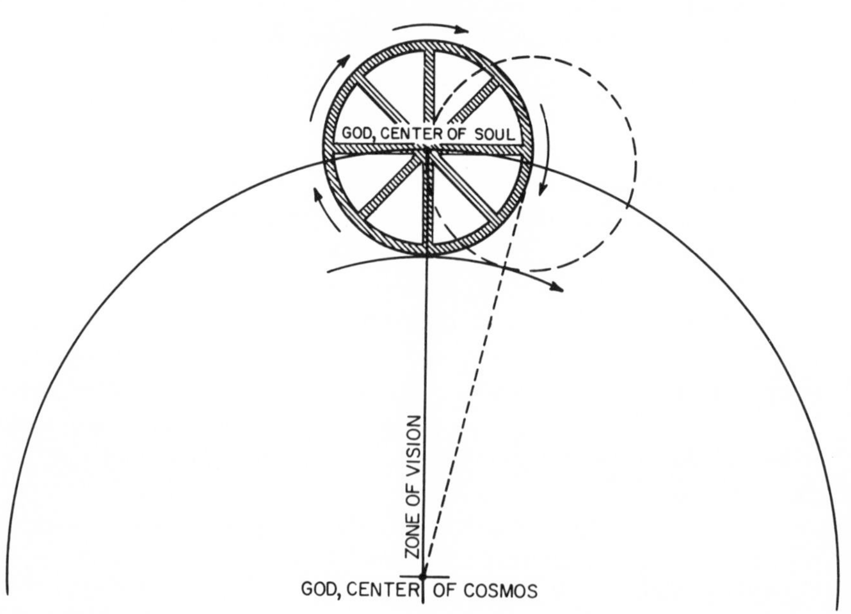

later in the Renaissance. Just as individuality could not be totally absorbed into divinity, so God could not be completely reduced to the proportions of the human soul. The dialectic was maintained by its synthesis, the Incarnation, which is to say that the final image maintains its coherence only by the grace of the vision that precedes it.

17. The Significance of *Terza Rima*

THE PERENNIAL PROBLEM IN LITerary interpretation is the problem of the relationship of form to content, or of poetics to thematics. In recent years there can be little doubt that formalism has occupied our attention, both in linguistics and in criticism, with Russian formalism, American new criticism, and the formalism of the French structuralists. The proper concern of poetics, according to Roman Jakobson, for example, is metalinguistic: not with the message itself, but rather with the message's awareness of itself as message. The most creative and interesting critical developments of the past few decades have been characterized by a concern for poetics, in Jakobson's sense, at least in the study of modern literature.

The single exception I can think of to this dominance of formal studies is in the field of medieval literature. Here the most significant contributions have involved taking content, particularly theology, very seriously. Perhaps Leo Spitzer was the precursor of this tendency, with his insistence on the importance of historical semantics for examining the coherence of the works he studied. In our own day, literary students, particularly in English, have found in the Bible and in the exegetical tradition a repository of semantic values and symbolic associations that seem essential for the coherence and meaning of medieval works. They have shown convincingly that it is impossible any longer to treat those works in the same way that we treat contemporary secular texts, written in our own cultural context.

In the field of Dante studies, it is the unique and permanent contribution of Charles Singleton to have brought poetics and thematics together in the interpretation of the poem. By refusing to accept the traditional dichotomy of poetry and belief, an older version of the opposition I have been describing, he demonstrated the relevance of theology not only to the literary archeologist, but also to the literary critic. His formal criticism represents a dramatic departure from the tradition of the *lectura dantis,* for it deals with the unity and coherence of the entire poem, rather than with single cantos or lyric passages. At the same time, that view of the whole necessarily involves accepting theology as part of that coherence. In this essay, I should like to extend his assertion of the relationship of theology to poetry in Dante's poem by offering one example where they are, quite literally, indistinguishable. I have deliberately chosen a title that brings together both meaning and form in a way that may sound simplistic but that I hope will prove nonetheless exact.

To say that poetry and theology are indistinguishable at a certain point in the poem is not to say that they should be indistinguishable in our analysis. As obvious as this remark sounds, there is still a great deal of critical confusion about the difference between what Dante believed and what we believe. Nowhere is this clearer than in discussions of Dante's allegory or "figural typology." Sometimes the word "allegory" is used to describe what Dante thought he was doing: writing a poem patterned on the Bible, for which a divine privilege was claimed in the Middle Ages. Because allegory is also a general literary term, however, others speak of it as though it were a formal characteristic of the poem, comparable to other examples of literary allegory. Erich Auerbach's otherwise masterly essay, "Figura,"[1] illustrates the confusion by first celebrating the mimetic power of Dante's representation, which is presumably a literary judgment, and then claiming to have found "the solid historical grounding" for this judgment in the theory of figural representation. It is as if the earlier critical perception required the medieval theory of *figura* in order to be validated or, conversely, as if the theological theory were somehow established by the power of Dante's poetry. The fact remains that any modern reader would accept Auerbach's literary judgment, but no modern reader could possibly accept the theory in which it is presumably grounded. This confusion, pervasive in Dante studies, can be resolved only by showing how a medieval conception of theological allegory can be reconciled to a formal pattern and so be made accessible to any reader, without theological presuppositions.

In my effort to show how theological meaning and poetic form are, in at least one instance, inseparable, I shall also have something to say concerning the *form* of theological allegory.

To begin with an abstract form is to proceed in a manner that is the reverse of what one might expect of a cultural historian. The coherence of Dante's poem is often taken to be a reflection of the coherence of his faith, which we take as the primary cultural reality, but the formula might well be reversed, by suggesting that the apparent coherence of Dante's belief is at least in part a projection of the coherence of his poem. The reversal is not meant to be cynically deconstructive; there are good historical grounds for maintaining a certain reversibility of terms. In a culture which called its central principle "the Word," a certain homology between the order of things and the order of words is strongly implied. This is another way of stating Kenneth Burke's "logological" principle. If theology is words about God, wherein linguistic analogies are used to describe a transcendent divinity, then "logology" is the reduction of theological principles back into the realm of words.[2] What ensures the possibility of the reversal is the central tenet of Christianity, the doctrine of the Word, according to which language and reality are structured analogously. We need not privilege either pole: thematics (that is, theology) and poetics might conceivably be joined in such a way as to offend neither historical understanding nor contemporary skepticism, for in either case we are discussing a coherence that is primarily linguistic. The traditional problem of poetry and belief would then be shifted onto a philosophical plane. Does the order of language reflect the order of reality or is "transcendent reality" simply a projection of language? What we had always taken to be a problem of Dante criticism turns out to be the central epistemological problem of all interpretation.

The formal aspect of the poem that I have chosen to discuss is Dante's rhyme scheme, *terza rima.* Its significance has rarely been questioned because it has seemed too obviously to represent the Trinity. While this may be true, it tells us very little. For one thing, virtually everything represents God in this poem; the abstraction is so remote as to be meaningless. Perhaps more important, a verse scheme is necessarily temporal, or at least a spatial representation of time. It is not self-evident that a temporal scheme could serve to represent a timeless deity.

Dante devised his rhyme scheme especially for the *Divine Com-*

edy. It is very simply expressed: ABA, BCB, CDC, etc. Some critics believe it to have been adapted from existing verse forms, *sirvente, sestina,* or sonnet, but most of their discussions are clearly attempts to deduce influence from metric analogies. In any case, the *terzina* is characterized by a basically triadic structure, like the *sirvente,* and by a forward *entrelacement,* like both the *sirvente* and the *sestina.* Unlike in the *sestina,* however, the rules for closure are not inherent in the form: the *terzina* as a metric pattern could theoretically go on forever and must be arbitrarily ended.

It is this open-endedness that has moved some theorists to object that pure *terza rima* does not exist, since it would have to violate its own rules in order to begin or end. So it is with Dante's *terzina,* which has a dyadic beginning and end. In each canto, it begins and ends with what are sometimes called *rime rilevate.* The rhyme A in the scheme ABA, BCB, CDC . . . appears only twice, rather than three times, while at the end, the last rhyme, Z, also appears only twice: XYX, YZY, Z (fig. 1). A and Z (or Alpha and Omega, to hint at a more accurate theological analogy) are *rime rilevate,* arbitrary beginnings and endings for an otherwise autonomous and infinite forward movement, whose progress is also recapitulation. So *terza rima* may be characterized as a movement that begins and ends arbitrarily. This heterogeneity of the form would seem to be incompatible with the idea that it might represent the Trinity (fig. 2).

Not only was Dante's rhyme form unique, but his organization of tercets into *canti* was also a formal innovation, transforming the arbitrary element of versification into a higher formal exigency. Since his verses are hendecasyllables, each of his *terzine* consists of 33 syllables. So too, each of his *cantiche* consists of 33 *canti,* if we except the first canto as prologue to the rest. We have then a formal structure which suggests a certain homology between the versification and the

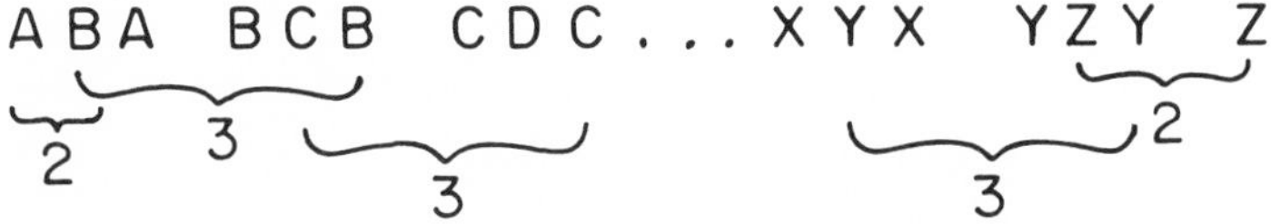

Figure 1.

Figure 2.

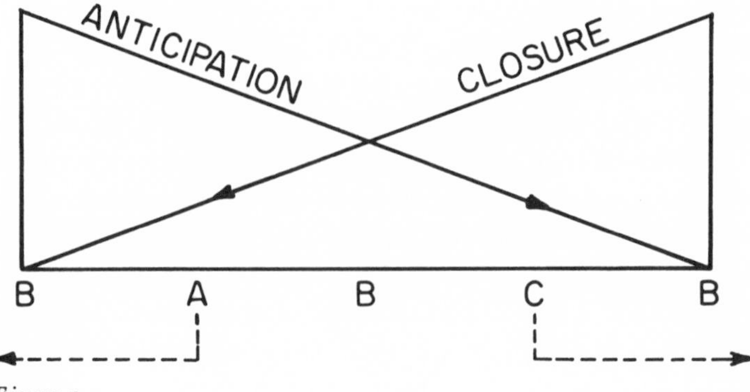

Figure 3.

formal divisions of the poem. The 33 syllables of a *terzina* are mirrored in the 33 *canti* of a *cantica* and the three *cantiche* thus represent a kind of cosmic tercet, an encyclopedic representation of the number three.

We are familiar with this kind of numerology from Dante himself who, in the *Vita Nuova,* refers to the mystic power of the number three and its square, nine. Here, however, I should like to stress not the static value of divisions by the number three, but rather the reconciliation of motion that *terza rima* implies: a forward motion, closed off with a recapitulation that gives to the motion its beginning and end. Any complete appearance of a rhyme . . . BA BCB . . . incorporates at the same time a recall to the past and a promise of the future that seem to meet in the now of the central rhyme (fig. 3).

The formal pattern of interlocking rhymes arbitrarily closed off in a way that is symmetrical with its beginning becomes more significant when we reflect for a moment on its thematic counterpart, the forward motion of the pilgrim toward a goal which is, at the same time, the narrative's logical point of departure. Readers have for centuries noted innumerable correspondences between the three *cantiche,* constituting retrospective recalls over the course of the poem, the most familiar of which, perhaps, is the recurrence of the word *stelle* at the end of each of them. So far as I know, however, Singleton's essay on the "Vistas in Retrospect" is the only full treatment of the subject at both the lexical and thematic levels.[3] Singleton brilliantly illustrates the manner in which the scheme proceeds by a gradual unfolding that is recaptured en route in a series of retrospectives that range from the minute (the retrospective gloss on the word *ruina,* for example) to the cosmic (as in the backward glance of the pilgrim from the Gemini in the starry heaven). The final recapitulation is at the same time the logical justification for the poem's beginning, the transformation of the pilgrim into the author, whose story we have just finished reading. When Singleton paradoxically suggests that the story must be read from the ending, as well as from the beginning, he confirms the analogy we have drawn between the movement of the verse and the movement of the theme.

Perhaps the most astonishing parallel between the theme and the formal pattern is established by the dramatic action of the poem, the pilgrim's path. The geometric representation of forward motion which is at the same time recapitulatory is the spiral. Whatever thematic importance we wish to attach to the spiral path in Dante's story (and I have said in chap. 4 above what I take that importance to be), it happens to be a geometric synthesis of the contradictory theses that are presented temporally by the verse pattern and thematically by the story line. From a purely geometric standpoint, the first two *cantiche* are replicas of each other, with the cavity of hell inversely symmetrical with the Mount of Purgatory, while the representation of paradise recapitulates both of these shapes with the celestial rose mirroring the God-head and the surrounding angels "come clivo in acqua . . . si specchia" (*Par.* XXX, 109–110). The geometric complexities of the spiral theme are spatial analogues of the temporal paradox of *terza rima* forward motion which recapitulates the beginning in the end.

We have seen that both the verse pattern and the theme proceed by a forward motion which is at the same time recapitulatory. I should now like to suggest that this movement also can serve as the spatial representation of narrative logic, particularly autobiography. The paradoxical logic of all such narratives is that beginning and end must logically coincide, in order for the author and his *persona* to be the same. This exigency, analogous to what Kenneth Burke in another context refers to as "the Divine tautology," takes the form, "I am I, but I was not always so." The whole of temporal sequence in such a narrative, then, is generated by some form of negation introduced into the principle of identity and then refined away. Logically, autobiography is a sequential narrative that moves toward its own origin. If that statement seems paradoxical, it is no more so than the premise of all autobiography—that one can judge one's own life as though that life were concluded. The ending of such a story implies its beginning, for the *persona's* experience must be concluded before the author's voice (and hence the story) can come into existence. The paradox of continuity/discontinuity in the formal representation of *terza rima* is matched by the paradox of continuity/discontinuity involved in the logic of autobiographical narrative: I am I, but I was not always so.

Thus far, we have traced a pattern in three conceptual orders: the formal, the thematic, and the logical. *Terza rima,* Dante's theme, and the logic of autobiographical narrative all may be represented as forward motion that moves toward its own beginning, or as a form of advance and recovery, leading toward a final recapitulation. All that is required in order to move from the realm of poetics to the realm of theology in this context is to assert that the pattern we have been describing has a necessary rather than arbitrary justification. Thus far we have been dealing with a formal characteristic of the poem that is discernible to any reader: the theological leap requires only that we ascribe this pattern, not simply to the poem, but to metaphysical reality. Notice, however, that our description of the pattern in either case remains the same. Doubtless Dante believed that his verse pattern reflected some transcendent reality, while a contemporary skeptic might claim that the verse pattern is constitutive of that imagined reality. Since we are dealing with a linguistic coherence, however, we need not decide that issue.

Let us turn now to the "theologizing" of this formal pattern. I shall begin with the theological counterpart of the logical structure of autobiography, because it is so clear. The narrative structure we have been describing, like the verse pattern, privileges the ending, the moment of closure and makes it coincide with the beginning. This logical reversal is theologically the movement of conversion, of death and resurrection. The Christian theme of conversion satisfies the contrary exigencies of autobiography by introducing a radical discontinuity into the sequence of a life, thanks to which one can tell one's life story as though it were true, definitive, and concluded. Death in life is closure in the story, but it is thanks to a spiritual resurrection that the story can be told. It was Augustine who set the pattern for this Christian thematization of narrative structure in his *Confessions,* although it might equally well be said that it was the Christian theme that gave rise to the narrative. The logic of definitive autobiography demands conversion, just as conversion, death, and resurrection imply the continuity/discontinuity of the autobiographical form. In this case, the formal pattern and the theology of conversion are identical.

The analogy between this Augustinian pattern and Dante's story is evident in the gap that separates pilgrim and poet. It is further reinforced by about twenty-three addresses to the reader, each of which suggests a progressive movement toward a goal that is the poem's beginning: the pilgrim's story leads to the establishment of the author's status as storyteller, so that the story of the *Divine Comedy* is in part the story of how the story came to be written. The addresses to the reader create a chronological illusion, leading us to understand the evolution of the pilgrim as preceding the telling of the story. In fact, however, the experience of the pilgrim and the telling of the story are one and the same: pilgrim and author are dialectically related by the action of the story, for the narrative voice is created by the action of the protagonist in the very act of interrupting it. It is only at the poem's ending that the retrospective illusion is completed, when pilgrim and poet become one. If we were to represent that dialectic in logical form, we would have to describe it as a movement forward in time that is simultaneously a recapitulation. That Dante thinks of this movement as a series of conversions can scarcely be doubted. The ending of the *Inferno* is marked by a literal conversion, a turning upside-down of the pilgrim and his guide, providing a continuity and discontinuity in spatial terms as well as in spiritual terms. The second part of the journey also ends in a conversion, with the theological motifs of sanctifying grace whose presence has been convincingly demonstrated by Singleton. Finally, in the transition between nature and supernature, the whole of the universe is turned to mirror the image of God surrounded by his angels.

The theology of conversion perfectly illustrates the tautological argument of autobiography: "I am I, but I was not always so." Here again, I must make reference to Singleton's work on the *Purgatorio,* where he explores the attempts in the Middle Ages to describe conversion, death, and resurrection, in Aristotelian terms, as a movement toward form.[4] Logically, conversion implies a destruction of a previous form and the creation of a new form. Like the process of autobiography, conversion begins with two subjects: the sinner who is and the saint who will be, like the pilgrim who is and the author who will be. The evolution of the sinner is toward destruction, the evolution of the saint is toward regeneration. Logically, the movement is twofold, chronologically it is one, for the first step toward salvation is the first away from sin. Like the dialectics of the poem, wherein pilgrim and narrator are created at the same time, conversion is a dialectic of death and resurrection. We may observe in passing that this theological paradox is illustrated in the poem by the symmetry and asymmetry of hell and purgatory. The center of the universe is no space-occupying place in the coordinates of moral theology, but simply the logical zero-point of a moral dialectic that leads from mountain-top to mountain-top, from the prologue scene to the ending of the *Purgatorio.* When the pilgrim says "Io non mori' e non rimasi vivo" (*Inf.* XXXIV, 25) (I did not die and I did not remain alive), he indicates a purely logical point that marks the destruction of an anterior form and the beginning of the generation of a new form, sanctifying grace. From the standpoint of theology, the two processes take place together.

We have discussed the theology of autobiographical structure. It remains for us now to discuss the theology of the movement represented in the formal pattern of both the verse and the pilgrim's path. *Conversion* is the technical term of the theologians to describe the way the Old Testament was transformed in the light of the New. That transformation is precisely in the form we have been describing, forward motion toward recapitulation. This movement is the essence of the Christian theory of history, referred to by the early Greek fathers of the Church as *anakephalaiōsis,* or *recapitulation.* Irenaeus is the Church father most often associated with the theory, which is defined by a modern theologian in words that might equally well describe *terza rima:* "It means not just flowing backward to the beginning, but movement forward in time as the integration of the beginning in the end, and this is the significance of the movement itself, insofar as it is at once in time and above time."[5]

The term itself, *anakephalaiōsis,* comes from Ephesians 1:10, where Christ is described as "the fullness of time." We are told that the eternal plan of the Father was realized by the Son: "and this His good pleasure He purposed in Him, to be dispensed in the fullness of time: to *re-establish* [recapitulate] all things in Christ, both those in the heavens and those on earth."[6] Thus, Christ is the recapitulation, the fulfillment of the promise and the return to the beginning, as is said in the Gospel of John: "In the beginning was the Word."

This theory of history is the foundation of biblical allegory, God's way of writing narrative, with things rather than signs. It is what Dante called the Allegory of Theologians. According to it, Christ, as the fullness of time, recapitulates all of the preceding history and gives to it its moment of closure. The New Testament must be understood as the fulfillment of the Old, which is to say, its ending. Thus history is the movement of time away from the Word and back to the Word, with all of the persons and events having their own autonomy, yet functioning prefiguratively as signs of their own truth: "di lor vero umbriferi prefazii" (*Par.* XXX, 78) (shadowy prefaces of their own truth). The moment of reversal was the *conversio* of the Old Testament into the New. Christian history or biblical allegory (they are one and the same) move in the same way as *terza rima* (fig. 4).

Dante gives us only one clue as to the significance of his verse form. The forward movement of *terza rima* is interrupted in the *Paradiso,* where the name of Christ, *Cristo,* appears in rhyme only with itself. It must not be imagined that this is merely pietistic reticence—the name of God, the Holy Spirit, and Mary all appear in rhyme at some point or other in the text. Even if it were, however, we should have to ask why rhyme would be inappropriate for the name of Christ. The answer must be that rhyme is the movement of temporality and Christ transcends time. The now of the Christ event is underscored even in the tenses of verbs in the *Paradiso* with lat-

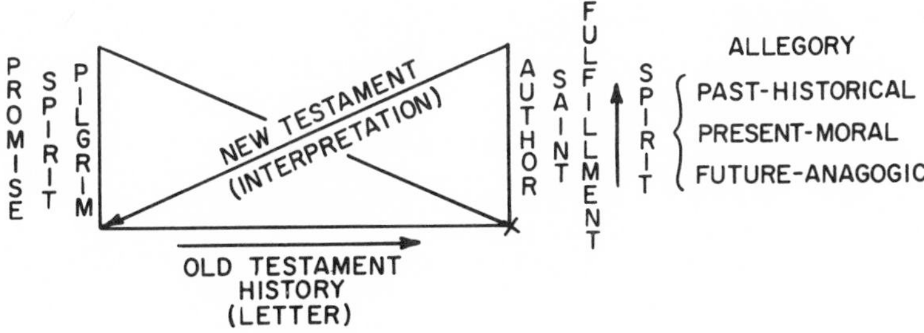

Figure 4.

inisms: "ciò che . . . fatto avea prima, e poi era fatturo" (VI, 82–83) (had done before and after was to do), said of the eagle, or again, Ripheus and Trajan, who lived in faith, "quel d'i passuri, e quel d'i passi piedi" (XX, 105) (the one in the Feet that were to suffer, and the other in the Feet that had suffered). The threefold appearance of "Cristo" in the tercet points unmistakably to a recapitulation of past, present, and future in His transcendence. Finally, the name of Christ rhymes with itself twelve times in the *Paradiso,* as if to underscore the zodiacal all-inclusiveness of the fullness of time.

The appearance of the name of Christ three times in a tercet suggests a further elaboration of biblical allegory. I have said that Old Testament time should be regarded as the unfolding of time toward its fullness, the New Testament, which is in a sense a recapitulation of all that went before. This structure is the basis of what is usually called figural typology or, to use the language of St. Paul, of the difference between the letter and the spirit. The spirit is the end-term, the moment of closure, the New Testament that gives meaning to the Old. Yet this moment was transcendent—it is the New *and Eternal* Testament, which means that it has three hypostases in time: past, present, and future. From this consideration, born in the tradition, no doubt, when it became clear that the fullness of time was not in fact the end of the world, there arose a further elaboration of Christian allegory—the so-called fourfold theory, which should be understood as one plus three: the literal, fulfilled by the Christ-event in history (allegory in the past), the Christ-event in the individual soul (allegory in the present or tropological sense) and finally, the Second Coming (allegory in the future or anagogic sense). In the interstices between the first coming and the second, there is the founding of the Church and the work of the redemption of individual souls, but history properly speaking is concluded with the First Coming (fig. 5).

With reference to the time after the Crucifixion, the word *recapitulatio* has a history in the Latin West. As originally used in the Greek church, it suggested above all universal restoration, a theory that survives in Latin exegesis in the idea of Christ as the new Adam. In the West, with the Donatist Tychonius, it comes to have a more specialized meaning, as one of the seven rules for the interpretation of Scripture. A recapitulation is made when a biblical writer speaks simultaneously of both the type and the anti-type, the promise and the fulfillment.[7] It was in this form that the term was passed on to

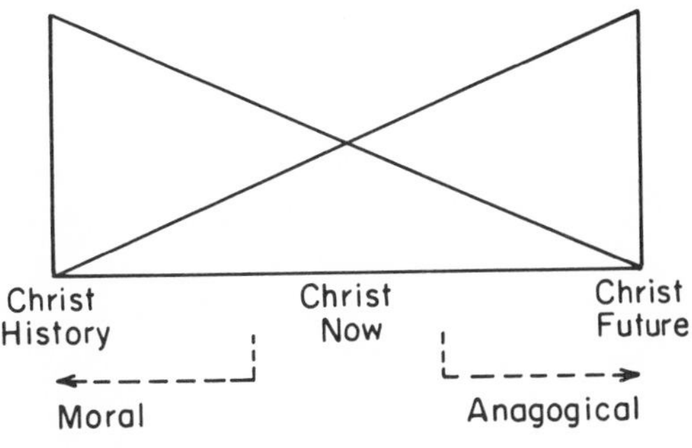

Figure 5.

the Latin West, through the extensive paraphrase made of Tychonius' remarks by Augustine in the *De doctrina christiana.* Like the story of the *Divine Comedy,* Christian history is a forward motion toward an end-term which is the beginning: "In the beginning was the Word . . . and the Word was made flesh."

We have examined a formal pattern in Dante's work and have explored theological parallels, ancient and medieval thematizations of that pattern. I do not by any means wish to suggest that these theological motifs are "solid historical grounding" for Dante's poetics, as does Auerbach in his search for an historical valorization of his critical judgment. On the contrary. I should like to suggest quite the reverse: the theological principles that seem to underlie Dante's formal pattern are themselves in turn derived from literary principles. The Christian theory of recapitulation is derived from linguistic categories. If one wished to trace the origins of the use of the word *anakephalaiōsis,* it would surely be in the realm of rhetoric. Both the orator Lysias and Aristotle use the word to mean a verbal summary, or the summation of a statement: "rerum congregatio et repetitio" (the recapitulation and repetition of things), to use the definition of Quintilian.[8] It would seem that the theory of history derives from the attempt to superimpose linguistic closure on the realm of temporality, transforming entropy, what Augustine would call fallen time, into formal discourse, the time redeemed. If it is possible to see in Dante's literary form a reflection of his theological beliefs, then it is equally possible to see in that theology the projection of literary forms.

Of all of the fathers of the Church, Augustine, orator and bishop, was most aware of the analogy between the realm of words and the theology of the Word. His discussion of the rule of recapitulation in the *De doctrina christiana* moves from an understanding of the term as a literary device to its application to biblical exegesis. There is no conflict in his mind between literary interpretation and salvation history; on the contrary, poetry was for him the emblem of intelligibility in the cosmos. Just as meter gave a pattern and a regularity to the otherwise open-ended flow of our words, so God's providential intent gave meaning to the flow of time. History itself might be said to be God's poem, saved from both the timeless eternity of the Platonists and the death of the fall by the Word, through whom the time was redeemed. In such a plan, human lives are the syllables, ordered to one another according to the meter of Providence, and death is no more than the syntactic silence necessary for meaning to emerge.[9]

One passage from the *Confessions* might well serve as a recapitulation of all that I have said. It is so suggestive for understanding the homologies in Dante's poem that Dante might well have had it in mind. It occurs as an illustration of the nature of time:

> Suppose that I am going to recite a song *(canticum)* that I know. Before I begin, my faculty of expectation is engaged by the whole of it. But once I have begun, as much of the song as I have removed from the province of expectation and relegated to the past now engages my memory, and the scope of the action which I am performing is divided between the two faculties of memory and expectation, the one looking back to the part which I have already recited, the other looking forward to the part which I have still to recite. But my faculty of attention is present all the while, and through it passes what was the future in the process of becoming the past. As the process continues, the province of memory is extended in proportion as that of expectation is reduced, until the whole of my expectation is absorbed. This happens when I have finished my recitation and it has all passed into the province of memory.[10]

This discussion of the nature of time conforms exactly to the movement of *terza rima*. If we think of the second of the triple rhyme as the now of recitation, it is equally divided between the memory of repetition and the anticipation of the third and last rhyme of the series (fig. 6). Augustine refers to the *canticum* as known by heart, which is another way of referring to its tautological character. The ending is the beginning, for recitation is the performance, or un-

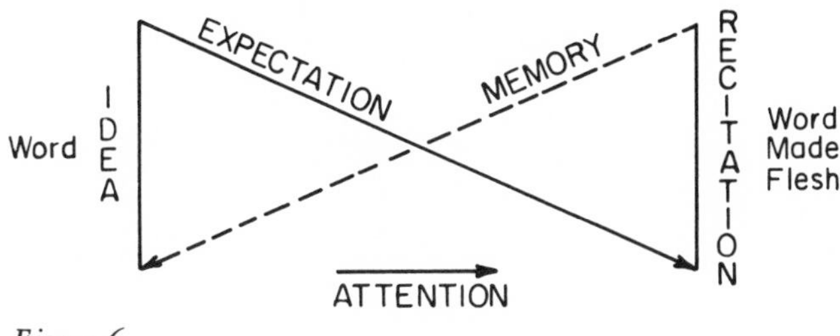

Figure 6.

folding, of a text previously known in its entirety. As in the act of speech, we move from the intentionality of the speaker to the performance of the speech, syllable by syllable, until it is completely sounded in time. The silence that follows the speech exactly corresponds to the silence that preceded it. Time, in such a context, is impressed, like syntax, into the service of significance.

This, of course, is the central metaphor of Christian history. God's Word, pre-existing for all time, is recited by all of history until, in the fullness of time, it is made flesh. The human spirit, which repeats this action with its three faculties of memory, attention, and expectation (or, to use later Augustinian terminology, memory, intelligence, and will) reflects, in this respect, the Trinity of Father, Son, and Holy Spirit. It is in the now of the Word, the Logos, that the present moment becomes all-encompassing.

Augustine's passage on the nature of time goes on to express the series of homologies, of ever-increasing dimension, from the syllabic to the autobiographical to the eschatological:

> What is true of the whole song is also true of all its parts and of each syllable. It is true of any longer action in which I may be engaged and of which the recitation of the song may be only a small part. It is true of a man's whole life, of which all his actions are parts. It is true of the whole history of mankind, of which each man's life is a part.

Whether the grounding of Dante's poem is in the formal, syllabic structure of its cantos or in the *canticum* of the universe, its rhyme scheme remains the same. It begins and ends in duality, for there can be no memory in the first instant nor any further expectation at the last. Like the Hegelian dialectic,[11] its modern analogue, *terza rima* represents a model for the synthesis of time and meaning into history.

NOTES

SOURCES

INDEXES

NOTES

1. The Prologue Scene

1. *Convivio* I, ii, 12.

2. See, for example, Natalino Sapegno. After quoting some early commentators, he concludes: "Qui insomma il nome esplicitamente pronunciato del protagonista non è segno di vanità, ma serve ad accrescer vergogna." *La Divina Commedia,* ed. N. S. (Milan-Naples: Ricciardi, 1957), ad loc.

3. Richard of St. Victor uses an analogous phrase in a context where "transitus" means "conversion": "Qui transit de malo ad bonum, bene quidem transit; et qui transit de bono ad optimum, bonum et ipse transitum facit." *De exterminatione mali* I (*PL* 196, 1074).

4. For Beatrice as guide for the second stage of Dante's spiritual progress, see Charles S. Singleton, *Dante Studies 2: Journey to Beatrice* (Cambridge, Mass.: Harvard University Press, 1958).

5. For the arguments against the *literal* historicity of the scene, see Pierre Courcelle, *Recherches sur les "Confessions" de Saint Augustin* (Paris: E. de Boccard, 1950), esp. pp. 188 ff. Courcelle answers some of his critics in *Les "Confessions" de Saint Augustin dans la tradition littéraire: Antécédents et postérité* (Paris: Etudes Augustiniennes, 1963), pp. 191 ff. Both works were essential in the preparation of this study. Indeed, the present article might be considered simply an application of Courcelle's conclusions to the *Divine Comedy.*

6. *Confessions* V, chap. 20, p. 72 of the translation used here, by E. B. Pusey (New York: Collier Books, 1961).

7. For the "region of unlikeness" from Plato to Gide, see Courcelle's "répertoire" in *Les "Confessions,"* pp. 623–640. For relevant bibliography, see, by the same author, "Tradition néo-platonicienne et traditions chrétiennes de la 'région de dissemblance,' " in *Archives d'histoire doctrinale et littéraire du Moyen Age,* 32 (1957–58), 5–33.

8. *Conf.* VII, 20; Pusey, p. 112.

9. Charles S. Singleton, *Dante Studies* 1: *Commedia, Elements of Structure* (Cambridge, Mass.: Harvard University Press, 1954), pp. 11–12.

10. Plotinus, *Enneads* I, 8, ed. E. Bréhier (Paris: Societé d'editions "Les belles Lettres," 1924–38). Courcelle's chap. 3 in his *Recherches* is dedicated to Ambrose's borrowing from Plotinus and the influence of these texts on Augustine. Section 2 (pp. 106 ff) in particular is devoted to the influence of chapter 8 from the *Enneads* on Ambrose and Augustine. The text we quote is cited by Courcelle, p. 111.

11. *Liber de Isaac et anima* VIII, 79 (*PL* 14, 559); Courcelle, *Recherches,* p. 111.

12. *Moralia* XXIV, cap. XI (*Rec.* VII); *PL* 76, 300. It is clear from the context that Gregory is talking about the first stage of conversion, presumably before the reception of sanctifying grace. In the figure of Exodus which he subsequently applies to his analysis (col. 301), this stage corresponds to the wandering in the desert, between the crossing of the Red Sea and the crossing of the Jordan. This is precisely the stage at which the pilgrim finds himself here. See Charles S. Singleton, "In Exitu Israel de Aegypto," *78th Annual Report of the Dante Society* (1960), reprinted in *Dante: A Collection of Critical Essays,* ed. John Freccero (Englewood Cliffs, N.J.: Prentice-Hall, 1965), p. 105, where Singleton quotes a passage further on in this chapter of the *Moralia.*

13. *Conf.* VIII, 8; Pusey, p. 126.

14. Ibid. VII, 10; Pusey, p. 107.

15. Ibid. VII, 17; pp. 109–110.

16. Courcelle, *Recherches,* pp. 157–167.

17. Plotinus, *Enneads* I, 6; Courcelle, *Les "Confessions,"* p. 49.

18. *Conf.* VII, 10; Pusey, p. 107. Courcelle (*Les "Confessions,"* p. 51) shows that in his insistence on the need for a guide, Augustine is much closer to Philo than to Plotinus. In the *De migratione Abrahami,* Philo states that it is precisely because they were not presumptuous but were guided by God that Moses and Abraham were able to see the light (*De migr. Abr.* VII, ed. Cadiou, *Sources chrétiennes,* 47 [Paris, 1957], 70).

19. St. Bernard, Letter to William, Patriarch of Jerusalem, No. 217 in his *Letters,* trans. B. S. James (London: Burns, Oates, 1953), p. 296.

20. *Conf.* VII, 21; Pusey, pp. 113–114. (I have corrected Pusey's rendering of the phrase "de silvestre cacumine.")

21. *Conf.* X, 35; Pusey, p. 181.

22. On Bernardus and the question of his dualism, as well as relevant bibliography, see Eugenio Garin, *Studi sul platonismo medievale* (Florence: Le Monnier, 1958) pp. 55 ff.

23. For a recent view, as well as bibliography, see the article by F. X. Newman, "St. Augustine's Three Visions and the Structure of the *Commedia,*" in *MLN,* 82, 1 (Jan. 1967), 56–78.

24. *Conv.* IV, xxiv, 12.

25. Singleton, "In Exitu," p. 105.

26. *Conf.* IX, 13; Pusey, pp. 151–152.

27. The annotation is contained in the translation of William Watts (1631), reprinted in the Loeb Library edition of the *Confessions* (Cambridge, Mass.: Harvard University Press, 1951), I, 399.

28. *PL* 196, 1073 (a propos of Psalm 113), cited in part by Courcelle, *Les "Confessions,"* p. 635.

29. Ibid., col. 1076.

30. William of St. Thierry, *De nat. et dign. amoris* XI, 34 (*PL* 184, 401); Courcelle, *Les "Confessions,"* p. 625.

31. Usually, *voluptas, concupiscentia, inanis gloria* or *concupiscentia carnis, concupiscentia oculorum, superbia vitae,* following Augustine in Book X. See the texts of Courcelle, *Les "Confessions,"* pp. 632–633.

32. St. Bernard, *De diversis sermo* XLII, 2 (*PL* 183, 661); Courcelle, *Les "Confessions,"* p. 627.

33. Giorgio Padoan, "Ulisse 'Fandi Fictor' e le vie della Sapienza," in *Studi danteschi,* 37 (1960), 21–61.

34. Rocco Montano, *Storia della poesia di Dante* (Naples: Quaderni di Delta, 1962), I, 520 n. 125.

35. Pierre Courcelle, "Quelques symboles funéraires du néo-platonisme latin: Le vol de Dédale—Ulysse et les Sirènes," in *Revue des études anciennes,* 46, 1 (1944), 65–93. See also, by the same author, "Les pères de l'Eglise devant les enfers virgiliens," *Archives d'histoire doctrinale et littéraire du Moyen Age,* 30 (1955), 10–11.

36. "Quelques symboles," p. 67 and n. 8, where Courcelle shows the influence of Ovid on the tradition of Daedalus' flight.

37. Ambrose, *De virginitate* XVIII, 115–116 (*PL* 16, 296) and *Hexam.* V, 14, 45 (*PL* 14, 225); Augustine, apart from the texts mentioned below, *De ordine* II, 12, 37; *Enar. in Psalm. Ps.* CXVIII, 14, 89; on which see Courcelle, "Quelques symboles," p. 68.

38. Bernardus Silvestris, *Commentum super sex libros Eneidos Virgilii,* ed. G. Riedel (Gryphiswaldae: J. Abel, 1924), p. 37.

39. This essentially favorable connotation of the phrase is demonstrated by the glosses of Ambrose and Augustine. For the former, "*Alarum* autem *remigium* non materialis compago pennarum, sed continuus ordo bonorum factorum est" (*De virgin.,* XVIII, 115–116). Augustine, on the other hand, identifies the wings as the wings of the dove, or charity (cf. Psalm 67:13; *Enar. in Psalm. Ps.* CXVIII, 14, 8).

40. Porphyry's *De regressu animae* was the standard neoplatonic text for the theme. Its possible influence on Augustine is a much debated question, for which see Courcelle's *Recherches,* Index, *s.v.* Courcelle remarks that phrases in Ovid's *Ars amandi* such as "Da *reditum* puero" (II, 29) and "*Regressus* non dabat ille viro" (II, 32) "se prètaient à merveille à un exposé des théories néo-platoniciennes sur le retour de l'âme" (*Revue des études anciennes,* p. 67, n. 8). Jerôme Carcopino has shown that Ulysses' *return* to Ithaca was used in gnostic iconography to represent the salvation of the soul: *De Pythagore aux Apôtres* (Paris: Flammarion, 1956), pp. 157–188.

41. Cf. David Thompson, *Dante's Epic Journeys* (Baltimore: The Johns Hopkins University Press, 1974). Thompson shows that it is more likely than not that Dante knew of Ulysses' return, as did many medieval mythographers and commentators long before the translation of Homer.

42. See, for example, Thomas Aquinas, *In IV Sent.* d. XVII, q.1 a.3, sol.3, quoting Augustine's *Enar. in Psalm. Ps.* CXVIII, 14, 8. For the relevance of the point in Dante's prologue, see chap. 2 below.

43. *Conf.* I, 18; Pusey, p. 24.

44. *Conf.* VIII, 8; Pusey, p. 126.

45. Plotinus, *Enneads* I, 8, cited by Courcelle in his *Recherches,* pp. 111–112 and compared with the text of Ambrose *De Isaac* VIII, 78.

46. In a text from the *Contra Academicos,* Augustine seems to be alluding to the voyage of Ulysses as an allegorical journey to the "port of wisdom." Interestingly enough, he recalls the flight of Daedalus as a similar journey: "No one ever crosses the Aegean sea without a ship or other means of transport, nor, if he does not wish to fear Daedalus himself, without appropriate means or without the help of some hidden power . . . The same may be said of him who wishes to reach the port of wisdom." (Translation mine.) (*Contra Acad.* III, 2, 3; quoted by Courcelle, *Revue des études anciennes,* pp. 68–69). The figure of Ulysses as *sapiens* was a commonplace. See, for example, Bernardus Silvestris (*Commentum,* p. 21) who etymologizes Ulysses' name: "Ulixes quasi olonsevos, omnium sensus, dicitur sapiens quia omnium peritiam habet."

47. *De beata vita* I, 1; Courcelle, in *Revue des études anciennes,* p. 87; Padoan, "Ulisse," p. 41.

48. I am translating from the text of R. Jolivet in *Dialogues philosophiques* (*Oeuvres* de St. Aug., 4, 1re série; Paris, 1948), p. 222, with the help of his French translation.

49. Ibid., p. 224.

50. Padoan, "Ulisse," p. 42, n. 1.

51. Jolivet, *Dialogues,* p. 224.

52. Ibid., p. 226.

53. Ibid., pp. 226–230. The theme of the shipwreck as an allegory for philosophical *curiositas* reoccurs in the anonymous *Disputatio adversus Abaelardum,* where "tempestuous" questions lead to "shipwreck" from which the writer flees with the "oars" of the fathers of the church: "caeterum, quoniam propitia divinitate profundissimarum quaestionum naufragia incolumni nave, non ingeniolo meo, sed sanctorum Patrum remis evasi." (*PL* 180, 328; referred to by Henri de Lubac, *L'Exégèse médiévale* [Paris: Aubier, 1959], I[1], 108).

54. Jolivet, *Dialogues,* p. 226.

55. *Conf.* XI, 28; Pusey, p. 204.

56. Ibid., 6, p. 190.

2. The Firm Foot on a Journey Without a Guide

1. Dante's poem differs from the innumerable visions of the Middle Ages, and from ancient *katabasis* literature, in that it contains a consistent philosophical allegory applicable to this life. The studies of Charles S. Singleton have examined this pattern in the poem and situated it in its historical context, and it is to those studies that this paper owes its view of the poem as a whole. See *Dante Studies 1: Commedia, Elements of Structure* (Cambridge, Mass.: Harvard University Press, 1957), and *Dante Studies 2: Journey to Beatrice* (Cambridge, Mass.: Harvard University Press, 1958).

2. Aristotle, *Nicomachean Ethics* VII, 2 (1145b, l. 27).

3. In the *Republic* (VII, 529c) Socrates says that the turning inward of the soul is the beginning of looking upwards: "in my opinion, that knowledge only which is

of being and of the unseen can make the soul look upwards," tr. B. Jowett (3rd ed., Oxford: Clarendon, 1925). See also the famous allegory of the cave, *Rep.* VII, 516a ff., and the "turning of the eye" in 519b, 533d and *Timaeus* 91d. According to Plotinus, death for the soul is to rest in matter. It must withdraw its eye from the mire and reascend (*Enneads* I, 8 and 13; Bréhier I, 128). These are the ancient ancestors of the theme to which Dante alludes in the last sentence of a chapter in the *Convivio* (III, 5): "O ineffabile sapienza che così ordinasti, quanto è povera la nostra mente a te comprendere! E voi a cui utilitade e diletto io scrivo, in quanta cechitade vivete, non levando li occhi suso a queste cose [the movements of the sun], tenedoli fissi nel fango de la vostra stoltezza!" For the influence of Plato's "turning of the eye" on the philosophical idea of conversion, see the succinct remarks of E. R. Dodds, ed., in *Proclus, The Elements of Theology* (Oxford: Clarendon, 1933), p. 218. Coupled with this strictly philosophical tradition there exists also the religious topos, common to pagan and Christian thought. See Psalm 120, I: "levavi oculos meos in montes, unde veniet auxilium meum." In *Conv.* III, xii, 7, Dante tells us that "Nullo sensibile in tutto lo mondo è più degno di farsi essemplo di Dio che il sole." For the conversion toward the light in St. Thomas, see *ST* I–II, 109, 6 resp.

4. "Pronus sum ad omne flagitium, ita me obruunt concupiscentiae fluctus, ut quotidie mergar, et in profundum peccatorum ruam." Augustine, Sermo CCCLXV (*PL* 39, 1645), quoted by Singleton, "Sulla fiumana ove 'l mar non ha vanto," *Romanic Review* 39, 4 (Dec. 1948), 274. This article explores the long patristic tradition evoked by Dante's simile. For the philosophical meaning of the "shipwrecked soul" in antiquity, see the notes of J. H. Waszink, ed., on Tertullian's *De anima* 52, 4 (Amsterdam: J. M. Meulenhoff, 1947), pp. 538–539. He quotes St. Ambrose's *De bono mort.* 8, 31: "denique iustis mors quietis est portus, nocentibus naufragium putatur" and suggests that such metaphoric shipwrecks may be dependent upon the helmsman-ship metaphor for the body and soul composite (*Phaedrus* 247c). In St. John Climacus' *Scala Paradisi,* translated by a contemporary of Dante's, we find the word "pelago" used repeatedly in the same sense as in *Inferno* I: "lo grave, profundo e lo crudele pelago della vita tempestosa"; *La Scala del Paradiso,* ed. Antonio Ceruti (Bologna, 1874), p. 5.

5. Dante quotes the *De finibus* at least nine times in his works. See Edward Moore, *Studies in Dante* (First Series): *Scripture and Classical Authors in Dante* (Oxford: Clarendon, 1896), pp. 353–354.

6. Cicero, *De finibus bonorum et malorum* III, xiv, 48.

7. Ibid., IV, xxiv, 65.

8. Augustine, *De sententia Jacobi liber,* Epistola CLXVII, 13 (*PL* 33, 738).

9. This translation is based upon the interpretation suggested by A. Pagliaro, of "lo passo che non lasciò già mai persona viva," in *Studi letterari: Miscellanea in onore di Emilio Santini,* Facoltà di lettere e filosofia dell' Università di Palermo (Palermo: U. Manfredi, 1956), p. 109: "È palese che *persona viva* costituisce una unità concettuale, poichè *viva* è attributo di *persona* e non ha il valore predicativo che l'interpretazione corrente vi attribuisce. Si tratterà perciò di 'persona viva' nel senso più proprio di uomo che sia in vita, anima e corpo." The quotation from the Psalms would seem to substantiate this reading, particularly since in the moral allegory, the summit of the mountain represents man's *justification.*

10. In the *Convivio* (III, vii, 5) Dante used water to symbolize corporeity. The

angels are free of it altogether, the animals are totally submerged, while man holds the *medius locus:* "da una parte sia da materia libera, da un' altra è impedita, sì come l'uomo ch'è tutto ne l'acqua fuor del capo, del quale non si può dire che tutto sia nè l'acqua nè tutto fuor da quella." Here the opposition body/soul is presented by the dyadic image of the Stoics. Man's mediate position in the ontological order corresponds to his position in the moral order—at least in this life.

11. See Singleton, *Commedia, Elements of Structure,* pp. 11–12.

12. For a long history of the question before 1904, see Francesco D'Ovidio, *Nuovi studi danteschi* (Milan: U. Hoepli, 1907), pp. 447–469. See also Domenico Guerri, *Di alcuni versi dotti della Divina Commedia* (Città di Castello: S. Lapi, 1908), pp. 51 ff., and Guido Mazzoni, *Lectura dantis* (Florence: Sansoni, 1914), pp. 23 ff., as well as many others. I have used D'Ovidio's study, pp. 452 ff., to summarize the various theories outlined in the following paragraph.

13. Natalino Sapegno, commenting upon this verse, settles for this "obvious" reading: "Di questo verso, tanto discusso, la spiegazione più ovvia resta tuttavia quella che ne dava il Boccaccio: 'Mostra l'usato costume di coloro che salgono, che sempre si ferman più in su quel piè che più basso rimane.' " *La Divina Commedia,* ed. Sapegno (Milan-Naples: Ricciardi, 1957), I, 5.

14. *De caelo* II, ii, 285a.

15. Glossing Ephesians I, 20 ("Et constituens illum in dextera sua coelis"), he explains: "Quoniam Christus Dei motus est; motus autem in operatione est; operatio vero motus semper in dextera est; id circo Christus in dextera Dei est constitutus" (*PL* 8, 1250–51).

16. *De anima* III, x, 433b24. Averroes' commentary assumes that it is the right which moves out first: "Quoniam autem motus animalis compositus est ex attractione et expulsione manifestum est, quoniam, quando pars dextra movetur a nobis et sustentati fuerimus super sinistram, tunc quedam partes illius partis erunt expulse ad anterius et quedam attracte, et sunt partes que sunt posterius." *Comment. Magnum in Arist. de anima lib.,* ed. F. Stuart Crawford, *Corpus Philosophorum Medii Aevi* VI, i (Cambridge, Medieval Academy of America, 1953), pp. 525–526.

17. *De motu animalium* 8, 702a21. St. Augustine alludes to this analysis in his *De Genesi ad litteram* (VIII, xxi, 41): "Denique nec in ambulando pes levatur, nisi alius fixus totum corpus ferat, donec ille qui motus est a loco unde fertur, ad locum quo fertur, immoto articulo sui cardinis innitatur" (*PL* 34, 388–389).

18. *De hist. animal.* II, ii, 498b.

19. *Naturalis Historiae* XI, 45. Similarly Joannes Philoponus recalled the principle that all motion begins on the right, when he commented upon *De anima* I, 3, 406b25, *In Arist. de anima lib. comment.,* ed. M. Hayduck, *Comment. in Arist. Graeca* (Berlin, 1897) XV, 119; II, 30–31. Aristotle says nothing about left or right in this context, however, speaking merely in a general way of the movement imparted to the body by the soul.

20. *Quaestiones super de animalibus* II, 3, ed. E. Filthaut, O.P. *Opera Omnia* (Monasterii Westfalorum, 1955), XII, 110.

21. Ibid., II, 7; pp. 112–113. He adds this remark which will prove to be of relevance for the allegory of Dante's verse: "Pes enim sinister magis stabilis est, et ideo illi magis est innitendum, propter quod *tardius movetur* nisi a casu."

22. *De caelo et mundo* II, ii (Arist. 285a15–15). *Opera Omnia* XIX, 82.

23. Ibid., p. 81.

24. *Inf.* I, 19–21. "Allor fu la paura un poco queta / che nel lago del cor m'era durata / la notte ch'i'passai con tanta pietà." In the *Vita Nuova* (II, 4), Dante refers to this cavity of the heart as the "secretissima camera del cuore," in which dwells "lo spirito della vita." Boccaccio's commentary on the line adds that in this receptacle "abitano li spiriti vitali." According to Aristotle, it was in the heart that the *pneuma* was gathered (*De motu* 8, 702a21) and, as we shall see, this *spiritus* applied alternate pushing and pulling forces to the muscles and tendons, enabling the body to move. For Albertus Magnus, the left foot was less agile because the heart "influit suam virtutem in partem dextram." The two expressions "lago del cor" and "piè fermo" both obviously allude to the Aristotelian physiology.

25. E. R. Curtius, *European Literature and the Latin Middle Ages,* trans. W. R. Trask (New York: Harper and Row, 1953), pp. 136 ff., discusses corporal metaphors and remarks that the subject is relatively unexplored: "An entire volume could be filled with examples from patristic literature, alone." He suggests that the source of such imagery is Plato's "eye of the soul," and collects some of the more "baroque" examples ("ears of the mind," "knees of the heart," "the hand of the tongue"), but does not mention the *pes animae.*

26. D'Ovidio (*Nuovi studi danteschi,* p. 461) doubted the existence of an allegorical significance in this verse, and seemed not at all disturbed by the fact that the commentators (except Boccaccio) were quick to find one. Had he known of the many "feet-of-the-soul" images in the patristic tradition, however, one feels that his skepticism would have been somewhat shaken. Furthermore, as soon as one grants that "fermo" means "left," there can be no doubt that the line is charged with allegorical meaning, for the distinction between right and left is very carefully made by Dante throughout his itinerary, as it was in nearly all vision literature, from the *Pistis Sophia* and the *Acts of Thomas* to the philosophical vision poems of Avicenna and their derivatives. By far the most famous of such distinctions derives from the use made of the Pythagorean "Y," or *bivium* to represent at once the topography of the other world and the crossroads of choice in this life. Servius' commentary on *Aeneid* VI, 136, is one of the most famous allegorizations of the left/right distinction in these terms (ed. Thilo [Leipzig, 1888], pp. 30–31), and the *Visio Tnugdali* admirably illustrates the use made of the ancient idea in medieval voyages to the other world: "Respondens angelus dixit ei: Benedicta sis, ne mireris; hec est mutatio dextere excelsi. Per aliam viam debemus redire in regionem nostram. Tu ergo benedic deum et sequere me" (ed. Wagner [Erlangen, 1882], p. 40). In the strictly philosophical allegory which Enrico Cerulli has suggested is one of the few antecedents of Dante's poem ("Les Pérégrinations de l'âme dans l'autre monde d'après un anonyme de la fin du XIIe siècle," ed. M. T. d'Alverny, *Archives d'histoire doctrinale et littéraire du Moyen Age,* 13 [1940–42], 283–284; Enrico Cerulli, "Il 'Libro della Scala,'" *Studi e testi* 150 [Città del Vaticano: Biblioteca apostolica vaticana, 1949], pp. 519–522), we find that heaven and hell represent the *dispositiones animae: dextra et sinistra et media* ("dicitur dispositio dextra felicitas et sinistra miseria"). Here the left and right of the cosmos are associated with the "left and right" of the soul. In the light of all these currents it seems rash in the extreme to dismiss the possibility of allegory in Dante's verse. For the importance of direction or "orientation" in gnostic literature and in Avicenna's poetry, see H. Corbin, "Avicenne et le récit

visionnaire," *Conferenze dell'Istituto Italiano per il medio ed estremo oriente,* 7 (Rome, 1955), 16–17. For the "Y" in the pagan otherworld, see Franz Cumont, *Lux Perpetua* (Paris: P. Geuthner, 1949), p. 287, and for the entire history of the idea, see Erwin Panofsky, *Herkules am Scheidenwege, Stud. der Bibl. Warburg* (Leipzig: B. G. Teubner, 1930), esp. p. 62 ff.

27. *Phaedrus* 253c.

28. *Timaeus* 44c, trans. Chalcidius, ed. Wrobel (Leipzig, 1876), p. 50.

29. Ibid., Commentarius IX, 211; p. 250.

30. See, for example, St. Cyprian, Epistola LXXVII—Ad Nemesianum; *PL* 4, 429.

31. *Stromatum* VII, 7; *PG* 9, 456.

32. *Liber de Isaac et anima* VIII, 79; *PL* 14, 559.

33. Jamblique, *Traité de l'âme,* trans. A. Festugière, O.P., in *La Révélation d'Hèrmes Trismégiste* (Paris: Lecoffre, 1953), III, 226–227. For the sources of such metaphors, and for their philosophical importance, see Festugière's lengthy notes.

34. *De peccatorum meritis et remissione* II, 13, 20. *Corpus Scriptorum Ecclesiasticorum Latinorum* 60 (Leipzig, 1902), 93.

35. *Ennaratio in Psalm.* XCIV, 1; *PL* 37, 1217.

36. Ibid. IX, 15; *PL* 36, 124

37. *De fuga saeculi* VII, 43; *PL* 14, 618.

38. Philo, glossing Gen. 49:16 ("Dan shall be a serpent by the way . . . that biteth the horse's heels"), suggested that the soul is our road and that the passions are likened to a horse: "For passion, like a horse, is . . . impulsive, full of willfulness, and naturally restive." (*Legum allegoria* II, 96; *Philo* I, trans. F. H. Colson and G. H. Whitaker, Loeb Classical Library [Cambridge, Mass.: Harvard University Press, 1929], p. 287.) This is obviously Plato's horse on the left. In Ambrose's day, it was thought that Gen. 3:15 ("he shall watch thy head, and thou shalt watch his heel") meant that the serpent wounded Adam's heel, and Philo notes the difficulty involved in the meaning of that verse (ibid., p. 429). It may be that Ambrose blended the two passages from Genesis, and associated them with the Phaedrus myth.

39. *De sacramentis* III, i, 4–7; *PL* 16, 452–453. For the ceremony of the washing of the feet, and the controversy it provoked, see A. Malvy, "Lavement des pieds," *Dictionnaire de théologie catholique* (Paris: Letouzey et ané, 1926), IX, cols. 16–36.

40. "Verum tamen cum in rebus humanis postea vivitur, utique terra calcatur. Ipsi igitur humani affectus, sine quibus in hac mortalitate non vivitur, quasi pedes sunt, ubi ex humanis rebus afficimur; et sic afficimur, ut si dixerimus quia peccatum non habemus, nos ipsos decipiamus." *In Joan. Evang.* XIII, 6–10, Tract. LVI, 4; *PL* 35, 1788–89.

41. "Respondemus peccatum quidem actum dici et esse, non rem. Sed etiam in corpore claudicatio eadem ratione actus est, non res, quoniam res pes ipse vel corpus vel homo est, qui pede vitato claudicat nec tamen vitare potest claudicationem, nisi habuerit sanatum pedem, quod etiam in interiore homine fieri potest, sed gratia dei per Iesum Christum dominum nostrum." *De perfectione iustitiae hominis* III, 5; *Corpus Scriptorum Ecclesiasticorum Latinorum* 42, 5.

42. Sermo V, 8; *PL* 38, 58.

43. *Homiliarum in Ezechielem,* lib. II, hom. II, 13; *PL* 76, 955–956.

44. A few representative citations will suffice: Rabanus Maurus, *De universo* IV, I; *PL* 3, 75; *Comment. in Genesim* III, 20 (where Gregory is quoted at length); *PL* 107, 610; Rupert Tuitiensis, *In Exodum comment.* II, 13 *(De Trinitate); PL* 167, 620; Hugh of St. Victor, *Miscellanea* III, 126; *PL* 697–98 (where Gregory is again quoted); all of Gregory's citations are quite naturally recalled by Garnerius of St. Victor, *Gregorianum* in his chapter 56: "De pedibus"; *PL* 193, 233 ff.; finally Alanus ab Insulis faithfully recalls Augustine: "*Lavi pedes meos,* id est affectus meos purgavi ab omni saeculari cura et concupiscentia," *Elucidatio in Cant. canticorum* V; *PL* 210, 86.

45. Pietro quoted Augustine, *Ennar. in Psalm.* IX, 15. He then concluded that the pilgrim was limping: "Igitur . . . pes auctoris, idest affectio in quo magis adhuc firmabatur, erat inferior, quod adhuc ad infimi terrena relicta aliquantulum magis inclinabatur, quamquam superior pes ad superiora ascenderet, et sicut claudus ibat." Benvenuto da Imola offered similar identifications for the pilgrim's feet: "pes inferior erat amor, qui trahebat ipsum ad inferiora terrena, qui erat firmior et fortior adhuc in eo quam pes superior, idest amor, qui tendebat ad superna. Amor enim est pes, quo anima graditur." Francesco da Buti followed the others: "come l'uomo ha due piedi, cosi due affetti erano in lui, l'uno ragionevole alle virtù, l'altro sensuale alle concupiscenzie." For all these comments, see G. Biagi, ed., *La Divina Commedia nella figurazione artistica e nel secolare commento* (Turin: Unione Tipografico-Editrice Torinese, 1924), I *(Inferno),* I, 30.

46. "Duos pedes habet anima, intellectum scilicet et affectum. Qui quando aequales sunt, quod scilicet affectus adaequatur intellectui veritatis, homo bene ambulat. Si autem vel ambo vel alter curvus est, intellectus scilicet per errorem et affectus per libidinem, homo claudus est." *Postilla super Isaiam,* XXV, 6, ed. F. Siepmann, *Opera Omnia* (Monasterii Westfalorum, 1952) XIX, 371.

47. "Sed quid per pedes? Intellectus utique et affectus"; *Homiliae Dominicales Aestivales* LXXXVI; *PL* 174, 371.

48. See, for example, Gregory the Great's gloss on Ezekiel 1:7: "Et pedes eorum pedes recti": "Quid per pedes nisi gressus actuum designatur?" *Hom. in Ezech.* lib. I, hom. III; *PL* 76, 806.

49. *De anima* III, x, 433b ff.

50. *De motu animalium* 8, 702a ff.

51. See Landino's exact remark, in his commentary on the verse: "come il corpo è portato da' piedi, così l'anima dall'appetito" (Biagi, *La Divina Commedia*).

52. See *Convivio* III, ii, 5: "quello che è causato da corpo circulare ne ha in alcuno modo circulare essere." Busnelli and Vandelli mention Albertus Magnus' use of this principle in the *De causis* (I, 4, 7), "applicandolo al moto e alla struttura degli animali, che si muovono per semicircoli, e hanno le articolazioni organate con dischi e cavità, perchè tutto è causato dal moto circolare dei cieli." *Convivio,* ed. Busnelli-Vandelli (Florence: Le Monnier, 1934), p. 266. We may add that Aristotle compares the heart's *motus girativus* to a "ball and socket joint" (trans. W. D. Ross, *Works of Aristotle* [Oxford: Clarendon, 1931], III, 433b21) in *De anima* III, x. Undoubtedly Albert had this type of articulation in mind.

53. Such an association is implicit in *Timaeus* 36c ff., where the "circle of the same" in the world soul (i.e., the celestial equator) and in the human soul (i.e., the reflective intellect) is given a motion *epi dexia;* cf chap. 4 below.

54. *Sermones:* Dominica tertia in Quadragesima II; *Opera Omnia* (Quaracchi, 1901), IX, 225.

55. Aristotle, *Problemata* XXVII, 10–11 (949a). Cf. Thomas, *ST* I–II, q.44: De effectibus timoris.

56. *ST* I–II, 44, 1, resp.

57. *Inf.* I, 90: "ch'ella mi fa tremar le vene e i polsi." The veins and arteries serve to transmit the vital and animal spirits.

58. *ST,* I–II, 44, art. 4, resp.

59. *Commedia: Elements of Structure,* p. 13.

60. "S'io ti fiammeggio nel caldo d'amore / di là dal modo che 'n terra si vede, / sì che del viso tuo vinco il valore, / non ti maravigliar; ché ciò procede / da perfetto veder, che, come apprende, / così nel bene appreso move il piede." *Par.* V, 1–6. Dante implies the analogy between the movement of the soul and the movement of the feet in *Purg.* XVIII, 43–45: "s'amore è di fuori a noi offerto, / e l'anima non va con altro piede, / se dritta o torta va non è suo merto."

61. *In IV Sent.* d.xvii, q.1, a.3, sol.3; quoted by Singleton, *Journey,* pp. 13–14.

62. According to Henri de Lubac, *Le mystère du surnaturel* (Paris: Aubier, 1965), p. 96, the maxim is not found in Augustine, but represents his thought accurately. The *locus classicus* is Peter Lombard, *Sent.* 2, 29, 1. We may add to the instance of the use of the formula given by de Lubac, the *Sententiae divinitatis* II, 11, 2nd ed. B. Geyer, *Beiträge zur Gesch. der Phil. d. M.A.* VII, 2–3 (1909), p. 24. One of the passages from Augustine which may have been influential in this formulation of the doctrine is *Ennar. in Psalm.* XCIV, 1: "Unus ergo idemque homo corpore stans uno loco, et amando Deum accedit ad Deum, et amando iniquitatem recedit a Deo: nusquam pedes movet, et tamen potest et accedere et recedere." (*PL* 37, 1217).

63. (Pseudo) Alexander of Hales, *Summa Theologica* I, 2, inq. IV, tr.3, q.4, 516 (Quaracchi, 1928), II, 762.

64. For a résumé of the history of the doctrine, see Odon Lottin, *Problèmes de Morale* III, 2: *Psychologie et Morale aux XIIe et XIIIe siècles* (Louvain: Abbaye du Mont César, 1954), IV, 272–275.

65. Manuscript Clm 7972 (Munich, Staatsbibliothek), f.6[r]; partially edited by Lottin, ibid., p. 71.

66. Hugo de Sancto Caro, *Liber Proverbiorum* II; *Opera Omnia* (Lugduni, 1645), III, 6, col. 4.

67. Perhaps the most convincing proof that the pattern we are suggesting—a progression from illness to partial health to final soundness—was indeed recognizable to a contemporary, is provided by the anonymous text edited by M. T. D'Alverny ("Les Pérégrinations"; see n. 26 above). We read there that the soul has three dispositions, right, left, and middle, just as the body has three states: health, illness, and neutrality. Further, the dispositions of the right are ten, and lead to paradise, as the ten on the left lead to hell. The first step toward happiness is union with the guidance of an angelic *intellectus agens.* The first step toward hell cannot fail to remind us of the Pauline struggle: "Prima est ut *non possit operari anima quod*

vult, quia non habet obediens sibi nec cui imperet, nec proprias operationes secundum creationem exercere potest, et cum hoc cupiat et non possit, torquetur. . . . Et quia sic impeditur anima ab operibus suis et ab his que multum cupit, dicitur ligata et in manibus et in pedibus, sicut dicitur homo ligatus qui detinetur ab his que vult facere" (p. 294). The greatest difficulty is posed by deciding what is the condition of man who dies with the *dispositio media,* and the text suggests a vague fusion of limbo and purgatory: "Status enim anime que perveniet ad felicitatem cum exuitur a corpore non est sine fine, sed ad tempus finibilis, eo quod creata est sapiens naturaliter et bona, quare potius tendit ad id quod est de natura sua quam ad contrarium, *nisi habeat impediens"* (p. 299). The halfway point along the dispositions of the right corresponds to the point reached by Dante's pilgrim at the end of *Purg.* XXVII, *justification:* "Sexta est ut dominetur anima sibi ipsi et obediat sibi ipsi et ut dominans et dominatum sint idem, quod est dicere ut ipsa sit equata sibi ipsi in velle et habere et posse et est sensus: tantum velit habere quantum habet vel habere potest et e contrario et tantum velle facere quantum facit vel facere potest et e contrario, et sic non erit diminutio in sua essentia, actu nec potentia, quia sua essentia eadem est suis formis et sue forme eedem cum ea et hanc equationem dominationemque felicem nemo habet in vita ista" (pp. 288–289). Here are all the elements of *justificatio impii,* whose relevance to the *Purgatorio* has been traced by Singleton (*Journey,* pp. 57–71). The anonymous author echoes the Aristotelian conception of *generatio (motus ad formam)* with the words "essentia eadem est suis formis" and associates it with Christian justification by adding "nemo habet in vita ista," which recalls Psalm 142, 2, and Dante's "lo passo che non lasciò già mai persona viva." For *generatio* as *praeparatio ad gratiam,* see Singleton, ibid., pp. 43–54.

68. "Libero, dritto e sano è tuo arbitrio, / e fallo fora non fare a suo senno: / per ch'io te sovra te corono e mitrio" *Purg.* XXVII, 140. Dante uses Boethius' definition of the *liberum arbitrium* in *De monarchia:* "liberum arbitrium esse liberum de voluntate iudicium" (I, xii, 2). He goes on to say, "dico quod iudicium medium est apprehensionis et appetitus: nam primo res apprehenditur, deinde apprehensa bona vel mala iudicatur; et ultimo iudicans prosequitur sive fugit" (I, xii, 3). Hence "arbitrio" is the act of choice midway between the "senno" (apprehensive) and the actual deed ("fare"). Dante, as a rationalist, had to believe in the priority of intellect in the act of choice. Thus the pilgrim begins the shorter journey with an apprehension of the truth, the glance up at the light. In the concatenation of apprehensive and appetitive movements, represented by the footsteps, one or the other foot had to step out first, and this was *intellectus.* But even the *intellectus* had to have a prime mover, and this, like the prime mover in every causal chain was God, who called the pilgrim to look up at the truth (cf. Thomas, *ST* I, 82, 4 ad 3; Singleton, *Journey,* pp. 48–56). Thus, grace is operative in some sense in every human act, and the complexities of this problem of actual grace were to vex Christian philosophers until well after the Renaissance.

69. Lottin, *Problèmes de Morale* IV, 274–275.

70. *Republic* IV, 440a ff. Cf. Arist. *Politics* II, 2, 1254b5 and Thomas, *ST* I–II, 17, 7.

71. The concept is set forth in detail by Lottin, *Problèmes de Morale* III, 283 ff.

72. *De anima* II, 3, 414b2; III, 9, 432b5 ff.

73. W. H. V. Reade, *The Moral System of Dante's Inferno* (Oxford: Clarendon, 1909), p. 116 ff.

74. Ibid., p. 118; John Damascene, *PG* 94, 928b; Lottin, I, 394 ff.

75. For an influential and typical statement of these divisions, see Albertus Magnus, who identifies them and describes their respective roles in the human act: "Si autem consideremus movens quodcunque movet, tunc sunt duo in genere moventia . . . Quorum unum in genere quidem movens est ut decernens motum, alterum sicut impetum faciens in motu . . . Si autem determinari habet movens, ut causans motum, tunc oportet duo esse ad minus, quorum unum determinat, et alterum facit impetum: & sic sunt duo moventia quae sunt vel intellectus & appetitus, vel phantasia & appetitus"; *De anima* III, IV, viii, text. 56; *Opera Omnia* (Lugduni, 1651), III, 178. After an analysis of the power of discernment, the appetitive power is similarly subdivided: "appetitus, sicut diximus, commune aliquod est, et dividitur in appetitivam rationalem, et in appetitivam sensibilem: et illa quidem est quae rationalis voluntas proprie vocatur. Illa autem quae est sensibilis pars animae, vocatur desiderium" (ibid., x, p. 181). The sensitive appetite is twofold: "Desiderativa autem est animae sensibilis pars appetitiva, dividitur in concupiscibilem et irascibilem . . . [Plato] vocavit autem concupiscibilem virtutem desiderativam eorum quae afficiunt secundum delectationem . . . Irascibile autem vocavit virtutem animae quae insurgit ad arduum quod est in ausu et gloria et victoria et in omni eo quod collocat in gloria et in gradu quodam sublimitatis et altitudinis secundum seipsum" (ibid., p. 182). Albertus is careful to state that these powers are formally distinct from the irascible and concupiscent powers in animals: *in homine enim sunt rationales.* They participate in the rational insofar as they are subject to the will. Man is free only when the will maintains its power over all: "hoc modo [voluntas] quasi motor est aliarum virium ad actum vel actus, et hoc modo dicimus, quando per voluntatem domini sumus nos nostrorum actuum, et sumus liberi: quia liberum vocamus, quia causa sui est et non causa alterius" (ibid.). This is the liberty which is conferred upon the pilgrim at the summit. Avicenna undoubtedly contributed much to these psychological doctrines. See Kitab al-Najat, VI in *Avicenna's Psychology,* trans. F. Rahman (London, 1952), p. 37 and Rahman's commentary, pp. 73–74.

76. *Conv.* IV, xxii, 10; xxvi, 6.

77. See Reade, *The Moral System of Dante's Inferno,* pp. 404–430 for a lengthy and somewhat inconclusive discussion.

78. The principle of mediation, a characteristic of much of Greek philosophy, was expressed by Thomas Aquinas as "natura in suo infimo contingit naturam in ejus supremo" (*Contra Gent.* II, 91). The importance of this principle for all phases of theological speculation remains to be explored. Among recent partial examinations of the problem is Rudolf Allers' "Triad and Mediation in Augustine," *The New Scholasticism,* 31, 4 (October 1957).

79. "Non ti rimembra di quelle parole / con le quai la tua Etica pertratta / le tre disposizion che 'l ciel non vole, / incontenenza, malizia e la matta / bestialitade?" *Inf.* XI, 79–83. Cf. *Nicomachean Ethics* VII, 1, 1145a16: "circa mores fugiendorum tres sunt species, malitia, incontinentia et bestialitas."

80. As in the discussions of the "firm foot," here too, D'Ovidio will serve as guide through the mass of bibliography. For his remarks on Casella's work, which has not been available to me, see in particular "Le Tre Fiere," *Studii sulla Divina Commedia* (Milan: R. Sandron, 1901), pp. 305 ff.

81. *ST* tract. III, q.2, mem.1, n.220 (Quaracchi III, pp. 232–233).

82. "Io avea una corda intorno cinta, / e con essa pensai alcuna volta, / prender la lonza a la pelle dipinta" *Inf.* XVI, 106. Just as Dante had hoped to catch the *lonza* with this girdle of self-reliance, so when he momentarily passes the *lonza* on the prologue scene, he seems almost confident about what appears to be an initial victory: "sì ch'a bene sperar m'era cagione / di quella fiera a la gaetta pelle / l'ora del tempo e la dolce stagione" *Inf.* I, 41–43.

83. "Ma perché frode è de l'uom proprio male, / più spiace a Dio; e però stan di sotto / li frodolenti e più dolor li assale" *Inf.* XI, 25–27.

84. "Ed una lupa, che di tutte brame / sembiava carca ne la sua magrezza, / e molte genti fé già viver grame" *Inf.* I, 49–51. In his *Commentary on the Nicomachean Ethics,* Thomas refers to the wolf as "vorax in omnibus" in a context which deals with various types of incontinence (*In Eth.* VII, vi).

85. "Alio modo potest corrumpi contemperantia humanarum affectionum alicujus bestiae, puta leonis aut porci. Et hoc est quod vocatur bestialitas" (VII, i.).

86. *De opere et eleemosynis* I; *PL* 4, 603.

87. *Ad Simplicianum* I, 1, 9; *PL* 40, 106. See also *Contra Julianum* VI, x, 29; *PL* 44, 839. For the later history of this doctrine, see Lottin IV, 55 ff.

88. *In Lucam* 10, 30; *PL* 92, 469.

89. *ST* IV, tract. III, q.3, 1, 510 (Quaracchi II, 746).

90. *ST* I–II, 85, 3; cf. *De malo* 2, 11.

91. D'Ovidio, *Studii,* pp. 305 ff.

92. *ST* I–II, 77, 3, ad 1.

93. D'Ovidio raised this objection to Casella's thesis: "contro lui sta la contradizione ov'ei s'impiglia di volere dall'un lato che le tre fiere siano una prefigurazione precisa dell'*Inferno,* e dall'altro che la fiera meno temibile rappresenti giusto il peccato più cupo" *Studii,* p. 311.

94. Twice the pilgrim refuses to enter into the flames, and submits only when Virgil reminds him: "Or vedi, figlio: / tra Beatrice e te è questo muro," *Purg.* XXVII, 35–36.

95. *In Eth.* VII, vi, end.

96. Lottin IV, 275.

97. For the most influential statement of the allegory see Augustine, *De trinitate* XII, 12 (*PL* 42, 1007–8). The temptation of the serpent was identified with the "primus motus" of the sensitive appetite, or concupiscence of the flesh.

98. "Perpetua corruptio sensualitas est intelligenda quantum ad fomitem, qui nunquam totaliter tollitur in hac vita: transit enim peccatum originale reatu, et remanet actu" Thomas, *ST* I–II, 74, 4, ad 2.

99. Bonaventure represented the causal chain in meteorological terms: "Et sicut in maiori mundo vapores elevati infrigidantur propter malitiam aeris et praepediunt aspectum solis; sic in minori mundo cogitationes de *sensualitate ascendentes* infrigidantur et calore gratiae privantur propter malitiam rationis peccato consentientis et impediunt aspectum solis iustitiae." *Sermones* II, *Opera* IX, 226.

100. *Ad Simplicianum,* I, 1, 6–17; *PL* 40, 104 ff.; *Serm. ad popul.* 30, 2–3; *PL* 38, 188–189; *Contra Jul.* 3, 26; *PL* 44, 733.

101. Thomas' exposition of Aristotle's *incontinentia* recalls Paul's *malum concupiscentiae:* "Si quidem igitur sit perversitas ex parte appetitus ut ratio practica

remaneat recta, erit incontinentia, quae scilicet est, quando aliquis rectam aestimationem habet de eo quod est faciendum vel vitandum, sed propter passionem appetitus in contrariam trahit" *In Eth.* VII, 1.

3. The River of Death

1. Erich Auerbach, "Figura," in *Scenes from the Drama of European Literature,* trans. Ralph Manheim (New York: Meridian, 1959), and comments on this essay by Dante della Terza in his Italian translation of Auerbach's Dante studies (*Studi su Dante,* Milan: Feltrinelli, 1963), esp. xiii–xv.

2. *Epistola* X, 7.

3. Charles S. Singleton, "In Exitu Israel de Aegypto," *78th Annual Report of the Dante Society of America* (Boston, 1960), rept. in *Dante: A Collection of Critical Essays,* ed. John Freccero (Englewood Cliffs, N.J.: Prentice-Hall, 1965), pp. 102–121.

4. Charles S. Singleton, "Su la fiumana ove 'l mar non ha vanto" (*Inf.* II, 108), *Romanic Review,* 39, 4 (Dec., 1948), 269–277, to which the reader is referred for the relevant bibliography. Since Singleton's essay, Antonino Pagliaro ("*. . . ove 'l mar non ha vanto.* Dante, *Inf.* II, 108," *Studi in onore di Angelo Monteverdi,* II [Modena: Società Tipografica Editrice Modenese, 1959], 543–548) has attempted a reading of the verse, the most valuable part of which is a survey of previous studies on the subject, excluding Singleton's. As for the reading itself, it is vitiated by an almost total incomprehension of figural principles. See the brief review by Francesco Mazzoni in *Studi danteschi,* 38 (1961), 383–384. Singleton identifies the "fiumana" with the wolf and produces a wealth of citations from the Fathers of the Church in order to show that the river is to be identified with the *fluctus concupiscentiae.* There is no contradiction between his thesis and mine: this study seeks only to apply some of the insights gained from a reading of Singleton's later work (cited above) to an understanding of the figural dimension of meaning—the view from the ending of the poem. From the pilgrim's perspective, the barrier seems indeed to be the formidable one of concupiscence, as Singleton demonstrates. To buttress his argument even further, we may point out that the topos of the *fluctus concupiscentiae* was not confined to Christianity. In Plato's *Timaeus,* it is precisely a *fluctus* of the senses to which the newly incarnate soul is subjected: "These circuits [of the mind], being thus confined in a strong river, neither controlled it nor were controlled, but caused and suffered violent motions" (*Tim.* 43a). Chalcidius (ed. Waszink in the series *Plato latinus* [Leyden: Brill, 1962], p. 233) identifies this "river" as *silva,* prime matter. It is precisely to bring these violent motions under control that the soul requires *paideia.*

5. In an interesting comparative study of "hermeneutic" and "structural" modes of interpretation, "Symbolique et temporalité," in *Ermeneutica e tradizione,* ed. Enrico Castelli, Archivio de Filosofia (Padua: Cedam, 1963), pp. 20–21, 29–31, Paul Ricoeur gives as an example of the former the retrospective exegesis of the Jews on their own history. He fails to note, it seems, the "detachment" required for such self-analysis, represented by the Jews as the crossing of Jordan. On the contrary, detachment is precisely what allows the self to take a "diachronic" view of itself. *Figura* is a necessarily diachronic way of looking at the self and the world.

6. Singleton ("In Exitu") has discussed these correspondences between the *Purgatorio* and the prologue scene at length. In an article published almost simultaneously with Singleton's and bearing the same title (in *American Benedictine Review*), Fr. Dunstan Tucker attempted an overall reading of the *Purgatorio* according to the figure of exodus. He did not, however, mention the correspondence to the prologue scene. For the general typology of exodus, I am most indebted to Jean Daniélou, *From Shadows to Reality,* trans. W. Hibberd (London: Newman Press, 1960), esp. chaps. 4 and5.

7. Joshua: 3–5.

8. Singleton, "Su la fiumana," pp. 271–272.

9. Attilio Momigliano, ed. *La Divina Commedia* (Florence: Sansoni, 1965): "Vi è ripresa in forma diretta e più impressionante l'immagine del 'pelago'."

10. On Oceanos, I have consulted the usual handbooks on classical literature. By far the most useful is the article by P. Weizsäcker in Röscher, *Lexikon* III, col. 890–820 (*s.v.*).

11. Werner Jaeger, *Paideia* (1934), I, 207, cited by G. M. A. Hanfmann in *Oxford Classical Dictionary, s.v.*

12. Per Lundberg, *La typologie baptismale dans l'ancienne église* (Leipzig: A. Lorentz, 1942), pp. 64–72.

13. Book of Enoch XVII, cited by Lundberg, p. 69.

14. Lundberg, pp. 151 ff.

15. See the chapter entitled "Der Paradiesjordan" in F. Ohrt, *Die ältesten Segen über Christi Taufe und Christi Tod . . .* Det. Kgl. Danske Videnskabernes Selskab. 25 (Copenhagen: Levin and Munksgaard, 1938), pp. 180 ff.

16. Lundberg has made much of the "Okeanos-Jordan" in Mandaean sects. The problem is crucial, for some (Reitzenstein, among others) have attempted to show that the importance of the Jordan in primitive Christianity reflects a Mandaean and ultimately oriental influence on Christianity. See Daniélou, *Shadows,* p. 272, Lundberg, *La Typologie,* pp. 155 ff.

17. Translation from Daniélou, *Shadows,* p. 273, quoted from Hippolytus, *Elenchos* V, 7; *PG* 16, 313f. Daniélou does not mention the fact that Hippolytus is here fusing a quotation from *Odyssey* XXIV, 9, with Psalm 82:6–7.

18. See the discussion of Ferdinand Piper, *Mythologie der Christlichen Kunst* (Weimar, 1851), II, 489–564, for an exhaustive account of the iconography of the river in Christianity. Throughout the chapter, the personification of the Jordan is discussed, the material being chronologically, rather than thematically, arranged.

19. Ohrt (177 ff.) reviews the history of cosmographical speculation about the Jordan in his chapter "Der Weltjordan." He notes that already in the Talmud the Jordan was imagined to continue its course from the Dead Sea into the great sea (B[e]khoroth 55[a]; Strack-Billerbeck 1:101). He continues the history of this speculation in the Arabic cosmographers of the Middle Ages. Of special interest to us is this conclusion: "der Jordan ist Haupstrom des ganzen iridischen Wassersystems" (177).

20. "If the Acheron is meant, the ocean can rightly be said to have no vaunt over it, as it does not empty into the sea, but runs down through Hell." *Divina Commedia,* ed. C. H. Grandgent (Boston: D. C. Heath, 1909–1913).

21. Quoted and translated by Daniélou, *Shadows,* p. 271, from *De baptismo* IV, 1; *PG* 12, 843a.

22. Lundbereg has demonstrated that the *abyssos* mentioned in Rom. 10:7 represents the realm of the dead: "Who shall descend into the deep? (That is, to bring up Christ again from the dead.)" This seems to be St. Paul's gloss of Deut. 30:13: "Who shall go over the sea for us." This is one scriptural passage among many adduced by Lundberg in support of his argument that the realm of the dead was represented by the waters. His second chapter is an exhaustive study of the theme of the waters of the dead associated with the Jordan. He goes on to explore in rich detail "les bases cosmologiques de l'idée du descensus dans le baptême" (64–72).

23. Philo Judaeus, *Legum Allegoriarum* II, 22; Origen, *Commentary on St. John,* VI, 42; thereafter a commonplace. See Daniélou, *Shadows,* p. 268. Cf. St. Jerome, *PL* 22, 722.

24. Singleton, "In Exitu," p. 109.

25. *ST* III, 39, art. 4 ad 2.

26. For Dante's knowledge of the *Georgics,* see Vladimiro Zabughin, *Vergilio nel Rinascimento Italiano* (Bologna: N. Zanichelli, 1921), p. 10, who affirms, against Edward Moore, *Studies in Dante,* Series I (Oxford: Clarendon, 1896), pp. 9 and 21, that Dante knew the *Georgics* very well.

27. Virgil, *Georgics* IV, 353 ff., trans. Wm. C. McDermott (New York: Modern Library, 1950), p. 347 (my italics). It is interesting to observe that in the famous simile about Glaucus, who became a consort of the gods (*Par.* I, 68), Dante is recalling the Ovidian story in which the fisherman calls upon the sea-divinities to ask "Oceanus and Tethys to purge [his] mortal nature all away." Here too, Oceanos is suggestive of Jordan. For the importance of the Ovidian story for Dante's allegory, see Singleton, *Dante Studies 2: Journey to Beatrice* (Cambridge, Mass.: Harvard University Press, 1958), p. 28.

28. Lactantius, *De. Div. Inst.* IV, 10, mentioned by Franz Dölger, "Der Durchzug duren den Jordan als Sinnbild der Christlichen Taufe," *Antike und Christentum* II, 71, n. 5. According to Servius (*In Georg.* IV, 373), Marius Victorinus, in a commentary now lost, interpreted the *purpureum mare* of this passage as the Red Sea. Servius was probably unaware that this reflected a reading of the passage according to exodus. See Pierre Courcelle, "Les pères de l'église devant les enfers virgiliens," *Archives d'histoire doctrinale et littéraire du Moyen Age,* 30 (1955), 70.

29. Badius Ascensius and Iodocus Clichtoveus both make the point. See *P. Virgilii Maronis Opera,* Bonello edition (Venice, 1566), p. 118.

30. *Commentary on St. John* VI, 43–44 (my italics), quoted and translated in Daniélou, *Shadows,* p. 263. Philo Judaeus had already stressed the moral dimension of the drama of exodus in *De migratione Abrahami,* 151. For Origen's reading, see Völker, *Das Vollkommenheitsideal des Origenes* (Tübingen: 1931).

31. *Commentary on St. John* I, 3; Daniélou, 269.

32. P. 270. Dölger's hypothesis was that the crossing of the Red Sea represented merely the negative effects of baptism, whereas the crossing of the Jordan represented the actual reception of grace. Daniélou seeks to qualify this assertion, p. 261.

33. Matthew 3:11, in the Authorized Version. Thomas Aquinas insists that

the baptism of John was the *baptismus poenitentiae* (Mark 1:4) and makes this statement which is essential for an understanding of what the baptism of John represented: "nihil in illo baptismo efficiebatur quod homo facere non posset." *ST* III, 38, art 2. resp.

34. Mark I:4 was the scriptural authority for distinguishing repentance from the actual forgiveness of sin. See also Gregory the Great's insistence that the baptism of John could not forgive sin: *In. Evang.* I, hom. 7 (*PL* 76, 1101). Also important is the figural role played by John as the frontier between Judaism and Christianity: "fuit enim terminus legis et initium evangelii"; *ST* III, 38, art. 1 ad 2.

35. Ibid., 39, art. 4 ad 1.

36. Ibid., art. 4 resp.

37. Bonaventure, *Collationes in Evangelium Joannis* XIII, coll. XLVIII *Opera* (Quaracchi) VI, 597. Probably the intermediary for this moral reading of Exodus between the Greek and the Latin tradition was Ambrose, *Hexam.* V, 4.

38. Ibid.

4. Pilgrim in a Gyre

1. See, for instance, Allan H. Gilbert, "Can Dante's *Inferno* Be Exactly Charted?" *PMLA,* 60 (June 1945), 302–304. Gilbert quite rightly objects to those who prefer "drawing" to poetry, and to "the refinements of geometric structure" produced "by the zeal of literal-minded commentators." At the same time, however, he seems to object to the search for allegorical meaning in the directions taken by the pilgrim (p. 304). It would appear from his article that the directions given by the poet neither convey a precise visual image, nor contribute to the "meaning" of the journey. One is left wondering why they are there.

2. As Dante and Virgil wheel downward close to the bank, the poet says "Io sentia già da la man destra il gorgo / far sotto noi un orribile scroscio" (*Inf.* XVII, 118–19). See H. D. Austin, "Clockwise or Counter-clockwise?—A Dante Study," *Italica,* 24 (March 1947), 201–205. If the pilgrim continually hears the pool *beneath* him at the right hand, this would seem to indicate that his *left* is close to the bank and his right is always toward the center in his downward flight.

3. See *Purg.* XIX, 79–81: "Se voi venite dal giacer sicuri, / e volete trovar la via più tosto, / le vostre destre sien sempre di fori," and XXII, 121–23: "Io credo ch'a lo stremo / le destre spalle volger ne convegna, / girando il monte come far solemo."

4. P. 203. According to Austin, it is now believed that this shift was due to the confusion of the prepositions *a(b)* and *ad.* As we shall see, there is no reason to hazard such a guess. Austin's discussion failed to take into account the fact that already in Attic Greek motion that we would normally describe as "from the right" was designated "to the right." See Alice F. Braunlich, " 'To the Right' in Homer and Attic Greek," *American Journal of Philology,* 57 (1936), 245–260. It is obvious that in archetypal circular motion, movement is both *to* and *from* the point of origin. Aristotle calls rightward circular movement *apo tōn dexiōn kai, epi ta dexia* (*De caelo,* 285b20). Dante was following the Aristotelian tradition when he used *a sinistra* rather than *da* (*de* + *ab*) *sinistra,* thus designating the movement by its final, rather than initial phase.

5. One must distinguish between circular movement along the ever-decreasing circumferences of hell's structure and movement toward the center, approximately at right angles, from circle to circle. Since the pilgrim moves in a clockwise direction throughout most of hell (i.e., with the left closest to the wall), in order to go down into the cavity toward the center he must generally turn to the right. See *Inf.* XVIII, 71–72: "E vòlti a destra . . . da quelle cerchie etterne *ci partimmo.*" This is not the case with *Inf.* IX, 132, where the pilgrim moves circularly "a la man destra," after having entered the city of Dis. On the contrary, in this circle he must descend to the left, in order to move to the center: "Appresso mosse a man sinistra il piede; / lasciammo il muro, e gimmo inver' lo mezzo" (*Inf.* X, 133–34). Cf. G. Agnelli, *Giornale dantesco,* 6 (1898), 401.

6. N. Sapegno remarks "nonostante le ingegnose elucubrazioni degli allegoristi, rimane per noi inesplicabile l'intendimento simbolico." *La Divina Commedia* ed. N. Sapegno (Milan-Naples: Ricciardi, 1957), I, 111.

7. The pilgrim and his guide have been walking along a dike toward the edge of the precipice which is the inner border of the seventh circle. They descend the bank by turning to the right (*Inf.* XVII, 31): "Però scendemmo a la destra mammella." They then walk a little further on to avoid the burning sand: "diece passi femmo in su lo stremo, / per ben cessar la rena e la fiammella." Virgil stops to talk to Geryon, but the pilgrim moves further on along the edge (this could only be "to the right"), to see the usurers. He then returns by retracing his steps back to the monster ("to the left"). Thus he has moved to fraud with his usual motion, in spite of the fact that Geryon was originally on the right side of the river, and the movement to fraud is continued in the same direction, clockwise, by the flight. Gino Rizzo was the first to point out to me the need for an explanation of this right turn.

8. Apart from the critical commonplace, there are excellent historical reasons for suspecting that these details are not important. The distinction between right and left turns was a familiar element of pagan as well as Christian topographies of the otherworld. The *biviium* of choice, the "Pythagorean Y," is the most famous example of distinctions of this kind. See *Aeneid* VI, 136, comm. Servius, ed. Thilo (Leipzig, 1888), p. 30; Franz Cumont, *Lux perpetua* (Paris: P. Guethner, 1949), p. 287; Vladimiro Zabughin, *L'Oltretomba classico medievale dantesco nel rinascimento* (Rome: Pontificia Accademia degli Arcadi, 1922), p. 27; Leo Spitzer, "Er hat einen Sparren (Span)," *Essays in Historical Semantics* (New York: S. F. Vanni, 1948), p. 80. The longest and most complete study of the theme is Erwin Panofsky, *Herkules am Scheidewege,* Studien der Bibliothek Warburg (Leipzig: G. Teubner, 1930), p. 62. In mystic visions of eastern origin, right and left and their cosmic equivalents, East and West, are also given symbolic meaning. From the history of religious or philosophical visions, it is safe to conclude that Dante's vision would have been an extraordinary exception if the poet had used such details gratuitously. For additional bibliography, see chap. 2.

9. *De caelo* II, 2, 285b. We would nevertheless call such a movement "to the left," for even granting Aristotle's definition of the right as the East, we would consider only the visible 180° arc of the heaven's motion, from dawn (the right) to sunset (the left). The philosopher, on the contrary, was faced with a double exigency: in the first place, there was his own definition of the right as the point *from which* motion begins, and in the second place, there was the Pythagorean convention,

founded upon the symbolic importance of both the sun and "the right," according to which the heavens moved *to* the right. Aristotle was forced to consider the full circuit, from dawn (the right) to sunset (the left) and thence around the other hemisphere to dawn (the right) once more: motion from the right and back *to the right.* It was also in keeping with his metaphysical concern for finality and completion that he described a motion in terms of its terminus.

10. Aristotle, ibid.: "Of the poles, the one which we see above us is the lowest part, and the one which is invisible to us the uppermost. For we give the name of righthand to that side of a thing whence its motion through space starts. Now the beginning of the heaven's revolution is the side from which the stars rise, so that must be its right, and where they set must be its left. If this is true, that it begins *from the right* and moves around *to the right* again, its upper pole must be the invisible one, since if it were the visible, the motion would be leftward, which we deny. Clearly therefore the invisible pole is the upper, and those who live in the region of it are in the upper hemisphere and to the right, whereas we are in the lower and to the left." Trans. W. K. C. Guthrie, Loeb Classical Library (Cambridge, Mass.: Harvard University Press, 1939), p. 147.

11. The argument is unclear because Aristotle does not supply a vantage point when he says that if north were "up" the movement of the heavens would be *ep'aristera.* A. E. Taylor imagines a man "looking to our visible pole" (*Commentary on the Timaeus,* Oxford: Clarendon, 1938, p. 150 f.); T. Heath imagines a man lying face down along the earth's axis (quoted by Guthrie, *De caelo,* p. 137); A. Braunlich disagrees with both and maintains that Aristotle considers the movement "from the standpoint of the heaven itself." She cites Simplicius *De caelo,* ad loc., in support (" 'To The Right'," p. 247). Braunlich suggests that Aristotle did not take the argument too seriously.

12. Thomas's explanation is clearer than that of many modern commentators: "Imaginemus enim hominem cujus caput sit in polo arctico, et pedes in polo antarctico: manus ejus dextra erit in occidente, et manu sinistra in oriente, *si tamen facies ejus sit versus hemisphaerium superius* quod est nobis apparens." *De caelo et mundo* II, lect. 111 (*Opera omnia,* Parma, 1864, XIX, 85).

13. *Confessions* IV, xii. Cf. Ephesians 4:7: "He also descended first into the lower parts of the earth."

14. *Inf.* XXXIV, 121–26. Unfortunately Bruno Nardi's complete study of the problem and its relationship to the *De caelo* ("La caduta di Lucifero", *Lectura dantis romana,* Rome, 1959, pp. 3–14) had not yet appeared when this article was written.

15. Dante says of the outermost sphere that "tutto quanto rape . . . seco" (*Par.* XXVIII, 70–71). In the *Convivio* (II, xiv, 16), he discusses the movement at length, and imagines what the movement of the other heavens would be if this movement were to cease. See M. A. Orr, *Dante and the Early Astronomers* (London: Wingate, 1913), pp. 433–438, for a discussion of the passage.

16. Orr (p. 18) describes these two apparent movements: "The daily revolution of the entire heavens, carrying with it every visible celestial body, in a little less than 24 hours [and] the revolutions of sun, moon, and five naked-eye planets, in seven different periods. The first of these is from east to west . . . All the others are in the main from west to east, though the progress of the planets is complicated by periodical retrograde movements." Alfraganus, in the fifth chapter of the work

that Dante calls "Il libro dell'aggregazione delle stelle" (*Conv.* II, v, 16), discusses "de duobus primis motibus coeli quorum unus est motus totius, quo fiunt nox et dies ab oriente ad occidentem, et alius est motus stellarum quae hac re videntur in orbe ab occidente ad orientem" (ed. R. Campani, *Collezione di opus. dant.* 87–90 [Città di Castello, 1910], p. 53). See also Ristoro d'Arezzo: "s'egli è uno movimento del cielo, lo quale muove tutto da oriente a occidente, lo quale è chiamato primo, e' è mestieri per forza di ragione, per maggiore operazione, ch'egli sia un altro movimento, lo quale sia suo opposito, e vada per opposito d'occidente ad oriente." *Composizione del mondo,* ed. E. Narducci (Rome, 1859), V, ii, 74. Belief in the existence of these two apparent movements remained basically the same, in spite of the difference between ancient and medieval cosmologies.

17. *De caelo* II, 2; 285b28; "Nevertheless in relation to the secondary revolution, i.e., that of the planets, we are in the upper and right-hand part."

18. Ibid. II, 3; 286b.

19. *Par.* XXXIII, 142: "A l'alta fantasia qui mancò possa; / ma già volgeva il mio disio e 'l velle, / sì come rota ch'igualmente è mossa, / l'amor che move il sole e l'altre stelle."

20. Cf. *Conv.* III, xii, 9, where it is said of God that "suo 'girare' è suo 'intendere'," and the lengthy note of Busnelli. He notes that in the *Liber de causis* the "girare" is attributed to all intellect.

21. *Par.* II, 121–123. "Questi organi del mondo cosi vanno, / come tu vedi omai, di grado in grado, / che di sù prendono e di sotto fanno." Cf. *Liber de causis,* VII, ed. Emil Orth (Rome, 1938), 28. In this passage one recognizes immediately the hierarchical continuity of the chain of being. See A. O. Lovejoy, *The Great Chain of Being* (Cambridge, Mass.: Harvard University Press, 1948), pp. 67 ff. Lovejoy notices that Dante came close to asserting "that the actual exercise of the creative potency extends of necessity through the entire range of possibility" (p. 70). For the influence of the *Liber de causis* on Dante see B. Nardi, "Le citazioni dantesche del *Liber de causis,* in *Saggi di filosofia dantesca* (Città di Castello, 1930), pp. 89–120.

22. *Purg.* XXV, 70 ff.: "lo motor primo a lui si volge lieto / sovra tant'arte di natura, e spira / spirito novo, di vertù repleto, / che ciò che trova attivo quivi, tira / in sua sustanzia, e fassi un'alma sola, / che vive e sente e sé in sé rigira."

23. *Timaeus* 36d (trans. Jowett). See the remarks on this passage by Rudolf Allers, "Microcosmus—from Anaximandros to Paracelsus," *Traditio* 2 (1944), esp. 353, 354, 361. For a more detailed treatment, see A. Ölerud, *L'Idée de macrocosmos et de microcosmos dans le Timée de Platon* (Uppsala: Almquist and Wiksell, 1951), pp. 32 ff. For the idea of *anima mundi* in the Middle Ages, see Tullio Gregory, *Anima mundi: La filosofia di Guglielmo di Conches e la scuola di Chartres* (Florence: Sansoni, 1955), p. 157, where it is suggested that by understanding the world-soul as the Holy Ghost the idea was made acceptable to orthodox Christians.

24. See A. Schneider, "Der Gedanke der Erkenntnis des Gleichen durch Gleiches in antiker and patristischer Zeit," *Beiträge zur Geschichte der Philosophie der Mittelalters,* Suppl. II (1923), p. 68, quoted by Allers, p. 352 n. 84. Adelard of Bath entitled a tract *De eodem et diverso* (ed. Willner, *Beitr.,* IV, 1 [1903], p. 3): "quoniam videlicet maximam orationis partem duabus personis, philosophiae scilicet atque philocosmiae, attribui, una quarum eadem, altera vero diversa a principe

philosophorum appellatur." This distinction is based upon one logically prior to it: God = unity, matter *(hyle)* = multiplicity. See Bernardus Silvestris: "Unitas deus. Diversum non aliud quam hyle eaque indigens forma." *De mundi universitate . . . sive Megacosmos et Microcosmos,* ed. Barach and Wrobel (Innsbruck, 1876), p. 61.

25. *In Platonis Timaeum Comment.,* 95, ed. Wrobel (Leipzig, 1876), p. 167.

26. *Timaeus* 44c-d. Cf. R. Grosseteste, *Quod homo sit minor mundus* in L. Baur, *Die Philosophie des R. Grosseteste* (*Beitr.,* 1912), IX, 59. Quoted by Allers, *Microcosmus,* p. 348. See also Bernardus Silvestris, *De mundi universitate,* p. 64.

27. *Timaeus* 44c. Cf. Chalcidius IX, 211; p. 250. For a typical use of the passage by a medieval writer, see John of Salisbury, *Metalogicon* IV, 17; *PL* 199, 926.

28. See chap. 2 above. It is uncertain whether Dante knew the *Timaeus* directly, even though he mentions it in *Par.* IV, 49. Edward Moore, *Studies in Dante,* Series I (Oxford: Clarendon, 1896), pp. 156–164, discusses the problem without definite conclusion. G. Fraccaroli, in an appendix to his translation of the *Timaeus* devoted to the problem ("Dante e il Timeo" in *Il Timeo* (Turin: Bocca, 1906, pp. 391–424), adds to Moore's observations and concludes: "Mentre da una parte sembra certo aver Dante veduta la traduzione di Calcidio, se non forse anche il commento, non si può dall'altra affermare che questo fosse uno dei testi ch'egli più studiasse e intendesse, e tanto meno ch'egli possedesse" (p. 422).

29. For a typical statement, see Plutarch, *De virtute morali* III, *Moralia* 441. I am indebted to A. B. Chambers of Johns Hopkins for this reference.

30. Philo Judaeus, "Quis rerum divinarum heres," 48; *Works,* ed. F. H. Colson (Classical Library, Cambridge, Mass.: Harvard University Press, 1932), Loeb IV, 399.

31. Consult B. Switalski, *Des Chalcidius Kommentar zu Platos Timaeus* (Münster, 1903), *Beitr.* III, 6, for the establishment of the neoplatonic current; E. Garin, *Studi sul platonismo medievale* (Florence: La Monnier, 1958), p. 46 ff. for the twelfth century; J. M. Parent, *La Doctrine de la création dans l'école de Chartres,* Publications de l'Institut d'études médiévales d'Ottawa, 8 (Paris-Ottawa, 1938), 139–142, 163–166, for texts and comments relative to Chartres. For a commentary from the early thirteenth century, T. Schmid, "Ein Timaeos-kommentar in Sigtuna," *Classica et Medievalia,* 10 (1949), 221–266; p. 249 in particular. See also pseudo-Rabanus Maurus, *Alleg. in S. Script.; PL* 112, 929 (on Gen. 1:6); Godfrey of St. Victor, *Microcosmos* I, 34, ed. P. Delhaye (Lille, 1951), p. 57, and comment of Delhaye, *Le 'Microcosmus' de Godfrey de St. Victor* (Lille, 1951), p. 113. Among the scholastics, Albertus Magnus discusses the passage most frequently: *Summa* II, 72, m.4, a.3; *Metaphysics* I, 4, 12; *De natura et origine animae* II, 7, 31; *Physics* VIII 2, 8; etc.

32. A. B. Chambers' dissertation (Johns Hopkins Univ.) on John Donne shows the relevance of the *Timaeus* theme to the interpretation of Donne's poetry.

33. *Liber de planctu naturae; PL* 210, 443. See also *Distinctiones (s.v. mundus); PL* 210, 866.

34. *Consolation,* III, m. 9: "Tu triplicis mediam naturae cuncta moventem / Conectens animam per consona membra resolvis. / Quae cum secta duos motum glomeravit in orbes, / In semet reditura meat mentemque profundam / Circuit et simili convertit imagine caelum." Trans. Richard H. Green. *The Consolation of Philosophy* (New York: Liberal Arts Press, 1962). For the relationship of this text to

that of the *Timaeus* and for the diffusion of both, see Garin, *Studi,* pp. 29–33, 46, 70 ff.

35. Sapegno (III, 31) annotates *Par.* II, 130 ff. with the quotation from Boethius: "I versi di Dante, sebbene esprimano un concetto sostanzialmente diverso, riecheggiano de vicino, e talora in modo letterale, un passo di Boezio, dove parla dell'anima del mondo secondo la dottrina dei neoplatonici."

36. *Il Boezio e l'Arrighetto nelle versioni del trecento,* ed. S. Battaglia, Coll. di classici italiani, 2nd ser., 14 (Turin, 1929), p. 110.

37. The comparison between the movements of the heavens and those of the mind was so popular that it was often mentioned even in scientific contexts. Sacrobosco interrupts his description of the celestial circles with this statement: "Be it understood that the 'first movement' . . . also is called 'rational motion' from resemblance to the rational motion in the microcosm, that is, in man, when thought goes from the Creator through creatures and back to the Creator and there rests. The second movement is of the firmament and planets contrary to this, from west through east back to west again, which movement is called 'irrational' or 'sensual' from resemblance to the movement of the microcosm from things corruptible to the Creator and back again to things corruptible." *The Sphere of Sacrobosco* II, ed. and trans. Lynn Thorndike (Chicago: University of Chicago Pres, 1949), p. 123. See the comments on the passage by Robertus Anglicus (p. 163); Michael Scot (?), where Plato is cited (pp. 303–304); and Cecco d'Ascoli (pp. 377–378). Cf. pseudo-Johannes Scotus, *In Boethius De consolatione* III, m. 9, ed. E. T. Silk, Papers and Monographs, American Academy in Rome, 10 (1935), 160–190.

38. *Timaeus* 40a; Thomas Aquinas, *Comm. super lib. Boetii* III, m. 9; *Opera,* XXIV, 82.

39. Pseudo-Dionysius, *De div. nom.* IV, 8; *PG* 3, 703.

40. Ibid. IV, 9; *PG* 3, 705. Cf. Aquinas, *Com. in div. nom., Opus* VII, 7, par. 509; *Opera* XV, 310. Dante knew the idea very well. In the *Convivio* (IV, xxi, 9) he attributes the three operations to the "anima nobile": "però è scritto nel libro de le Cagioni: 'Ogni anima nobile ha tre operazioni, cioè animale (linear), intellettuale (spiral) e divina' (circular)." See Busnelli-Vendelli, notes ad loc. For a Renaissance version see M. Ficino, *Theologia Platonica* IV, ii (Paris, 1559), f: 57.

41. *Itinerarium mentis in Deum* I, 2, in *Tria Opuscula* (Quaracchi, 1938), p. 295. Also operative is the neoplatonic theme of the downward movement of love from God to creatures and its return from creatures to God, throughout the chain of being. See pseudo-Dionysius IV, 9; *PG* 3, 705. Cf. Dante, *Par.* II, 21–23 and above, n. 21. The creative potency comes from above, is transmitted below, and is shared by members of the same hierarchy in the chain. Thus the intelligences can convert to God *(supra nos),* communicate *(intra nos),* or distribute goodness to the world below *(extra nos).* Dante outlines the doctrine in *Conv.* III, vi, 4–5. Proclus described the movement of cosmic love as one of Progression and Reversion (*In primum Alcibiadem,* ed. Victor Cousin [Paris: 1820–27], II, 153; E. R. Dodds, *Proclus, the Elements of Theology* [Oxford: Clarendon, 1933], pp. 35–37 and Dodds's note, p. 218), and hence as the archetype of all movement. The idea of the *circulatio rerum* was transmitted to the later Middle Ages via Dionysius (*De div. nom.* IV, 15) and the *Liber de causis* VII. For a typical statement see St. Thomas, *In IV Sent.* 49, q.1, a.3, sol.3.

42. *De Monarchia* III, xvi, 3, where Dante echoes *Liber de causis* II to show that man is the horizon between time and eternity. Bruno Nardi has shown that this is originally a notion applied to the *anima mundi,* transposed by Dante to apply to the soul of man. The comparison between man and the planets is originally Aristotelian. See Aristotle, *De caelo* II, xii (292b).

43. Chalcidius, commenting on *Tim.* 39a (p. 182), gives a minute description of the path followed by Venus, for example: "Quos quidem gyros Gracei helicas adpellant, quorum incrementa ab inminutionibus, imminutiones porro ab incrementis notantur." The sketch used to describe the movement could be used equally well to illustrate the pilgrim's path (see *descriptio* XXVI, p. 410). Cf. Dante, *Conv.* III, v, 13–14: "a guisa d'una vite dintorno," and Ristoro, I, 23, p. 28 ff.

44. *De anima* III, 11 (434a), trans. Foster and Humphries, *Aristotle's "De anima" in the Version of William of Moerbeke and the Commentary of St. Thomas Aquinas* (New Haven: Yale University Press, 1951), p. 478. I have used this translation because of William of Moerbeke's influential mistranslation of *akrasia* as *continentia;* see Foster-Humphries' note.

45. See, for instance, Themistius *De anima* III, XI, trans. Wm. Moerbeke; ed. G. Verbeke, *Corpus lat. comment. in Arist. Graec.,* I (Louvain, 1957), 271. Averroes, *Comment magnum in Arist. de anima* 50, ed. F. S. Crawford (Cambridge, 1953), p. 72. Averroes describes the parallelism between the movement of the heavens and the movement of the soul in paragraph 46 (p. 63). Albertus Magnus, *De anima* III, tr. IV, c. IX, com. 57; *Opera Omnia* (Lugduni, 1651), III, 180; Thomas Aquinas (?) *De motibus corporum caelestium, Opera* XXIV, 218.

46. Aquinas, *De motibus;* Foster-Humphries, *Aristotle's "De anima,"* p. 481.

47. *Par.* VIII, 127. Cf. *Conv.* III, ii, 5.

48. Plato, *Republic* IV, 440a ff; Aristotle, I *Polit.* 2, ii, 1254b5; Thomas, *ST* I–II, 17, 7; all describe justice in the soul and compare it to right order in the state. The music of the spheres is often compared to the "music" of the soul in medieval discussions of the microcosm (e.g., Honorius d'Autun, *De imagine mundi* I, 82; *PL* 172, 140). Chalcidius calls the soul's harmony "Justice": "optima porro symphonia est in moribus nostris iustitia" (*Com.* 267, p. 298). In the school of Chartres, the *Republic* was thought of as a treatise concerned with justice in the state, whereas the *Timaeus* treated "de naturali justitia, id est rerum omnium concordia." William of Conches, Paris mss. 16579, fol. 55, quoted by J. M. Parent, *La doctrine de la création* (Paris: Vrin, 1938), p. 139. He says that the school was "unanime à dire que le *Timée* traite de la justice naturelle.") Cf. Bonaventure, *Quaest. disp. de perf. evangelica* IV, iii: "Requirebat enim hoc *ordo universalis iustitiae* et quantum ad iustitiam *naturalem* et quantum ad *civilem* et quantum ad *caelestem* sive spiritualem" (*Opera omnia,* Quaracchi, 1891, v, 194). For the theological concept of Justice and its relevance to Dante's poem, see C. S. Singleton, *Dante Studies 2: Journey to Beatrice* (Cambridge, Mass.: Harvard University Press, 1958), pp. 55–71.

49. For "right" in the cosmos, *De caelo* II, 2, 285a, and *De anima* III, x, 433b24; for human motion, *De motu animalium* VIII, 702a21 and *De hist. animal.,* II, ii, 498b. See also chap. 2 above.

50. See the remarks of the Casini-Barbi commentary on this passage: "Alcuni commentatori, Lana, Ottimo, Cassinese, Benvenuto, ecc. credono che i cerchi accennino allegoricamente le virtù cardinali e le croci le teologiche, a significare che

la grazia divina risplende più viva e propizia là ove sono insieme congiunte le virtù" (*La Divina Commedia,* Florence: Sansoni, 1938, p. 691).

51. *Par.* X, 7–9: "Leva dunque, lettore, a l'alte ruote / meco la vista, dritto a quella parte / dove l'un moto e l'altro si percuote."

52. Aristotle uses a similar comparison in *Nich. Ethics* I, xiii, 10 (1102^b).

53. Augustine, *In psalm.* CXVIII, serm. viii, quoted by Thomas, *In IV Sent.* d.xvii, q.1, a.3, sol.3; Dante, *Par.* XIII, 120, although the poet is using the expression in a different context.

54. *Liber de contritione cordis* VII; *PL* 40, 947–948. See also cap. X: "Obvolvere, aerumnose, iterum volens horridis in tenebris inconsolabilis luctus, qui volens provulutus [sic] es in voragine tam sordidi fluctus. Volutere in gurgite amaritudinis, qui delectatus es in volutabro turpitudinis." Dante's spiral dramatizes this type of "involvement." For the Latin use of "wind-unwind" as metaphorically applied to moral behavior, see the examples given by the *Thesaurus Linguae Latinae* V, 871 (*s.v. devolvo* C^2).

55. St. Paul gave the most famous expression of the situation in Rom. 7:18–19. Cf. Aristotle, *Nich. Ethics* VII, 2 (1145b).

56. *De caelo* II, 3, 286b; *Par.* X, 14–15.

57. Cf. *Par.* XI, 37–39. The warmth and light of the sun serve to symbolize the ardor and splendor of the *Spiriti Sapienti* in the *Paradiso,* and at the same time are associated with the Seraphim and Cherubim. See J. B. Fletcher, "Dante's 'Image' in the Sun," *Romanic Review,* 24 (April–June 1933), 99–128; esp. p. 106.

58. According to Thomas, heresy is a species of *infidelitas:* "falsitas veritati opponitur. Sed haereticus est qui falsas vel novas opiniones vel gignit vel sequitur. Ergo opponitur vertati, cui fides innititur. Ergo sub infidelitate continetur" (*ST,* II–IIae, q.11, a.1 contra). Infidelity, and its various species, resides "in the intellectu sicut in subiecto" (ibid., q.10, a.2).

59. W. H. V. Reade says of the sin of heresy, "Aristotle and the moral philosophers had never conceived of a sin residing in the *intellectus speculativus.*" He continues: "the sixth circle owes its unexplained position to the fact that moral philosophy, which Virgil represents, makes no provision for any sin which is in *intellectu speculativo sicut in subiecto.*" Given Dante's moral system, "with heresy there were only two alternatives, (1) to omit it altogether, (2) to make it isolated and, in a sense, extraneous to the moral scheme of the *Inferno.* The former course was impossible for a good Catholic: the latter is actually adopted, and is embodied in the circle of the Heresiarchs" (*The Moral System of Dante's Inferno* [Oxford: Clarendon, 1909], pp. 374–375). Reade's chap. 22 is devoted to an analysis of "The Circle of Heresy," pp. 367–381.

60. Ibid., p. 429: "St. Thomas always teaches that in Usury an art is put to an unnatural purpose, and when proving that Justice is thus outraged, he alludes to the *Politics* (i, 10): 'et Philosophus naturali ratione ductus dicit quod 'usuraria acquisitio pecuniarum est maxime praeter naturam' (S. 2. 2. lxxviii. I ad 3)."

61. *Conv.* II, xiii, 2: "Dico che per cielo io intendo la scienza e per cieli le scienze, per tre similitudini che li cieli hanno con le scienze massimamente; e per l'ordine e numero in che paiono convenire, sì come trattando quello vocabulo, cioè 'terzo,' si vedrà." See Busnelli's excellent note ad loc. André Pézard has seen the

importance of the *Convivio* metaphor for the interpretation of Canto XI's exposition, but finds it impossible to believe that Dante had chosen usury as the sole example of violence against art; see *Dante sous la pluie de feu* (Paris: Vrin, 1950), p. 229.

62. In the state of continence, reason dominates sense appetite, against the force of the latter, whereas in the virtue of *temperantia,* the two are in harmony. See Thomas, *ST* I–II, 155, 4 and Foster-Humphries, *"Aristotle's De anima,"* p. 481.

63. *Timaeus* 40a; cf. Plotinus, *Enneads* II, ii, 2.

64. Cf. *Paradiso* XIV. 1–3; for basic discussions of the theme and necessary bibliography, see Georges Poulet, "Le Symbole du cercle infini dans la littérature et la philosophie," *Revue de métaphysique et de morale,* 3 (1959), esp. pp. 259–264; H. R. Patch, "The Last Line of the Commedia," *Speculum,* 14 (1939), 56–65; Bruno Nardi, "Sì come rota ch'igualmente è mossa" in *Nel mondo di Dante* (Rome: Edizioni di Storia e Letteratura, 1944), pp. 337–350.

5. Infernal Irony

1. The Augustinian tradition dominates medieval discussions, of course, but it is also clearly alluded to by Marsilio Ficino in his *De raptu Pauli* in E. Garin, ed., *Prosatori Latini del Quattrocento* (Milan: Ricciardi, 1952), pp. 932 ff.

2. The title was common in nineteenth-century editions. See Cary's remarks in his preface to the 1814 edition, *The Vision of Dante Alighieri* (London, 1814).

3. The discussion to which most refer is by F. X. Newman, "St. Augustine's Three Visions and the Structure of the *Comedy,*" *MLN* (1967), 56–78.

4. Marguerite Chiarenza, "The Imageless Vision and Dante's *Paradiso,*" *Dante Studies,* 90 (1972), 77–91.

5. Augustine, *In Ioannem,* tr. XXIV, 2 (John 6:6–14).

6. Erich Auerbach, *Mimesis* (Princeton: Princeton University Press, 1953).

7. "The Substance of Things Seen," in C. S. Singleton, *Dante Studies* 1 (Cambridge: Harvard University Press, 1954), pp. 61–83.

8. Benedetto Croce, *La poesia di Dante* (Bari: Laterza, 1921).

9. Augustine, *De Genesi ad litteram,* XII, 11.

10. For an understanding of Peirce's categories in the context of semiotics, I am indebted to Michael Shapiro, *The Sense of Grammar* (Bloomington: University of Indiana Press, 1983).

11. The idea of the gate as a funerary inscription was suggested to me by a reading of "The Mnemonics of History" (*Yale Italian Studies,* I, 4 [1977]) by my dear friend Eugenio Donato, to whose memory this essay is dedicated.

12. C. S. Singleton, "The Irreducible Dove," *Comparative Literature* 9 (1957), 129–135.

13. Augustine, *In Ioannem,* XXVII, 5.

14. C. S. Singleton, "*Inferno* X: Guido's Disdain," *MLN,* 77 (1962), 49–65.

15. Augustine, *Confessions* III, 7, trans. R. S. Pine-Coffin (Baltimore: Penguin Books, 1961).

16. Michel Foucault, *Discipline and Punish,* trans. Alan Sheridan (New York: Pantheon, 1979), p. 30.

17. Quoted by Foucault, p. 45.

18. Paul de Man, "The Rhetoric of Temporality," in *Interpretation and the Languages of Criticism,* ed. Singleton et al. (Baltimore: Johns Hopkins University Press, 1969).

19. Dan Sperber and Deirdre Wilson, "Irony and the Use—Mention Distinction," in *Radical Pragmatics,* ed. Peter Cole (New York: Academic Press, 1981). I am indebted to David Wellbery for pointing out this work to me.

20. Marianne Shapiro, "The Status of Irony," forthcoming in *Stanford Literature Review.* I should like to acknowledge my general indebtedness on the subject of irony to this important work.

6. The Neutral Angels

1. The standard terminology derives from St. Augustine. He wonders what Genesis means when it refers to God's separating the light from the darkness, when in fact the sun had not yet been created: "qualis illa sit lux et quo alternante motu qualem que vesperam et mane fecerit, remotum est a sensibus nostris." He then hits upon Paul's statement, "Omnes enim vos filii lucis estis et filii diei; non sumus noctis neque tenebrarum" (I Thess. 5:5). He continues: "Quoniam scientiae creaturae in compartione scientiae Creatoris quodam modo vesperascit, itemque lucescit et mane fit, cum et ipsa refertur ad laudem dilectionemque Creatoris; nec in noctem vergitur, ubi non Creator creaturae dilectione relinquitur" (*De civ. Dei* XI, 7, lines 6–20; cf. *De Genesi ad litteram* IV, 22; *PL* 34, 312). Thereafter, the *cognitio matutina et vespertina* was applied to the first moments of cognition with the added support of the light imagery of the Epistles to the Corinthians (I Cor. 13:12: "Nunc per speculum in aenigmate: tunc autem facie ad faciem"; II Cor. 4:6; II Cor. 6:14). Thomas systematized the metaphor with regard to the angels in his article "Utrum in angelis sit cognitio matutina et vespertina" (*ST* I, 58, 6); he fused the light imagery with the idea of introspection according to the pseudo-Dionysius: "[the angel] se in seipsam convertit per vespertinam cognitionem . . . [Some] per matutinam cognitionem ad laudem Verbi sunt conversi . . . [others] in seipsis remanentes, facti sunt nox" (ibid. 63, 6 ad 4). Hence, the angels who could not wait became night. The being of the creature is fulfilled in glory, and hence the "unripeness" of Satan (*Par.* XIX, 46–48).

2. Dante, *The Inferno,* trans. John Ciardi (New York: New Americana Library, 1954), p. 43. One might hazard the guess that Ciardi calls this the canto of "The Opportunists" (ibid., p. 4) on the basis of his translation of "per sè."

3. *The Comedy of Dante Alighieri: Cantica I,* trans. Dorothy L. Sayers (New York: Penguin, 1949), p. 86.

4. *The Divine Comedy of Dante Alighieri,* trans. Charles E. Norton (Boston: Houghton Mifflin, 1892), I, 12.

5. "Inferno," *The Divine Comedy,* trans. Carlyle-Wicksteed (New York: Modern Library, 1950), p. 23.

6. *The Vision of Dante Alighieri,* trans. Henry F. Cary, 3rd ed. (London: Smith, 1844), p. 60.

7. Aischa Hell uses this unnamed German translation: "Vermischt sind sie mit jenem bösen Chore / Der Engel, die einst, weder abgefallen / Von Gott, noch ihm getreu, allein gestanden" ("Dante und die Unentschiedenheit," *Deutsches Dante-*

jahrbuch, 32 [XXIV Neue Folge], [Weimar, 1954], 110). I would consider this a more faithful rendering of Dante's verses. Among others who have eschewed the translation of "per sè" as "for themselves" are: I. C. Wright ("who stood aloof," *The Divine Comedy of Dante Alighieri*, 5th ed. [London, 1875], p. 12) and E. H. Plumptre ("who . . . dwelt in isolated shame," *The Commedia and Canzoniere of Dante Alighieri* [London, 1866], I, 14).

8. Apoc. 3:15: "Scio opera tua: quia neque frigidus es, neque calidus: utinam frigidus esses, aut calidus: sed quia tepidus es, et nec frigidus, nec calidus, incipiam te evomere ex ore meo."

9. The famous lines describing all the spirits of the vestibule are spoken by Virgil, and they suggest that God shares the contempt of Virgil and the pilgrim: "Fama di loro il mondo esser non lassa; / misericordia e giustizia li sdegna: / non ragioniam di lor, ma guarda e passa" (*Inf.* III, 49–51).

10. The shift in interpretation during the Renaissance is strikingly illustrated by the fact that Matteo Palmieri, in his long cosmological poem "La Città di Vita," made these angels his heroes, and looked upon their neutrality as the essence of the human condition. The human soul was created when these angels were sent to earth to make up their minds once and for all; see *Libro del poema chiamato Città di Vita composto da Matteo Palmieri florentino,* transcribed by Margaret Rooke, Smith College Studies in Modern Languages, VIII, 1–4 (Oct. 1926–June 1928). This reflects a judgment of the angels' relative innocence much like that expressed by Francesco da Buti: "chì è più vizioso è più basso, e chi è men vizioso è men basso" (*Commento di Francesco da Buti sopra la Divina Commedia,* ed. Crescentino Biannini [Pisa, 1858–62], I, 89). Using this reasoning, the vestibule spirits would be less culpable than the virtuous pagans.

11. *De civ. Dei* XII, 6.

12. Triadic speculation is characteristic of hierarchical thinking, and hierarchy is part of the subject matter of angelology. According to the pseudo-Dionysius, love makes the cosmos a unity, for the lower loves the higher, converting to it; those of the same order love each other, and the higher loves the lower (*De div. nom.* IV, 15; *PG* 3, 707). This was a principle that Proclus had set forth in his commentary on the *Alcibiades* (ed. V. Cousin, II, 153), and in the *Elements of Theology* (ed. E. R. Dodds, pp. 35–37). The downward movement, from the One to the many (Progression), is the emanation in a neoplatonic scheme. The upward movement, from the many to the One (Reversion) is the return. According to E. R. Dodds (*Elements of Theology*, p. 218), the idea arose in middle Platonism, possibly with Poseidonius, and may be described as a combination of many elements: Plato's idea of conversion, the Hellenistic religious teaching about a flight to the heavens, etc. The idea is found also in Plotinus (*Enneads* IV, 4, 2). Plato spoke of the circularity of contemplation and the rectilinear movement of action in *Timaeus* 40a. He was thinking of planetary motion, but the pseudo-Dionysius transposed this language to angelology, adding a third or oblique movement, so that the angels moved circularly around God, directly when administering to men, and in a combination of these two movements (*De div. nom.* IV, 8; *PG* 3, 703). Thus the movement of the cosmos and of the individual angelic soul was threefold: upward, inward, and downward (cf. *Liber de causis* VII, ed. Orth, p. 28). In the text of the pseudo-Alexander, the three alternates "sive . . . sive . . . sive" reflect a mistaken transposition of the threefold

movement to the ethical sphere. Precisely the same shift was made in the late fifteenth century by Marsilio Ficino in his commentary on the pseudo-Dionysius: "Tres, ut Platonici loquar, actus in angelicis mentibus esse possunt, scilicet trina conversio, vel ad Deum, vel ad se, vel ad sequentia. Itaque angeli . . . ad ipsum Deum . . . conversi, semper evasere beati. Nonnulli vero conversi ad se . . . facti sunt e vestigio miser . . . Quidam rursus, ad infima . . . conversi . . . omnium evasere miserrime" *Opera Omnia* (Basel, 1576), II, 1080.

13. *Summa,* par. 171; II, 223.

14. Ibid. II, 224.

15. "Quelli che vedi qui furon modesti / a riconoscer sè da la bontate / che li avea fatti a tanto intender presti; / per che le viste lor furo essaltate / con grazia illuminante e con lor merto, / sì c'hanno ferma e piena volontate; / e non voglio che dubbi, ma sia certo, / che ricever la grazia è meritorio, / secondo che l'affetto l'è aperto" (*Par.* XXIX, 58–66).

16. "E ciò fa certo che 'l primo superbo, / che fu la somma d'ogni creatura, / per non aspettar lume, cadde acerbo" (*Par.* XIX, 46–48).

17. *Inf.* III, 64. Similarly, it may be said that the human beings in the vestibule never were alive since they failed to make the commitment which is the beginning of moral life. The single moment of angelic choice recapitulates the whole of man's moral existence; thus angelology was the "control laboratory" for the analysis of human action.

18. *Sermones de sanctis, In purif. Mariae* 2; *PL* 183, 368.

19. In *Convivio* IV, 8, 11f., Dante distinguishes irreverence from non-reverence according to the Aristotelian theory of logical opposition: "Lo inreverente dice privazione, lo non reverente dice negatione." An Aristotelian logician would have recognized "ribelli/fedeli" as a third type of opposition, that of contrariety. In contrariety, there can be no mean or intermediate position, unless it be exclusion of both contradictory qualities. In the opposition of good and evil, on the other hand, because these stand in the relationship *habitus/privatio,* there is always an intermediate, which is equally composed of the two opposed qualities. It is clear then that exclusion from the opposition "fedeli/ribelli" does not at the same time imply an exclusion from the category of moral good or evil.

20. See L. B. Gillon, *La Théorie des oppositions et la théologie du péché au XIII*[e] *siècle* (Paris: Vrin, 1937), p. xv: "Sans doute le péché reçoit de la privation sa dénomination ultime de mal. Mais ce *defectus,* pour être péché et non un mal quelconque, réclame absolument l'acte humain dans lequel il se fonde. Et c'est cette 'substance' de l'acte, accompagnée par la privation, que le péché désigne immédiatement non comme mal, mais comme péché."

21. St. Augustine had established that evil could only stem from a *defectus:* "Nemo igitur quaerat efficientem causam malae voluntatis; non enim est efficiens sed deficiens, quia nec illa effectio sed defectio. Deficere namque ab eo, quod summe est, ad id, quod minus est, hoc est incipere habere voluntatem malam"; *De civ. Dei* XII, 7. Note, however, that the beginning of sin consists of two moments: the first is the *adversio* from that which is paramount; the second is the *conversio* to that which is lower. The first is the *defectus,* the second is the *actus.* The first is a rational nonconsideration, the second is the action itself. It will not do to confuse the *adversio* with a sin of omission, according to St. Thomas, for this sin too is composed of two

moments. The first is the aversion of the mind, the second is the act of abstention from acting. In the first moment of the sin of omission, the sinner fails to consider that which should be considered, in the second he decides not to act. For this distinction, see Thomas, *De malo* II, 1, resp.

22. In a sense, this episode of the spirits of the vestibule might be called the canto of exclusion. The language throughout the scene derives much of its harsh tone from the great number of oppositions and antitheses, poles which contain all of the universe within them. These are the beings who lived "sanza infamia" and "sanza lodo." The angels were neither "ribelli" nor "fedeli," both they and their human counterparts are scorned by "misericordia" and "giustizia," and finally, they are hateful both to God and "a' nemici sui." This leaves only cosmic isolation. An Italian manual of rhetoric quotes some of the verses of this canto as an example of a classic figure of speech: " 'Caccianli i ciel per non esser men belli / ne lo profondo inferno li riceve, / ch'alcuna gloria i rei avrebber d'elli.' This is called *aetiology,* that is, the figure which is 'ad propositum subiecta ratio' "; see A. Salvagni, *Figure Grammaticali,* Manuali Hoepli 374–75 (Milan, 1907), p. 237. It might be added that the first terzina conforms to the figure called by Salvagni *antitheton* ("la contrapposizione di parola a parola, di concetto a concetto, tra loro opposti"), ibid. It is clear that Dante isolates these spirits as totally as he can.

7. Medusa: The Letter and the Spirit

1. Charles S. Singleton, *Dante Studies 1: Commedia, Elements of Structure* (Cambridge, Mass.: Harvard University Press, 1954); "Allegory." For general bibliography on Dante's allegory, see Robert Hollander, *Allegory in Dante's "Commedia"* (Princeton: Princeton University Press, 1969).

2. *Convivio* IV, xv, 11. Cf. II, i, 4.

3. See R. P. C. Hanson, *II Corinthians* (London, 1954), p. 39, commenting on II Cor. 3 and 4.

4. On the word and its history, see J. A. Robinson, *St. Paul's Epistle to the Ephesians* (London, 1914), pp. 264–274.

5. *Glossa Ordinaria; PL,* 114, 55.

6. Fulgentius, *Mythologicon* I, 26, in A. Van Staveten, *Mythographi Latini* (Amsterdam, 1742), p. 657.

7. Quoted by Hermann Gmelin, *Kommentar: Die Göttliche Komödie* (Stuttgart: Klett, 1954), ad loc.

8. Among the encyclopedias, I have found W. H. Röscher, *Ausführliches Lexikon der griechishen und römischen Mythologie* (Munich, 1884–1937) to be most helpful on the subject of Medusa's beauty. Arnolf d'Orléans says of her: "illa autem mutabat homines in saxum quia pre amore illius obstupebant." Arnulfi Aurelianensis, *Glosule super Lucanum,* ed. Berthe M. Marti, Papers and Monographs, American Academy of Rome, 18 (1958), 470. Cf. Boccaccio, *Genealogie* X, 9, ed. V. Romano (Bari: Laterza, 1951), p. 496. See especially on the subject, A. A. Barb, "The Mermaid and the Devil's Grandmother," *Journal of the Warburg and Courtauld Institutes,* 29 (1966), and "Diva Matrix," in the same journal, 16 (1953).

9. *Odyssey* XI, ll. 634 ff.

10. See the possibly interpolated passage in *Aeneid* VI, 289, ed. J. W. Mackail (Oxford: Clarendon, 1930), p. 233n.

11. *Troilus and Creseyde* I, 6–11, and note, in F. N. Robinson (ed.), *The Works of Geoffrey Chaucer* (Boston: Houghton Mifflin, 1961).

12. *Roman de la Rose,* ed. Ernest Langlois (Paris: Firmin-Didot, 1914), V, 107. The interpolation occurs at vv. 20810–11. (Translation is by Matilda Bruckner.)

13. A. A. Barb, "Mermaid," p. 9.

14. For the temporality of allegory, see Paul de Man, "The Rhetoric of Temporality," in *Interpretation: Theory and Practice,* ed. Charles S. Singleton (Baltimore: The Johns Hopkins University Press, 1969), pp. 190–191.

15. *Confessions* VIII, xi.

16. John B. Friedman, *Orpheus in the Middle Ages* (Cambridge, Mass.: Harvard University Press, 1970), pp. 104–109.

17. "Introduction to Dante's *Rime*" (trans. Yvonne Freccero) in *Dante: A Collection of Critical Essays,* ed. J. Freccero (Englewood Cliffs, N.J.: Prentice-Hall, 1965), p. 36.

18. Gianfranco Contini, "Dante come personaggio-poeta della *Commedia,*" in *Approdo,* N.S. 4, no. 1 (1958), 19, rept. in *Varianti e altra linguistica* (Turin: Einaudi, 1970).

19. Text and trans. by K. Foster and P. Boyde, *Dante's Lyric Poetry* (Oxford: Clarendon, 1967) I, p. 163.

20. For the adaptation of Augustinian theology to the medieval love lyric, see Frederick Goldin, *The Mirror of Narcissus in the Courtly Love Lyric* (Ithaca: Cornell University Press, 1967), pp. 207 ff.

21. See Jacques Lacan, *Ecrits* (Paris: Editions du Seuil: 1966), p. 40, for a neo-Freudian restatement of the tyranny of the letter, or "signifier."

22. *Purg.* VIII. If, as I have suggested, the arrival of the messenger is an *interpretive* descent, then the identification of that messenger with Mercury (from Statius, *Thebaid* II, 2; cf. Pietro di Dante) is peculiarly apt: the *Hermes* of a new Christian *hermeneutics*. The angel fulfills this and other roles of the classical messenger of the gods.

8. Dante's Ulysses

1. Robert Hollander, *Allegory in Dante's "Commedia"* (Princeton, N.J.: Princeton University Press, 1969), pp. 76 ff.

2. David Thompson, "Dante's Ulysses and the Allegorical Journey," *Dante Studies,* 85 (1967), 33–58.

3. E. R. Curtius, *European Literature and the Latin Middle Ages* (Princeton, N.J.: Princeton University Press, 1953), pp. 128–130.

9. Bestial Sign and Bread of Angels

1. Marianne Shapiro, "An Old French Source for Ugolino?" *Dante Studies,* 92 (1974), 129–147, following Gianfranco Contini's brief but masterful reading in "Filologia ed esegesi dantesca," *Varianti e altra linguistica* (Turin: Einaudi, 1970), pp. 409–432.

2. Shalom Spiegel, *The Last Trial,* trans. by Judah Goldin (New York: Pantheon, 1967), p. 15.

3. This is the interpretation of C. S. Singleton in his *Inferno* commentary, p. 617.

4. *Aeneid* II, 3–6.

5. Augustine, *Confessions* VII, x, 16.

6. Henri de Lubac, *Corpus Mysticum* (Paris: Aubier, 1948).

7. Augustine, *In Johannis Evangelium,* tract. XXVII, 5; John 5:62.

10. The Sign of Satan

1. "Dante," in T. S. Eliot, *Selected Essays* (New York: Harcourt, Brace, 1934), p. 212.

2. For the significance of the word as it applies to Dante's journey, see Charles S. Singleton, *Dante Studies 2: Journey to Beatrice* (Cambridge, Mass: Harvard University Press, 1958), chap. 4. In a sense, of course, the pilgrim's justification begins when he first sees Virgil. This is the sense of *justificatio impii,* which not only requires a *conversio in causam justificantem* (that is, God), but also requires that a man be converted *ad destructionem peccati praeteriti.* Justification *simpliciter,* however, is simply the infusion of grace, the preparation for which begins at the "zero-point." See Thomas Aquinas, *De veritate* XXVIII, art. v. resp.

3. W. Bousset investigates the association of an analogous cosmological point, the vernal equinox, with the Christian cross. According to him, Plato's letter *chi* was taken by early Christians to represent the cross. W. Bousset, "Platons Weltseele und das Kreuz Christi," *Zeitschrift für die Neutestamentliche Wissenschaft,* 14 (1913), 273–285. Dante's modified use of the theme occurs at *Par.* I, 37 and again at *Par.* X, 7–15; see chap. 4 above. The passage from Ephesians was believed to refer to the dimensions of the cross. A. E. Schönbach collected many of the commentaries on the passage in his *Altdeutsche Predigten* (Graz, 1888), II, 177–189.

4. *In Hexaem.* I, 21–24; *Opera* (Quaracchi, 1882–1902) V, 333. See the commentary on the passage by Etienne Gilson, *La Philosophie de St. Bonaventure* (Paris: Vrin, 1943), p. 222, and the remarks by Georges Poulet, *Les Métamorphoses du cercle* (Paris: Plon, 1961), p. xviii. It seems clear that Bonaventure here alludes to the cosmological tree located *in medio terrae* (Dan. 4:7–14), Jerusalem, the *umbilicus terrae* (Ezech. 38:12), where tradition placed the cross. The ambiguity of the phrase *medium terrae* allowed him to conceive of the cross also at the earth's center and thus associated the Crucifixion with the harrowing of hell. Here we have in germ the juxtaposition of Calvary and the earth's center (cf. *Inf.* XXXIV, 113–114). On the *umbilicus terrae* and the cosmological tree of the cross, see E. S. Greenhill, "The Child in the Tree," *Traditio,* 10 (1954), 335 ff.

5. Charles S. Singleton, *Dante Studies 1: Commedia, Elements of Structure* (Cambridge, Mass: Harvard University Press, 1954), p. 37. Singleton's extensive discussion of the figure of Satan is fundamental and is this essay's point of departure. For the full text of the *Vexilla Regis,* see F. Leo's edition of Fortunatus' *Opera* (Berlin, 1881), p. 34.

6. Ubertino da Casale, *Arbor Vitae Crucifixae Jesu,* introduction by C. T. Davis (Turin: Bottega d'Erasmo, 1961), p. 317.

7. Ambrose, *In Lucam* VIII, 29; *PL* 15, 1774.

8. Augustine, II *Quaes. Evangelior.* q.39, n.2. An analogous gloss turns up un-

expectedly in the tradition of the *Ovidius moralizatus* as an allegorical explanation of the story of Pyramus and Thisbe. See, for example, Pierre Bersuire, for whom Pyramus is Christ and Thisbe is *anima humana*. They meet *sub more arbore, idest sub cruce,* the tree which is stained with blood. *Ovidius Metamorphoseos moralizatus a Fratre P. Berchorii,* appendix to F. Ghisalberti, "Ovidius moralizatus," *Studi romanzi,* 23 (1933), 114–115. Cf. *Ovide moralisé* IV, 1176, edited by C. De Boer (*Kongl. akad. van Wetenschappen, Amsterdam, Verhand.* Afdeeling Lett. N. R. Deel XXI [1920], II, 37).

9. The *Glossa Ordinaria* gives both (*PL* 114, 318); Bede (*Corpus Christ.* 120, 310) sides with Augustine, while Chrysostom's gloss resembles Augustine's. For a convenient survey of exegetical opinion, see Cornelius a Lapide's commentary *Commentarius in Quat. Evang.* (Venice, 1700), II, 146, but it is by no means exhaustive. Bonaventure distinguishes the tropological and allegorical interpretations of the verse; see *Opera* VII, 430–431.

10. For a survey of the bibliography on Satan's three heads, three colors, and three winds, see H. Gmelin, *Die Göttliche Komödie,* Kommentar I (Stuttgart: Klett, 1954), pp. 483–486. Among the most interesting passages he refers to is one by Hugo de Sancto Caro on Jeremiah I, which discusses and names three winds of the devil. The passage recalls Hildegard von Bingen, whose works are full of suggestive glosses to Dante's poem. See especially, for our purposes, a passage from the *Liber vitae meritorum* which discusses a three-colored fire tormenting those who were bitter toward their neighbors. The flames are precisely black, red, and white. *Nova S. Hildegardis Opera—Analecta Sacra Spicilegio Solesmensi Parata,* ed. by J.-B. Pitra (Paris, 1883), p. 587. The analogy with Dante's devil was noticed by A. Battandier, "Ste. Hildegarde, sa vie et ses oeuvres," *Revue des questions historiques,* 33 (1883), 422–423. The most interesting discussion of the colors in Italian criticism, so far as I have been able to determine, is by Giovanni Busnelli, *I tre colori del Lucifero dantesco* (Rome, 1910), which associates the colors with the horses of the Apocalypse, but fails to go beyond the literal meaning of the Apocalypse. The classic piece associating Dante's devil with iconographic traditions is Arturo Graf, "La Demonologia di Dante," in *Miti, leggende e superstizioni del medio evo* (Turin: E. Loescher, 1925; rept. Bologna: Forni, 1965), pp. 300 ff.

11. Bartholomeus Anglicus, *De rerum proprietatibus* (Frankfurt, 1601; rept. Frankfurt, 1964, p. 1139). Plato seems to have taken white, black, and red as primary colors in *Timaeus* 67e (cf. Cornford's note ad loc.). Aristotle sets his spectrum as white and black (although he does not specifically mention red) in the *De sensu* II, iii, the *locus classicus* for medieval theorists of color, on which see Averroes' paraphrase (*Comment.,* Venice, 1574, vol. VI[2]) and Albertus Magnus (*Opera,* ed. Jammy, V).

12. Bartholomeus, *De rerum,* pp. 1150–1151. Albertus agrees that *pallidus* is the first stage in the blackening process.

13. Singleton, *Dante Studies 2,* chap. 4.

14. For a discussion of these points and appropriate references to the *Physics,* see M. Flick, "L'Attimo della giustificazione," *Analecta Gregoriana* XL, B (Rome, 1947), esp. pp. 23–26: "Il passaggio dallo stato di peccato allo stato di grazia."

15. According to Aristotle (*Physics* I, vii), there are three species of mutation: generation, corruption, and motion. Motion is a mutation from one affirmation to

another, whereas generation is from negation to affirmation and corruption is from affirmation to negation. It follows that motion involves the two other mutations. As Thomas says: "nam quod movetur de albo in nigrum, corrumpitur album et fit nigrum" (*Opera* [Leonine] II, 46). Here, as throughout the *Physics,* the opposition of black and white is the standard example of contrariety.

16. The cross as tree is one of the most venerable of all exegetical traditions, for which see Greenhill, "The Child in the Tree," *passim.* On p. 365, Greenhill suggests that the origin of the *arbor vitiorum,* the tree of the devil, may be found in the tradition of the *crux diaboli* (see n. 17 below) by a development analogous to that of the *crux Christi,* but the devil as tree may be a tradition quite as old as the *crux diaboli,* ultimately dependent on the two trees of Paradise. T. Silverstein (*Visio Sancti Pauli,* Studies and Documents IV [London: Christophers, 1935], p. 139) quotes Gregory the Great (*Moralia* XXXIV, 23, 47; *PL* 76, 664) as a probable source of the tree of vices and suggests that a literal reading of "radix omnia malorum est superbia" may have been influential as well.

17. Schönbach (*Altdeutsche Predigten,* pp. 187–189) has collected examples of the *crux diaboli* in the works of Hugo de Folieto (pseud. Hugh of St. Victor), Peter Damian, and Dungal, Abbot of Pavia. He suggests that the last is one of the oldest, but Robert Kaske has pointed out to me that the *crux diaboli* already appears in Origen's Homily 8 on Josue 8:29, which we have here paraphrased.

18. Schönbach (p. 188) cites this passage from *PL* 176, 1017.

19. Sermo 2, *PL* 210, 225; Schönbach, p. 187. Among others whom Schönbach mentions for the three crosses are Hugh of St. Victor (*PL* 177, 499) and Lucas Tudensis (*Bibl. Max. Patr.* 25,233).

20. A number of details in Canto XXXIV are reminiscent of phrases used in contexts concerning the cross. For the cross as the Trinity, see Honorius D'Autun: "per tria cornua superiora Trinitas Patris et Filii et Spritus sancti denotatur" (*PL* 172, 945; Schönbach, p. 184). For the devil as "vermo reo" (XXXIV, 108) transfixed by the cross, see Arnoldus Carnotensis: "hoc in profundo cordis crux agit . . . subterque Leviathan verme venenato hoc vecte transfixo, intrinseca nostra pacificat" (*Bibl. Max. Patr.* 22, 1273; Schönbach, pp. 184–185). For the cross as bird (cf. "tanto uccello," v. 47) which speads its wings, ibid., p. 185: "expansisque alis pullos inplumes [crux] aggregat et fovet et protegit."

21. Isidore first established the folk etymology with a pun that was taken seriously by some: "*Sycomorus,* sicut et morus Graeca nomina sunt . . . Hanc Latine *celsam* appellant" *Etymol.* XVII, vii (*PL* 82, 63). See, for example, Albertus Magnus: "Sycomorum autem quidam virtutem vocabuli ignorantes, dicunt arborem quae est sicut mous. . . ." *In Evang. D. Luc.* XIX, *Opera* X, 261. The interpretation which became accepted was that of Augustine: "Sycomora fici fatuae Latini interpretatur" (Sermo 174, [8 *de Verbis Apostoli*] c.3, n.3), althugh Bede is sometimes cited. Because of its late flowering, the *morus* was called *sapientissima* by Pliny (*Naturalis Historiae* XVI, 25); thus it was said to be foolish *per antiphrasin.* See Cornelius a Lapide, *Commentarius in quat. Evang.,* p. 146.

22. See St. Jerome, *Liber interpr. Hebr. Nom.:* "Zacheus interpretatur iustus vel iustificatus seu iustificandus" (*Corpus Christ.* 72, 138). He is quoted verbatim by many compilers, such as Papias Grammaticus (Venice, 1484), *s.v.*

23. *In Evang. D. Luc.,* p. 259.

24. Ibid., p. 263.

25. Ibid., p. 262.

26. On the phrase "inde erat transiturus," see Hugo de Sancto Caro, *Opera* (Basel, 1504), V, 222v.

11. Infernal Inversion and Christian Conversion

1. Bruno Nardi, "Al Lettore," *Dante e la cultura medievale: Nuovi saggi di filosofia dantesca* (Bari: Laterza, 1942), p. ix.

2. Werner Jaeger, *Early Christianity and Greek Paideia* (Cambridge, Mass.: Harvard University Press, 1961).

3. *Timaeus* 43e; trans. F. M. Cornford, *Plato's Cosmology* (New York: Liberal Arts Press, 1957), p. 149.

4. *Timaeus* 44c. *Commentarius* IX, 211, ed. Wrobel (Lepizig, 1876), p. 250. On the passage, see chap. 2 above.

5. Wilhelm Bousset, "Platons Weltseele und das Kreuz Christi," *Zeitschrift für die Neutestamentliche Wissenschaft* 14 (1913), 275 ff.

6. *Apocryphal Acts of Paul, Peter,* etc., trans. B. Pick (Chicago, 1909), pp. 118–119.

7. Jacobus a Voragine, *Legenda Aurea,* ed. Th. Graesse (Leipzig, 1850), cap. 89 (p. 375).

8. Ibid.

12. Casella's Song

1. For the question of the *poet* as pilgrim, see Gianfranco Contini, "Dante come personaggio-poeta della *Commedia,*" in *Approdo,* n.s., 4, no. 1 (1958), 19–46, repr. in *Varianti e altra linguistica* (Turin: Einaudi, 1970), pp. 335–361.

2. Quoted by Natalino Sapegno, ed., Dante, *La Divina Commedia* (Milan-Naples: Ricciardi, 1957), p. 415.

3. For the myth of Casella as inventor of the madrigal, see Leonard Ellenwood, "Origins of the Italian *Ars Nova,*" Papers Read by Members of the American Musicological Society (Pittsburgh: Dec. 29–30, 1937; privately printed), pp. 30–31. Ellenwood discusses the "timeworn" reference to the phrase, "e Casella diede il suono," supposedly attached to a "madrigal" of Lemmo da Pistoia.

4. For the phrase, "amoroso canto," see Sapegno, p. 414, who correctly observes "non si tratta di amore per donne, ma dell'elogio in forma allegorica della Filosofia." For the theme and genre of "Consolation," see *Dictionnaire de Spiritualité ascétique et mystique,* ed. G. Viller (Paris: Beauschesne, 1953), *s.v.*

5. Boethius, *The Consolation of Philosophy,* trans. V. E. Watts (Hammondsworth, England: Penguin Books, 1969), p. 54.

6. For the iconography of Boethius and music, see Pierre Courcelle, "*La Consolation de philosophie" dans la tradition littéraire: Antécédents et postérité de Boèce* (Paris: Etudes Augustiniennes, 1967), pp. 92–93 and especially the iconographical appendix.

7. Boethius, *The Consolation of Philosophy,* ed. H. F. Stewart, Loeb Classical Library (Cambridge, Mass.: Harvard University Press, 1953), p. 234.

8. Ibid., p. 132.

9. See Sapegno, p. 414.

10. *Confessions* I, 1. See C. S. Singleton's remarks in *An Essay on the Vita Nuova* (Cambridge, Mass.: Harvard University Press, 1953), p. 61.

11. The parallelism between "disio . . . voler" in *Inferno* V and "disio . . . velle" in *Paradiso* XXXIII was first pointed out to me by C. S. Singleton. See chap. 16 below.

12. William R. O'Connor, *The Eternal Quest: The Teaching of St. Thomas Aquinas on the Natural Desire for God* (London: Longmans, Green, 1947), pp. 147 ff.

13. For Bonagiunta, see Maria Simonelli, "Bonagiunta Orbicciani e la problematica dello stil nuovo (*Purg.* XXIV)," in *Dante Studies,* 86 (1968), 65–83.

14. "Omo ch'è saggio non corre leggero," Sonnet XIX[b], *Poeti del Duecento,* ed. Gianfranco Contini (Milan: Ricciardi, 1960), II, 482.

13. Manfred's Wounds

1. Erich Auerbach, *Mimesis,* trans. Willard Trask (Princeton: Princeton University Press, 1953), p. 3.

2. Ibid., pp. 4–5.

3. Northrop Frye, *Anatomy of Criticism* (Princeton: Princeton University Press, 1957), p. 189.

4. On Frederick, see Ernst Kantorowicz, *Frederick the Second,* trans. W. Trask (Princeton: Princeton University Press, 1948).

5. Ibid., p. 421.

6. Ibid., p. 75.

7. Meyer H. Abrams, *The Mirror and the Lamp* (New York: Norton, 1958).

8. Robert Klein, "L'Enfer de Marsile Ficin," in *L'umanesimo e esoterismo;* ed. E. Castelli (Padua: 1955), p. 264.

9. *Roman de la Rose* XXXIV, 72.

15. The Dance of the Stars

1. Emanuele Tesauro, *Il Cannocchiale aristotelico* (Venice: 1655), p. 493, quoted by Eugenio Donato, "Tesauro's Poetics: Through the Looking Glass," *MLN,* 77 (Jan. 1963), 19: "Reduced to this level of reality, the concepts expressed by the metaphor are nothing but 'argomenti urbanamente fallaci,' because 'ad urdirle sorprendono l'intelletto, parendo concludenti di primo incontro, ma esaminate, si risolvono in una vana fallacia: come le mele nel Mar Negro, di veduta son belle e colorite, ma se le mordi, ti lasciano le fauci piene di cenere e di fumo.' "

2. Charles S. Singleton, *Dante Studies 1: Commedia, Elements of Structure* (Cambridge, Mass.: Harvard University Press, 1957), chap. 1. For the various figurative modes of the *literal* level of Scripture, see P. Synave, "La Doctrine de St. Thomas d'Aquin sur le sens littéral des Ecritures," *Revue biblique,* 35 (1926), 40 ff.

3. G. Fraccaroli, trans., *Il Timeo* (Turin: Bocca, 1906); "Dante e il Timeo," pp. 391–424. Fraccaroli is certain that Dante knew the text in the translation of Chalcidius and possibly a commentary. For a more recent view of the diffusion of the *Timaeus* in Dante's time, see Guillaume de Conches, *Glosae super Platonem,* ed. E. Jeauneau (*Textes philosophiques du Moyen Age,* 13 [Paris: Vrin, 1965]), pp. 29–

31. Jeauneau utilized, among others, a thirteenth-century ms. from Ss. Annunziata in his collection.

4. See E. Jeauneau, "L'usage de la notion d'*integumentum* à travers les glosses de Guillaume de Conches," *Archives d'histoire doctrinale et littéraire du moyen âge,* 24 (Paris, 1957), 35–100. Cf. Guillaume de Conches, *Glosae,* p. 19.

5. Ibid., pp. 24–25 and bibliography.

6. Ibid., pp. 210–211.

7. Guillaume de Conches, *Commentary on Boethius,* III, m. 9. Ms. Troyes 1381, fol. 57, published in part by C. Jourdain, "Des Commentaires inédits," *Notices et extraits de la Bibliothèque Impériale* XX (Paris, 1865), pp. 77–78. The selection from the manuscript published by Jourdain containing Guillaume's explanation of the myth of Orpheus is extremely suggestive for a reading of Canto IX, *Inferno.* Guillaume sees in the story of Eurydice an echo of Luke 9:62, a passage frequently related to the story of Lot's wife turned to salt. According to J. Hatinguais ("En marge d'un poème de Boèce: L'interprétation allégorique du mythe d'Orphée par Guillaume de Conches," *Congrès de Tours et Poitiers: Actes* [Paris: "Belles Lettres," 1954], pp. 285 ff.), in the allegorical descent into Hell Orpheus faces a "tentation du passé." So does the pilgrim when he comes upon Medusa. The echoes of the *rime petrose* in the rhyme words of *Inf.* IX, 50, 52, 54 (*alto, smalto, assalto;* cf. *Rime,* c, vv. 55, 58, and 59 suggest a "tentation du passé" that might well be glossed as Guillaume glosses the story of Orpheus (cf. "Medusa," chap. 7 in this book).

8. The difficulty with any philosophical reconciliation stems from the fact that the Platonic myth suggests a *decadence* to the world of matter and hence a metaphysical dualism incompatible with Christianity.

9. *Inf.* XXXIV, 139: "a riveder le stelle"; *Purg.* XXXIII, 145: "a salire a le stelle"; *Par.* XXXIII, 145: "il sole e l'altre stelle."

10. Ernout and Meillet, in the *Dictionnaire Etymologique de la langue latine* (Paris: Klincksieck, 1951) *s.v.,* acknowledge that "A *sidus* les anciens rattachaient déjà *considerare, desiderare,*" cf. Paulus Festus, 66, 7; "desiderare et considerare a sideribus dici certum est." But they then conclude "Ce sont sans duote d'anciens termes de la langue augurale." The Pythagorean idea of the intellectual quality of sidereal movement as enunciated by Timaeus (*Timaeus* 40a ff.) seems to me a more plausible hypothesis, indicating a familiar *moral* distinction: *desiderare* = a fall to *temporalia* (Ernout and Meillet: "cesser de voir"). The moral force of *consideratio* seems to survive in the Middle Ages. See, for example, Johannes Sacrobosco, *Sphaera* II: "motus rationalis . . . id est . . . quando fit *consideratio* a creatore per creaturas in creatorem ibi sistendo," referring to the movement of the stars; see Lynn Thorndike, *The "Sphere" of Sacrobosco* (Chicago: University of Chicago Press, 1949), p. 86. At any rate, there can scarcely be any doubt of the celestial associations in antiquity. Franz Boll's essay on the astronomical origins of the theme of contemplation ("Vita Contemplativa," *Kleine Schriften zur Sternkunde des Altertums,* ed. V. Stegemann [Leipzig: Koehler & Amelang, 1950], pp. 303–331) has gathered together many texts suggesting the astronomical force of *contemplatio* (see below, n. 56), some of which illustrate a similar force for *consideratio:* see, for example, Cicero, *Acad.* II, 127: "Est. enim animorum ingeniorumque naturale quoddam quasi pabulum *consideratio contemplatioque* naturae; erigimur, altiores fieri videmur, humana despicimus cogitantesque supera atque caelestia haec nostra ut exigua et minima contemnimus,"

Boll, "Vita," p. 323. St. Bernard's treatise, *De consideratione* (*PL* 182, 727), gave the word the technical force that it surely has, resonances apart, in Dante's description of Richard of St.-Victor, for whom, however, the key word was *contemplatio.* See Richard of Saint-Victor, *Selected Writings on Contemplation,* trans. C. Kirchberger (London: Faber & Faber, 1957), pp. 269 ff.

11. Sapegno describes the medieval "ballata" upon which this description is based. See *La Divina Commedia,* ed. N. Sapegno (Milan-Naples: Ricciardi, 1957), ad loc, with bibliography. See also A. H. Lograsso, "From the *Ballata* of the *Vita Nuova* to the Carols of the *Paradiso*" in *83rd Annual Report of the Dante Society* (1965), pp. 23–48, and Bruno Nardi, "Il canto decimo del *Paradiso,*" *Convivium,* 24 (1956), 650 ff.

12. Augustine, Letter to Ceretius *PL* 33, 1034 ff.), referred to by Theodor Zahn, *Acta Joannis* (Erlangen: Deichert, 1880), p. 220.

13. *Acta Joannis,* ed. Zahn, p. 220, trans. B. Pick, *The Apocryphal Acts of Paul, Peter, John, Andrew and Thomas* (Chicago: Open Court, 1909), p. 181. For the gnostic sources, see R. A. Lipsius, *Die Apokryphen Apostelgeschichten und Apostellegenden* (Braunschweig: Schwetschke, 1883), I, 520. For similar dances in antiquity, see Lipsius' notes as well as Erwin Rohde, *Psyché,* trans. A. Reymond (Paris: Payot, 1928), pp. 270 ff, and Robert Eisler, *Weltenmantel und Himmelszeit* (München: Beck, 1910), pp. 462 and 472, where "star-dances" of antiquity are cited.

14. For the number 8, its significance and its sources, see Hugo Rahner, who quotes the saying "all things are eight," *Greek Myths and Christian Mystery,* trans. B. Battershaw (London: Burns and Oates, 1957), pp. 74–78 and bibliography.

15. Almost all of the standard works on the history of astrology attempt to trace the origins of the idea, beginning with the fundamental A. Bouché-Leclercq, *L'Astrologie grecque* (Paris: Leroux, 1899), *s.v.* and Franz Boll, *Sternglaube und Sterndeutung* (Leipzig-Berlin: Teubner, 1919), *s.v.* and subsequent editions. I have found W. Gundel, *Dekane und Dekansternbilder* (Studien der Bibliothek Warburg; Hamburg: Augustin, 1936) *s.v.* particularly useful. For a fuller bibliography, see J. Baltrusaitis, "L'Image du monde celeste du IXe au XIIe siècle," *Gazette des Beaux-Arts,* 20 (1938), 138, n. 1.

16. The illustration is reproduced after a sketch of the pavement of the baptistry published by G. B. Befani, *Memorie storiche di San Giovanni Battista di Firenze* (Florence: Pia Casa di Patronato, 1884), frontispiece. A palindrome encircles the solar disc: "En giro torte sol ciclos et rotor igne." The fact that the phrase can be read in both directions is an ingenious way of conveying the two-fold motion of the sun. For further details, see Befani, *Memorie,* p. 38. For the prevalence of such schemata, see J. Baltrusaitis, "L'Image du monde celeste."

17. The wealth of citations from the Old and New Testaments, classical and gnostic sources are brought together in Franz Dölger's *Sol Salutis* (Münster: Aschendorff, 1925), pp. 445 ff., as well as "Sonne und Sonnenstrahl als Gleichnis in der Logostheologie des Christlichen Altertums," *Antike und Christentum* (1929), 271.

18. For the importance of solar mysticism at the time of the Copernican revolution, see Eugenio Garin, *Studi sul Platonismo medievale* (Florence: Le Monnier, 1958), pp. 190 ff: "La Letteratura 'solare' e l'orazione al Sole di Giuliano," and bibliography cited there.

19. Jean Daniélou, "Les Douze Apôtres et le zodiaque," *Vigiliae Christianae,* 13 (1959), 14 ff. One of the key texts cited by Daniélou to document the transference of the number 12 from the Jewish to the Christian tradition is from Clement of Alexandria: "The twelve gems [of the grand priest] arranged in groups of four on his chest describe the Zodiac with the four changes of the seasons. One may also discern there . . . the prophets who denote the just men of each of the alliances. We will not be deceived if we say that in fact the Apostles are both prophets and just men" (*Stromata* V, 6, 38; quoted by Daniélou, p. 21).

20. F. Piper, *Mythologie und Symbolik der christlichen Kunst* (Weimar: Landes-industrie-comptoir, 1847–1851), II, 292 ff. See in particular his tables on pp. 305 and 306, listing the transformation of the significances of the various signs of the Zodiac.

21. See Eisler, *Weltenmantel,* pp. 264 ff., where "twelves" from Greek, Jewish, Etruscan, Roman and Germanic traditions are cited as possible examples of astrological survivals.

22. For the zodiacal origins of these verses, see Franz Boll, *Aus der Offenbarung Johannes* (Leipzig: Teubner, 1914), p. 39. For a typical gloss, see Hugo de S. Caro, *Commentum in Apocalypsim* (Lugduni, 1669), ad loc.: "Hae sunt duodecim Apostoli, qui dicuntur *corona* quia quodammodo Christus per ipsos devicit mundum," f. 400v.

23. For the invention of the mechanical clock, see Lynn Thorndike, "Invention of the Mechanical Clock about 1271 A.D.," *Speculum,* 16 (1941), 242.

24. It is not my intention in this essay to discuss the propriety or the rationale of the ordering or selection of the characters in this representation. The classical discussion concerning the presence of Siger is by Etienne Gilson, *Dante and Philosophy,* trans. D. Moore (New York: Harper, 1963), p. 275.

25. For the liturgical day, see Odon Casel, *Le Mystère du culte* (Paris: Editions du Cerf, 1946), chap. 5, and Dölger, *Sol Salutis,* chap. 22.

26. See Sapegno, ad loc.

27. *In Lucam* VII, 222, *Sources Chrétiennes,* p. 92, quoted by Daniélou, pp. 14–15.

28. For the theme, see Georges Poulet, "The Metamorphoses of the Circle" in *Dante: A Collection of Critical Essays,* ed. J. Freccero; Englewood Cliffs, N.J.: Prentice-Hall, 1965), pp. 151–169.

29. Dölger, *Sol Salutis.*

30. Benevenuti de Rambaldis de Imola, *Comentum super Dantis Aldigherij Comoediam,* ed. Lacaita (Florence: Barbera, 1887), V, ad loc.

31. See Rahner, *Greek Myths,* p. 158.

32. For a typical comment see Guillaume de Conches, *De mundi constitutione:* "De iride: sunt aliquando etiam duo arcus, quia luna similter arcum facit, plenum tamen, quia non est ipsa Iris, et solet esse imminentibus ventis aut pluviis." In Bede, *Opera dubia et spuria, PL* 90, 888. Dante alludes to the two types of "rainbows" in *Purg.* XXIX, 78, in a context which suggests the heavenly couple: "onde fa l'arco il Sole e Delia il cinto."

33. Rahner, chap. 4.

34. Ibid., p. 111, quoting Origen, *On Prayer,* p. 7.

35. Aldo Scaglione, "Imagery and Thematic Patterns in *Paradiso* XXIII," *From Time to Eternity,* ed. T. Bergin (New Haven: Yale University Press, 1967), p. 163.

36. Ibid., pp. 156–157.

37. Ibid., p. 160.

38. Casel, *Le Mystère*, and Dölger, *Sol Salutis*.

39. *Timaeus a Calcidio translatus*, ed. J. H. Waszink (*Plato latinus*, IV; Leyden: Brill, 1962), p. 33, *Timaeus* 40c; Guillaume de Conches, *Glosae*, p. 197.

40. *Glosae*, p. 186.

41. On the theme of harmony, see Leo Spitzer, *Classical and Christian Ideas of World Harmony*, ed. A. G. Hatcher (Baltimore: The Johns Hopkins University Press, 1963).

42. *Timaeus* 39b. Francis Cornford, *Plato's Cosmology* (New York: Liberal Arts Press, 1957), p. 115.

43. See *La Divina Commedia*, ed. Isidoro del Lungo (Florence: Le Monnier, 1931), III, 763: "l'una al 'prima' e l'altra al 'poi,' secondo il concetto e il linguaggio aristotelico (cf. *Convivio* IV, ii, 5–6), che 'il tempo è numero di movimento secondo *prima e poi*.'" See the notes of Busnelli and Vandelli, *Convivio* II, 16.

44. Tullio Gregory, *Anima Mundi* (Florence: Sansoni, 1955), esp. p. 123.

45. For an outline of the apparent movement of the sun along the Zodiac, see M. A. Orr, *Dante and the Early Astronomers*, 2nd ed. (London: Wingate, 1956), pp. 172–181.

46. *Timaeus* 36b ff. and Cornford's notes ad loc.

47. Boethius, *Consolation of Philosophy* (New York: Liberal Arts Press, 1962), p. 72.

48. These identifications are commonplace in the commentaries. I chose for an example the commentary published by E. T. Silk, *Saeculi nonis Auctoris in Boetii Consolationem philosophiae commentarius* (Papers and Monographs of the American Academy in Rome, 1935). For the association of Mind with the Son, see p. 175: "Dicit Boetius mundum Perpetua Ratione regi, quia intellexit illum per *sapientiam* Dei, id est per Filium Dei, non tantum factum esse sed etiam gubernari." For the various arguments in the controversy concerning the identification of *Anima* with the Holy Spirit, see Gregory, *Anima Mundi*, pp. 146 ff.

49. Z. Hayes, *The General Doctrine of Creation in the Thirteenth Century* (München: Schöningh, 1964), p. 88.

50. "Platons Weltseele und das Kreuz Christi," *Zeitschift für die Neutestamentliche Wissenschaft*, 14 (1913), 273.

51. Pick, *Acta Joannis*, p. 184.

52. *Theologia Christiana in Petri Abaelardi Opera*, ed. V. Cousin (Paris: Durand, 1859), II, 406–407.

53. Macrobius (I, 14) is a *locus classicus* for a résumé of the neoplatonic doctrine of emanation and creation. See Macrobius, *Commentary of the Dream of Scipio*, trans. W. H. Stahl (New York: Columbia University Press, 1952), pp. 142–148, and Stahl's notes.

54. For the astronomical details of zodiacal inclinations, their effects and their sources, see the parallel discussions in *Conv.* III, v, 23 ff. and Busnelli-Vandelli notes. See also below, n. 56.

55. For the religious theme of the glance up at the sun, see Dölger, *Sol Salutis*, especially chap. 18.

56. Macrobius I, 14; Stahl, p. 144. In this chapter Macrobius derives *contem-*

platio from "the temple of God"; see Stahl, p. 142 and notes. Dante echoes the tradition in *Par.* XXVIII, 53: "questo miro e angelico templo." The poet seems to blend elements of both the Platonic and religious traditions when he describes the divine providence of the twofold motion: "O ineffabile sapienza che così ordinasti . . . ! E voi a cui utilitade e diletto io scrivo, in quanta cechitade vivete, non levando li occhi suso a queste cose, tenendoli fissi nel fango de la vostra stoltezza!" (*Conv.* III, v, 22).

57. The circular movement of a "corona" (Ariadne's garland—*corona borealis, Par.* XIII, pp. 14–15) is identified as the movement of the Zodiac by Remi d'Auxerre's commentary of Martianus Capella (I, 30.14): "Per coronam, zodiacus . . . in modum coronae spheram caelestem quasi Iovis verticem cingit." *Commentum in Martianum Capellam,* ed. Cora Lutz (Leyden: Brill, 1962), p. 121.

58. *Par.* XI, 37–39:

L'un fu tutto serafico in ardore;
  l'altro per sapïenza in terra fue
  di cherubica luce uno splendore.

The source of the exhortation to conform human conduct to the angelic hierarchies is Gregory the Great, *In Evangel. sermo XXXIV* (*PL* 76, 1252). Alanus ab Insulis identifies the Seraphim with "viri contemplativi qui divino amori omnino sunt dediti, ut viri claustrales," while the Cherubim are the "magistri in sacra pagina," *Hierarchia Alani,* in Alain de Lille, *Textes inédits,* ed. M. T. d'Alverny (*Etudes de philosophie médiévale,* 52; Paris: Vrin, 1965), pp. 230–231. See d'Alverny's comments, p. 107. The importance of the comparison is not only doctrinal but poetic as well, for the angels are in fact the archetype for the circular movement of the blessed in the Empyrean; see chap. 16. Furthermore, they are in fact the movers of the Primum Mobile and the sphere of the fixed stars respectively, i.e., the intelligences which cause the celestial movement which is the counterpart of this movement in the physical world.

59. "[Conviene] esso sole girar lo mondo intorno giù a la terra . . . come una mola de la quale non paia più che mezo lo corpo suo." *Conv.* III, v, 14; ed. Busnelli-Vandelli, I, 313.

60. For the assimilation of the muses to the "Sirens of the Spheres" in the *Republic* (X, 617b) see Pierre Boyancé, "Les Muses et l'harmonie des sphères," *Mélanges dédiés à la mémoire de Félix Grat* (Paris: Pecqueur-Grat, 1946), pp. 3 ff.

61. *Conv.* III, xii, 6; ed. Busnelli-Vandelli, I, 399; see H. Gmelin, ed., *Die Göttliche Komödie, Kommentar, III Teil: Das Paradies* (Stuttgart: Klett, 1957), ad loc. For the importance of the Sun in Aries as an *essemplo* of Christ, see Rahner, *"Greek Myths,"* pp. 109–112.

16. The Final Image

1. *La Divina Commedia,* ed. N. Sapegno (Milan-Naples: Ricciardi, 1957), p. 1197.

2. For a summary of critical opinion, see Siro A. Chimenz, "Il canto XXXIII del *Paradiso,*" *Nuova "Lectura dantis"* (Rome: A. Signorelli, 1956), esp. p. 33.

3. Benedetto Croce, "L'ultimo canto della Commedia," in *Poesia antica e moderna* (Bari: Laterza, 1943).

4. See Chimenz, "Il canto," pp. 1 ff.

5. Ezek. 1:16 and 10:2.

6. For a convenient résumé of the history of exegetical opinion, see Cornelius a Lapide, *Commentaria in quatuor prophetas maiores* (Antwerp, 1703), pp. 994–945 and 960–964.

7. Ibid., p. 944: "Erant ergo hae quatuor currus Dei rotae quasi quatuor coluri"; or "erat modiolus, qui solet esse in rotis."

8. Bruno Nardi, *Nel mondo di Dante* (Rome: Edizione di "Storia e Letteratura," 1944), pp. 339 ff.

9. Pseudo-Dionysius, *De caelesti hierarchia* XV, 9 (my translation). Because Nardi's essay studies the subsequent history of this passage in scholastic thought, I have not thought it necessary to repeat the survey here.

10. Thomas Aquinas, *Opera Omnia (Commentaria in libros Arist. de caelo et mundo;* Rome, 1886), III, p. 11 (I, 2, lect. 3, n. 27). Italics added. The passage is quoted and briefly discussed in Thomas Litt, *Les corps célestes dans l'univers de saint Thomas d'Aquin* (*Philosophes médiévaux,* 7; Louvain and Paris, 1963), p. 342.

11. Werner Jaeger, *Early Christianity and Greek Paideia* (Cambridge, Mass.: Harvard University Press, 1961). According to Jaeger, it was Gregory of Nyssa who was primarily responsible for the Christian adaptation of these themes.

12. *Timaeus* 40a–b, trans. by F. M. Cornford in *Plato's Cosmology: The Timaeus of Plato* (New York: Liberal Arts Press, 1957; reprinted from original ed., Cambridge: 1937), p. 118.

13. *Platonis Timaeus interprete Chalcidio,* ed. J. Wrobel (Leipzig, 1876), pp. 40–41. Italics added.

14. See, for instance, pseudo-Honorius (William of Conches?), *De philosophia mundi,* II, 7, entitled "De infixis stellis utrum moveantur," where the following statement is rejected: "Alii dicunt eas etiam proprio motu moveri quia igneae sunt naturae, nec aliquid in aethere vel in acre sine motu possit sustineri sed semper in codem loco et circum se moveri" (*PL* 172,59).

15. The following résumé is taken from A. E. Taylor, *Commentary on Plato's Timaeus* (Oxford: Clarendon, 1928), p. 225. For the dissenting view of the *Timaeus* and a general view of motion in the dialogue (apart from that of Cornford, *Plato's Cosmology*), see J. B. Skemp, *The Theory of Motion in Plato's Later Dialogues* (Cambridge: Cambridge University Press, 1942), esp. pp. 81, 83, 101.

16. See the résumé of Aristotle's doctrine in B. Nardi, *Nel mondo di Dante* pp. 344 ff.

17. Ibid.; see also Pierre Duhem, *Le système du monde* (Paris: A. Hermann et Fils, 1916), IV, 422–559.

18. *De caelo* II, 3; 286b.

19. Nardi, *Nel mondo di Dante,* pp. 347–348.

20. See, for example, Averroës' résumé of the theme of the *Timaeus:* "idest quod actiones celi sunt eedem cum actionibus anime," in *Averrois Cordubensis commentarium magnum in Aristotelis de anima libros,* ed. F. Stuart Crawford (*Corpus commentariorum Averrois in Aristotelem* VI, 1; Cambridge, Mass.: Medieval Academy of America, 1953), p. 63.

21. See, among others, B. Nardi, *Nel mondo di Dante,* pp. 295 ff. For man in his fallen state, cf. Thomas Aquinas, *In IV Sent.* d.XVII, q.1, a.3, sol.3, and esp. his

citation of Augustine: "Praecedit intellectus, sequitur tardus aut nullus affectus."

22. For Thomas's doctrine of the will's fruition, see *ST,* I–II, q.11: "De fruitione, quae est actus voluntatis."

23. Aristotle, *Metaphysics* V, 4, n. 1 (1027b 25). Thomas uses the distinction to show that in itself the intellect is a higher power than the will. When, however, "res in qua est bonum est nobilior ipsa anima, in qua est ratio intellecta . . . voluntas est altior intellectu." In the poem, the blinding vision "equalizes" the two powers, so that intellect and will are equally matched.

24. The famous lines of the ninth meter of Book III of the *Consolation of Philosophy* are interpreted in this epistemological sense by Erigena (?). Of the lines, "In semet reditura meat mentemque profundam / Circuit et simili convertit imagine caelum," he says, ". . . melius est in hoc loco animam humanam intelligamus." Thus the germ of Dante's interpretation of the *Timaeus* analogy is already contained in Erigena, *Saeculi nonis auctoris in Boetii Consolationem philosophiae commentarius,* ed. E. T. Silk (Papers and Monographs of the American Academy in Rome, 1935), p. 186.

25. Nardi, *Nel mondo di Dante,* pp. 349–350, effectively refuted previous attempts to interpret the word *igualmente* in terms of some other unspecified wheel. He suggested that the word *aequaliter* in scholastic texts simply means "uniform." But because the intellect is brought to superhuman vision at this point, it is also true to say that the soul is *equally* moved by its now *equal* intellect and will. The motion of the soul is uniform precisely because of the exact correspondence of the poet's vision and fruition.

26. For example, *Purg.* V, 85; *Par.* II, 40; XXVIII, 52; XXX, 70; and so on. Charles Singleton discussed in his Gauss lectures (Princeton, 1961) the importance of these two words here and in Canto V of the *Inferno,* where Dante describes a movement antithetical to this.

27. See Nardi's remarks on the passage, *Nel mondo di Dante,* pp. 43–46.

28. For the sense of *velle* in Thomas Aquinas, see W. R. O'Connor, *The Eternal Quest* (New York: Longmans, Green, 1947), pp. 121–125. My reading of the literal image may help somewhat in the understanding of what has always seemed to me the cryptic interpretation offered by Pietro di Dante: "unde ejus desiderium ex parte objecti, et ejus velle ex parte sui, volvebatur in non plus velle," in *Petri Allegherii commentarius,* ed. V. Nannucci (Florence, 1845), III, p. 739. The object here can only mean God, at the center of the soul, whereas *velle* signifies the wheel itself. The singular verb denotes the essential unit of the two powers of the soul.

29. I am indebted to my friend David I. Grossvogel of Cornell University for this drawing.

30. Georges Poulet, *Les Métamorphoses du cercle* (Paris: Plon, 1961), p. xv.

31. The phrase whose history Poulet has traced, "Deus est sphaera cujus centrum ubique, circumferentia nusquam," is quoted by Cornelius a Lapide (who attributes it to Parmenides) in his remarks on the wheel of Ezekiel, *Commentaria in quator prophetas maiores.*

17. The Significance of *Terza Rima*

1. Erich Auerbach, "Figura," in *Scenes from the Drama of European Literature,* trans. Ralph Manheim (New York: Meridian, 1959), pp. 11–76

2. Kenneth Burke, *The Rhetoric of Religion: Studies in Logology* (Berkeley: University of California Press, 1970), pp. 1–7.

3. Charles S. Singleton, "The Vistas in Retrospect," in *Atti del Congresso internazionale di studi danteschi 20–27 Aprile 1965* (Florence: Sansoni, 1965), pp. 279–303.

4. Charles S. Singleton, *Dante Studies 2: Journey to Beatrice* (Cambridge, Mass.: Harvard University Press, 1958), pp. 57–71.

5. Hans Urs von Balthasar, *Man in History* (London: Sheed and Ward, 1968), p. 116.

6. For the doctrine, see E. Scharl, *Recapitulatio mundi,* Freiburger Theologische Studien, LX (Frieberg im Breisgau: Herder, 1941).

7. St. Augustine, *On Christian Doctrine* III, 30, trans. D. W. Robertson (New York: Liberal Arts Press, 1958), p. 104 and the notes on Tychonius ad loc. I am grateful to my friend Robert Kaske for calling this passage to my attention.

8. See Scharl, *Recapitulatio,* pp. 6–7.

9. Augustine, *Confessions* IV, 10, trans. R. S. Pine-Coffin (London: Penguin, 1961), p. 80.

10. Ibid., XI, 28; p. 278. I have changed the word "psalm" to "song," which I believe to be more accurate.

11. The analogy between the theory of history of Ephesians and Hegel's dialectic is implicit in the title used by the theologian A. Lindemann, *Die Aufhebung der Zeit* (Gütersloh: Gütersloher Verlagshaus, 1975).

SOURCES

The following is a list of the original titles, places, and dates of publication of the essays in this collection; they are listed in order of publication and are reprinted by permission of the publishers.

"Dante's Firm Foot and the Journey Without a Guide," *Harvard Theological Review,* 52, no. 3 (1959), 245–281.

"Dante and the Neutral Angels," *Romanic Review,* 51 (1960), 3–14.

"Dante's Pilgrim in a Gyre," *PMLA,* 76 (1961), 168–181. Reprinted by permission of the Modern Language Association of America.

"The Final Image: *Paradiso* XXXIII, 144," *MLN,* 79 (1964), 14–27. Published by The Johns Hopkins University Press.

"The Sign of Satan," *MLN,* 80 (1965), 11–26. Published by The Johns Hopkins University Press.

"Infernal Inversion and Christian Conversion (*Inferno* XXXIV)," *Italica,* 42 (1965), 35–41.

"Dante's Prologue Scene," *Dante Studies,* 84 (1966), 1–25. Published by the Dante Society of America.

"The River of Death: *Inferno* II, 108," pp. 25–42 in *The World of Dante: Six Studies in Language and Thought,* ed. S. Bernard Chandler and J. A. Molinaro (Toronto: University of Toronto Press, 1966).

"*Paradiso* X: The Dance of the Stars," *Dante Studies,* 86 (1968), 85–111. Published by the Dante Society of America.

"Introduction" to *The Paradiso,* from *The Paradiso* by Dante, translation by John Ciardi. Copyright © 1961, 1965, 1967, 1970 by John Ciardi. Introduction copyright © 1970 by New American Library. Reprinted by arrangement with New American Library, New York, New York.

"Medusa: The Letter and the Spirit," *Yearbook of Italian Studies,* 2 (1972), 1–18.

"Casella's Song (*Purg.* 11, 112)," *Dante Studies,* 91 (1973), 73–80. Published by the Dante Society of America.

"Dante's Ulysses: From Epic to Novel," pp. 101–119 in *Concepts of the Hero in the Middle Ages and the Renaissance* (Papers of the Fourth and Fifth Annual Conferences of the Center for Medieval and Renaissance Studies, State University of New York at Binghamton), ed. Norman T. Burns and Christopher J. Reagan (Albany: SUNY Press, 1975).

"Bestial Sign and Bread of Angels (*Inferno* 32–33)" *Yale Italian Studies,* 1 (1977), 53–66.

"Manfred's Wounds and the Poetics of the *Purgatorio,* in *Centre and Labyrinth: Essays in Honour of Northrop Frye,* ed. E. Cook, C. Hosek, J. Macpherson, P. Parker and J. Patrick (Toronto: University of Toronto Press, 1983).

"The Significance of *Terza Rima,*" pp. 3–17 in *Dante, Petrarch, Boccaccio: Studies in the Italian Trecento in Honor of Charles S. Singleton,* ed. Aldo S. Bernardo and Anthony L. Pellegrini, Medieval and Renaissance Texts and Studies XXII (Binghamton, N.Y.: SUNY Press, 1983).

"Infernal Irony: The Gates of Hell," *MLN,* 98 (1983), 769–786. Published by The Johns Hopkins University Press.

Note on Translations

Throughout this book the text and translation of the *Commedia,* with a few exceptions, are from *The Divine Comedy,* translated and with a commentary by Charles S. Singleton, Bollingen Series 80 (Princeton, N.J.: Princeton University Press, 1970–1975), quoted by permission of the publisher. The text of the *Convivio* is from the edition of G. Busnelli and G. Vandelli (Florence: Le Monnier, 1934–1937). The Latin text of the *Aeneid* is from the edition of J. W. MacKail (Oxford: Clarendon, 1930), and translations, unless otherwise specified, are by John Freccero. The Latin text for Augustine's *Confessions* is from the edition of Pierre de Labriolle (Paris: Gainier frères, 1945–1946). Translations from the Bible are from the Douay edition (Baltimore, Md.: John Murphy Co., 1914).

Index of Cantos and Verses

General Index